A CIP catalogue record for this book is
available from the British Library

10 9 8 7 6 5 4 3 2 1

ISBN: 978-1-78097-395-1

Editor: Martin Corteel
Designers: Luke Griffin & Katie Baxendale
Picture research: Paul Langan
Production: Rachel Burgess

Printed in Dubai

Right: Brazil captain Thiago
Silva holds aloft the FIFA
Confederations Cup after his
team's 3-0 victory over Spain
in the 2013 final.

Next pages (left to right): Top:
Yaya Toure (Ivory Coast), Xavi
Hernandez (Spain): Middle:
Cristiano Ronaldo (Portugal),
Philipp Lahm (Germany), Andrea
Pirlo (Italy); Bottom: Wayne
Rooney (England), Neymar (Brazil),
Lionel Messi (Argentina).

WORLD FOOTBALL RECORDS

FIFTH EDITION

KEIR RADNEDGE

CARLTON
BOOKS

CONTENTS

THE 2014 FIFA World Cup finals are just around the world football corner. However, not only will the eyes of fans, officials and players in 31 other competing nations be on events in Brazil in June and July 2014: the global sporting domination of the world's greatest game ensures that all 200-plus nations will be tuning in to the drama.

All are featured, in one way or another, in this latest edition of the *World Football Records*. These pages feature the major worldwide international tournaments for men and woman and within their varying age categories, too.

Also included is the 2013 FIFA Confederations Cup which whetted appetites for Brazil 2014 with a winning revival by the hosts – as well as fine performances from other star-laden national teams such as Spain, Italy and Uruguay.

The outcome – victory in the final for Brazil over Spain – raised the pressure which must be shouldered by the hosts as record five-times world champions when they pursue the greatest prize of them all in front of their own fans.

Much of the fascination and attraction of football is due to the mixture of individual brilliance with the frame of a team. Hence the national team achievements of a Neymar, a Messi and a Cristiano Ronaldo will depend on the strength of partnerships with their team-mates from Brazil, Argentina and Portugal.

The 2014 FIFA World Cup kicked off on 15 June 2011, at the Ato Boldon Stadium in Couva, Trinidad and Tobago. Belize beat Montserrat 5-2 in the first of a scheduled 824 qualifying ties. Deon McCaulay of Belize wrote his name into football history with the first goal of the entire tournament in the 24th minute.

Here was solid evidence that the FIFA World Cup is not only about the giants. The international game is bubbling with other national team as well as club tournaments while domestic leagues and knockout cup competitions also have an unshakable grip on fans' thirst for information.

Within these pages readers can find the main events and the sideshows, the giants and the giant-killers, the greatest players and the eager debutants ... from Belize to Brazil.

Keir Radnedge
London, July 2013

Fred celebrates his second goal and his country's third during Brazil's surprise 3-0 victory over reigning world and European champions Spain in the 2013 FIFA Confederations Cup final.

PART 1: THE COUNTRIES

SOME call it soccer, others say futbol or calcio or futebol – but go to virtually any country on earth and someone will be speaking about this game by whatever label. Association football knows no boundaries of race or politics or religion.

The structure is simple, helping ensure the sport's international success. At the head of the world football pyramid is FIFA, the world federation. Supporting FIFA's work are the six regional geographical confederations representing Africa, Asia, Europe, Oceania, South America, plus the Caribbean, Central and North America. Backing up the regions in turn are the national associations of 209 countries – and thus FIFA can boast more member countries than even the United Nations or the Olympic movement.

The countries are pivotal. They field the national teams who have built sporting history through their many and varied achievements in world-focused competitions such as the FIFA World Cup. But they also oversee the growth of football in their nation – from professional leagues to the game at grass-roots level.

Representative teams from England and Scotland played out the first formal internationals in the late 19th century, thus laying the foundation for the four British home nations' unique independent status within a world football family otherwise comprised of nation states. The original British Home Championships was the first competition for national teams but its demise, as a result of a congested fixture list, has left the Copa America in South America as the oldest survivor – apart from the Olympic Games.

The trend-setting example of the Olympic Games in the 1920s led directly to the creation of the FIFA World Cup and its launch in 1930. Already South America had its own national team championship and all the other five FIFA regions followed in due course. The winners meet once every four years in the FIFA Confederations Cup which is the rehearsal event for the extravaganza, one year later, which is the FIFA World Cup itself – the ultimate celebration of the planet's favourite sport.

The opening ceremony of the 2013 FIFA Confederations Cup in Brazil meant the countdown to the 2014 FIFA World Cup in the same country had well and truly begun.

EUROPE

As soon as modern association football's rules were written in England the game's growth was rapid – enthusiasm spreading swiftly across Europe, the cradle of the game. UEFA, the European football confederation, now boasts 54 member states, from tiny Andorra to world giants, Spain, Italy, England, the Netherlands, Germany and France. The game is played and followed with a fervent passion across the continent, at club and national levels, with two-times European champions Spain the dominant force.

Andres Iniesta (6) has been a mainstay of Spain's all-conquering teams in recent years. The 2010 World Cup final match-winner also claimed European Championship winners medals in 2008 and 2012.

ENGLAND

England is where football began; the country where the game was first developed, which saw the creation of the game's first Football Association and the first organized league, and which now plays host to the richest domestic league in the world. But England have not had it all their own way on the international scene. Far from it. One solitary FIFA World Cup win apart, as hosts in 1966, the Three Lions have found it hard to shake off the "underachievers" tag when it comes to major tournaments.

IF THE CAP FITS

England's players in the historic first game against Scotland all wore **cricket-style caps** while the Scots wore hoods. England's "fashion statement" prompted the use of the term "cap" to refer to any international appearance. The tradition of awarding a cap to British international footballers still survives today.

HAVE A BASH, ASH

Chelsea left-back **Ashley Cole** is one of only seven England footballers to reach a century of caps but – goalkeeper Peter Shilton aside – is the only one to reach the mark without ever having scored a goal. He overtook Kenny Sansom as England's most-capped full-back when he represented his country for the 87th time, against Denmark in February 2011, and made his 100th appearance against Brazil at Wembley in March the following year. He holds the record for the most outfield appearances for England without scoring – ahead of Gary Neville (85). Cole's 98th international, against Italy in the Euro 2012 quarter-final, ended unhappily, as he missed England's final penalty in the shoot-out. But he did set another record that day: his 22nd finals match is more than any other of his compatriots. Cole has also won more domestic English FA Cup medals than any other player, after three triumphs with Arsenal and four with Chelsea.

RUNAWAY SUCCESS

England have hit double figures five times: beating Ireland 13-0 and 13-2 in 1882 and 1899, thrashing Austria 11-1 in 1908, crushing Portugal 10-0 in Lisbon in 1947 and then the United States 10-0 in 1964 in New York. The ten goals were scored by Roger Hunt (four), Fred Pickering (three), Terry Paine (two) and **Bobby Charlton**.

IN THE BEGINNING

The day it all began ... 30 November 1872, when England played their first official international match, against Scotland, at Hamilton Crescent, Partick. The result was a 0-0 draw in front of a then massive crowd of 4,000, who each paid an admission fee of one shilling (5p). In fact, teams representing England and Scotland had played five times before, but most of the Scottish players had been based in England and the matches are considered unofficial. England's team for the first official game was selected by Charles Alcock, the secretary of the Football Association. His one regret was that, because of injury, he could not pick himself to play. In contrast, the first rugby union international between England and Scotland had been played in 1871, but England's first Test cricket match was not played until March 1877, against Australia in Melbourne.

FIRST DEFEAT

Hungary's 6-3 win at Wembley in 1953 was the first time England had lost at home to continental opposition. Their first home defeat by non-British opposition came against the Republic of Ireland, who beat them 2-0 at Goodison Park, Liverpool, in 1949.

STEVIE G FORCE

Steven Gerrard won his 100th cap in a 4-2 friendly defeat to Sweden in November 2012 and could have secured more but injury. He scored at the 2006 and 2010 FIFA World Cups and was the only Englishman named in the Euro 2012 "team of the tournament". His next international brought an unwanted record: his red card against Ukraine in September 2012 saw him become the oldest player ever sent off for England.

ENGLAND'S BIGGEST WINS

1882	Ireland 0 England 13
1899	England 13 Ireland 2
1908	Austria 1 England 11
1964	United States 0 England 10
1947	Portugal 0 England 10
1982	England 9 Luxembourg 0
1960	Luxembourg 0 England 9
1895	England 9 Ireland 0
1927	Belgium 1 England 9
1896	Wales 1 England 9
1890	Ireland 1 England 9

ENGLAND'S BIGGEST DEFEATS

1954	Hungary 7 England 1
1878	Scotland 7 England 2
1881	England 1 Scotland 6
1958	Yugoslavia 5 England 0
1964	Brazil 5 England 1
1928	England 1 Scotland 5
1882	Scotland 5 England 1
1953	England 3 Hungary 6
1963	France 5 England 2
1931	France 5 England 2

NAUGHTY BOYS

Alan Mullery was the first player to be sent off for England in a senior international, in a 1-0 semi-final loss to Yugoslavia at the 1968 UEFA European Championship in Italy. Of 13 dismissals since then, David Beckham and **Wayne Rooney** have had two apiece. Paul Scholes was the only England player sent off at the old Wembley Stadium, against Sweden in June 1999, before it was demolished and rebuilt.

SENIOR MOMENT

Goalkeeper David James became the oldest player to make his FIFA World Cup debut, aged 39 years and 321 days, when he appeared for England at the 2010 competition in South Africa. He kept a clean sheet in a goalless Group C draw against Algeria after coming into the side to replace Robert Green, who had made an embarrassing error in England's opening game against the USA.

HEAD FOR GOAL

Robust and commanding centre-backs had the honour of scoring both the last England goal at the old Wembley stadium, closed down in 2000, and the first in the new version, which was finally opened in 2007. Tony Adams scored England's second in a 2-0 win over Ukraine in May 2000 – Germany's Dietmar Hamann hit the only goal of the final international at the old Wembley, four months later – and captain John Terry headed his side ahead in the new stadium's showpiece June 2007 friendly against Brazil, which ended 1-1. Terry shares the honour of scoring the most England goals (six) by a defender with 1966 FIFA World Cup winner **Jack Charlton**.

BLANKS OF ENGLAND

A goalless draw against Algeria in Cape Town in June 2010 made England the first country to finish 10 different FIFA World Cup matches 0-0. Their first was against Brazil in 1958, while the tally also includes both second-round group games in 1982 against eventual runners-up West Germany and hosts Spain.

BEST GERMANY

England suffered their heaviest-ever FIFA World Cup finals defeat when losing 4-1 to Germany in Bloemfontein, South Africa, in the second round of the 2010 tournament. Before then, their largest loss had been 4-2 against Uruguay in a 1954 quarter-final. Germany managed more goals in one match than England scored in the entire 2010 tournament – defender Matthew Upson scored England's consolation goal in Bloemfontein, after only **Steven Gerrard** and Jermain Defoe had scored in three first-round matches. Back in September 2001, England enjoyed a 5-1 away win over Germany, in a FIFA World Cup qualifier in Munich, thanks to Michael Owen's hat-trick and goals by Steven Gerrard and Emile Heskey. Germany still progressed further at the following year's FIFA World Cup in South Korea and Japan, though, losing to Brazil in the final after England were knocked out by the same opponents in the quarter-finals.

THE LONG AND THE SHORT OF IT

At 6ft 7in, centre-forward **Peter Crouch** is the tallest player ever to stretch above opposing defences for England – while **Fanny Walden**, the Tottenham winger who won two caps in 1914 and 1922, was the shortest at 5ft 2in. Sheffield United goalkeeper Billy "Fatty" Foulke became the heaviest England player at 18st when he played against Wales on 29 March 1897.

TEENAGE PROMISE

Theo Walcott became England's youngest full international when he played against Hungary at Old Trafford on 30 May 2006 at the age of 17 years 75 days. On 10 September 2008, he became England's youngest hat-trick scorer in a 4-1 win away to Croatia, aged 19 years 178 days. The previous youngest international was Wayne Rooney, who was 17 years 111 days old when he made his debut against Australia in February 2003.

WAITING FOR THE CALL

Four England internationals played at the 1966 FIFA World Cup yet missed out on the triumphant final against West Germany – Ian Callaghan, John Connelly, Jimmy Greaves and Terry Paine. Liverpool winger Callaghan would then endure the longest wait between England appearances, when he went 11 years and 49 days between his showing in a 2-0 win over France at that 1966 tournament and his return to international action in a goalless draw with Switzerland in September 1977. The game against the Swiss was his third – and penultimate – outing for England.

FRANK'S A LOT

Frank Lampard has scored more penalties for England than any other player, successfully striking nine since his debut in October 2005 – despite missing another two. The prolific ex-West Ham United and Chelsea midfielder should have had another goal to add to his international tally, but his potential equalizer against Germany during the two countries' 2010 FIFA World Cup second-round match was wrongly deemed not to have crossed the line – prompting the eventual introduction of goal-line technology. Lampard became then-reigning European champions Chelsea's all-time leading scorer in May 2013 with his 203rd goal for the West London club, despite being a midfielder.

BECKHAM'S RECORD

David Beckham played for England for the 109th time when he appeared as a second-half substitute in the 4-0 win over Slovakia in a friendly international on 28 March 2009. That overtook the record number of England games for an outfield player, which had been set by Bobby Moore, England's 1966 FIFA World Cup-winning captain. Beckham, born on 2 May 1975, in Leytonstone, London, made his first appearance for his country on 1 September 1996, in a FIFA World Cup qualifying match against Moldova. He was appointed full-time England captain in 2001 by the then manager Sven-Goran Eriksson – stepping down after England's quarter-final defeat by Portugal at the 2006 FIFA World Cup. He ended his England career on 115 caps and hung up his boots in May 2013, at the age of 38, having just won the league in a fourth different country with French club Paris Saint-Germain. His 68 competitive matches for England are also a national record. Also retiring from the game in summer 2013 was England's fourth highest scorer **Michael Owen**, who netted a stunning solo goal against Argentina at the 1998 FIFA World Cup – only for Beckham to be sent off in a 2-2 draw before England lost on penalties.

ALEXANDER THE LATE

The oldest player to make his debut for England remains Alexander Morten, who was 41 years and 114 days old when facing Scotland on 8 March 1873 in England's first home game, at The Oval in Kennington, London. He was also captain that day and is still the country's oldest-ever skipper.

THE GOOD SONS

Eighteen-year-old winger Alex Oxlade-Chamberlain became the fifth son of a former England international to earn a cap for his country when he made his debut against Norway in May 2012 – 28 years after the last of his father Mark Chamberlain's eight appearances. Oxlade-Chamberlain became England's youngest scorer in a FIFA World Cup qualifier with his strike against San Marino in October 2013. The earlier pairings were George Eastham Snr (one cap, 1935) and George Eastham Jnr (19, 1963–66); Brian Clough (two, 1959) and Nigel Clough (14, 1989–93); Frank Lampard Snr (two, 1972–80) and **Frank Lampard Jnr** (90, 1999–date); and Ian Wright (33, 1991–98) and his adopted son Shaun Wright-Phillips (36, 2004–10). The only grandfather and grandson to play for England are Bill Jones, who won two caps in 1950, and Rob Jones, who won eight between 1992 and 1995.

GRAND OLD MAN

Stanley Matthews became England's oldest-ever player when he lined up at outside-right against Denmark on 15 May 1957 at the age of 42 years 104 days. That was 22 years and 229 days after his first appearance. Matthews was also England's oldest marksman. He was 41 years eight months old when he scored against Northern Ireland on 10 October 1956.

TOP SCORERS

1	Bobby Charlton	49
2	Gary Lineker	48
3	Jimmy Greaves	44
4	Michael Owen	40
5	Wayne Rooney	36
6	Tom Finney	30
=	Nat Lofthouse	30
=	Alan Shearer	30
9	Frank Lampard	29
=	Vivian Woodward	29

CAPTAIN SOLO

Claude Ashton, the Corinthians centre-forward, set a record when he captained England on his only international appearance. This was a 0-0 draw against Northern Ireland in Belfast on 24 October 1925.

TOP CAPS

1	Peter Shilton	125
2	David Beckham	115
3	Bobby Moore	108
4	Bobby Charlton	106
5	Billy Wright	105
6	Ashley Cole	103
7	Steven Gerrard	102
8	Frank Lampard	97
9	Bryan Robson	90
10	Michael Owen	89

CAPTAINS COURAGEOUS

The international careers of Billy Wright and **Bobby Moore**, who both captained England a record 90 times, very nearly overlapped. Wright, from Wolves, played for England between 1946 and 1959 and Moore, from West Ham, between 1962 and 1973, including England's FIFA World Cup win in 1966.

SHARED RESPONSIBILITY

Substitutions meant the captain's armband passed between four different players during England's 2-1 friendly win over Serbia and Montenegro on 3 June 2003. Regular captain David Beckham was missing, so Michael Owen led the team out, but was substituted at half-time. England's second-half skippers were Owen's then-Liverpool team-mates Emile Heskey and Jamie Carragher and Manchester United's Philip Neville. The first time three different players have captained England in one FIFA World Cup finals match was against Morocco in 1986, when first-choice skipper Bryan Robson went off injured, his vice-captain Ray Wilkins was then sent off and goalkeeper Peter Shilton took over leadership duties.

CAMEO ROLE

Tottenham Hotspur striker **Jermain Defoe** has come on as substitute for England more often than any other player in history, 31 times since his debut in March 2004 – and his initial 17 starting appearances all ended in him being replaced before the end of 90 minutes.

SEVEN UP

Roy Hodgson's England equalled a national record when they trounced San Marino 8-0 in a March 2013 FIFA World Cup qualifier: the seven different goalscorers were as many who found the net when England defeated Luxembourg 9-0 in December 1982. This time, though, thanks to the opening own goal by Alessandro Della Valle, only six of the scorers were Englishmen. Adding to the tally were a Jermain Defoe brace and single strikes by **Alex Oxlade-Chamberlain**, Ashley Young, Frank Lampard, Wayne Rooney and Daniel Sturridge.

WHO'S THE GREATEST?

Fabio Capello is the most statistically successful England manager over a prolonged period, with a win ratio of 67 per cent, followed by **Sir Alf Ramsey (below)** and Glenn Hoddle tied on 61 per cent. Sir Alf's 1966 FIFA World Cup victory, however, puts him head and shoulders above all the rest. Technically, caretaker manager Peter Taylor has the worst record – a 100 per cent record of defeat. But then, he was in charge for only one game – a 1-0 defeat to Italy in Turin, a game that saw David Beckham making his first appearance as England captain. Don Revie, in the 1970s, and Steve McClaren, in the 2000s, are the only full-time managers to have failed to qualify for any international tournament. Terry Venables was spared the need to qualify for his only tournament, UEFA Euro 1996, since England were hosts. McClaren's 16-month tenure (during which Venables served as his assistant) is also the shortest full-time reign as national team manager.

COMING OVER HERE

Argentina were the first non-UK side to play at Wembley – England won 2-1 on 9 May 1951 – while Ferenc Puskas and the "Magical Magyars" of Hungary were the first "foreign", or "continental", side to beat England at home, with their famous 6-3 victory at Wembley in 1953. This humiliation marked Alf Ramsey's last game as an England player. England first tasted defeat to a "foreign" side when they lost 4-3 to Spain in Madrid on 15 May 1929. Two years later England gained their revenge with a 7-1 win at Highbury.

WRONG WAY!

Though the goal is sometimes credited to Scottish striker John Smith, it is believed that Edgar Field was the first England player to score an "own goal", which was his fate as Scotland crushed England 6-1 at The Oval on 12 March 1881. By the time Field put the ball in his own net, Scotland were already 4-1 up. The full-back, who was an FA Cup winner and loser with Clapham Rovers, is in good company. Manchester United's Gary Neville has scored two own goals "against" England.

ROLL UP, ROLL UP

The highest attendance for an England game came at Hampden Park on 17 April 1937, when 149,547 spectators crushed in to see Scotland's 3-1 victory in the British Home Championships. Only 2,378 turned up in Bologna, Italy, to see San Marino stun England after nine seconds in Graham Taylor's side's 7-1 victory that was not enough to secure qualification to the 1994 FIFA World Cup.

FIRST AND FOREMOST

England's first official international was a 0-0 draw against Scotland in Glasgow on 30 November 1872, though England and Scotland had already played a number of unofficial representative matches against each other prior to that. Given that England's only opponents for four decades were the home nations – and only Scotland for the first seven years, it is not surprising that England's first draw, win and defeat were all against their northern neighbours. After the goalless first game, the second fixture – played at The Oval on 8 March 1873 – proved a more exciting affair: England won 4-2 in a six-goal thriller. In their third game, back in Glasgow almost exactly a year later, Scotland evened things up with a 2-1 win. These fixtures completed the trio of first wins, defeats and draws for the oldest participants in international football. The Football Association's 150-year anniversary celebrations in 2013 included a 2013 Wembley friendly against Scotland, the first time the two sides were scheduled to meet since a two-leg play-off to qualify for Euro 2000 in October 1999. England won that tie 2-1 on aggregate, after a 2-0 victory at Hampden Park and a 1-0 defeat at home.

ROY'S BOYS

After Fabio Capello faced criticism for his struggles with the English language, his successor **Roy Hodgson** could claim fluency in not only his mother tongue but also Swedish, Norwegian, Italian and German. Much-travelled Hodgson – a former Switzerland, Finland and Inter Milan manager – was appointed England boss just six weeks before the 2012 UEFA European Championship, but his side topped their group before losing to Italy in the quarter-finals on penalties. First-round victories came against Sweden – England's first competitive victory over them at the eighth attempt – and co-hosts Ukraine, the first time England had beaten the hosts at a major tournament since Switzerland in 1954.

YOUR COUNTRY NEEDS YOU

The first England teams were selected from open trials of Englishmen who responded to the FA's adverts for players. It was only when these proved too popular and unwieldy that, in 1887, the FA decided that it would be better to manage the process through an International Selection Committee, which continued to pick the team until Sir Alf Ramsey's appointment in 1962.

MANAGERIAL ROLL OF HONOUR

Walter Winterbottom	(1946–62)
Sir Alf Ramsey	(1962–74)
Joe Mercer	(1974)
Don Revie	(1974–77)
Ron Greenwood	(1977–82)
Bobby Robson	(1982–90)
Graham Taylor	(1990–93)
Terry Venables	(1994–96)
Glenn Hoddle	(1996–98)
Howard Wilkinson	(1999–2000)
Kevin Keegan	(1999–2000)
Peter Taylor	(November 2000)
Sven-Goran Eriksson	(2001–06)
Steve McClaren	(2006–07)
Fabio Capello	(2008–2012)
Stuart Pearce	(March 2012)
Roy Hodgson	(2012–)

THE ITALIAN JOB

Italian Fabio Capello became England's second foreign coach when he took over from Steve McClaren in January 2008 and led the country to the 2010 FIFA World Cup in South Africa. Capello already had happy memories of national stadium Wembley from his playing days – he scored the only goal for Italy there on 14 November 1973, giving them their first-ever away win against England. He steered England through qualifiers for the 2012 UEFA European Championship, but suddenly resigned in February 2012, in protest at the Football Association stripping John Terry of the captaincy.

WONDERFUL WALTER

Walter Winterbottom was the England national team's first full-time manager – and remains both the longest-serving (with 138 games in charge) and the youngest-ever England manager, aged just 33 when he took the job in 1946 (initially as a coach and then, from 1947, as manager). The former teacher and Manchester United player led England to four FIFA World Cups.

FRANCE

France – nicknamed "Les Bleus" – are one of the most successful teams in the history of international football. They are one of only three countries to be World and European champions at the same time. They won the FIFA World Cup in 1998 as tournament hosts, routing Brazil 3-0 in the final. Two years later, they staged a sensational, last-gasp recovery to overhaul Italy in the Euro 2000 final. The French equalized in the fifth minute of stoppage time, then went on to win 2-1 on a golden goal. France had previously won the UEFA European Championship in 1984, beating Spain 2-0 in the final in Paris. They reached the 2006 FIFA World Cup final too, but lost to Italy in a penalty shoot-out. France also won the 2001 and 2003 FIFA Confederations Cup and took the Olympic football gold medal in 1984.

KOPA – FRANCE'S FIRST SUPERSTAR

Raymond Kopa (born on 13 October 1931) was France's first international superstar. Born into a family of Polish immigrants (the family name was Kopaszewski), he was instrumental in Reims's championship successes of the mid-1950s. He later joined Real Madrid and became the first French player to win a European Cup winner's medal. He was the playmaker of the France team that finished third in the 1958 FIFA World Cup finals. His performances for his country that year earned him the European Footballer of the Year award.

PLATINI'S GLITTERING CAREER

Michel Platini (born in Joeuf on 21 June 1955) has enjoyed a glittering career, rising from a youngster at Nancy to become one of France's greatest-ever players, a hero in Italy, and now the president of UEFA. He was also joint organizing president (along with Fernand Sastre) of the 1998 FIFA World Cup finals in France. Platini was the grandson of an Italian immigrant who ran a café in Joeuf, Lorraine. He began with the local club, Nancy, before starring for Saint-Etienne, Juventus and France. He was instrumental in France's progress to the 1982 FIFA World Cup semi-finals and was the undisputed star of the UEFA European Championship two years later, when France won the tournament on home soil.

LIGHTNING RUN

Goals by **Jeremy Menez** and Yohan Cabaye gave France a 2-0 first-round win over Euro 2012 co-hosts Ukraine, after an hour-long delay caused by a lightning storm. It was also France's first ever victory at a UEFA European Championship without either Michel Platini or Zinedine Zidane in the side. France had not won a match in a tournament since beating Portugal in their 2006 FIFA World Cup semi-final, ending a national-record eight finals games without a win. The result also extended the team's unbeaten run under coach Laurent Blanc to 23 games, France's second-longest sequence without defeat – though they lost the two games that followed – a final first-round Group D match, 2-0 to Sweden, and a quarter-final against Spain by the same scoreline. France's best unbeaten run was the 30 games without loss between February 1994 and October 1996, when managed by Aime Jacquet. This did, however, include a goalless draw followed by defeat on penalties in a 1996 UEFA European Championship semi-final against the Czech Republic.

CROSSING THE BARRIERS

France's teams have usually included a high proportion of players from immigrant backgrounds or ethnic minorities. Three of France's greatest players – Raymond Kopa, Michel Platini and Zinedine Zidane – were the sons or grandsons of immigrants. In 2006, 17 of France's 23-man FIFA World Cup squad had links to the country's former colonies.

KISSING COLLEAGUES

Marseille colleagues centre-back **Laurent Blanc** and goalkeeper **Fabien Barthez** had a special ritual during France's run to the 1998 FIFA World Cup crown. Before the game, Blanc would always kiss Barthez's shaven head, even when the veteran defender was suspended for the final. Blanc was on the winning side when France won the 2000 UEFA European Championship final, after which he announced his international retirement. He said at the time: "The French team has been my life and has led me to do things I shouldn't have. It has been my mistress – a beautiful mistress."

TO BE FRANCK

Franck Ribery has become one of modern-day France's most important and influential footballers. His displays off both wings helped them reach the 2006 FIFA World Cup final as well as helping lift Bayern Munich to success in the 2013 UEFA Champions League. He is the first man to have been named Footballer of the Year in both France and Germany. Yet he was rejected as a teenager by French club Lille, with 1.7m-tall Ribery later claming they deemed him too short. Ribery was severely injured in a car crash as a two year old, leaving him with lifelong scars across the right side of his face.

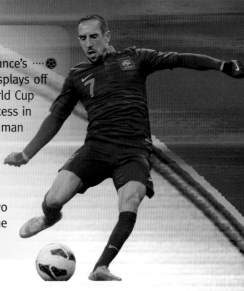

IT'S A SHAME ABOUT RAY

France's failure to win a match at the 2010 FIFA World Cup meant coach Raymond Domenech equalled but failed to exceed Michel Hidalgo's record of 41 victories in charge of the national side. Domenech did at least end his six-year reign having surpassed Euro 84-winning Hidalgo's tally of matches in the job. Domenech's final game, against South Africa, was his 79th as coach, four more than Hidalgo achieved. Domenech, a tough-tackling defender who was picked for France by Hidalgo, proved eccentric as national coach. He admitted partly judging players by their star signs and responded to being knocked out of the 2008 UEFA European Championship by proposing to his girlfriend on live television.

MICHEL PLATINI (league and national career)

Duration	Team	Appearances	Goals
1972–79	Nancy	181	98
1979–82	Saint-Etienne	104	58
1982–87	Juventus	147	68
1976–87	France	72	41

WRONG KIND OF STRIKERS

During France's disastrous 2010 FIFA World Cup campaign, the players went on strike, refusing to train two days before their final Group A match, in protest at striker Nicolas Anelka being sent home early for insulting coach Raymond Domenech. France finished bottom of the group after a goalless draw with Uruguay and defeats to Mexico and hosts South Africa. The country's president Nicolas Sarkozy ordered an investigation into all that had gone wrong, while former French international defender Lilian Thuram called for captain **Patrice Evra** to be banned from playing for the team ever again. New coach Laurent Blanc refused to consider any members of the 23 in the 2010 FIFA World Cup squad for France's first match after the finals, a friendly in Norway, and they lost 2-1.

FRANCE AND FIFA

France were one of FIFA's founding members in 1904. Frenchman Robert Guerin became the first president of the governing body. Another Frenchman, Jules Rimet, was president from 1921 to 1954. He was the driving force behind the creation of the FIFA World Cup and the first version of football's most coveted trophy was named in his honour.

HENRY BENCHED

France's record scorer Thierry Henry missed out on an appearance in the 1998 FIFA World Cup final because of Marcel Desailly's red card. Henry was France's leading scorer in the competition with three goals and coach Aime Jacquet planned to use him as a substitute in the final. But Desailly's sending-off forced a re-think: Jacquet decided to reinforce the midfield, with Arsenal team-mate Patrick Vieira going on instead, so Henry spent the full 90 minutes of the final on the bench. But Henry does have the distinction of being the only Frenchman to play at four different FIFA World Cups (1998, 2002, 2006 and 2010). He passed Michel Platini's all-time goal-scoring record for France with a late brace against Lithuania in October 2007.

TOP CAPS

1	Lilian Thuram	142
2	Thierry Henry	123
3	Marcel Desailly	116
4	Zinedine Zidane	108
5	Patrick Vieira	107
6	Didier Deschamps	103
7	Laurent Blanc	97
=	Bixente Lizarazu	97
9	Sylvain Wiltord	92
10	Fabien Barthez	87

TOP SCORERS

1	Thierry Henry	51
2	Michel Platini	41
3	David Trezeguet	34
4	Zinedine Zidane	31
5	Just Fontaine	30
=	Jean-Pierre Papin	30
7	Youri Djorkaeff	28
8	Sylvain Wiltord	26
9	Jean Vincent	22
10	Jean Nicolas	21

DESCHAMPS THE LEADER

Compatriot Eric Cantona contemptuously dismissed him as a mere "water-carrier" in central midfield but **Didier Deschamps** provided his infamous critic with the perfect riposte in becoming the most successful captain in French football history. He lifted both the 1998 FIFA World Cup and 2000 UEFA European Championship trophies as an inspirational skipper and wore the captain's armband a record 55 times during his 103 international appearances before retiring in July 2000. After successful managerial spells with AS Monaco, Juventus and Marseille, Deschamps was given the job of France manager after Laurent Blanc's resignation following the 2012 UEFA European Championship. He holds France's highest decoration, as a Chevalier, or Knight, of the Légion d'honneur, awarded after the 1998 FIFA World Cup triumph.

UNITED FOR ABIDAL

Defender **Eric Abidal**, a key member of the French teams at the 2006 and 2010 FIFA World Cups, was enjoying his best form for Spanish club Barcelona when he was diagnosed with liver cancer in March 2011 – but managed to recover in time for a surprise return to action by the season's end. Club rivalries were put aside when players from rivals Real Madrid wore T-shirts bearing the supportive message "Animo Abidal" after their UEFA Champions League tie against Abidal's former club Olympique Lyonnais a few days later. Barcelona fans then clapped throughout the 22nd minute of their La Liga game against Getafe, in recognition of Abidal's shirt number. Remarkably, he was fit enough to return to action, as a substitute, in Barcelona's UEFA Champions League semi-final victory over Madrid in May 2011. Abidal started in the final and, although not the captain, was given the armband to lift the cup after their 3-1 win over Manchester United. Abidal came through further trauma in March 2012, when he was told he needed a liver transplant. Yet again Abidal would return to action with Barcelona, taking the field again towards the end of the 2012–13 season.

BITTERSWEET FOR TREZEGUET

Striker David Trezeguet has bittersweet memories of France's clashes with Italy in major finals. He scored the "golden goal" that beat the Italians in extra-time in the Euro 2000 final but, six years later, he was the man who missed as France lost the FIFA World Cup final on penalties. Trezeguet's shot bounced off the bar and failed to cross the line.

PRESIDENTIAL PARDON

Imperious centre-back Laurent Blanc was known as "Le President" during his playing days and went on to become national coach when he succeeded Raymond Domenech after the 2010 FIFA World Cup. He was unlucky to miss the 1998 FIFA World Cup final after being sent off in the semi-final for pushing Slaven Bilic in the face, though replays showed Bilic had over-reacted. Blanc did enjoy some redemption by being part of the French team that won the UEFA European Championship two years later. He became national coach 12 months after leading Bordeaux to the 2008–09 domestic championship, ending Olympique Lyonnais's run of seven league titles in a row.

ARMBAND FINALLY IN SAFE HANDS

After Patrick Evra lost the French captaincy for his role in their 2010 FIFA World Cup fiasco, new coach Laurent Blanc used four different skippers during qualifying for the 2012 UEFA European Championship. Midfielders Florent Malouda, Alou Diarra and Samir Nasri took turns wearing the armband, as did goalkeeper **Hugo Lloris** who was finally confirmed as permanent captain ahead of Euro 2012. He was the only man to play every single minute of the qualifying campaign for France, while also being ever-present for teams which played in the qualifying tournament and finals – keeping seven clean sheets in France's 14 matches.

THE FULL SET

Five France stars have a full set of top international medals as FIFA World Cup, UEFA European Championship and UEFA Champions League winners. Didier Deschamps, Marcel Desailly, Christian Karembeu, Bixente Lizarazu and Zinedine Zidane all played for France's winning teams in 1998 and 2000. Desailly won the European Cup with Marseille in 1993 and AC Milan the following year. Deschamps won with Marseille in 1993 and Juventus in 1996; Lizarazu did so with Bayern Munich in 2001, Karembeu with Real Madrid in 1998 and 2000, and Zidane with Real Madrid in 2002. While Karembeu ended the 1999–2000 season with UEFA Champions League and UEFA European Championship winners' medals, he was an unused substitute in both finals – making him the only player to have achieved that particular bittersweet double.

LILIAN IN THE PINK

Defender **Lilian Thuram** made his 142nd and final appearance for France in their defeat by Italy at Euro 2008. His international career had spanned nearly 14 years, since his debut against the Czech Republic on 17 August 1994. Thuram was born in Pointe a Pitre, Guadeloupe, on 1 January 1972. He played club football for Monaco, Parma, Juventus and Barcelona before retiring in the summer of 2008 because of a heart problem. He was one of the stars of France's 1998 FIFA World Cup-winning side and scored both goals in their semi-final victory over Croatia – the only international goals of his career. He gained another winner's medal at Euro 2000. He first retired from international football after Euro 2004, but was persuaded by coach Raymond Domenech to return for the 2006 FIFA World Cup campaign and made his second appearance in a FIFA World Cup final. He broke Marcel Desailly's record of 116 caps in the group game against Togo.

ALBERT THE FIRST

Albert Batteux (1919–2003) was France's first national manager. Before his appointment in 1955, a selection committee had picked the team. Batteux was also the most successful coach in the history of French football. He combined managing France with his club job at Reims. His biggest achievement was guiding the national team to third place at the 1958 FIFA World Cup finals. The team's two big stars, Raymond Kopa and Just Fontaine, had both played under his charge at Reims.

REVEILLERE REMAINS

Anthony Reveillere is the only player to be picked by all of the last four France managers: Jacques Santini, Raymond Domenech, Laurent Blanc and Didier Deschamps. Yet in a decade the full-back has only made 19 appearances since his debut against Israel in October 2003.

OVAL BALL

The father of France's most capped goalkeeper Fabien Barthez was also a French international. Alain Barthez was a fine rugby union player who won one cap for France.

JACQUET'S TRIUMPH

Aime Jacquet, who guided France to FIFA World Cup glory in 1998, was one of their most controversial national coaches. He had been attacked for alleged defensive tactics despite France's run to the semi-finals of Euro 96 and a record of only three defeats in four years. A month before the 1998 finals, the sports daily *L'Equipe* claimed he was not capable of building a successful team!

NO TIME FOR FONTAINE

Former striker **Just Fontaine** spent the shortest-ever spell in charge of the France team. He took over on 22 March 1967 and left on 3 June after two defeats in friendlies. More happily, he still holds the record for most goals at a single FIFA World Cup – 13 across all six games he played at the 1958 tournament, including four in France's 6-3 victory over West Germany to finish third.

FRANCE MANAGERS

Albert Batteux	1955–62
Henri Guerin	1962–66
Jose Arribas/Jean Snella	1966
Just Fontaine	1967
Louis Dugauguez	1967–68
Georges Boulogne	1969–73
Stefan Kovacs	1973–75
Michel Hidalgo	1976–84
Henri Michel	1984–88
Michel Platini	1988–92
Gerard Houllier	1992–93
Aime Jacquet	1993–98
Roger Lemerre	1998–2002
Jacques Santini	2002–04
Raymond Domenech	2004–10
Laurent Blanc	2010–12
Didier Deschamps	2012–

VALBUENA NOTTE

France's unbeaten away record against Italy stretched to 50 years after a 2-1 victory in Parma in November 2012, thanks to goals by Mathieu Valbuena and substitute Bafetimbi Gomis. The win extended Marseille midfielder Valbuena's record of never having lost a game when starting for France (on 16 occasions). Previously Italy's last home victory over France had been back in May 1962 when the *Azzurri* beat *Les Bleus* with two goals from Brazilian-born Jose Altafini in a 2-1 win.

WINNING WITH YOUTH

In the early 1990s, France became the first European country to institute a national youth development programme. The best young players were picked to attend the national youth academy at Clairefontaine. Then they went on to the top clubs' academies throughout the nation. The scheme has produced a rich harvest of stars. FIFA World Cup winners Didier Deschamps, Marcel Desailly and Christian Karembeu started at Nantes. Lilian Thuram, Thierry Henry, Manu Petit and David Trezeguet began with Monaco and **Zinedine Zidane** and Patrick Vieira were graduates from Cannes.

BLINK AND YOU'LL MISS HIM

Unfortunate defender Franck Jurietti's international debut proved bittersweet – it lasted just five seconds and he never won another cap. The Bordeaux full-back came on just before the final whistle of France's match against Cyprus in October 2005, amounting to an international career even shorter than fellow defender Bernard Boissier's two minutes against Portugal in April 1975.

PACKING THEM IN

A record home crowd of 80,051 people were inside the Stade de France, in Saint-Denis, to see France take a major step towards qualifying for the 2008 UEFA European Championship with a 2-0 defeat of Ukraine in June 2007. The goals were scored by Franck Ribery and **Nicolas Anelka**.

EARNING THEIR STRIPES

France are the only country to play at a FIFA World Cup wearing another team's kit. In the 1978 tournament in Argentina, for a first-round match at Mar del Plata, *Les Bleus* were forced to wear the green and white stripes of a local club side, Atletico Kimberley, when they met Hungary. France brought their second, white, kit instead of their normal blue, while Hungary turned up in their second strip, white, too. The quick-change did not seem to affect France, who won the match 3-1.

WHAM BAM THANK YOU SAM

Samir Nasri scored the winner to give France a 2-1 victory over Spain in the final of the UEFA European U-17 Championship on home soil in 2004, the only time France have lifted that trophy. They have also won the UEFA European U-19 Championship seven times, most recently in 2010 with another final triumph over Spain, and the UEFA European U-21 Championship once, in 1988, when Laurent Blanc was named player of the tournament. Midfielder Nasri is one of the successful graduates from that acclaimed "Generation '87" team that won in 2004, also featuring Jeremy Menez, Hatem Ben Arfa and Karim Benzema. All four were also involved, though, when France's senior side lost to Spain in the quarter-finals of the 2012 UEFA European Championship – with Cesc Fabregas and Gerard Pique, also veterans of that earlier clash, now on the winning side. Nasri was then criticized by French sports minister Valerie Fourneyron – and given a three-match suspension – for his petulant post-match response to journalists' questions.

GERMANY

Politics may have divided the country in two for more than 40 years, but few countries can match Germany's record in international football. Three-time winners of the FIFA World Cup (all as West Germany, in 1954, 1974 and 1990) and three-time UEFA European Championship winners (1972, 1980 and 1996), in 1974 they became the first country in history to hold the World and European titles at the same time – and have remained a fearsome opponent in top-level football matches ever since.

SHOOT–OUT SURE–SHOTS

German teams have always put in hours of preparation for penalty shoot-outs. Their last two major successes – at the 1990 FIFA World Cup and Euro 96 – both came after shoot-out victories in the semi-finals. England were the Germans' victims on both occasions.

BELITTLE ITALY

Germany may have become England's bogey-team, but their own unlucky run against Italy goes on. They have never managed to beat the Italians in an international tournament. This sequence was stretched to eight games after a Germany side – featuring such stars as midfielder **Bastian Schweinsteiger** and goalkeeper Manuel Neuer – lost 2-1 in their 2012 UEFA European Championship semi-final. Perhaps the most dramatic clash was Italy's 4-3 victory, after extra-time, in the semi-finals of the 1970 FIFA World Cup. Italy also reigned triumphant in the 2006 FIFA World Cup semi-finals and the 1982 FIFA World Cup final. Germany can at least celebrate one recent success over their Italian rivals – albeit at club level. Since 2011–12, the German Bundesliga has had four clubs eligible for the UEFA Champions League, gaining their extra space at the expense of Italy's Serie A.

NO LOSS

Germany maintained their record of never losing their opening game at a UEFA European Championship by beating Portugal 1-0 at Euro 2012, thanks to a header by **Mario Gomez**. Their 4-2 quarter-final victory over Greece that same summer set a new world record of 15 consecutive wins in competitive matches, one more than the best tallies set by both Spain and the Netherlands.

BOTH SIDES NOW

Eight players appeared for both the old East Germany and then Germany after reunification in October 1990.

Player	East Germany	Germany
Ulf Kirsten	49	51
Matthias Sammer	23	51
Andreas Thom	51	10
Thomas Doll	29	18
Dariusz Wosz	7	17
Olaf Marschall	4	13
Heiko Scholz	7	1
Dirk Schuster	4	3

2010 FIFA WORLD CUP SOUTH AFRICA

EAST GERMANY – TOP APPEARANCES AND GOALS

Appearances
1	**Joachim Streich**	98
2	Hans-Jurgen Dorner	96
3	Jurgen Croy	86
4	Konrad Weise	78
5	Eberhard Vogel	69

Goals
1	Joachim Streich	53
2	Eberhard Vogel	24
3	Hans-Jurgen Kreische	22
4	Rainer Ernst	20
5	Henning Frenzel	19

PARTY LIKE IT'S MATCHDAY 99

Germany (and West Germany) have now played more FIFA World Cup finals matches than any other country. Their 2010 semi-final defeat to Spain was their 98th in the competition, one ahead of losing quarter-finalists Brazil. **Germany's third-place play-off win** took their overall tally to 99 matches – comprising 60 wins, 19 draws and 20 losses, with 203 goals scored and 115 conceded.

BERLIN ALL

German capital Berlin has been awarded hosting rights for the 2015 UEFA Champions League final. This will make it the second German city, after Munich, to have hosted an Olympic Games, a FIFA World Cup final and a UEFA European Cup final. Berlin hosted the Olympics in 1936 and the FIFA World Cup in 2006, while Munich staged the Olympics in 1972, the FIFA World Cup two years later and European Cup finals in 1979, 1993, 1997 and 2012.

GERMANY JOIN THE 200 CLUB

Thomas Muller's third-minute goal for Germany against Argentina in their 2010 FIFA World Cup quarter-final, set his side on the way to a 4-0 victory, and made Germany the second country to score 200 World Cup goals. Joachim Low's side ended the 2010 finals on 203 goals, seven behind Brazil. Germany's first finals goal was scored by Stanislaus Kobierski in a 5-2 victory over Belgium in 1934. Germany's 2010 team became the first since Brazil in 1970 to enjoy three separate four-goal sprees at one FIFA World Cup, trouncing Australia 4-0, England 4-1 and Argentina 4-0.

HISTORY MAN

East and West Germany met only once at senior national team level. That was on 22 June 1974, in the FIFA World Cup finals. Drawn in the same group, East Germany produced a shock 1-0 win in Hamburg, but both teams advanced. Jurgen Sparwasser, scorer of East Germany's winning goal, defected to West Germany in 1988 – two years before the two countries reunited.

SCHNELL, SCHNELL

Lukas Podolski scored one of the fastest goals in international football history when he gave Germany the lead after just nine seconds in their May 2013 friendly away to Ecuador. When Lars Bender added another shortly afterwards, it was the first time ever that Germany had scored twice in the opening four minutes of a match. Both Podolski and Bender scored again by the time 24 minutes were on the clock and Germany ultimately went on to win the match 4-2.

GOLDEN WONDER

Germany became the first team to win a major title thanks to the now-discarded golden goal system when they beat the Czech Republic in the UEFA Euro 96 final at Wembley. **Oliver Bierhoff's** equalizer forced extra-time after Patrik Berger scored a penalty for the Czechs. Bierhoff grabbed Germany's winner five minutes into extra-time to end the game and the championship.

MEIN BENDERS

You could have thought you were seeing double when manager Joachim Low made a double substitution with 12 minutes remaining during Germany's 5-3 defeat to Switzerland in May 2012. His two midfield substitutes were twin brothers **Lars** and **Sven Bender**. Born on 27 April 1989, they both began their careers with 1860 Munich before Lars (the elder by 12 minutes) moved to Bayer Leverkusen and Sven to Borussia Dortmund. Both were members of Germany's 2008 UEFA U-19 European Championship-winning side, but only Lars was selected for Euro 2012. They were were the second twins to play for Germany after Erwin and Helmut Kramers. Striker Erwin scored three goals in 15 games between 1972 and 1974, while full-back Helmut played eight times without scoring. Erwin was part of the 1972 UEFA European Championship-winning squad, but was overlooked for the triumphant 1974 FIFA World Cup-winning squad, a set-up that included Helmut.

"DER BOMBER"

Gerd Muller was the most prolific scorer of the modern era. Neither tall nor graceful, he was quick, strong and had a predator's eye for the net. He also had the temperament to score decisive goals in big games, including the winner in the 1974 FIFA World Cup final, the winner in the semi-final against Poland and two goals in West Germany's 1972 UEFA European Championship final victory over the USSR. He netted 68 goals in 62 appearances for West Germany and remains the leading scorer in the Bundesliga and all-time record scorer for his club, Bayern Munich.

KING OTTO

Mario Gomez was the last man to score a hat-trick for Germany, thanks to his four goals in a 7-2 friendly victory over the United Arab Emirates in June 2009. Gerd Muller has more hat-tricks than any other German international – eight in all, four of which were four-goal hauls. But Otto Siffling remains the only player to score five in one match for Germany, during an 8-0 triumph over Denmark on 16 May 1937, in the Polish city of Wroclaw – then a German territory known as Breslau.

A LAHM CALL

Versatile full-back **Philipp Lahm**, who can play on either flank, is the youngest man to captain Germany at a FIFA World Cup. He was 26 when he stood in for the injured Michael Ballack at the 2010 tournament in South Africa, though he was unable to repeat his spectacular long-range strike against Costa Rica at the 2006 FIFA World Cup on home turf – the opening goal of the competition. Lahm played every minute of every Germany match at the 2006 FIFA World Cup and in qualifiers for the 2010 event, but was finally given a rest for the third-place play-off match against Uruguay in South Africa.

DER KAISER

Franz Beckenbauer is widely regarded as the greatest player in German football history. He has also made a huge mark as a FIFA World Cup-winning coach, administrator and organizer. Beckenbauer (born on 11 September 1945) was a 20-year-old attacking wing-half when West Germany reached the 1966 FIFA World Cup final. He later defined the role of attacking sweeper, first in the 1970 FIFA World Cup finals, and then as West Germany won the 1972 UEFA European Championship and the 1974 FIFA World Cup. When West Germany needed a coach in the mid-1980s, they turned to Beckenbauer, despite his lack of experience. He delivered a FIFA World Cup final appearance in 1986, a Euro 88 semi-final and 1990 FIFA World Cup triumph in his final game in charge. He later became president of Bayern Munich, the club he captained to three consecutive European Cup victories between 1974 and 1976. He also led Germany's successful bid for the 2006 FIFA World Cup finals and headed the organizing committee. No wonder he is known as "Der Kaiser" ("the Emperor") for his enormous influence on German football.

MAGICAL MATTHAUS

Lothar Matthaus is Germany's most-capped player. He appeared in five FIFA World Cup finals – 1982, 1986, 1990, 1994 and 1998 – a record for an outfield player. Versatile Matthaus could operate as a defensive midfielder, an attacking midfielder, or as a sweeper. He was a FIFA World Cup winner in 1990, a finalist in 1982 and 1986 and a UEFA European Championship winner in 1980. His record 150 appearances – spread over a 20-year international career – were split 87 for West Germany and 63 for Germany. He also scored 23 goals and was voted top player at the 1990 FIFA World Cup.

TOP CAPS
(West Germany & Germany)

1	Lothar Matthaus	150
2	Miroslav Klose	127
3	Lukas Podolski	110
4	Jurgen Klinsmann	108
5	Jurgen Kohler	105
6	Franz Beckenbauer	103
7	Thomas Hassler	101
8	Michael Ballack	98
=	Philipp Lahm	98
=	Bastian Schweinsteiger	98

TOP SCORERS
(West Germany & Germany)

1	Gerd Muller	68
2	Miroslav Klose	67
3	Jurgen Klinsmann	47
=	Rudi Voller	47
5	Lukas Podolski	46
6	Karl-Heinz Rummenigge	45
7	Uwe Seeler	43
8	Michael Ballack	42
9	Oliver Bierhoff	37
10	Fritz Walter	33

KLOSE ENCOUNTERS

Miroslav Klose drew level with  Gerd Muller as the country's most prolific FIFA World Cup scorer when he took his tournament tally to 14 in South Africa in 2010. He had opened his overall account with a hat-trick against Saudi Arabia in 2002, scoring five goals that summer, before winning the Golden Boot with five strikes in his homeland four years later. His four goals at the 2010 FIFA World Cup included the opener against England in the second round and two in the quarter-final against Argentina. Polish-born Klose managed more goals for Germany at the 2010 FIFA World Cup than his meagre three during what had been a disappointing 2009–10 domestic season for Bayern Munich. Klose also holds a rather more unenviable FIFA World Cup record, having been substituted an unlucky 13 times – more than any other player.

GOLDEN GLOVES

Sepp Maier was at the heart of West Germany's triumphs of the early 1970s, including the 1972 UEFA European Championship and the 1974 FIFA World Cup. He remains West Germany's most-capped goalkeeper, winning 95 caps in an international career lasting from 1965 to 1979. He played his whole club career for Bayern Munich and helped them win the European Cup three times. A car crash in 1979, in which he received life-threatening injuries, ended his playing days, but he went on to become a goalkeeping coach for both Germany and his old club.

YOUNGEST CENTURION LUKAS

Lukas Podolski became the youngest European footballer to reach 100 caps when, aged 27 years and 13 days old, he appeared in Germany's third first-round game of the 2012 UEFA European Championship, against Denmark. He marked the occasion by scoring the opener in a 2-1 win – his 44th goal for his country. Podolski was born in Gliwice in Poland, but opted to play for Germany – his family having emigrated there when he was two years old. He was voted best young player of the tournament when Germany hosted and finished third at the 2006 FIFA World Cup.

STRENGTH IN DIVERSITY

Germany is increasingly cosmopolitan, not only as a country but also as a national football team – as shown by the fact that 11 of their 23 squad players at the 2010 FIFA World Cup could have qualified to play for at least one other country instead. These included Polish-born forwards Lukas Podolski and Miroslav Klose, Turkish-descended playmaker **Mesut Ozil**, half-Tunisian midfielder Sami Khedira, Brazilian-born striker Cacau, and full-back Dennis Aogo, whose father is Nigerian.

KEEPING A LOW PROFILE

Until **Joachim Low**, Germany had followed a recent trend of being led into FIFA World Cup finals by former playing legends who had already starred in the competition on the field rather than on the touchline: 1974 FIFA World Cup winners Franz Beckenbauer (coach in 1986 and 1990) and Berti Vogts (1994 and 1998), and 1990 FIFA World Cup winners Rudi Voller (coach in 2002) and Jurgen Klinsmann (2006). Low, Klinsmann's assistant in 2006, then became the first man to coach Germany at a FIFA World Cup without having been to any finals as a player since Jupp Derwall in 1982. Derwall had at least won two international caps during his player career, both in 1954 – but missed out on a call-up for that year's FIFA World Cup, which West Germany won.

THE WORST OF STARTS

Goalkeeper Marc-Andre ter Stegen had an international debut to forget when Switzerland beat Germany 5-3 in a May 2012 friendly. He became the first German goalkeeper to concede more than three goals on debut for 58 years. The last to do so was Heinrich Kwiatowski, who was in goal when Hungary won 8-3 in West Germany's opening game of the 1954 FIFA World Cup – it was Kwiatowki's only appearance of the tournament (and he would make only three further appearances), but he still ended up with a winners' medal when they beat the same opponents 3-2 in the final. Despite ter Stegen's promise, Germany's current undisputed number one is 38-cap Manuel Neuer.

GERMANY'S MANAGERS

Otto Nerz	1928–36
Sepp Herberger	1936–64
Helmut Schon	1964–78
Jupp Derwall	1978–84
Franz Beckenbauer	1984–90
Berti Vogts	1990–98
Erich Ribbeck	1998–2000
Rudi Voller	2000–04
Jurgen Klinsmann	2004–06
Joachim Low	2006–

BONUS BATTLE

Helmut Schon's 1974 FIFA World Cup winners came close to walking out before the finals started. Schon was prepared to send his squad home in a row over bonuses. A last-minute deal was brokered between Franz Beckenbauer and federation vice-president Hermann Neuberger. The vote among the squad went 11-11, but Beckenbauer persuaded the players to accept the DFB's offer. It was a great decision: they beat Holland 2-1 in the final.

GOAL RUSH

Germany's biggest win was 16-0 against Russia in the 1912 Olympic Games in Stockholm. Karlsruhe's Gottfried Fuchs scored ten of the goals, still a national team record.

SCHON IN SAARLAND

Helmut Schon is remembered as one of Germany's most successful managers. He started his international coaching career with Saarland, now part of Germany, but which had been made a separate state (with a population of 970,000) after the country's post-war division. Saarland's greatest moment came in the 1954 FIFA World Cup qualifiers, when they beat Norway 3-2 in Oslo to top their qualifying group. They were eventually eliminated by Sepp Herberger's West Germany.

NEW BOYS REUNION

Borussia Dortmund midfielder **Mario Gotze** and Mainz striker Andre Schurrle jointly became the first German football internationals to be born after the reunification of East and West Germany in 1990, when they appeared as 79th-minute substitutes in a November 2010 friendly against Sweden. Gotze became the most expensive German transfer of all time in April 2013 when he decided to join Bayern Munich from Borussia Dortmund for 37 million euros. Injury denied him a final game for Dortmund in the 2013 UEFA Champions League final – coincidentally against Bayern.

GERMANY'S BRONZE AGES

The 2010 FIFA World Cup third-place play-off between Germany and Uruguay was a rematch of the same tie at the 1970 tournament, when West Germany won 1-0. The German side again took third place 40 years later, thanks to a dramatic 3-2 victory in Port Elizabeth's Nelson Mandela Bay stadium. The result, secured by Sami Khedira's late goal, meant Germany had a record four third-place finishes at FIFA World Cups, having also come third in 1934 and 2006.

PRESSURE ON JULIAN

Julian Draxler became Germany's fifth-youngest player when he made his debut against Switzerland in May 2012, aged 18 years 248 days old. Team-mate Mario Gotze is third on that list, having been 18 years and 166 days old when he made his first appearance, against Sweden in November 2010, at the age of 18 years and 166 days. Germany's youngest-ever player remains Oskar Ritter, who was 17 years and 254 days old when he made his debut, also against Sweden, in June 1925. Uwe Seeler was 90 days older when he debuted against France in October 1954. Olaf Thon was 63 days older than Gotze when he made his first international appearance, against Malta, in December 1984.

SEPP'S SURPRISE

Sepp Herberger (1897–1977) was one of the most influential figures in Germany's football history. He was their longest-serving coach (28 years at the helm) and his legendary status was assured after West Germany surprised odds-on favourites Hungary to win the 1954 FIFA World Cup final – a result credited with dragging the country out of a post-war slump. Herberger took charge in 1936 and led the team into the 1938 FIFA World Cup finals. During the war years he used his influence to try to keep his best players away from the heavy fighting. When organized football resumed in 1949, the federation decided to advertise for a national coach, but Herberger persuaded DFB chief Peco Bauwens to give him back his old job. He had a clause in his contract guaranteeing him a totally free hand in organization and selection policy. Among Herberger's favourite sayings was: "The ball is round and the match lasts 90 minutes. Everything else is just theory."

ITALY

Only Brazil (with five victories) can claim to have won the FIFA World Cup more times than Italy. The *Azzurri* became the first nation to retain the trophy (through back-to-back successes in 1934 and 1938), snatched a surprise win in Spain in 1982, and collected football's most coveted trophy for a fourth time in 2006 following a dramatic penalty shoot-out win over France. Add the 1968 UEFA European Championship success to the mix and few nations can boast a better record. The success story does not end there. Italian clubs have won the European Cup on 11 occasions and the country's domestic league, Serie A, is considered among the strongest in the game. Italy are a true powerhouse of world football.

ROTTEN RETURN

Italy's players were pelted with tomatoes by angry fans when they returned home after crashing out of the 1966 FIFA World Cup at the group stages. After a nervy and unconvincing 2-0 opening victory over Chile, they slumped to a 1-0 defeat to the Soviet Union – and then crashed to a humiliating reverse against North Korea, by the same scoreline.

OFF THE SPOT

Only England have lost as many FIFA World Cup penalty shoot-outs as Italy – three apiece. **Roberto Baggio**, nicknamed "The Divine Ponytail", was involved in all three of Italy's spot-kick defeats, in 1990, 1994 and 1998. Left-back Antonio Cabrini is the only man to have missed a penalty during normal time in a FIFA World Cup final – the score was 0-0 at the time but, fortunately for him, Italy still beat West Germany 3-1 in 1982.

COMEBACK CASSANO

Many feared **Antonio Cassano** would never play football again after he collapsed with brain damage in November 2011 and needed heart surgery. Yet he was back in action for AC Milan by April the following year and started every game for Italy at the 2012 UEFA European Championship. Along with defender Giorgio Chiellini, Cassano was one of only two ever-presents for Italy as they reached Euro 2012 with 26 points from ten games – a national record for any qualification campaign. Cassano was top scorer in qualifying with six goals and was also on the scoresheet at the finals in a 2-0 victory over the Republic of Ireland. Having scored twice at Euro 2004, he shares with Mario Balotelli the all-time record for Italian goals at UEFA European Championships. Less enviably, he has been substituted eight times in UEFA European Championship finals matches – one more than closest challengers Dennis Bergkamp, of the Netherlands, and German striker Mario Gomez.

IN SAFE KEEPING

During World War Two, the Jules Rimet Trophy, the FIFA World Cup – won by Italy in 1938 – was hidden in a shoebox under the bed of football official Ottorino Barassi. He preferred to keep it there, rather than at its previous home – a bank in Rome. The trophy was handed back to FIFA, safe and untouched, only when the FIFA World Cup resumed in 1950.

BLUE BOYS

Internazionale full-back Davide Santon became Italy's second-youngest international of the post-war era when he played against Northern Ireland in a June 2009 friendly, aged just 18 years and 155 days and following just 20 first-team appearances for his club. Another Internazionale defender, the richly moustachioed Giuseppe Bergomi, was 42 days younger when he made his debut against East Germany in April 1982, just three months before helping Italy win the FIFA World Cup. Even more junior were Casale midfielder Luigi Barbesino, 18 years and 61 days old against Sweden in July 1912, and record-holder Renzo De Vecchi, an AC Milan defender who was aged just 16 years and 112 days when he lined up against Hungary in May 1910.

BOSSI DE ROSSI

Combative central midfielder **Daniele de Rossi** was roundly condemned when he was sent off for elbowing the United States' Brian McBride during Italy's second match of the 2006 FIFA World Cup. He returned from suspension in time to come on as a substitute in the final, which Italy won against France. Yet earlier that year, in March, he had won widespread praise for his honesty during a Serie A match for AS Roma against Messina. Roma were awarded a goal when he diverted the ball into the net using his hand, but De Rossi persuaded the referee to disallow his strike – Roma went on to win 2-1. His international honours for Italy include a bronze medal at the 2004 Summer Olympics – not long before he made his international debut.

TOP DRAW

No team has drawn more FIFA World Cup matches than Italy, who took their tally to 21 with 1-1 draws against both Paraguay and New Zealand in Group F at the 2010 competition in South Africa. Their first draw had also been 1-1, against Spain in a 1934 quarter-final tie. Italy's Giuseppe Meazza scored the only goal of a replay the following day, and Italy went on to lift the trophy for the first time that year.

TOURNAMENT SPECIALISTS

FIFA WORLD CUP: 17 appearances – winners 1934, 1938, 1982, 2006
UEFA EUROPEAN CHAMPIONSHIP: 8 appearances – winners 1968
FIRST INTERNATIONAL: Italy 6 France 2 (Milan, 15 May 1910)
BIGGEST WIN: Italy 9 USA 0 (Brentford, London, 17 August 1948 – Olympic Games)
BIGGEST DEFEAT: Hungary 7 Italy 1 (Budapest, 6 April 1924)

FLYING HIGH

Vittorio Pozzo is the only man to have won the FIFA World Cup twice as manager – both times with Italy, in 1934 and 1938 (only two players, Giuseppe Meazza and Giovanni Ferrari, were selected in both finals). Pozzo also led Italy to the 1936 Olympics title. Born in Turin on 2 March 1886, Pozzo learned to love football as a student in England, watching Manchester United. He returned home reluctantly when his family bought him a return ticket for his sister's wedding and then refused to let him leave Italy again. Pozzo fired up his Italian team ahead of their 1938 semi-final against Brazil by revealing their opponents had already booked their plane to Paris for the final – Italy won 2-1.

CHAMPS TO CHUMPS

Italy's dismal 2010 FIFA World Cup campaign was the worst in their history, despite going into the tournament as defending world champions. Their two draws and 3-2 defeat to Slovakia meant they ended a FIFA World Cup without a win for the first time ever. Finishing bottom of their first-round group was also unprecedented. The poor showing must have left 2006 World Cup-winning coach **Marcello Lippi** regretting his decision to resume control in 2008. Immediately after the Slovakia match, which ended the defending champions' run, Lippi insisted the players should not be faulted and he should take all the blame. He had already announced his intention to resign after the finals.

ITALY'S NATIONAL COACHES

Vittorio Pozzo	1912, 1924
Augusto Rangone	1925–28
Carlo Carcano	1928–29
Vittorio Pozzo	1929–48
Ferruccio Novo	1949–50
Carlino Beretta	1952–53
Giuseppe Viani	1960
Giovanni Ferrari	1960–61
Giovanni Ferrari/Paolo Mazza	1962
Edmondo Fabbri	1962–66
Helenio Herrera/Ferruccio Valcareggi	1966–67
Ferruccio Valcareggi	1967–74
Fulvio Bernardini	1974–75
Enzo Bearzot	1975–86
Azeglio Vicini	1986–91
Arrigo Sacchi	1991–96
Cesare Maldini	1997–98
Dino Zoff	1998–2000
Giovanni Trapattoni	2000–04
Marcello Lippi	2004–06
Roberto Donadoni	2006–08
Marcello Lippi	2008–10
Cesare Prandelli	2010–

COMEBACK KID

Paolo Rossi was the unlikely hero of Italy's 1982 FIFA World Cup triumph, winning the Golden Boot with six goals – including a memorable hat-trick against Brazil in the second round, and the first of Italy's three goals in their final win over West Germany. But he only just made it to the tournament at all, having completed a two-year ban for his alleged involvement in a betting scandal only six weeks before the start of the tournament.

HELPING HANDS

Goalkeeper Angelo Peruzzi was a 14-year-old ballboy at the 1984 European Cup final between Roma and Liverpool. He made 16 appearances for Roma before playing for Juventus, Internazionale and Lazio as well as 31 times for Italy between 1995 and 2006.

HOME GROWN

More than 80 years separated the first and most recent foreign-born players to wear the *Azzurri* shirt. Argentina-born Julio Libonatti made the first of his 17 appearances in a 3-1 defeat by Czechoslovakia in Prague on 28 October 1926. One of the latest is Sao Paulo-born defensive midfielder **Thiago Motta**, who even played twice for Brazil's U-23 side at the 2003 CONCACAF Gold Cup. But he was later able to switch to Italy due to Italian grandparents on both parents' sides. Motta made his full international debut for Italy in February 2011 and came on as a substitute in the 2012 UEFA European Championship final. His Italy breakthrough was followed by an October 2011 debut for Buenos Aires-born striker Pablo Osvaldo, though he did not make the Euro 2012 squad.

TOP CAPS

1	Fabio Cannavaro	136
2	Gianluigi Buffon	133
3	Paolo Maldini	126
4	Dino Zoff	112
5	Andrea Pirlo	102
6	Gianluca Zambrotta	98
7	Giacinto Facchetti	94
8	Alessandro Del Piero	91
9	Daniele De Rossi	90
10	Franco Baresi	81
=	Giuseppe Bergomi	81
=	Marco Tardelli	81

TOP SCORERS

1	Luigi Riva	35
2	Giuseppe Meazza	33
3	Silvio Piola	30
4	Roberto Baggio	27
=	Alessandro Del Piero	27
6	Alessandro Altobelli	25
=	Adolfo Baloncieri	25
=	Filippo Inzaghi	25
9	Francesco Graziani	23
=	Christian Vieri	23

MISTER INTER, GIACINTO

No Internazionale footballer will ever wear the No.3 shirt after it was retired in tribute to the legendary full-back **Giacinto Facchetti**, following his death in 2006 at the age of 64. He spent his entire senior career at Inter, between 1960 and 1978, and later served as the club's technical director and president. In his playing days he helped pioneer the role of a full-back as a stampeding, attacking presence – though favoured his right foot despite advancing on the left. He captained Italy 70 times, during his 94-cap international career and lifted the UEFA European Championship trophy in 1968.

ZOFF THE SCALE

Goalkeeper **Dino Zoff** set an international record by going 1,142 minutes without conceding a goal between September 1972 and June 1974. Zoff was Italy's captain when they won the 1982 FIFA World Cup – emulating the feat of another Juventus goalkeeper, Gianpiero Combi, who had been the victorious skipper in 1934. Zoff coached Italy to the final of the 2000 UEFA European Championship, which they lost 2-1 to France thanks to an extra-time "golden goal" – then quit a few days later, unhappy following the criticism levelled at him by Italy's then prime minister, Silvio Berlusconi.

SOMETIMES SUPER MARIO

Mario Balotelli is one of football's most explosive footballers – and not only because the fire brigade had to be called when fireworks were set off from the bathroom of his home the night before he scored in his club Manchester City's 6-1 trouncing of local rivals United. He marked his opening goal by revealing a T-shirt under his club kit bearing the question: "WHY ALWAYS ME?" His turbulent time in Manchester included a Premier League title but also a training-ground fight with manager Roberto Mancini and a reported £100,000 in parking fines. He was born in Palermo to Ghanaian parents, but health problems as a child prompted him to be adopted by an Italian couple when he was three, changing his name from Mario Barwuah to Mario Balotelli. He was given clearance to play for Italy when given citizenship at the age of 18 and was one of the country's star players at the 2012 UEFA European Championship, when he scored his first three international goals – including a decisive double against Germany in the semi-finals. But his volatile nature brought him a red card in a 2014 FIFA World Cup qualifier against the Czech Republic in June 2013 – and he lashed out at water bottles and then a brick wall after making his way off the pitch.

RIGHT CALL

Italy captain Giacinto Facchetti called correctly when their 1968 UEFA European Championship semi-final against the Soviet Union ended in a draw after extra-time (in the days before penalties) and had to be settled by the toss of a coin. The attacking left-back had luck on his side that time, then lifted the trophy after a 2-0 replay victory in the final against Yugoslavia. Facchetti, who also won the European Cup with Internazionale in 1964 and 1965, had an impressive scoring record for a defender, ending his career with 59 goals in 476 league appearances. He played on the left flank, even though he was a naturally right-footed player.

ROLLING RIVA

Italy's all-time top scorer is **Luigi "Gigi" Riva**, who scored 35 goals in 42 appearances for his country. One of his most important strikes was the opening goal in the 1968 UEFA European Championship final win over Yugoslavia. Despite his prolific form after having switched from left-winger to striker, he never played for one of Italy's traditional club giants. Instead, Riva – born in Leggiuno on 7 November 1944 – spent his entire league career with unfashionable Sardinian club Cagliari, and at one point turned down a move to the mighty Juventus. His goals (21 of them) fired the club to their one and only league championship in 1970. Riva suffered his fair share of bad luck with injuries, breaking his left leg while playing for Italy in 1966, then his right leg in 1970, again when he was away on international duty.

HAPPY CENTENARY

After captaining Italy to the 2006 FIFA World Cup title, **Fabio Cannavaro** was named FIFA World Player of the Year – at 33, the oldest winner of the prize, as well as the first defender. Cannavaro, born in Naples in 1973, played every minute of the 2006 tournament and the final triumph against France was the ideal way to celebrate his 100th international appearance.

WHEN THE GOING GETS BUFF

Italy goalkeeper **Gianluigi Buffon** has not only been one of the finest modern-day goalkeepers in the world but has also even surpassed some of the achievements of legendary Italian predecessor Dino Zoff. Buffon emulated 1982 world champion Dino Zoff by being part of Italy's 2006 FIFA World Cup-winning side – only conceding two goals during the tournament, one an own goal and the other a penalty. Italy's progress to the 2012 UEFA European Championship final allowed him to play his 25th game at a finals for Italy, one more than Zoff – and behind only defenders Paolo Maldini (36) and Fabio Cannavaro (26). Italy's dismal first-round exit at the 2010 FIFA World Cup could be blamed at least more than a little on Buffon's back injury in the first half of their first match that ruled him out of the rest of the tournament. Unlike fellow veterans Cannavaro and Gennaro Gattuso, who retired from internationals after the finals, Buffon insisted he would go on and was rewarded with the captaincy by incoming coach Cesare Prandelli.

CLEAN SWEEP

Italian clubs won all three UEFA trophies in the 1989–90 season, a unique treble. AC Milan took the European Cup (beating Benfica 1-0 in the final), Juventus the UEFA Cup (beating Fiorentina 3-1) and Sampdoria the Cup-Winners' Cup (beating Anderlecht 2-0 in the final).

GLOVE CONQUERS ALL

Walter Zenga went 517 minutes without conceding a goal at the 1990 FIFA World Cup – a tournament record.

ITALY'S GREATEST PLAYERS

(as chosen by the Italian football association)

1	Giuseppe Meazza	5	Giacinto Facchetti
2	Luigi Riva	6	Sandro Mazzola
3	Roberto Baggio	7	Giuseppe Bergomi
4	Paolo Maldini	8	Valentino Mazzola

KEEPING IT IN THE FAMILY

Cesare and **Paolo Maldini** are the only father and son to have hoisted the European Cup as winning captains – both with AC Milan and both for the first time in England. Cesare lifted the trophy after his team beat Benfica at Wembley, London, in 1963. Paolo repeated the feat 40 years later, when Milan defeated Juventus at Old Trafford, Manchester. Cesare was Italy coach and Paolo Italy captain at the 1998 FIFA World Cup, and they both featured at the 2002 tournament – though by now Cesare was in charge of Paraguay. The Maldini dynasty may not end there – Paolo's son, Christian, is emerging through the youth ranks at Milan. If he makes it into the first team, Christian will be the only player allowed to wear Paolo's famous No. 3 jersey. Although retired as Italy's second most-capped player, Paolo never managed to win an international tournament – he played for Italy sides that finished third and runners-up at the FIFA World Cup and runners-up in the UEFA European Championship.

TRAVELLING TRAPATTONI

Italian **Giovanni Trapattoni** has won domestic league titles as a coach in Italy, Germany, Portugal and Austria – with Juventus, Bayern Munich, Benfica and Salzburg. Only Portugal's Jose Mourinho has also coached teams in four different top countries to league title success. Trapattoni is the only manager to have won all three UEFA club competitions as well as the World Club Cup, all with the great Juventus sides of the 1980s.

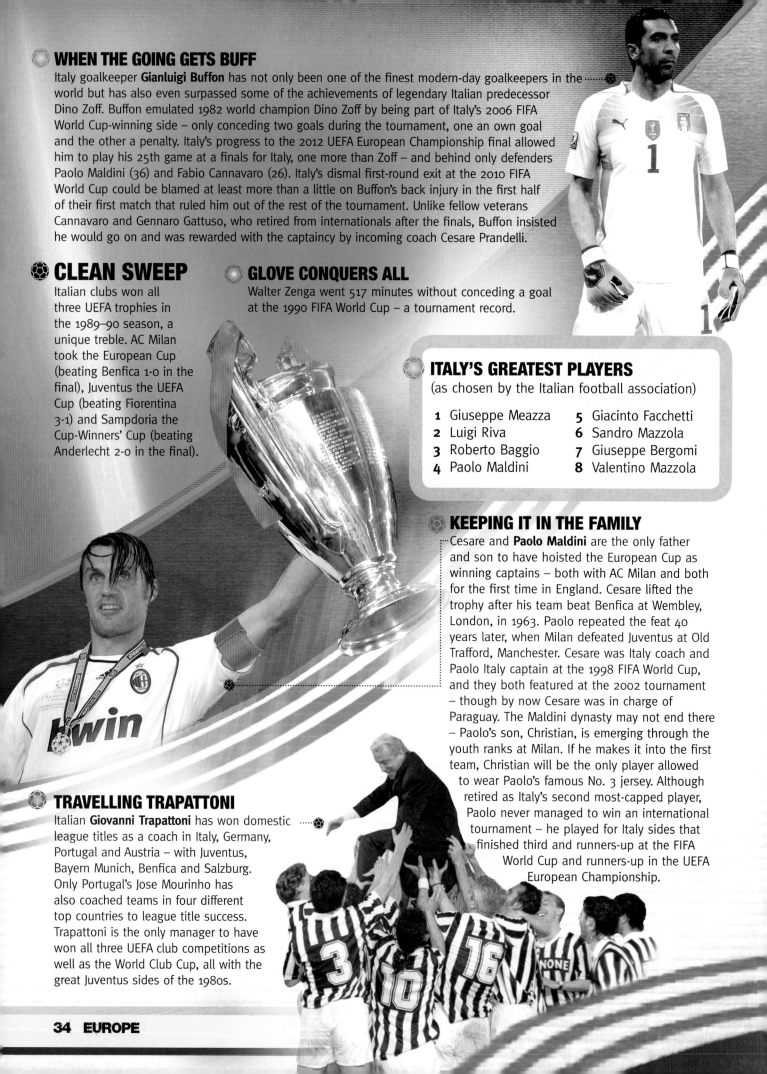

PEERLESS PIRLO

Deep-lying playmaker **Andrea Pirlo** is one of the finest passers of a football in the modern era. He was one of the stand-out performers when Italy won the 2006 FIFA World Cup and the only player to win three man-of-the-match prizes at the 2012 UEFA European Championship. Perhaps his finest moment of Euro 2012 was the "Panenka" penalty he audaciously chipped down the centre of the goal in Italy's quarter-final shoot-out victory over England. Pirlo came to the tournament having gone through the Italian league season unbeaten, helping Juventus lift the Serie A title after joining them in 2011 from AC Milan on a free transfer.

MEDAL COLLECTORS

Giovanni Ferrari not only enjoys the status of having won both the 1934 and 1938 FIFA World Cups with Italy, he also shares the record for most Serie A titles, with eight triumphs. Five were with Juventus, two with Internazionale and one with Bologna. He shares the record of eight league championship medals with Virginio Rosetta, twice with Pro Vercelli and six times with Juventus, and Giuseppe Furino, all with Juventus.

ITALIAN LEAGUE TITLES

Juventus	28	Lazio	2
Internazionale	18	Napoli	2
AC Milan	18	Cagliari	1
Genoa	9	Casale	1
Bologna	7	Hellas Verona	1
Pro Vercelli	7	Novese	1
Torino	7	Sampdoria	1
Roma	3	Spezia	1
Fiorentina	2		

GRAND OLD TEAM TO PLAY FOR

Every Italian FIFA World Cup squad has featured at least one Juventus player. The Turin team, known as the "Grand Old Lady" of Italian club football, were relegated a division in 2006 after being found guilty of match-fixing – and, as a result, were forced to endure their first season outside the top division since the club's foundation in 1897. Their 55 trophies are an Italian club record, following consecutive league title triumphs in 2012 and 2013 – and, in 1985, they became the first team to have won the European, UEFA and Cup Winners' Cups.

PRANDELLI'S PLEDGE

Cesare Prandelli was in Africa during the 2010 FIFA World Cup tournament, before he succeeded Marcello Lippi as Italy coach. But the ex-Fiorentina boss went there not only to watch football; he and his daughter went to Zanzibar, Tanzania, to open a school in memory of his wife Manuela, who had died of cancer three years earlier. Prandelli's first competitive home match in charge of Italy was in Florence, and his new team crushed the Faroe Islands 5-0. The coach exceeded most expectations by leading Italy to the 2012 UEFA European Championship final. The defeat that day to Spain was Prandelli's first in 16 competitive matches in charge. Prandelli's son Nicolo, a fitness coach, became part of the national team's back-up staff in the build-up to Euro 2012.

BEEFING UP

The stadium shared by AC Milan and Internazionale is popularly known as the San Siro, after the district in which it is located. Its official title, however, is Stadio Giuseppe Meazza, named after the star inside-forward on the pitch and dance enthusiast off it who played for both clubs as well as Italy's 1934 and 1938 FIFA World Cup-winning sides. Meazza, born in Milan on 23 August 1910, was first spotted by an Inter scout while playing keepy-uppy in the street with a ball made of rags – but he was so thin he had to be fattened up with plenty of steaks. His last goal for Italy was a penalty in the 1938 World Cup semi-final against Brazil – taken while trying to pull up his shorts, whose elastic had broken.

TRAGIC TORINO

Torino were Italy's most successful club side when their first-team squad was wiped out in an air crash at Superga, above Turin, on 4 May 1949. The club has only won the Serie A title once since then, in the 1976–77 season.  Among the victims was star forward Valentino Mazzola, who had gone along on the trip despite being ill. His son **Sandro Mazzola**, only six at the time of the disaster, went on to star in the Italy teams that won the 1968 UEFA European Championship and finished as FIFA World Cup runners-up two years later.

NETHERLANDS

The walled banks of orange-shirted Netherlands fans may have become a regular feature at the world's major football tournaments, but that has not always been the case. It wasn't until the 1970s, with Johan Cruyff and his team's spectacular brand of Total Football, that the country possessed a side worthy of the modern legend. They won the UEFA European Championship in 1988 and have regularly challenged for the game's major honours.

NETHERLANDS MANAGERS (SINCE 1980)

Jan Zwartkruis	1978–81
Rob Baan	1981
Kees Rijvers	1981–84
Rinus Michels	1984–85
Leo Beenhakker	1985–86
Rinus Michels	1986–88
Thijs Libregts	1988–90
Nol de Ruiter	1990
Leo Beenhakker	1990
Rinus Michels	1990–92
Dick Advocaat	1992–95
Guus Hiddink	1995–98
Frank Rijkaard	1998–2000
Louis van Gaal	2000–02
Dick Advocaat	2002–04
Marco van Basten	2004–08
Bert van Marwijk	2008–12
Louis van Gaal	2012–

MICHELS THE MASTER

Rinus Michels (1928–2005) was named FIFA's Coach of the Century in 1999 for his achievements with the Netherlands and Ajax. The former Ajax and Netherlands striker took over the manager's job at his old club in 1965 and began creating the side that would dominate European football in the early 1970s. Michels built the team around Johan Cruyff – as he later did with the national side – and introduced the concept known as "Total Football". He moved to Barcelona after Ajax's 1971 European Cup victory, but he was called back to mastermind the Netherlands' 1974 FIFA World Cup bid. Nicknamed "The General", he was known as a disciplinarian who could impose order on the many different factions within the Dutch dressing room. Michels used that skill to great effect after taking over the national team again for their 1988 UEFA European Championship campaign. In the finals, the Dutch beat England and the Republic of Ireland to reach the last four, then knocked out hosts West Germany before beating the Soviet Union 2-0 in the final. Michels tookcharge for a third spell as manager when the Netherlands reached the semi-finals of Euro 92. He retired straight after the tournament.

CRUYFF THE MAGICIAN

Johan Cruyff's footballing achievements have made him the most famous living Dutchman. Cruyff (born in Amsterdam on 25 April 1947) was the catalyst for the rise of both Ajax and the national team. As one Dutch paper wrote before the 1974 FIFA World Cup final: "Cruyff woke up the Netherlands and took us to a world-class level." His great opponent, Franz Beckenbauer, said: "He is the best player to have come from Europe." Cruyff joined Ajax as a ten-year-old and made his league debut at 17. He led them to eight championships and the European Cup three years in a row. He and coach Rinus Michels also developed the style of playing known as "Total Football", which became a trademark for club and country. Cruyff made his national debut, against Hungary, on 7 September 1966. He scored 33 goals in 48 appearances and captained his country 33 times. He was named Player of the Tournament in the 1974 FIFA World Cup finals and was voted European Player of the Year three times.

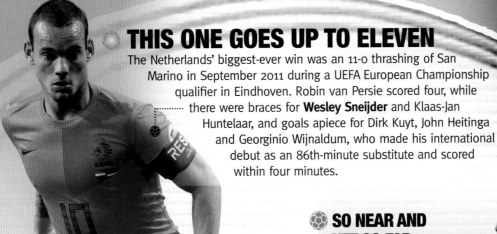

THIS ONE GOES UP TO ELEVEN

The Netherlands' biggest-ever win was an 11-0 thrashing of San Marino in September 2011 during a UEFA European Championship qualifier in Eindhoven. Robin van Persie scored four, while there were braces for **Wesley Sneijder** and Klaas-Jan Huntelaar, and goals apiece for Dirk Kuyt, John Heitinga and Georginio Wijnaldum, who made his international debut as an 86th-minute substitute and scored within four minutes.

SO NEAR AND YET SO FAR

The Netherlands lost all three first-round matches at the 2012 UEFA European Championship – Denmark (1-0), Germany (2–1) and Portugal (2-1) – and became the third country in a row to go from losing a FIFA World Cup final to departing the next UEFA European Championship in the first round two years later. 2006 FIFA World Cup runners-up France did the same at the 2008 UEFA European Championship, as did 2002 FIFA World Cup runners-up Germany at the 2004 UEFA European Championship. Italy had suffered a similar fate following their 1994 FIFA World Cup final loss; they also fell at the first hurdle at Euro 96. The Dutch failure in 2012 meant they failed to reach the knockout stages of a major tournament for the first time since 1984, when they failed to qualify for that year's UEFA European Championship finals tournament. They only scored twice in three games at Euro 2012, the first courtesy of striker **Robin van Persie**. Ten of the 11 men who started the 2010 FIFA World Cup final were in the Euro 2012 squad, with only the retired Giovanni van Bronckhorst missing.

LOUIS LOUIS

Louis van Gaal returned as the Netherlands manager after Bert van Marwijk's side flopped at the 2012 UEFA European Championship. This was van Gaal's second stint in charge, having previously served between 2000 and 2002. His club triumphs include a UEFA Champions League with Ajax Amsterdam in 1995, two La Liga titles with Barcelona in Spain and one Bundesliga crown with Germany's Bayern Munich. The Dutch are no strangers to reappointing former coaches: Karel Kaufman, Friedrich Donenfeld, Leo Beenhakker and Dick Advocaat have all been the boss more than once, while Euro 1988 winner Rinus Michels had four separate stints in the job.

GOALS GALORE

Only four players have scored five goals in a game for the Netherlands: Jan Vos, as Finland were crushed 9-0 in July 1912; Leen Vente, in a 9-3 defeat of Belgium in March 1934; John Bosman, in an 8-0 home trouncing of Cyprus in October 1987; and Marco van Basten, in an 8-0 win in Malta in December 1990. Bosman scored three separate hat-tricks for the Dutch, as did Mannes Francken, Beb Bakhuys and Faas Wilkes. Two of Wilkes' trebles were scored in 1946 – the third came a full 13 years later.

VAN BASTEN'S TOURNAMENT

Marco van Basten was the hero of the Netherlands' 1988 UEFA European Championship success. He netted a hat-trick to see off England in the group games, scored a semi-final winner against West Germany, and then cracked a spectacular flying volley to clinch a 2-0 victory over the Soviet Union in the final. The Dutch forward also starred in Italy's Serie A with AC Milan, and was twice the league's top scorer before persistent ankle trouble ended his career prematurely.

HERO HAPPEL

Ernst Happel is second only to Rinus Michels for his coaching achievements with Dutch teams. The former Austria defender made history by steering Feyenoord to the European Cup in 1970 – the first Dutch side to win the trophy. He was drafted in to coach the Netherlands at the 1978 FIFA World Cup finals after guiding Belgian side Brugge to the European Cup final. In Johan Cruyff's absence, Happel drew the best from Ruud Krol, Johan Neeskens and Arie Haan as the Netherlands reached the final before losing in extra-time to Argentina in Buenos Aires.

HANGING AROUND

Sander Boschker waited a long time for his full introduction to international football, but set two Dutch records when finally coming on as a second-half substitute against Ghana in a June 2010 friendly. At the age of 39 years and 256 days, he was not only the oldest Dutchman to win his first cap – but also the oldest Dutch international ever. That remains his only cap ... so far.

FLYING FEAR DENIED BERGKAMP MORE CAPS

Dennis Bergkamp would have won many more than 79 caps, but for his fear of flying. Bergkamp refused to board aircraft after the Netherlands squad were involved in a bomb hoax incident during the 1994 FIFA World Cup in the United States. He missed every away game for the Netherlands and his clubs unless he could reach the venue by road, rail or boat.

NEESKENS'S EARLY GOAL

The Netherlands took a first-minute lead in the 1974 World Cup final without a West German player having touched the ball. The Dutch built a move of 14 passes from the kick-off and Johan Cruyff was tripped in the box by Uli Hoeness. Johan Neeskens converted the first penalty in a World Cup final history ... but they still went on to lose.

KEEPING IN WITH THE IN–LAWS

Midfield enforcer **Mark van Bommel** was left out of coach Marco van Basten's Dutch squad for the 2008 UEFA European Championship, but was ever-present at the 2010 FIFA World Cup. Van Basten's replacement Bert van Marwijk is his father-in-law: van Bommel being married to van Marwijk's daughter Andra. Van Bommel retired from international football after the 2012 UEFA European Championship, during which he was dropped for the Netherlands' final game. He responded by saying: "Before I was a hero. Now I am only van Marwijk's son-in-law."

NETHERLANDS' DOUBLE LOSERS

Nine Netherlands players were on the losing side in both the 1974 (2-1 to West Germany) and 1978 (3-1 to Argentina) FIFA World Cup finals. Jan Jongbloed, Ruud Krol, Wim Jansen, Arie Haan, Johan Neeskens, Johnny Rep and Rob Rensenbrink started both games. Wim Suurbier started in 1974 and was a substitute in 1978. Rene van de Kerkhof was a sub in 1974 and started in 1978.

DIFFERENT SIDES OF SNEIJDER

Wesley Sneijder was hoping to achieve an unprecedented quintuple when his Netherlands team took on Spain in the 2010 FIFA World Cup final. No footballer had ever before won the FIFA World Cup in the same season as a domestic league and cup double and the UEFA Champions League or European Cup – let alone adding the FIFA World Cup Golden Boot. Sneijder won the 2009–10 treble with his club side Internazionale before only just missing out on the FIFA World Cup and the Golden Boot. Despite his FIFA World Cup final heartbreak, Sneijder did enjoy some romantic solace six days after defeat to Spain, when he married Dutch actress and TV presenter Yolanthe Cabau van Kasbergen.

BRAVING THE PAIN

Dutch defender Khalid Boulahrouz insisted on playing in his country's 2008 UEFA European Championship quarter-final against Russia despite the death of his prematurely-born baby daughter Anissa just days earlier. He and his team-mates all wore black armbands in her honour during the game.

THE WINNING CAPTAIN

With his distinctive dreadlocks, Ruud Gullit cut a swathe through world football through the 1980s and '90s. Twice a European Cup winner with AC Milan and a former European Footballer of the Year, he will always be remembered fondly by the Dutch fans as being the first man in a Netherlands shirt to lift a major trophy – the 1988 UEFA European Championship.

NETHERLANDS' EURO STARS

Three Dutch players have won the European Footballer of the Year award: Johan Cruyff, **Ruud Gullit** and Marco van Basten. Cruyff picked up the award in 1971, 1973 and 1974; Gullit was honoured in 1987, and Van Basten was chosen in 1988, 1989 and 1992.

TOP SCORERS

1	Patrick Kluivert	40
2	Dennis Bergkamp	37
3	Ruud van Nistelrooy	35
=	Robin van Persie	35
=	Faas Wilkes	35
6	Klaas-Jan Huntelaar	34
7	Johan Cruyff	33
=	Abe Lenstra	33
9	Beb Bakhuys	28
10	Kick Smit	26

DE BOER BOYS SET RECORD

Twins Frank and Ronald de Boer hold the record for the most games played by brothers together for the Netherlands. Frank won 112 caps, while Ronald won 67.

TOP CAPS

1	Edwin van der Sar	130
2	Frank de Boer	112
3	Gio van Bronckhorst	106
4	Rafael van der Vaart	105
5	Phillip Cocu	101
6	Dirk Kuyt	94
7	Wesley Sneijder	93
8	Clarence Seedorf	88
9	John Heitinga	87
10	Marc Overmars	86

WORK OF VAART

Rafael van der Vaart became the fifth player to reach a century of caps for the Netherlands, following goalkeeper Edwin van der Sar, defenders Frank de Boer and Giovanni van Bronckhorst and midfielder Philip Cocu. Yet for a spell it looked as though he might just miss out: he ended the 2012 UEFA European Championship on 99 caps and manager Bert van Marwijk signalled he may be left out of future squads. But Van Marwijk's departure that summer was a boost for van der Vaart and he went on to make his 100th appearance in a 4-2 friendly defeat to Belgium in August 2012. The ex-Ajax Amsterdam, Real Madrid and Tottenham Hotspur playmaker had marked his 99th cap with a stunning long-range opening goal against Portugal in the Netherlands' final first-round game at Euro 2012, and also hit the post as his side lost 2-1 and departed the tournament earlier than expected.

SIXTH SENSE

Maarten Stekelenburg, Edwin van der Sar's successor as the Netherlands' first-choice goalkeeper, impressed many with his performances at the 2010 FIFA World Cup, conceding just six goals in seven games – two of them penalties. His rise is all the more startling because he is deaf in one ear. He also has the unenviable distinction of being the first Dutch international goalkeeper to be shown a red card. On 6 September 2008, in a 2-1 friendly defeat against Australia in Eindhoven, he was sent off for fouling Josh Kennedy.

ALL-TIME LEADING SCORER

Born in Amsterdam on 1 July 1976, centre-forward Patrick Kluivert made his Netherlands debut in 1994. In the following ten years he made 79 appearances for the national side, scoring an all-time Dutch record 40 goals.

KOEMAN PEOPLE

The only man to both play for and manage all of Dutch domestic football's "big three" of Ajax Amsterdam, PSV Eindhoven and Feyenoord is **Ronald Koeman**. He won the UEFA European Cup twice, with PSV Eindhoven in 1988, and with Barcelona four years later – a game in which he scored the winning goal, a ferocious long-range free-kick. Despite largely playing in defence, he scored 14 goals in 78 games for the Netherlands. Elder brother Erwin played 31 times for the Netherlands and their father Martin won one cap for his country in 1964. Both Ronald and Erwin were part of the Netherlands' 1988 UEFA European Championship-winning side.

EARLY DAYS

The Netherlands played their first international against Belgium in Brussels on 30 April 1905. Eddy de Neve scored all the goals in the Netherlands' 4-1 win. The Dutch and their Belgian neighbours have been arch-rivals ever since.

NETHERLANDS – MODERN GREATS

The Netherlands have been one of the strongest nations in world football for the past 35 years. The Dutch "Total Football" team – led by Johan Cruyff – reached the 1974 FIFA World Cup final, only to lose 2-1 to West Germany. Four years later, the Dutch lost the final against Argentina, 3-1 in extra-time in Buenos Aires. In between, they reached the UEFA European Championship semi-finals in 1976. Coach Rinus Michels steered the Netherlands to their one major honour, in 1988, when they beat the Soviet Union 2-0 in the UEFA European Championship final. They had gained revenge over West Germany for the 1974 defeat by winning 2-1 in the semi-finals. Before reaching the 2010 FIFA World Cup final, the Dutch suffered a series of semi-final setbacks: they lost the 1998 FIFA World Cup semi-final on penalties to Brazil, and were also beaten in UEFA European Championship semi-finals in 1992, 2000 and 2004.

JETRO POWERED

Left-back **Jetro Willems** became the youngest player  in UEFA European Championship tournament history when he started for the Netherlands against Denmark in their opening Group B game in the Ukrainian city of Kharkiv on 9 June 2012. He was 18 years and 71 days old, 44 days younger than Belgium's Enzo Scifo had been at the 1984 finals. Willems is the fourth-youngest player to be capped by the Netherlands, with the record held by Jan van Breda Kolff, who was 17 years and 74 days old when making his debut against Belgium on 2 April 1911. Van Breda Kolff's goal in a 3-1 win, the only one of his 11-cap career, means he remains his country's youngest scorer.

NETHERLANDS SO CLOSE

The Netherlands came within a post's width of winning the 1978 FIFA World Cup final. A Rob Rensenbrink shot bounced off an upright in the last minute of normal time. It was 1-1 after 90 minutes and Argentina went on to win 3-1 in extra-time, shattering Dutch final dreams for the second FIFA World Cup in a row.

PENALTY PLAGUE

Missed penalties have become a nightmare for the Netherlands, causing their downfall in several major tournaments. The jinx started in the Euro 92 semi-final when Peter Schmeichel saved Marco van Basten's kick, enabling Denmark to win the penalty shoot-out. The Netherlands lost their Euro 96 quarter-final to France 5-4 on penalties and, two years later, went down 4-2 to Brazil in a FIFA World Cup semi-final shoot-out. Worse followed when the Dutch co-hosted Euro 2000. They missed two penalties in normal time in the semi-final against Italy. *Azzurri* keeper Francesco Toldo then saved two spot-kicks to eliminate the Dutch in the shoot-out.

KEY PLAYER

Maintaining harmony has often been a tricky task for Dutch coaches at major international tournaments – but Bert van Marwijk managed to do so at the 2010 FIFA World Cup, despite rumoured tension between several of his star players. When not conducting his team from the touchline, van Marwijk could occasionally be found playing the piano in the lobby of the squad's Johannesburg hotel.

VAN DER SAR TOPS THE LOT

Goalkeeper **Edwin van der Sar** (born in Voorhout on 29 October 1970)  is the Netherlands' most-capped player, having made 130 appearances for the national side. He joined Ajax in 1990 and helped them win the European Cup five years later. He made his Netherlands debut on 7 June 1995, against Belarus, and was their first-choice keeper for 13 years. He quit international football after the Netherlands' elimination at Euro 2008, but new coach Bert van Marwijk persuaded him to return briefly after injuries to his successors, Maarten Stekelenburg and Henk Timmer. Van der Sar has also won the UEFA Champions League with Manchester United, as well as spending spells with Juventus and Fulham.

GOING DUTCH FULL-TIME

Professionalism was not introduced into Dutch football until 1954. The Netherlands' emergence as a major power came even later, after Ajax and Feyenoord decided to go full-time professional in the early 1960s. Until then, even stars such as Ajax left-winger Piet Keizer – who worked in a tailor's – had part-time jobs outside the game.

DUTCH CLOGS

The Netherlands became the first team to be shown as many as nine cards during a single FIFA World Cup match when they received eight yellows, including a lenient one for Nigel de Jong's chest-high challenge on Xabi Alonso, and a red during the 2010 final against Spain. The Netherlands were also involved in the FIFA World Cup game with the most cards: their second-round defeat to Portugal four years earlier, when 20 cards were shown in total – 16 yellows and four reds.

WHOLE LOTTA SCHAKEN

Feyenoord winger Ruben Schaken netted the Netherlands' 1,500th international goal to complete a 3-0 victory over Estonia in a FIFA World Cup qualifier in March 2013. It was his second goal in three appearances for his country.

SPAIN

Spain is home to some of Europe's strongest club sides (boasting 13 European Cup/UEFA Champions League wins between them) and has produced some of football's biggest names. For years, however, the national team was considered the world game's biggest underachievers (*La Roja's* only success being the 1964 UEFA European Championship). Things changed in 2008, when Spain won the UEFA European Championship, its first taste of international success for 44 years and a first-ever top position in the Coca-Cola/FIFA World Rankings. Even better came with their first FIFA World Cup in 2010, then an unprecedented third consecutive major trophy when they retained their European crown at Euro 2012 – cementing Spain's place as the world's best.

"FALSE NINE"

Spain not only began and ended their Euro 2012 campaign against Italy, but also became the first team to win a UEFA European Championship fielding the same starting XI in their opening game as in the final. Perhaps even more surprising was that Vicente del Bosque's men won the tournament so convincingly despite kicking off without an orthodox striker, preferring a 4-6-0 formation with midfielder **Cesc Fabregas** deployed as a "false nine".

DOUBLING UP

Spain's 2010 FIFA World Cup triumph made them the first country since West Germany in 1974 to lift the trophy as the reigning European champions. When France combined the two titles, they did it the other way around, by winning the 1998 FIFA World Cup and then the UEFA European Championship two years later. Yet no country had won three major tournaments in a row until Spain won Euro 2012, trouncing Italy 4-0 in the final. This also made Spain the first team to make a successful defence of their UEFA European Championship title. That scoreline was also the largest victory in a FIFA World Cup or UEFA European Championship final. The clean sheet in the final also stretched their run without conceding a goal in knockout games at major tournaments to 990 minutes.

THREE AND EASY

Only three players have scored for Spain in three separate FIFA World Cup final tournaments – Raul (in 1998, 2002 and 2006), Julio Salinas (1986, 1990 and 1994) and Fernando Hierro (1994, 1998 and 2002). Hierro is also Spain's fourth leading goalscorer, despite spending a large part of his career as a defender.

GROUNDS FOR APPEAL

No single country has provided more venues when hosting a FIFA World Cup finals than the 17 stadiums – in 14 cities – used by Spain in 1982. The 2002 tournament was played at 20 different venues but ten were in Japan and ten in South Korea. The 1982 competition was the first FIFA World Cup to be expanded from 16 to 24 teams. The final was played in Madrid's Estadio Santiago Bernabeu.

RIGHT SAID FRED

When Spain came back from 2-0 and then 3-2 down to win 4-3 in Madrid in May 1929, they became the first non-British team to beat England. Spain's victory, in the Estadio Metropolitano, came with the help of their English coach Fred Pentland, who had moved to Spain in 1920. He had most success with Athletic Bilbao, leading them to league and cup doubles in 1930 and 1931 – and inflicting Barcelona's worst-ever defeat, a 12-1 rout in 1931.

NOT TOO SHABY XABI

Passmaster **Xabi Alonso** scored both goals as Spain beat France 2-0 in their 2012 UEFA European Championship quarter-final – an ideal way for him to celebrate a day in which he became the fifth Spaniard, after Iker Casillas, Raul, Xavi and Andoni Zubizarreta, to make 100 international appearances. The central midfielder's father Periko Alonso won 21 Spanish caps as well as three La Liga titles – two with Real Sociedad and one with Barcelona, though Xabi would later play for Barca's arch-rivals Real Madrid. Xabi's brother Mikel and half-brother Marcos are both professional footballers, while another brother Jon is a referee.

MAJOR TOURNAMENTS

FIFA WORLD CUP:
13 appearances – winners 2010

UEFA EUROPEAN CHAMPIONSHIP:
9 appearances – winners 1964, 2008, 2012

FIRST INTERNATIONAL:
Spain 1 Denmark 0 (Brussels, Belgium, 28 August 1920)

BIGGEST WIN:
Spain 13 Bulgaria 0 (Madrid, 21 May 1933)

BIGGEST DEFEAT:
Italy 7 Spain 1 (Amsterdam, Holland 4 June 1928); England 7 Spain 1 (London, England, 9 December 1931)

RED ALERT

Spain refused to play in the first UEFA European Championship in 1960, in protest at having to travel to the Soviet Union, a Communist country. But they changed their minds four years later, not only hosting the tournament but also winning it – by beating the visiting Soviets 2-1 in the final. Spain were captained by Fernando Olivella and managed by Jose Villalonga, who had been the first coach to win the European Cup, with Real Madrid in 1956.

WORLD BEATERS

Spain have not lost a FIFA World Cup qualifier since Denmark beat them 1-0 in March 1993. Their unbeaten run stretched to 50 games and 20 years with a 1-0 victory over France in Paris in March 2013 thanks to Pedro Rodriguez's 58th-minute goal.

WISE HEAD, OLD SHOULDERS

Luis Aragones became the oldest coach to win the UEFA European Championship when Spain won the 2008 tournament, a month short of his 70th birthday. Aragones, a former centre-forward and known only as "Luis" during his playing days, had lined up for Spain in the run-up to the 1964 finals, but had to watch the team win the competition from the sidelines after being left out of the squad. During his time as national coach between 2004 and 2008, the so-called "Wise Man of Hortaleza" won more matches than any other Spanish boss – 38. Aragones, born in Hortaleza, Madrid, on 28 July 1938, spent most of his playing career with Atletico Madrid, where he was surprisingly appointed as club coach (at the surprisingly young age of 36) immediately after retiring in 1974.

TORRES! TORRES!

Fernando Torres originally wanted to be a goalkeeper as a child before becoming a striker. Torres, born in Madrid on 20 March 1984, was only 19 when he was made captain of his boyhood heroes Atletico Madrid. He has a knack for scoring the only goal in tournament finals – most famously in the 2008 UEFA European Championship, for Spain against Germany in Vienna. He had already achieved the feat in the Under-16 UEFA European Championship in 2001 and for the Under-19s the following year. Torres became the most expensive Spanish footballer ever when Chelsea paid ¤58.5million to sign him from fellow English club Liverpool in January 2011 – eight months after his international strike partner David Villa cost Barcelona ¤40million in joining from Valencia. In 2012, Torres became the first player to score in the final of two different UEFA European Championships, when he came on as a substitute and found the net against Italy.

TOP CAPS

1	Iker Casillas	148
2	Xavi Hernandez	126
=	Andoni Zubizarreta	126
4	Sergio Ramos	108
5	Xabi Alonso	107
6	Fernando Torres	106
7	Raul Gonzalez	102
8	Carles Puyol	100
9	David Villa	92
10	Fernando Hierro	89

TOP SCORERS

1	David Villa	56
2	Raul Gonzales	44
3	Fernando Torres	36
4	Fernando Hierro	29
5	Fernando Morientes	27
6	Emilio Butragueno	26
7	Alfredo Di Stefano	23
8	Julio Salinas	22
9	Michel	21
10	David Silva	20
=	Telmo Zarra	20

HAPPY HERNANDEZ

Relentlessly precise passer **Xavi Hernandez** has proved himself a more than worthy heir to Pep Guardiola at the heart of the Barcelona and Spain midfields. As well as winning the UEFA Champions League with his club in 2006, 2009 and 2011, he was voted Player of the Tournament when Spain won the 2008 UEFA European Championship, and starred as *La Roja* claimed the FIFA World Cup crown two years later and retained their European crown in 2012. Xavi was third in the 2010 and 2011 FIFA Ballon d'Or voting, both times behind winning club mate Lionel Messi. Yet he nearly left Barcelona for Italy's AC Milan when aged just 17 – though Xavi was not keen on the proposed move and later expressed his relief at staying in Spain.

GIFT OF THE FAB

Arsenal's Cesc Fabregas became Spain's youngest-ever FIFA World Cup player – and the country's youngest international for 70 years – when he came on as a substitute against Ukraine at the 2006 FIFA World Cup aged 19 years 41 days.

BEST CAS SCENARIO

Spain suffered a rare defeat when goalkeeper and captain **Iker Casillas** equalled the national record for most international appearances, in a 1-0 friendly defeat to England in November 2011. *La Roja* then drew 2-2 with Costa Rica three days later when he broke the record. Seven months later Casillas was lifting a third trophy in a row, at Euro 2012 – and extending not just his international appearances record but several more. The 4-0 Euro 2012 final victory over Italy made him the first footballer to reach a century of international wins. It was also his 78th clean sheet for his country, more than any other goalkeeper has achieved – the closest challenger was the Netherlands' Edwin van der Sar, on 72. The pair now share the record – nine – for the most UEFA European Championship clean sheets. Casillas went 821 minutes without conceding a goal for Spain until Olivier Giroud scored for France in a FIFA World Cup qualifier in October 2012.

VILLA FILLS HIS BOOTS

David Villa became Spain's all-time top scorer in FIFA World Cups with his first-round goal against Chile, his sixth overall across the 2006 and 2010 tournaments – then knockout-round strikes against Portugal and Paraguay took his FIFA World Cup tally to eight. Emilio Butragueno, Fernando Hierro, Fernando Morientes and Raul had each scored five FIFA World Cup goals for Spain. Villa also became the first Spaniard to miss a penalty in a FIFA World Cup match, when he wasted the chance of a hat-trick against Honduras by shooting his spot-kick wide. Spain had scored their previous 14 FIFA World Cup penalties, not counting shoot-outs. Villa pulled ahead of Raul in Spain's all-time scoring stakes with a brace against the Czech Republic in March 2011, but a broken leg ruled him out of the 2012 UEFA European Championship, while a knee injury meant Barcelona team-mate Carles Puyol joined him in missing out on adding to their Euro 2008 and 2010 FIFA World Cup winners' medals.

SERGING SERGIO

Sergio Ramos became the youngest-ever European player to reach 100 international caps, in March 2013, at the age of 26 years and 358 days – and marked the occasion by scoring the opening goal in a 1-1 draw with Finland. He claimed the record from Germany's Lukas Podolski, who was 21 days older when he reached his century of caps. South Korea's Cha Bum-Kun, who was 24 years and 139 days old when he achieved the landmark, holds the global record. Ramos, who can play both at right-back or in central defence, was a member of the Spain team that won the 2008 and 2012 UEFA European Championships, as well as the 2010 FIFA World Cup. He held those trophies in safer hands than he had done when he raised the Spanish Copa del Rey, won by his club Real Madrid, during an open-top bus tour in April 2011: on that occasion, he dropped the cup from the upper deck and saw it crushed beneath the bus's wheels.

FIT FOR PURPOSE

Luis Suarez played through injury for Spain in the 1964 UEFA European Championship final – luckily for his team-mates, since he set up both goals in a 2-1 triumph. He was named European Footballer of the Year in 1960 – the only Spanish-born player to have taken the prize.

TRI-NATIONS

Ladislav Kubala played for not one, not two, but three different countries – though he never appeared in the finals of a major international tournament. Despite being born in Budapest on 10 June 1927, he made his international debut for Czechoslovakia in 1946 – winning five more caps for the country of his parents' birth. He then appeared three times for birthplace Hungary after moving back to the country in 1948, before playing 19 games for Spain after leaving Hungary as a refugee and securing a transfer to Barcelona in 1951.

VICTORY MARCH

Centre-back Carlos Marchena became the first footballer to go 50 internationals in a row unbeaten, when he played in Spain's 3-2 victory over Saudi Arabia in May 2009 – one more than Brazil's 1950s and 1960s winger Garrincha. Marchena was a member of Spain's successful 2010 FIFA World Cup squad, ending the tournament on 54 consecutive internationals without defeat. Marchena's 57-game unbeaten run came to an end when Argentina beat Spain 4-1 in September 2010.

TREASURE CHEST

The Spanish first division goalkeeper who concedes the fewest goals per game each season is awarded the Zamora Trophy. This is named after legendary keeper **Ricardo Zamora**, who played 46 times for Spain between 1920 and 1936 – including the legendary 4-3 win over England in Madrid in 1929. Zamora was the first Spanish star to play for both Barcelona and Real Madrid. Later he was league title-winning coach of ... Atletico Madrid.

LUCKY JUAN

Only one player has failed to score in a FIFA World Cup penalty shoot-out with a spot-kick that would have won the game had it gone in: Spain's Juan Carlos Valeron, whose effort went wide against the Republic of Ireland in 2002. The shoot-out score was 2-1 in Spain's favour, with just an Irish attempt to follow, when he missed – but his team went on to win anyway.

LEADING LIGHTS

Spain have become experts in holding onto a lead, winning 43 games in a row having opened the scoring – including all six of their victories at the 2010 FIFA World Cup. The last team to go a goal down to Spain but end up winning the game were Northern Ireland, who secured a 3-2 success in a Euro 2008 qualifier in September 2006.

SPANISH LEAGUE CHAMPIONSHIPS

Real Madrid	32
Barcelona	22
Atletico Madrid	9
Athletic Bilbao	8
Valencia	6
Real Sociedad	2
Deportivo de la Coruna	1
Sevilla	1
Betis	1

THE RAUL THING

Raul Gonzalez Blanco – known as Raul – is not only Spain's second-most prolific scorer, with 44 goals from 102 games, but also holds the records for the most UEFA European Cup/Champions League goals (66) and for the most goals for Real Madrid (323), having passed Alfredo di Stefano's tally of 309 in 2008-09. But despite his glittering career, he just missed out on international glory for Spain: he was controversially left out of their 2008 UEFA European Championship-winning squad and was also overlooked for the FIFA World Cup two years later.

SUPER PED

Spanish winger **Pedro** is the only player to have scored in six separate official club tournaments in one calendar year, managing to hit the net for Barcelona in Spain's Primera Liga, Copa del Rey and Super Cup in 2009, as well as the UEFA Champions League, UEFA European Super Cup and FIFA Club World Cup. He was also in the starting line-up for the 2010 FIFA World Cup final – less than two years after being a member of the Barcelona reserve team in Spain's third division and needing new club manager Pep Guardiola's intervention to prevent him being sent home to Tenerife.

SEMI PRECIOUS

Centre-back **Carles Puyol**'s thumping header not only gave Spain victory in their 2010 FIFA World Cup semi-final – it was also the country's first win over Germany in four FIFA World Cup matches. West Germany had won 2-1 in both 1966 and 1982, before a 1-1 draw at the 1994 tournament. But Spain's 1-0 win in 2010 was a repeat of their triumph over Germany in the UEFA European Championship final two years earlier. Nineteen members of the two 2010 FIFA World Cup squads had played in that Euro 2008 showdown, 11 Spanish and eight German.

PERFECT PICHICHI

The annual award for top scorer in La Liga is called the "Pichichi" – the nickname of Rafael Moreno, a striker for Athletic Bilbao between 1911 and 1921. He scored 200 goals in 170 games for the club, and once in five matches for Spain. Pichichi, who often took the field wearing a large white cap, died suddenly in 1922 aged just 29.

MORE THAN JUST A CLUB

Barcelona, founded in 1899 by a Swiss businessman, Hans Gamper, prides itself on being "more than a club". The club's famous blue and purple resisted the march of commercialism for more than a century until 2006, when the club signed a deal with (and gave money to) the United Nations Children's Fund (UNICEF) in exchange for using the charity's logo on its shirts.

TOP BOSS DEL BOSQUE

Vicente Del Bosque was an unused substitute during Ladislao Kubala's 68th and final match in charge of Spain in 1980. He was on Spain bench again when *La Roja* played Denmark in March 2013, but this time as manager, and for the 69th time, enabling him to surpass Kubala's record. Del Bosque won the 2010 FIFA World Cup and the 2012 UEFA European Championship as Spain manager, adding to the two UEFA Champions League titles he claimed as Real Madrid boss. He and Italy's Marcelo Lippi are the only men to have won both the UEFA Champions League or European Cup and the FIFA World Cup – but Del Bosque's Euro 2012 triumph gave him an unprecedented hat-trick. Another unmatched feat was his 13 victories in his first 13 matches as Spain manager after he succeeded Luis Aragones in 2008.

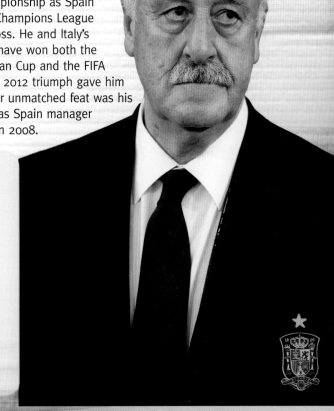

SPAIN'S PLAYERS IN EURO 2008/FIFA WORLD CUP 2010/EURO 2012 SQUADS

Iker Casillas*
Sergio Ramos*
Andres Iniesta*
Xabi Alonso*
Xavi Hernandez*
Cesc Fabregas*
Fernando Torres*
David Silva
Alvaro Arbeloa
Raul Albiol
Pepe Reina

* = appeared in all three finals.

WHO CAN TELMO

Telmo Zarraonaindia, commonly known as "Zarra", scored a Spanish championship record of 251 goals in 277 games for Athletic Bilbao between 1940 and 1955 – and 20 goals in 20 games for Spain between 1945 and 1951. He was nicknamed the "finest head in Europe after Churchill".

FIFA FIRST

Real Madrid were the only Spanish club formally represented at FIFA's first meeting in Paris in 1904 – though the club was then known simply as Madrid FC. Spanish clubs, such as Real Madrid and Real Betis, dropped the word "Real" – meaning "Royal" – from their names during the Second Spanish Republic, between 1931 and 1939.

BELGIUM

Belgium – nicknamed 'The Red Devils' – embarked on a golden period in the Eighties after eight decades spent on the fringes of international competition: first a runners-up finish at the 1980 UEFA European Championship, followed by a run to the semi-finals of the 1986 FIFA World Cup. The last time they qualified for a tournament was the 2002 FIFA World Cup but an emerging generation of talented young players is inspiring greater hopes for the future and if they qualify for Brazil 2014, they will be dark horses for glory.

BELGIAN LEAGUE CHAMPIONSHIP WINS

31	Anderlecht
13	Club Brugge
11	Union Saint-Gilloise
10	Standard Liege
7	Beerschot
6	Racing de Bruxelles
5	RFC de Liege
5	Daring de Bruxelles
4	Antwerp
4	Mechelen
4	Lierse
3	Genk
3	Cercle Brugge
2	Beveren
1	Molenbeek

ERWIN–WIN SITUATION

Belgium caused a sensation in the opening match of the 1982 FIFA World Cup by defeating the reigning champions Argentina, 1-0, thanks to a 62nd-minute goal by striker **Erwin Vandenburgh** in Barcelona's Camp Nou stadium. The same opponents had their revenge four years later, when two unanswered goals by Diego Maradona were enough to put Argentina into the 1986 FIFA World Cup final. Vandenburgh had also scored in Belgium's opening game of that tournament, a 2-1 Group B defeat to hosts Mexico.

SIXTH SENSE

By qualifying for the 2002 FIFA World Cup, Belgium became the first country to reach six successive tournaments without benefiting once from being either hosts or defending holders.

HE'S OUR GUY

Unquestionably Belgium's greatest manager – as well as their longest-serving – was **Guy Thys**. He led them to the final of the 1980 UEFA European Championship and – with a team featuring the likes of Enzo Scifo and Nico Claesen – the semi-finals of the FIFA World Cup six years later. He spent 13 years in the job from 1976 to 1989, then returned for a second spell just eight months after quitting. He stepped down again after managing Belgium at the 1990 FIFA World Cup. During his playing days in the 1940s and 1950s, he was a striker and won two caps for Belgium. He died at the age of 80 in August 2003.

TRIUMPHS AND TRAGEDY

The largest football venue in Belgium is the 50,000-capacity **King Baudouin Stadium** in Brussels, which opened under its previous name of the Jubilee Stadium on 23 August 1930 then took the name of Heysel in 1946. It was the scene of tragedy in 1985 when a wall collapsed and 39 fans died in disturbances while attending the European Cup final between Liverpool and Juventus. The stadium was rebuilt and given its current name in 1995. When Belgium and Holland co-hosted the 2000 UEFA European Championship, the stadium staged the opening ceremony and first match, Belgium's 2-1 victory over Sweden. It is now used for Belgium's home internationals.

CUP CONSOLATIONS

Belgium lost in the second round of the 2002 FIFA World Cup, beaten 2-0 by eventual champions Brazil. But there was some solace as Belgium won the tournament's fair play prize, and they were complemented by coach Luiz Felipe Scolari, who said Belgium were Brazil's toughest opponents en route to lifting the trophy.

LIEGE'S LEAGUE – AND LOSSES

The first Belgian league championship in 1896 was won by FC de Liege, who would later win another four and have the prefix "Royal" added to their name. RFC de Liege have suffered financial turmoil and several relegations since the 1990s and were dissolved in 2011 – only to be re-established in the Belgian fourth tier. The club was at the centre of the legal battle that led to major changes in the transfer of out-of-contract players, when midfielder Jean-Marc Bosman took them to court after being denied a move to French club Dunkerque in 1990.

BARON RUN

The first man given honorary membership of world football's governing body FIFA was Baron Edouard de Laveleye. The Belgian was rewarded for persuading The Football Association in England to join FIFA in 1905 rather than remain independent. De Laveleye was the first chairman of the Belgian FA, founded in 1895, and stayed in post for 29 years. He was also the founder and first chairman of the Belgian Olympic Committee and successfully campaigned for Antwerp to stage the Games in 1920.

CLUB MATES

Belgium ended a 1964 match against neighbours and rivals Holland with a team entirely comprised of Anderlecht players, after Liege goalkeeper Guy Delhasse was substituted by the Brussels club's Jean Trappeniers.

LONGEST–SERVING COACHES

1   Guy Thys (1976–89, 1990–91)
2   William Maxwell (1910–13, 1920–28)
3   Constant Vanden Stock (1958–68)
4   Raymond Goethals (1968–76)
5   Bill Gormlie (1947–53)
6   Jack Butler (1935–40)
7   **Paul Van Himst** (1991–96)
8   Hector Goetinck (1930–34)
9   Aime Anthuenis (2002–05)
10 Rene Vandereycken (2006–09)

FROM GOOD STOCK

Belgium's most successful club, with 31 league titles and five European trophies, are Anderlecht, who play at the 28,000-capacity Constant Vanden Stock Stadium in Brussels. This was built in 1917 and initially known as Emile Verse Stadium, but renovated and renamed in 1983 after the club's former player and later president Constant Vanden Stock. As well as running a successful brewery after retiring from playing, he coached the Belgian national team between 1958 and 1968. He died at the age of 93 in 2008 and his son Roger Vanden Stock is now Anderlecht's president. The club's honours include the UEFA Cup Winners' Cup and the UEFA Super Cup in both 1976 and 1978 and the UEFA Cup in 1983. Their 1983 triumph featured players such as international striker Franky Vercauteren and Denmark captain Morten Olsen, and they were managed by Belgium's joint leading scorer Paul van Himst.

SWINE FEVER

The man nicknamed "The Bull from Dongelberg" and "The Fighting Pig" has hogged more goals for Belgium than all but two compatriots, Paul van Himst and Bernard Voorhoof. **Marc Wilmots**' 28 goals in 70 international appearances between 1990 and 2002 included five scored at FIFA World Cups – the most by any Belgian player. After retiring, he spent a short spell as an elected Belgian senator before becoming assistant coach for the national team 2009. And, when Georges Leekens suddenly resigned as Belgium coach in 2012, Wilmots was promoted to the top job.

SPECS APPEAL

Most footballers with poor vision make do with contact lenses before going out to play, but Belgium captain Jef Jurion stood out in the late 1950s and early 1960s by wearing a pair of specially-made glasses during matches.

VOORHOOF'S A JOLLY GOOD FELLOW

Belgium's scoring record is shared by Bernard Voorhoof and Paul van Himst, both on 30 goals – though Voorhoof's came in 61 games between 1928 and 1940, compared to van Himst's 81 matches from 1960 to 1974. Voorhoof is one of only five players to feature at all three of the pre-Second World War FIFA World Cups, in 1930, 1934 and 1938. The others were Edmond Delfour and Etienne Mattler of France, Nicolae Kovacs of Romania and Brazil's Patesko. Voorhoof's only FIFA World Cup goals were the two he scored in 1934. Van Himst went into management after retiring as a player in 1977, managing Anderlecht when they won the UEFA Cup in 1983 and taking Belgium to the 1994 FIFA World Cup.

SAINT MICHEL

Belgium goalkeeper Michel Preud'homme was the first man to win the Lev Yashin Award for the best goalkeeper at a FIFA World Cup, when it was introduced in 1994. Preud'homme's four displays – conceding four goals – impressed the panel of judges even though Belgium were knocked out in the second round in the USA. He was dubbed "Saint Michel" by supporters when playing for Portuguese club Benfica.

PRINCE FERNAND

Fernand Nisot was part of the Belgium team that won the football gold medal when Antwerp hosted the Olympic Games in 1920. He still holds the record for Belgium's youngest international, being just 16 years and 19 days old on his debut.

THE EDEN PROJECT

Dazzling playmaker **Eden Hazard** made himself one of the hottest properties in world football with his performances for French club Lille. In 2011 he became the youngest footballer to be named the country's player of the year and retained the award 12 months later, just before joining the then-reigning European champions Chelsea. The London club also signed Hazard's brother Thorgan, two years younger than him and a Belgium under-21 international. Eden Hazard – who has been compared to Belgian great **Enzo Scifo** – made his full international debut at the age of 17 years and 316 days, becoming the eighth-youngest player to represent Belgium at full international level. The brothers are the sons of not just one former footballer but two. Their father, Thierry, played as a semi-professional and his mother Carine only retired from the women's game when she was pregnant with Eden.

TROUBLE A–VERT–ED

Defender **Jan Vertonghen** first found national fame when he score a spectacular – and entirely accidental – goal for Dutch club Ajax reserves' team in 2006. He blasted the ball down the pitch towards the goalkeeper of opponents Cambuur Leeuwarden, aiming to grant them possession after a player was treated for injury – but the ball ended up in the back of the Leeuwarden net. Apologetic Vertonghen and his team-mates agreed to immediately allow their rivals to score a goal back. Vertonghen's move to England in 2012 was a recent addition to what has become something of a Belgian invasion of the Premier League. Among his compatriots plying their trade in England's top flight are Tottenham Hotspur team-mate Mousa Dembele, Vincent Kompany at Manchester City, Everton's Marouane Fellaini, Chelsea pair Eden Hazard and Romelu Lukaku and Arsenal's Thomas Vermaelen.

TOP CAPS

1	Jan Ceulemans	96
2	Timmy Simons	91
3	Eric Gerets	86
=	Franky van der Elst	86
5	Enzo Scifo	84
6	Paul van Himst	81
7	Bart Goor	78
8	Georges Grun	77
9	Lorenzo Staelens	70
=	Marc Wilmots	70

MOTHER'S BOY

Belgium's most-capped player, **Jan Ceulemans**, is unusual in having turned down a move to Italian giants AC Milan – and he did so on the advice of his mother. He opted to stay loyal to Club Brugge, where he spent most of his playing career, and became a national hero with his linchpin displays at three consecutive FIFA World Cups in 1982, 1986 and 1990. He scored three goals and was captain at Mexico 1986 as Belgium finished fourth. The Lier-born midfielder retired from international football after Belgium's second-round exit at the 1990 FIFA World Cup.

TOP SCORERS

1	Bernard Voorhoof	30
=	Paul van Himst	30
3	Marc Wilmots	29
4	Joseph Mermans	27
5	Raymond Braine	26
=	Robert De Veen	26
7	Wesley Sonck	24
8	Jan Ceulemans	23
=	Marc Degryse	23
10	Henri Coppens	21

KOMPANY MAN

Belgium's current captain **Vincent Kompany** has emerged as one of the most commanding centre-backs in world football, and one of the most respected and articulate off the football field. He combines his professional career with part-time business administration studies at Manchester Business School. He captained Manchester City to their first English league title for 44 years in 2012-13. Kompany was recalled by his club, SV Hamburg of Germany, and was forced to miss the semi-final of the men's Beijing 2008 Olympic Games Football tournament. Without him, Belgium lost 4-1 to Nigeria and, after losing 3-0 to Brazil in the third-place match, Belgium were denied a medal to add to the Olympic gold they won as hosts at Antwerp in 1920. Kompany was named Belgium's permanent captain in November 2011, replacing fellow centre-back Thomas Vermaelen.

BULGARIA

The glory days of the "golden generation" apart – when Bulgaria finished fourth at the 1994 FIFA World Cup in the United States, sensationally beating defending champions Germany 2-1 in the quarter-finals – a consistent pattern emerges with Bulgarian football. Regular qualifiers for the game's major competitions, and the birthplace of some of the sport's biggest names (such as Hristo Stoichkov and Dimitar Berbatov), the country has too often failed to deliver on the big occasions and make its mark on world football.

TOP CAPS

1	Stiliyan Petrov	106
2	Borislav Mikhailov	102
3	Hristo Bonev	96
4	Krasimir Balakov	92
5	Dimitar Penev	90
=	Martin Petrov	90
7	Radostin Kishishev	88
8	Hristo Stoichkov	83
9	Nasko Sirakov	82
10	Zlatko Yankov	80

MAYOR WITH NO HAIR

Balding Yordan Letchkov headed the winning goal against holders and defending champions Germany in the 1994 FIFA World Cup quarter-final in the United States. At the time, he played for German club Hamburg. He later became mayor of Sliven, the Bulgarian town where he was born in July 1967.

TEETHING TROUBLES

Martin Petrov suffered a terrible start to his international career when he was sent off for two yellow cards just eight minutes into his debut as a substitute in a Euro 2000 qualifier against England. He broke down in tears when leaving the field, but recovered from the experience to become one of his country's most-capped players and enjoyed spells with top clubs such as Atletico Madrid in Spain and Manchester City in England. His 90 caps and 19 goals included Bulgaria's only strike at the 2004 UEFA European Championship, against Italy.

A NATION MOURNS

Bulgaria lost two of its most popular footballing talents when a June 1971 car crash claimed the lives of strikers Georgi Asparukhov (28) and Nikola Kotkov (32). Asparukhov scored 19 goals in 50 internationals, including Bulgaria's only goal of the 1966 FIFA World Cup finals in a 3-1 defeat to Hungary.

MOB RULES

Fulham and Bulgaria centre-forward **Dimitar Berbatov** claims to have learned English by watching the *Godfather* movies. Berbatov joined United from Tottenham in 2008 for a club and Bulgarian record fee of £30.75m. Before joining Spurs, he had been a member of the Bayer Leverkusen side who narrowly missed out on a treble in 2002. They lost in the final of both the UEFA Champions League and the German cup and finished runners-up in the German Bundesliga. Berbatov surprised and disappointed fans back home when he announced his international retirement aged just 29, in May 2010, having scored a national-record 48 goals in his 78 appearances for Bulgaria. He briefly considered a return to the national team in 2012, but ultimately opted against the idea, saying that he wanted to "give chances to younger players". After joining Fulham in the summer of that year, he raised eyebrows during one match by revealing a T-shirt with the slogan: "Keep calm and pass me the ball."

STAN THE BURGER VAN MAN

Stiliyan Petrov – nicknamed "Stan" by fans of his English club Aston Villa – was applauded onto the field when he became Bulgaria's first outfield player to reach 100 caps, against Switzerland in March 2011. The midfielder and Bulgaria captain has been playing in Britain since 1999, when he joined Scottish giants Celtic as a 20-year-old – but had to fight hard against a bout of homesickness. He later revealed that his English only improved when he started work behind the counter of a Scottish friend's burger van. Petrov said: "Some of the customers used to stare, thinking: 'That looks like Stiliyan Petrov, but it can't be.' But soon I started to understand things better." Tributes from across football and around the world poured in for Petrov when, in March 2012, he revealed he had been diagnosed with acute leukaemia. After 19 minutes of every home game for the rest of the season Villa fans stood and applauded for 60 seconds – 19 being his squad number.

PLAYING LUBO

Bulgaria's current coach is Lubo Penev, nephew of Dimitar Penev who had coached the country to their best-ever FIFA World Cup finish of fourth in 1994. Lubo, a centre-forward, missed out on that tournament after being diagnosed with testicular cancer, but he recovered to play for his country at both the 1996 UEFA European Championship and 1998 FIFA World Cup. He also finished top scorer as his Spanish club Atletico Madrid won the league and cup double in 1995–96. After coaching CSKA Sofia and Litex Lovich he was given the job of national manager in 2011 – becoming the fourth boss of Bulgaria's failed campaign to qualify for the 2012 UEFA European Championship. Compatriots Stanimir Stoilov and Michael Madanski had previously served in the post, either side of a stint by former German international Lothar Matthaus. From a record-low position of 96th in the FIFA rankings, Bulgaria improved enough under Penev's leadership to reach 40th in November 2012.

ALL–ROUNDER ALEKSANDAR

Defender Aleksandar Shalamanov played for Bulgaria at the 1966 FIFA World Cup, six years after representing his country as an alpine skier at the Winter Olympics. He also went to the 1964 Olympics as an unused member of the volleyball squad. Shalamanov was voted Bulgaria's best sportsman in both 1967 and 1973.

TOP SCORERS

1	Dimitar Berbatov	48
=	Hristo Bonev	48
3	Hristo Stoichkov	37
4	Emil Kostadinov	26
5	Ivan Kolev	25
=	Petar Zhekov	25
7	Atanas Mihaylov	23
=	Nasko Sirakov	23
9	Dimitar Milanov	20
10	Georgi Asparuhov	19
=	Dinko Dermendzhiev	19
=	Martin Petrov	19

HRISTO'S HISTORY

Hristo Stoichkov, born in Plovdiv, Bulgaria, on 8 February 1968, shared the 1994 FIFA World Cup Golden Boot, awarded to the tournament's top scorer, with Russia's Oleg Salenko. Both scored six times, though Stoichkov became the sole winner of that year's European Footballer of the Year award. Earlier the same year, he had combined up-front with Brazilian Romario to help Barcelona reach the final of the UEFA Champions League. He was banned for a year after a brawl earlier in his career, during the 1985 Bulgarian cup final between CSKA Sofia and Levski Sofia. Stoichkov won trophies with clubs in Bulgaria, Spain, Saudi Arabia and the United States before retiring as a player in 2003.

HEAD BOY

Bulgaria's second most-capped player is **Borislav Mikhailov**, born in Sofia on 12 February 1963, who sometimes wore a wig while playing and later had a hair transplant. After retiring in 2005, he was appointed president of the Bulgarian Football Union. His father Bisser was also a goalkeeper and Borislav's son, Nikolay, made his international debut in goal against Scotland in May 2006. All three have played for Levski Sofia.

CROATIA

Croatia's distinctive red-and-white chequered jersey has become one of the most recognized in world football – just ask England. Croatia broke English hearts not once but twice in the UEFA Euro 2008 qualifying tournament. First Croatia beat England 2-0 in Zagreb and then they shocked them 3-2 at Wembley to secure qualification. Croatia's march to the quarter-finals at the 2008 UEFA European Championship was followed by failure to qualify for the 2010 FIFA World Cup, but they impressed again at Euro 2012, though were edged out in the first round by Spain and Italy.

TOP SCORERS

1	Davor Suker	45
2	Eduardo da Silva	27
3	Darijo Srna	20
4	Ivica Olic	16
5	Niko Kranjcar	15
=	Goran Vlaovic	15
7	Niko Kovac	14
8	Mladen Petric	13
9	Zvonimir Boban	12
=	Ivan Klasnic	12

BILIC BEAT

Slaven Bilic and **Igor Stimac** formed a formidable partnership in central defence as Croatia finished third at the 1998 FIFA World Cup. And it was Stimac who succeeded his old team-mate when Bilic's six-year spell as Croatia manager ended after Euro 2012. Fashion-conscious, diamond-earring-wearing Bilic had taken his country to the 2008 and 2012 UEFA European Championships. The pair also have a love of music in common: Bilic's rock band released a single called "*Vatreno Ludilo*" ("Fiery Madness"), which topped the Croatian charts, while Stimac had a pop hit with "*Mare i Kate*".

LUKA LOOPY

Luka Modric scored the fastest penalty in UEFA European Championship history: his fourth-minute strike was the only goal of Croatia's first-round victory against co-hosts Austria at the 2008 tournament. But he would miss one of the spot-kicks as Croatia lost a shoot-out to Turkey in the quarter-finals. His much-loved status back home remains unaffected, though, as the diminutive playmaker – dubbed "the Croat Cruyff", and not just because he wears the number 14 – is now widely seen as one of the world's most skilful midfielders. Modric spent four years with English club Tottenham Hotspur from 2008 until he successfully manoeuvred a move to Spain's Real Madrid in the summer of 2012.

HAPPY OPENINGS

Few national teams have been as successful in their infancy as Croatia. Formerly part of Yugoslavia, Croatia reached the quarter-finals in their very first senior competition (UEFA Euro 96) and then came third at the 1998 FIFA World Cup. Since becoming eligible to participate in 1993, Croatia qualified for every FIFA World Cup (except for 2010), and missed only one UEFA European Championship (in 2000). Croatia have scored four goals at each of the four UEFA European Championships for which they have qualified, in 1996, 2004, 2008 and 2012. Three of the goals at Euro 2012 came from **Mario Mandzukic**, the first after just two minutes and 38 seconds against the Republic of Ireland – the sixth fastest UEFA European Championship finals goal of all-time. Mandzukic joined German giants Bayern Munich that summer, scoring their first goal in the UEFA Champions League triumph over Borussia Dortmund in May 2013.

SUPER SUKER

Striker Davor Suker won the Golden Boot for being top scorer at the FIFA World Cup in 1998, scoring six goals in seven games as Croatia finished third. His strikes included the opening goal in Croatia's 2-1 semi-final defeat to eventual champions France, and the winner in a 2-1 triumph over Holland in the third-place play-off. Suker, by far his country's leading scorer of all time, had hit three goals at the UEFA European Championship in 1996 – including an audacious long-distance lob over Denmark goalkeeper Peter Schmeichel. Suker was named president of the Croatian Football Federation in July 2012.

DEER DARIJO

Darijo Srna is Croatia's third top scorer of all time despite ·······
playing many games as a right-back or wing-back. He has a tattoo on his calf in the shape of a deer, the Croatian word for which is "srna". He also has a tattoo on his chest – the name of his brother Igor, who has Down's syndrome and to whom he dedicates each goal he scores. Srna shared the honour of making his 100th appearance, against South Korea in February 2013, with two team-mates also reaching their centuries: goalkeeper Stipe Pletikosa and defender Josip Simunic.

THE KIDNEYS ARE ALL RIGHT

Striker Ivan Klasnic returned to international duty with Croatia despite suffering kidney failure in early 2007. A first attempt at a transplant failed when his body rejected a kidney donated by his mother, but follow-up surgery – using a kidney from his father – proved successful. He recovered enough to play for Croatia again in March 2008 and represented his country in that summer's UEFA European Championship, scoring twice – including a winning goal against Poland.

FAMILY AFFAIR

Niko Kranjcar is the son of former Croatian coach Zlatko Kranjcar, but it wasn't always an easy affiliation. "Two days before he became Croatia's head coach everyone said I should get a call-up," Niko once said. "Then when Dad picked me for UEFA Euro 2004 suddenly it was because I was his son." No such problems for the Kovac brothers, Robert and Niko, both of whom are part of Croatian footballing folklore. The siblings were born in Berlin but are proud Croats. Both brothers have now hung up their boots at international level, though Robert went on for a year after Niko retired from Croatian duty.

TOP CAPS

1	Darijo Srna	104
2	Stipe Pletikosa	103
3	Josip Simunic	102
4	Dario Simic	100
5	Ivica Olic	85
6	Robert Kovac	84
7	Niko Kovac	83
8	Robert Jarni	81
9	Niko Kranjcar	79
10	Davor Suker	69

DOUBLE IDENTITY

Robert Jarni and Robert Prosinecki both have the rare distinction of playing for two different countries at different FIFA World Cup tournaments. They both represented Yugoslavia in Italy in 1990, then newly independent Croatia eight years later in France. Full-back Jarni actually played for both Yugoslavia and Croatia in 1990, then only Yugoslavia in 1991, before switching back – and permanently – to Croat colours in 1992 after the country officially joined UEFA and FIFA. He retired with 81 caps for Croatia, seven for Yugoslavia.

MLAD ALL OVER

Mladen Petric is the only player to score four goals in one game for Croatia – in their 7-0 trouncing of Andorra in October 2006. That equalled Croatia's record victory, having previously beaten Australia by the same scoreline in August 1998. **Davor Suker** ·············
scored a hat-trick that day, making him the only Croatian to complete two trebles – his first came in a 7-1 defeat of Estonia in September 1995.

CZECH REPUBLIC

The most successful of the former Eastern Bloc countries, as Czechoslovakia they finished as runners-up in the 1934 and 1962 FIFA World Cups, and shocked West Germany in a penalty shoot-out to win the 1976 UEFA European Championship. Playing as the Czech Republic since 1994, they came very close to victory at UEFA Euro 96, and lost out in the semi-finals eight years later. Recent times have been tougher, and although one of Europe's stronger nations, the Czechs did not qualify for the 2010 FIFA World Cup, but were UEFA Euro 2012 quarter-finalists.

EURO-VER AND OVER AND OVER AGAIN

Vladimir Smicer, now general manager of the Czech national team, is one of only seven players to score at three different UEFA European Championships – along with Germany's Jurgen Klinsmann, France's Thierry Henry, Portugal's Nuno Gomes, Helder Postiga and Cristiano Ronaldo, and Sweden's Zlatan Ibrahimovic. Smicer struck at the finals in 1996, 2000 and 2004. Perhaps his other greatest achievement came in his final game for English club Liverpool, during which he scored as a second-half substitute as his team came back from 3-0 down to beat AC Milan in the 2005 UEFA Champions League final. Smicer's wife Pavlina is the daughter of former Czechoslovakia striker Ladislav Vizek, who won footballing gold with his country at the 1980 summer Olympics but who was then sent off against France at the FIFA World Cup two years later.

CHIP WITH EVERYTHING

One of the most famous penalties ever taken was Antonin Panenka's decisive spot-kick for Czechoslovakia against West Germany in the final of the 1976 UEFA European Championship, giving the Czechs victory in the shoot-out. Despite the tension, and the responsibility resting on him, Panenka cheekily chipped the ball into the middle of the goal – as goalkeeper Sepp Maier dived to the side. That style of spot-kick is now widely known as a "Panenka", and has been replicated by the likes of France's Zinedine Zidane, in the 2006 FIFA World Cup final.

POPULAR KAREL

UEFA Euro 96 gave the frizzy-haired **Karel Poborsky** the perfect platform to take his career to new heights as he helped the Czech Republic reach the final and then sealed a dream move to Manchester United. His lob against Portugal in the quarter-finals was rated as one of the finest opportunist goals in the tournament's history. His 118 appearances is a record for his country.

CECH CAP

Goalkeeper **Petr Cech** has worn a protective cap while playing ever since suffering a fractured skull during an English Premier League match in October 2006. He later added a chin protector after requiring a facial operation following a training accident. Cech was born as a triplet, along with sister Sarka and brother Michal, who sadly died of an infection at the age of two. Cech served early notice of his talents by only conceding one penalty in a decisive shoot-out against France in the final of the 2002 UEFA U-21 European Championship, a performance that helped the Czechs to the trophy. He was also on the winning side as Chelsea won both the 2012 UEFA Champions League and the 2013 UEFA Europa League. In the 2012 showdown, in which Chelsea beat Bayern in Munich on penalties, Cech was named man of the match after saving a spot-kick in normal time from Arjen Robben.

PASSING THE PUC

The final of the 1934 FIFA World Cup was the first to go into extra-time, with Czechoslovakia ultimately losing 2-1 to hosts Italy despite taking a 76th-minute lead through Antonin Puc. Puc was Czechoslovakia/the Czech Republic's top international scorer when he retired in 1938 until he was passed, first by Jan Koller, 67 years later, and, latterly, by Milan Baros.

WALK-OUT

Belgium's 1920 victory in the Olympic Games was overshadowed when Czechoslovakia walked off the pitch after half an hour in protest following what they saw as biased refereeing. Czechoslovakia are the only team in the history of Olympic football to have been disqualified.

KEY MIDFIELDER

Czech Republic captain and playmaker **Tomas Rosicky** has long been nicknamed "Little Mozart", even though his favoured instrument is the guitar. And, due to bad luck with injuries (including 18 months out of action with hamstring problems in 2008 and 2009), he has had plenty of time to practise. He was installed as Czech skipper in 2009 following the appointment of coach Michal Bilek – a former midfielder who scored two minutes into his international playing career, against Poland in 1987. Rosicky, by now with English club Arsenal, was unfortunate again at the 2012 UEFA European Championship: he went off injured at half-time during the Czechs' second match, against Greece, and did not reappear at the tournament, even though his team-mates reached the quarter-finals.

THE CANNON COLLECTS

Pavel Nedved's election as European Footballer of the Year in 2003 ended an impatient wait for fans in the Czech Republic who had seen a string of outstanding players overlooked since Josef Masopust had been honoured back in 1962. Masopust, a midfield general, had scored the opening goal in the FIFA World Cup final that year before Brazil hit back to win 3-1 in the Chilean capital of Santiago. Years later, Masopust was remembered by Pele and nominated as one of his 125 greatest living footballers. At club level, Masopust won eight Czechoslovak league titles with Dukla Prague, the army club. He was also the winner, in 1962, of the first Czech Golden Ball as domestic footballer of the year. It was another day and in another age. Masopust was presented with his award before the kick-off of a European Cup quarter-final with Benfica – with a minimum of fuss. Years later, Masopust said: "Eusebio just shook hands with me, I put the trophy in my sports bag and went home on the tram."

TOP SCORERS

1	Jan Koller	55
2	Milan Baros	41
3	Vladimir Smicer	27
4	Pavel Kuka	22
5	Tomas Rosicky	20
6	Patrik Berger	18
=	Pavel Nedved	18
8	Vratislav Lokvenc	14
9	Marek Jankulovski	11
10	Karel Poborsky	8

TOP CAPS

1	Karel Poborsky	118
2	Petr Cech	101
3	Milan Baros	93
4	Jan Koller	91
=	Pavel Nedved	91
=	Tomas Rosicky	91
7	Jaroslav Plasil	84
8	Vladimir Smicer	80
9	Tomas Ujfalusi	78
10	Marek Jankulovski	77

TEN OUT OF TEN

Giant striker **Jan Koller** is Czech football's all-time leading marksman with 55 goals in 91 appearances. Koller scored on his senior debut against Belgium and struck ten goals in ten successive internationals. He scored six goals in each of the 2000, 2004 and 2008 UEFA European Championship qualifying campaigns. He began his career with Sparta Prague, who converted him from goalkeeper to goalscorer. Then, in Belgium, he was top scorer with Lokeren, before scoring 42 goals in two league title-winning campaigns with Anderlecht. Later, with Borussia Dortmund in Germany, he once went in goal after Jens Lehmann had been sent off and kept a clean sheet – having scored in the first half.

DENMARK

Denmark have been playing international football since 1908, but it was not until the mid-1980s that they became competitive at the game's major tournaments. The country's crowning moment came in 1992 when, after being called up as a replacement just ten days before the start of the tournament, they walked away with the UEFA European Championship crown, shocking defending world champions West Germany 2-0 in the final. They may not have been able to repeat that success, but remain a significant player in the world game.

TOP CAPS

1	Peter Schmeichel	129
2	Dennis Rommedahl	126
3	Jon Dahl Tomasson	112
4	Thomas Helveg	108
5	Michael Laudrup	104
6	Martin Jorgensen	102
=	Morten Olsen	102
8	Thomas Sorensen	101
9	Christian Poulsen	92
10	John Sivebaek	87

GOLDEN GLOVES

Peter Schmeichel was rated as the world's best goalkeeper in the early 1990s, winning many club honours with Manchester United and, famously, the UEFA European Championship with his native Denmark. His son Kasper Schmeichel was a member of Denmark's squad at the 2012 UEFA European Championship. Kasper was called up after first-choice Thomas Sorensen suffered a back injury, though began and ended the tournament still waiting for his first cap.

LEADERSHIP STYLE

Morten Olsen captained Denmark at the 1986 FIFA World Cup and later became the first Dane to reach a century of caps, eventually stepping down from the national team with four goals in 102 international appearances between 1970 and 1989. After he retired from playing all football that year, he switched to coaching, first at club level with Brondby, FC Koln and Ajax Amsterdam, before taking on the job as Danish national coach in 2000 and leading them to the 2002 and 2010 FIFA World Cups. Denmark's 2-1 defeat to England in a February 2011 friendly was his 116th international in charge – taking him past the previous record set between 1979 and 1990 by his former national team boss Sepp Piontek. Olsen planned to step down after the 2012 UEFA European Championship, but changed his mind and agreed a new deal extending his stay to the 2014 FIFA World Cup. Posters bearing Olsen's image can often be seen across Denmark – though these are advertising hearing aids, approved by the manager who suffers from deafness.

CHRISTIAN AID

Creative Danish talents have long enjoyed an association with Ajax Amsterdam, from Soren Lerby and Frank Arnesen in the 1970s and 1980s to the Laudrup brothers in the late-1990s. Later, the darling of the Dutch giants was diminutive playmaker Christian Eriksen, who was one of the inspirations behind the Amsterdam outfit's hat-trick of title triumphs. He made his full Danish debut in March 2010, having turned 18 the previous month, making him his country's fourth youngest debutant of all-time and the youngest since Michael Laudrup. Eriksen went to the 2010 FIFA World Cup as the youngest player among the tournament's 32 squads. His first goal did not come until April 2011, in a victory over Iceland. This made him Denmark's youngest goalscorer in a UEFA European Championship qualifying match – nine days younger than the same Laudrup to whom he is often compared had been in 1983.

DANISH DYNAMITE

Denmark's 6-1 defeat of Uruguay in the 1986 FIFA World Cup finals first-round group stage in Neza, Mexico, ranks among the country's finest performances. Sadly, Denmark's adventure was ended by Spain in the last 16, losing 5-1 after a horrendous back pass by Manchester United's Jesper Olsen allowed the Spanish to open the scoring. The Danes had already been hampered by the loss of playmaker Frank Arsesen through suspension, after he was sent off during their final group game, a victory over eventual runners-up West Germany. The side – popularly known as "Danish Dynamite" – was captained by future national coach Morten Olsen and managed by Sepp Piontek, a German who became the Danish national team's first professional coach when appointed in 1979. Michael Laudrup, a star member of the classic mid-1980s side, described them as "Europe's answer to Brazil".

PENALTY REDEMPTION

Former Dundee, Celtic and Brondby midfielder **Morten Wieghorst** is the only player to be sent off twice while playing for Denmark – yet has also received a special award for fair play. His first international red card came just three minutes after entering the field as a substitute, against South Africa in the 1998 FIFA World Cup. He was again dismissed after coming on as a sub against Italy in the 2000 UEFA European Championship, though this time he managed a whole 28 minutes of action – and scored a goal in Denmark's 3-2 victory. But the other side of his character was shown during a Carlsberg Cup match against Iran in February 2003, when he deliberately missed a penalty. The spot-kick had been awarded after Iranian defender Jalal Kameli Mofrad had picked the ball up, thinking wrongly that a whistle from the crowd was actually the referee blowing for half-time. The International Olympic Committee later presented Wieghorst with a special fair play prize for deliberately striking his penalty wide – a gesture which looked all the more sporting since Denmark went on to lose the game 1-0.

TOP SCORERS

1	Poul Nielsen	52
=	Jon Dahl Tomasson	52
3	Pauli Jorgensen	44
4	Ole Madsen	42
5	Preben Elkjaer Larsen	38
6	Michael Laudrup	37
7	Henning Enoksen	29
8	Nicklas Bendtner	22
=	Michael Rohde	22
=	Ebbe Sand	22

QUICK DRAW

Ebbe Sand scored the fastest FIFA World Cup goal ever scored by a substitute, when he netted a mere 16 seconds after coming onto the pitch in Denmark's clash against Nigeria at the 1998 FIFA World Cup.

TAKING THE MICHAEL

One Danish player with unhappy memories of a spell with Ajax Amsterdam is Michael Krohn-Dehli, who made just four appearances for the club between 2006 and 2008. But if he felt any resentment for the Netherlands – and the injuries that hampered his progress there and also contributed to his omission from the 2010 FIFA World Cup – then the 2012 UEFA European Championship brought some redemption. Krohn-Dehli scored the only goal in Denmark's surprise opening victory over the Netherlands. He said afterwards: "It's a little bit special for me as I played for eight years in Holland and I have a Dutch girlfriend, so I think the whole family was cheering in Holland." Manager Morten Olsen admitted afterwards that he should have taken Krohn-Dehli to the FIFA World Cup two years earlier. The only other Dane to score – and twice – at Euro 2012 was Nicklas Bendtner, though he was later fined $100,000 and banned for a game after celebrating his second by displaying underpants bearing the name of a betting firm.

THE UNEXPECTED IN 1992

Few Danish football fans are ever likely to forget June 1992, their national team's finest hour, when they managed to win the UEFA European Championship. Denmark had not qualified for the final round in Sweden, but ten days before the opening match UEFA asked them to take the place of Yugoslavia, who were thrown out of the tournament in the wake of international sanctions over the Balkan War. The Danes had come second in their qualifying group, behind Yugoslavia, and they took over their spot at the tournament proper. Expectations were minimal, but then the inconceivable happened. Relying heavily on goalkeeper Peter Schmeichel, his defence, and the creative spark of Brian Laudrup, Denmark crafted one of the biggest shocks in modern football history by winning the tournament, culminating in a 2-0 victory over world champions Germany. Their victory was all the more remarkable in that Brian's brother Michael, their finest player, quit during the qualifying competition after falling out with coach Richard Moller Nielsen. He revived his international career in 1993, only for Denmark to fail to qualify for the subsequent FIFA World Cup in the United States.

BROTHERS IN ARMS

Brian (left) and Michael Laudrup are among the most successful footballing brothers of modern times. As well as making a combined 186 international appearances, they played across Europe at club level. Michael (104 caps, 37 goals) played in Italy with Lazio and Juventus and in Spain with Barcelona and Real Madrid. Brian (82 caps, 21 goals) starred in Germany with Bayer Uerdingen and Bayern Munich, Italy with Fiorentina and Milan, Scotland for Rangers and England for Chelsea.

GREECE

There is no argument about Greece's proudest footballing moment – their shock triumph at the 2004 UEFA European Championship, one of the game's greatest international upsets. Guided by their long-serving German coach Otto Rehhagel, it was only the Greeks' second appearance at a UEFA Euro finals – while the 2010 tournament in South Africa marked just their second qualification for a FIFA World Cup. Their recent good run continued when they made it to the quarter-finals at UEFA Euro 2012.

TOP SCORERS

1	Nikos Anastopoulos	29
2	Angelos Charisteas	25
3	Theofanis Gekas	24
4	Dimitris Saravakos	22
5	Mimis Papaioannou	21
6	Nikos Machlas	18
7	Demis Nikolaidis	17
8	Panagiotis Tsalouchidis	16
9	Giorgos Sideris	14
10	Nikos Liberopoulos	13

SIMPLY THEO BEST

Theodoros "Theo" Zagorakis – born near Kavala on 27 October 1971 – was captain of Greece when they won the UEFA European Championship in 2004 and the defensive midfielder was also given the prize for the tournament's best player. He is the second most-capped Greek footballer of all time, with 120 caps. But it was not until his 101st international appearance – 10 years and five months after his Greek debut – that he scored his first goal for his country, in a FIFA World Cup qualifier against Denmark in February 2005. He retired from international football after making a 15-minute cameo appearance against Spain in August 2007.

PARTY CRASHERS

Shock UEFA Euro 2004 winners Greece became the first team to beat both the holders and the hosts on the way to winning either a UEFA European Championship or FIFA World Cup. In fact, they beat hosts Portugal twice – in both the tournament's opening game and the final, with a quarter-final victory over defending champions France in between.

SOT'S NEW

At 18 years and 46 days old, **Sotiris Ninis** became Greece's youngest scorer on his international debut, in a 2-0 friendly win over Cyprus in May 2008 – just 18 months after he had been happy to be working as a ballboy for his club side Panathinaikos. The second half of the 2006–07 season brought a stunning breakthrough for the attacking midfielder, who made his club debut, became a Greek team's youngest player in any UEFA club competition and then inspired Greece to a runners-up finish in the UEFA U-19s European Championship. The Albanian-born player was voted most valuable player of the summer 2007 tournament – making his first full international call-up only a matter of time.

ALL WHITE NOW

The surprise triumph at UEFA Euro 2004 brought a major change to Greek international football – they switched the national team's kit from blue to white. The former colours had been used since the Hellenic Football Federation was formed in 1926, but the success of Otto Rehhagel's men in their second kit prompted a permanent change of colours.

TOP CAPS

1	Giorgos Karagounis	125
2	Theodoros Zagorakis	120
3	Kostas Katsouranis	103
4	Angelos Basinas	100
5	Stratos Apostolakis	96
6	Antonis Nikopolidis	90
7	Angelos Charisteas	88
8	Dimitris Saravakos	78
9	Stelios Giannakopoulos	77
=	Anastassios Mitropoulos	77

DIMI MORE

Striker **Dimitrios Salpingidis** not only struck the only goal of Greece's 2010 FIFA World Cup qualifying play-off victory against Ukraine, sealing their place in South Africa, he also then became the first Greek ever to score at a FIFA World Cup, with a 44th-minute deflected strike in the 2-1 Group B triumph over Nigeria. Yet another notable achievement was added with his equalizer against Poland in the opening game of UEFA Euro 2012: this made him the first Greek ever to score at a FIFA World Cup and a UEFA European Championship.

WHEN EXPERIENCE DOESN'T COUNT

Ioannis Fetfatzidis, already nicknamed "the Greek Messi", had just seven Greek Superleague matches for Olympiacos to his name when he made his full international debut as a 19-year-old against Latvia in October 2010. Like Messi, Fetfatzidis was given growth hormones as a 13-year-old by his club Olympiacos, just as the Argentine had been by Barcelona.

HONESTY PAYS

Greece's 500th goal in international football was scored by Demis Nikolaidis at Manchester's Old Trafford in October 2001, giving them an unexpected 2–1 lead away to England in a final 2002 FIFA World Cup qualifier – although David Beckham would go on to equalize with a famous last-minute free-kick. In March the following year, striker Nikolaidis was formally acclaimed by the International Committee for Fair Play for admitting to the referee that he handled the ball when scoring for AEK Athens in the final of the Greek Cup. His team still won the match, and the trophy.

TOP KAT

Greek football has enjoyed various Portuguese connections. National coach Fernando Santos is Portuguese and took charge in 2000 after being the Greek league's most successful manager in the 1990s. He also spent some time as boss of Portuguese giants Benfica, whose signings this century have included Greek mainstays **Kostas Katsouranis** and Giorgios Karagounis. Both those players were part of the triumphant Greek side that lifted the 2004 UEFA European Championship trophy at Benfica's Estadio da Luz stadium in Lisbon. Katsouranis also played at UEFA Euro 2012, but squandered his best chance of a first goal in a finals tournament when he missed a penalty in the opening game against Poland.

GRIEF AND GLORY FOR GIORGOS

It was a bittersweet day for captain **Giorgos Karagounis** when he equalled the Greek record for international appearances, with his 120th cap against Russia in their final Group A game at the UEFA Euro 2012. The midfielder scored the only goal of the game, giving Greece a place in the quarter-finals at Russia's expense – but a second yellow card of the tournament ruled him out of the next match, in which the Greeks lost to Germany. Karagounis was one of three survivors from Greece's Euro 2004 success, along with fellow midfielder Kostas Katsouranis and goalkeeper Kostas Chalkias – though it was only in Poland that Chalkias made the first of his UEFA European Championship appearances, having been understudy in 2004 and 2008. Manager Fernando Santos also surprised many by leaving the winning goalscoring hero of Euro 2004, Angelos Charisteas, out of the squad. Chalkias, at 38 Euro 2012's oldest player, announced his international retirement once the tournament ended.

KING OTTO

German coach Otto Rehhagel became the first foreigner to be voted "Greek of the Year" in 2004, after leading the country to glory at that year's UEFA European Championship. He was also offered honorary Greek citizenship. His nine years in charge, after being appointed in 2001, made him Greece's longest-serving international manager. The UEFA Euro 2004 triumph was the first time a country coached by a foreigner had triumphed at either the UEFA European Championship or FIFA World Cup. Rehhagel was aged 65 at UEFA Euro 2004, making him the oldest coach to win the UEFA European Championship – though that record was taken off him four years later, when 69-year-old Luis Aragones lifted the trophy with Spain.

HUNGARY

For a period in the early 1950s, Hungary possessed the most talented football team on the planet. They claimed Olympic gold at Helsinki in 1952, inflicted a crushing first-ever Wembley defeat on England the following year, and entered the 1954 FIFA World Cup, unbeaten in almost four years, as firm favourites to win the crown. They lost to West Germany in the final and Hungary's footballing fortunes on the world stage have never been the same again.

TOP SCORERS

1	Ferenc Puskas	84
2	Sandor Kocsis	75
3	Imre Schlosser	59
4	Lajos Tichy	51
5	Gyorgy Sarosi	42
6	Nandor Hidegkuti	39
7	Ferenc Bene	36
8	Tibor Nyilasi	32
=	Gyula Zsengeller	32
10	Florian Albert	31

RETURN TO SANDOR

An estimated 1,000 success-starved fans thronged Budapest airport in October 2009 to welcome home the players and staff behind perhaps Hungary's finest footballing feat in decades. The country's youngsters clinched a surprise third place at that autumn's FIFA World U-20 Championship, beating Costa Rica on penalties in a play-off. Then-Liverpool striker Krisztian Nemeth scored the decisive spot-kick, having hit the late extra-time winner against Italy in the quarter-finals. Only Ghana and beaten finalists Brazil performed better. The reward for coach **Sandor Egervari** was promotion to the same role with the full international side the following summer. Egervari had been assistant coach the last time Hungary competed in a FIFA World Cup finals, in 1986.

GERA'S SHARE OF THE SPOILS

While none could compare with Ferenc Puskas, the elegant left-footed playmaker **Zoltan Gera** has been one of Hungary's most noted footballers of recent decades – not only with his performances in the English Premier League (with Fulham and West Bromwich Albion), but also on the international stage. His tally of 77 caps could have been higher but for a brief international retirement in 2009 after a dispute with then-manager Erwin Koeman after Gera arrived late for a team meeting. He returned to the fold when Sandor Egervari took over the following year and was made captain. The first three of his 23 international goals all came in the same game, a 3-0 victory over San Marino in October 2002, eight months after his international debut.

GOLDEN HEAD

Sandor Kocsis, top scorer in the 1954 FIFA World Cup finals with 11 goals, was so good in the air he was known as "The Man with the Golden Head". In 68 internationals he scored an incredible 75 goals, including a record seven hat-tricks. His tally included two decisive extra-time goals in the 1954 FIFA World Cup semi-final against Uruguay, when Hungary had appeared to be on the brink of defeat.

GALLOPING MAJOR

Ferenc Puskas was one of the greatest footballers of all time, scoring a remarkable 84 goals in 85 international matches for Hungary and 514 goals in 529 matches in the Hungarian and Spanish leagues. Possessing the most lethal left-foot shot in the history of football, he was known as the "Galloping Major" – by virtue of his playing for the army team Honved before joining Real Madrid and going on to play for Spain. During the 1950s he was top scorer and captain of the legendary "Mighty Magyars" (the nickname given to the Hungarian national team), as well as of the army club Honved.

HUNGARY FOR IT

Hungary's 6-3 win over England at Wembley in 1953 remains one of the most significant international results of all time. Hungary became the first team from outside the British Isles to beat England at home, a record that had stood since 1901. The Hungarians had been undefeated for three years and had won the Olympic tournament the year before, while England were the so-called "inventors" of football. The British press dubbed it "The Match of the Century". In the event, the match revolutionized the game in England, Hungary's unequivocal victory exposing the naivete of English football tactics. England captain Billy Wright later summed up the humiliation by saying: "We completely underestimated the advances that Hungary had made, and not only tactically. When we walked out at Wembley ... I looked down and noticed that the Hungarians had on these strange, lightweight boots, cut away like slippers under the ankle bone. I turned to big Stan Mortensen and said: 'We should be all right here, Stan, they haven't got the proper kit.'"

EUROPEAN PIONEERS

While Argentina's match against Uruguay in July 1902 was the first international outside the British Isles, Hungary's 5-0 defeat to Austria in Vienna three months later was the first in Europe between two non-UK sides. Ten of Hungary's first 16 internationals were against Austria, with the Hungarians winning four, drawing one and losing five of them. In total, Hungary have won 66, drawn 30 and lost 40 against their Austrian neighbours.

GLORIOUS FAILURE

Hungary were runaway favourites to win the 1954 FIFA World Cup in Switzerland. They arrived for the finals having been unbeaten for four years. In the first round they thrashed West Germany 8-3, despite finishing with ten men after skipper Ferenc Puskas injured an ankle.

GOODISON LESSON

In the 1966 FIFA World Cup, Hungary gave Brazil a footballing lesson at Goodison Park, running out 3-1 winners before their progress was stopped by the Soviet Union in the quarter-finals. It was Brazil's first defeat in the FIFA World Cup since the 1954 quarter-finals, when they had lost 4-2 to ... Hungary.

YEARS OF PLENTY

Hungary's dazzling line-up of the early 1950s was known as the "*Aranycsapat*" – or "Golden Team". They set a record for international matches unbeaten, going 31 consecutive games without defeat between May 1950 and their July 1954 FIFA World Cup final loss to West Germany – a run that included clinching Olympic gold at Helsinki in Finland in 1952. That 31-match tally has been overtaken since only by Brazil and Spain. Hungary in the 1950s also set a record for most consecutive games scoring at least one goal – 73 matches – while their average of 5.4 goals per game at the 1954 FIFA World Cup remains an all-time high for the tournament.

THE RIGHT TROUSERS

Four-time Hungarian footballer of the year, goalkeeper **Gabor Kiraly**, is notable for playing in tracksuit trousers – yet his performances have enabled him to surpass the 86-cap tally of another famed Hungarian goalkeeper, "*Aranycsapat*" mainstay Gyula Grosics. Kiraly had a dramatic start to his international career, saving a penalty just four minutes into his debut against Austria in 1998. Despite reaching 89 caps, ex-Crystal Palace stopper Kiraly has lately been battling for a starting-place between the posts with another player boasting English league experience: 2012 Hungarian footballer of the year Adam Bogdan (Bolton).

TOP CAPS

1	Jozsef Bozsik	101
2	Laszlo Fazekas	92
3	Gabor Kiraly	89
4	Gyula Grosics	86
5	Ferenc Puskas	85
6	Imre Garaba	82
7	Sandor Matrai	81
8	Zoltan Gera	77
=	Ferenc Sipos	77
10	Laszlo Balint	76
=	Ferenc Bene	76
=	Mate Fenyvesi	76
=	Roland Juhasz	76

NORTHERN IRELAND

Northern Ireland have played as a separate country since 1921 (before that there had been an all-Ireland side). They have qualified for the FIFA World Cup finals on three occasions: in 1958 (when they became the smallest country to reach the quarter-final stage), 1982 (when they reached the second round) and 1986.

GEORGE BEST

One of the greatest players never to grace a FIFA World Cup, **George Best** (capped 37 times by Northern Ireland) nevertheless won domestic and European honours with Manchester United – including both a European Champions Cup medal and the European Footballer of the Year award in 1968. He also played in the United States, Hong Kong and Australia before his "final" retirement in 1984.

GIANT JENNINGS

Pat Jennings's record 119 appearances for Northern Ireland also stood as an international record at one stage. The former Tottenham Hotspur and Arsenal goalkeeper made his international debut, aged just 18, against Wales on 15 April 1964, and played his final game in the 1986 FIFA World Cup, against Brazil, on his 41st birthday.

"PETER THE GREAT"

Former Manchester City and Derby County striker Peter Doherty, one of the most expensive players of his era, won the English league and FA Cup as a player, and earned 19 caps for Northern Ireland in a career interrupted by World War Two. His late goal to earn a 2-2 draw in 1947 ensured Northern Ireland avoided defeat against England for the first time. As manager, he led Northern Ireland to the quarter-finals of the 1958 FIFA World Cup – Northern Ireland remain the smallest country ever to reach that stage of the competition. They were defeated 4-0 by France, who went on to finish third.

OH DANNY BOY

Northern Ireland's captain at the 1958 FIFA World Cup was Tottenham Hotspur's cerebral **Danny Blanchflower** – the first twentieth-century captain of an English club to win both the league and FA Cup in the same season, in 1960–61. When asked the secret of his national team's success in 1958, he offered the explanation: "Our tactic is to equalize before the others have scored." More famously, he offered the philosophy: "The great fallacy is that the game is first and foremost about winning. It's nothing of the kind. The game is about glory. It's about doing things in style, with a flourish, about going out and beating the other lot, not waiting for them to die of boredom."

TOP SCORERS

1	David Healy	36
2	Colin Clarke	13
=	Billy Gillespie	13
4	Gerry Armstrong	12
=	Joe Bambrick	12
=	Iain Dowie	12
=	Jimmy Quinn	12
8	Olphie Stanfield	11
9	Billy Bingham	10
=	Johnny Crossan	10
=	Jimmy McIlroy	10
=	Peter McParland	10

KEEPING CONNECTED

Maik Taylor is Northern Ireland's fourth most-capped player, though he has no family connection to the country. Born in Germany, to an English father and German mother, his British passport meant he could represent any of the Home Nations – and he chose Northern Ireland. The goalkeeper was skipper for his 88th and final appearance, against Italy, in October 2011.

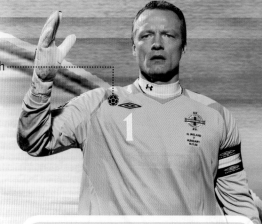

TOP CAPS

1	Pat Jennings	119
2	David Healy	95
3	Mal Donaghy	91
4	Sammy McIlroy	88
=	Maik Taylor	88
6	Keith Gillespie	86
=	Aaron Hughes	86
8	Jimmy Nicholl	73
9	Michael Hughes	71
10	David McCreery	67

"PETER THE LATE"

Poor Peter Watson is thought to have had the shortest Northern Ireland international career, thanks to the two minutes he spent on the pitch in a 5-0 UEFA European Championship qualifying win over Cyprus in April 1971. Coventry-born Watson was playing that season for Northern Irish club Distillery, in a side featuring law student and future international **Martin O'Neill** – who would go on to win 64 caps, including captaining his country at the 1982 FIFA World Cup before enjoying successful career in management. Paul Williams played only seven minutes for his country, as Northern Ireland drew 1-1 with the Faroe Islands in another Euro qualifier in May 1991.

THE BOY DAVIS

Midfielder Steven Davis became Northern Ireland's youngest post-war captain when he led out the side against Uruguay in May 2006, aged just 21 years, five months and 20 days.

YOUNG GUN

Norman Whiteside became the then-youngest player at a FIFA World Cup finals (beating Pele's record) when he represented Northern Ireland in Spain in 1982 aged 17 years and 41 days. He went on to win 38 caps, scoring nine goals – before injury forced his retirement aged just 26.

STRIFE OF BRIAN

Brian McLean's Northern Ireland career began and ended with his second-half appearance against Estonia in March 2006. The Scottish-born player had been thought eligible to play for Northern Ireland through family links, but it later transpired that he had played for Scotland Under-17s in a UEFA competition four years earlier and had not officially changed his allegiance until after his 21st birthday – which is the official deadline.

HERO HEALY

Northern Ireland's record goalscorer **David Healy** has scored almost three times as many international goals as the next highest player on the list. He scored two goals on his debut against Luxembourg on 23 February 2000, and scored all three as Northern Ireland stunned Spain 3-2 in a qualifier for UEFA Euro 2008 on 6 September 2006. He also hit the winner against Sven-Goran Eriksson's England in September 2005, Northern Ireland's first victory over their neighbours since 1972. But he more recently endured a four-year, 24-game drought between scoring against San Marino in October 2008 and his next international goal, versus Azerbaijan, in November 2012.

NORWAY

Although they played their first international, against Sweden, in 1908 and qualified for the 1938 FIFA World Cup, it would take a further 56 years, and the introduction of a direct brand of football, before Norway reappeared at a major international tournament. Success in such competitions has been rare – they have never progressed beyond the second round – but Norway retains the distinction of being the only nation in history never to have lost to Brazil.

BRAZIL RESISTANCE

Norway are the only nation never to have lost – so far – to Brazil, enjoying a record of two victories and two draws. Their most memorable match against the Samba Kings came in the first round of the 1998 FIFA World Cup, when Norway triumphed 2-1 against a side who would go on to reach that year's final. Norway actually went a goal down, but came back to win thanks to strikes in the last seven minutes from Tore Andre Flo and Kjetil Rekdal.

GOALS FOR EITHER IVERSEN

Steffen Iversen scored the only goal of Norway's only win at a UEFA European Championship – against Spain at the 2000 tournament. Iversen's father Odd had previously been one of the country's leading strikers, hitting memorable strikes in unexpected victories over Yugoslavia in a 1966 FIFA World Cup qualifier and away to France ahead of the 1970 tournament. Odd scored a total of 19 times in 45 games for Norway between 1967 and 1979. Steffen equalled his father's international scoring tally with a hat-trick against Malta in November 2007 – then scored his next two goals against Iceland the following September. He was still playing for Norway in 2011, aged 34, having reached 79 caps and scoring 21 goals.

YOUR BOYS TOOK A HELL OF A BEATING

Bjorge Lillelien's famous commentary after Norway beat England 2-1 in a qualifier for the 1982 FIFA World Cup remains one of the iconic moments of European football. A commentator from 1957 until just before his death from cancer in 1987, he concentrated on winter sports and football. Roughly translated, it sounded as follows: "Lord Nelson, Lord Beaverbrook, Sir Winston Churchill, Sir Anthony Eden, Clement Attlee, Henry Cooper, Lady Diana, Maggie Thatcher, can you hear me? Your boys took a hell of a beating." Although the commentary was for Norwegian radio, it soon made its way to an English audience and has achieved cliché status. In 2002, Lillelien's words were designated the greatest piece of sports commentary ever by the *Observer* newspaper's sports supplement. Such is its place in British sporting culture, parodies of the commentary have been written to celebrate a vast array of domestic sporting victories.

TOP SCORERS

1	Jorgen Juve	33
2	Einar Gundersen	26
3	Harald Hennum	25
4	John Carew	24
5	Tore Andre Flo	23
=	Ole Gunnar Solskjaer	23
7	Gunnar Thoresen	22
8	Steffen Iversen	21
9	Jan Age Fjortoft	20
10	Odd Iversen	19
=	Oyvind Leonhardsen	19
=	Olav Nilsen	19

LONG–DISTANCE RIISE

Fierce-shooting, ex-Liverpool, AS Monaco and AS Roma left-back Jon Arne Riise marked the game in which he matched Thorbjorn Svenssen's Norwegian appearances record, against Greece in August 2012, by getting onto the scoresheet, though the game ended in a 3-2 defeat. He was also on the losing side when claiming the record for himself, in a 2-0 loss in Iceland the following month, before scoring his 16th international goal in his 106th match four days later as Norway beat Slovenia 2-1. His younger brother, Bjorn Helge Riise, a midfielder, has joined him in both the national team and at their current club, Fulham.

FOOT FAULT

Norway striker Mohammed Abdellaoue, scorer of six goals in 25 internationals, was born with only four toes on his left foot. His younger brother Mos has followed him into the national team, making his debut in January 2012.

ERIK THE VIKING

Goalkeeper Erik Thorstvedt was among the Norway footballers taking part at the 1984 Olympic Games in Los Angeles when they qualified as late replacements after tournament boycotts by Iron Curtain countries Poland and East Germany. He was also a key member of the team that qualified for the 1994 FIFA World Cup (their first appearance since 1938) and played a Norwegian goalkeeping record of 97 internationals between 1982 and 1996.

TOP CAPS

1	John Arne Riise	110
2	Thorbjorn Svenssen	104
3	Henning Berg	100
4	Erik Thorstvedt	97
5	John Carew	91
6	Oyvind Leonhardsen	86
7	Brede Hangeland	84
8	Kjetil Rekdal	83
9	Steffen Iversen	79
10	Erik Mykland	78

LONG STAY TRAVELLERS

Norway's best finish at an international tournament was the bronze medal they clinched at the 1936 Summer Olympics in Berlin, having lost to Italy in the semi-finals but beaten Poland 3-2 in a medal play-off thanks to an Arne Brustad hat-trick. That year's side has gone down in Norwegian football history as the "*Bronselaget*", or "Bronze Team". However, they had entered the tournament with low expectations and were forced to alter their travel plans ahead of the semi-final against Italy on 10 August – Norwegian football authorities had originally booked their trip home for the previous day, not expecting their team to get so far. Italy beat Norway 2-1 in extra-time not only in that summer's Olympic semi-final, but also in the first round of the FIFA World Cup two years later – going on to win both tournaments.

GOAL HANGE

Norway's captain and seventh most-capped player, is commanding centre-back **Brede Hangeland**. He was actually born 5,000 miles from Norway in Houston, Texas, where his father worked for two years for an oil firm, but spent most of his childhood in Stavanger, Norway, making his name with local side Viking and then Danish club Copenhagen. His former Viking manager Roy Hodgson signed him in 2008 for English Premier League team Fulham, where Hangeland has become a fans' favourite. He made his international debut in November 2002, but did not score his first goal until his 62nd appearance, against Iceland in September 2010. Another wait followed before his second, third and fourth came in quick succession between August 2012 and October 2012.

BOOT CAMPER

Egil Olsen, one of Europe's most eccentric coaches, was signed up for a surprise second spell as national manager when Norway put their faith in the direct-football specialist along the road towards the 2010 FIFA World Cup finals in South Africa – 15 years after he had led the unfancied Scandinavians to the 1994 finals. That had been Norway's first finals appearance since 1938 and they followed it up by beating Brazil in the first round in France in 1998, making a hero out of the man in Wellington boots who guided his country to an impressive No. 2 in FIFA's official rankings. Before answering his country's call for a second stint as manager, Olsen's last job had been as manager of Iraq, but he left after only three months in charge. Remarkably, in his first match back at the helm for Norway, he masterminded a 1-0 win away to Germany with his route-one tactics. But life was not quite as happy for Olsen during his time at Wimbledon in the 1999–2000 Premier League season. The Norwegian, a firm believer in sports science, imposed a zonal marking system, which he was convinced would work. Critics held it responsible for Wimbledon's collapse in the second half of the season.

POLAND

The history of Polish football is littered with tremendous highs and depressing lows. Olympic gold-medal success in 1972, and third-place finishes in the 1974 and 1982 FIFA World Cup competitions were followed by failure to qualify for any tournament until 1992. Poland made it to the UEFA European Championship for the first time in 2008 and co-hosted the tournament with Ukraine in 2012, though went out in the first round both times.

TOP SCORERS

1	Wlodzimierz Lubanski	48
2	Grzegorz Lato	45
3	Kazimierz Deyna	41
4	Ernest Pol	39
5	Andrzej Szarmach	32
6	Gerard Cieslik	27
7	Zbigniew Boniek	24
8	Ernest Wilimowski	21
9	Dariusz Dziekanowski	20
=	Euzebiusz Smolarek	20

STAYING ON LATER THAN LATO

Record-breaking Polish stalwart **Michal Zewlakow** bowed out of international football on familiar turf, even though his country were playing an away game. The versatile defender's 102nd and final appearance for his country was a goalless friendly in Greece in March 2011, at the Karaiskakis stadium in Piraeus where he used to play club football for Olympiacos. Zewlakow had overtaken Grzegorz Lato's appearances record for Poland in his previous match, an October 2010 friendly against Ecuador. He had already helped make footballing history for his homeland when he and brother Marcin, a striker, became the first twins to line up together for Poland, against France in February 2000. Marcin would end his international career with 25 appearances and five goals.

TYTON THE TITAN

Two 1-1 draws in a row at the 2012 UEFA European Championship extended Poland's unbeaten run to eight games and filled the tournament co-hosts with high hopes of reaching the knock-out stages for the first time – only for a 1-0 defeat to the Czech Republic to seal their fate. But among those players to emerge from the tournament with credit was goalkeeper **Przemyslaw Tyton**. The stopper, with only five caps to his name, saved a penalty from Greece's Giorgos Karagounis just moments after coming on in the competition's opening match following a red card for first-choice goalkeeper Wojciech Szczesny, and kept his place in the team for the next two games. Szczesny had already conceded an equalizer to Greece's Dimitrios Salpingidis – ending a Polish record run of 512 minutes without allowing opponents to score, stretching back to a 2-1 victory over Hungary in November 2011.

O COME, O COME, EMMANUEL

Poland were the first European country to qualify for the 2002 FIFA World Cup in South Korea and Japan, largely thanks to the eight goals scored by striker **Emmanuel Olisadebe** – setting a Polish record for a FIFA World Cup qualifying campaign. Nigerian-born Olisadebe had been awarded Polish citizenship during a successful four-year stint at Polonia Warsaw. He was actually given special permission by the president of Poland to become a citizen a year before completing the official qualification period.

TOP CAPS

1	Michael Zewlakow	102
2	Grzegorz Lato	100
3	Kazimierz Deyna	97
4	Jacek Bak	96
=	Jacek Krzynowek	96
6	Wladyslaw Zmuda	91
7	Antoni Szymanowski	82
8	Zbigniew Boniek	80
9	Wlodzimierz Lubanski	75
10	Tomasz Waldoch	74

LATO'S MISSION

Grzegorz Lato is not only second in both the tallies of Poland's most-capped and top-scoring players, the only Polish winner of the Golden Boot with his seven goals at the 1974 FIFA World Cup, and a member of the gold medal-winning team at the 1972 Summer Olympics. He was also a leading figure in Poland's co-hosting with Ukraine of the 2012 UEFA European Championship, having become president of the country's football federation in 2008. He vowed: "I am determined to change the image of Polish football, to make it transparent and pure."

SUPER ERNEST

Ernest Wilimowski wrote his name into FIFA World Cup history in 1938 when he scored four goals but still finished on the losing side. Poland went down 6-5 after extra-time to Brazil in a first-round tie in Strasbourg, France.

PUNCTUALITY PUNISHMENT

Kazimierz Gorski was the coach – capped once as a player – who led Poland to third place at the 1974 FIFA World Cup, having won gold at the Olympics in Munich, Germany, two years earlier. While winning a reputation for closeness with his players, Gorski could also be ruthless – key player Adam Musial was dropped from the team for a second-round game against Sweden at the 1974 tournament as punishment for turning up 20 minutes late to training. Poland still won the game, 1-0.

"LITTLE FIGO"

Jacub Blaszczykowski was one of the Polish players to come out of Euro 2012 with the most credit – he scored a spectacular equalising goal against Russia – despite having gone into the tournament in testing circumstances. Before joining the rest of the squad in their training camp, he attended the funeral of his father. His presence at the event was all the more noteworthy because, as a ten-year-old child, Blaszyzkowski had witnessed his mother Anna being stabbed to death by his father, who served a 15-year prison sentence as a result. Polish great Zbigniew Boniek has dubbed Blaszczykowski "Little Figo" – after the Portuguese winger Luis Figo – though he is more commonly known as "Kuba", the name he often wears on the back of his shirt. He had been encouraged to pursue football as a teenager by his uncle Jerzy Brzeczek, who also played for Dortmund and captained Poland, winning 42 caps between 1992 and 1999 and picking up an Olympic silver medal in 1992.

FIVE ASIDE

Poland had five different goalscorers when they beat Peru 5-1 at the 1982 FIFA World Cup: Wlodzimierz Smolarek, Grzegorz Lato, Zbigniew Boniek, Andrzej Buncol and Wlodzimierz Ciolek. The feat was not repeated until Phillip Cocu, Marc Overmars, Dennis Bergkamp, Pierre van Hooijdonk and Ronald de Boer gave Holland a 5-0 victory over South Korea at the 1998 FIFA World Cup.

COOL KEEPER

What is it with Polish goalkeepers? The country's outfield players may not always be household names worldwide, but Jerzy Dudek (Liverpool), Artur Boruc and Lukasz Zaluska (both Celtic), Lukasz Fabianski and Wojciech Szczesny (both Arsenal), and Tomasz Kuszczak (Manchester United) have all played roles at four of Britain's most successful clubs.

BONIEK

Zbigniew Boniek, arguably the best player Poland has ever produced, earned a place among football's legends for his role in the country's progress to third place at the 1982 FIFA World Cup. However, his absence from the tournament's semi-final will go down as one of the great "what ifs" of the competition. Robbed of their star forward through suspension, could Poland have upset both Italy and the odds and reached the final? Instead they lost the match 2-0.

PORTUGAL

Portugal's first experience of international competition almost ended in triumph. Inspired by Eusebio, they marched through to the semi-finals of the 1966 FIFA World Cup, only to lose to eventual champions England. A standout performance in the 1984 UEFA European Championship apart, more than 30 years would pass before Portugal enjoyed such giddy heights again. A "golden" generation of players arrived on the scene and since the turn of the century Portugal have become a consistent force on the world football stage.

TOP CAPS

1	Luis Figo	127
2	Fernando Couto	110
3	Cristiano Ronaldo	104
4	Rui Costa	94
5	Pauleta	88
6	Simao	85
7	Joao Pinto	81
8	Vitor Baia	80
9	Nuno Gomes	79
=	Ricardo	79

TOP SCORERS

1	Pauleta	47
2	Eusebio	41
3	Cristiano Ronaldo	39
4	Luis Figo	32
5	Nuno Gomes	29
6	Rui Costa	26
=	Helder Postiga	26
8	Joao Pinto	23
9	Nene	22
=	Simao	22

HAPPY HUNDREDTH BIRTHDAY

Portugal celebrated their 100th birthday as a republic by beating newly crowned world champions Spain in a specially-arranged friendly in November 2010. The match not only marked the anniversary, but also celebrated the two countries' union in an ultimately unsuccessful bid to co-host the 2018 FIFA World Cup. Yet there was little equality in the match, Portugal sweeping to a 4-0 triumph – slight consolation for losing to Spain in the FIFA World Cup second round five months earlier.

GOODISON GLORY

At the 1966 FIFA World Cup Portugal beat North Korea 5-3 in an incredible quarter-final at Everton's Goodison Park. The sensational Eusebio spurred an amazing comeback after the Koreans had gone 3-0 ahead in the first 25 minutes. He scored four goals to take Portugal to the semi-finals in their first-ever FIFA World Cup appearance. Despite the tears that flowed after defeat to eventual winners England, Portugal rallied to claim third place with a **2-1 victory over the Soviet Union**.

THE BLACK PANTHER

Born in Mozambique, **Eusebio** da Silva Ferreira was named Portugal's "Golden Player" to mark UEFA's 50th anniversary in 2004. Signed by Benfica in 1960 at the age of 18, he scored a hat-trick in only his second game – against Santos in a friendly tournament in Paris – outshining the opponents' young star, Pele. He helped Benfica win the second of their European Cups in 1962, was named European Footballer of the Year in 1965 and led Portugal to third place in the 1966 FIFA World Cup, finishing the tournament as top scorer with nine goals. A phenomenal striker, Eusebio scored 320 goals in 313 appearances in the Portuguese league, won the first European Golden Boot in 1968 (and earned a second in 1973). His 41 goals for Portugal – in 64 matches – has been bettered only by Pauleta, who scored 47, but in 24 more appearances.

PRESIDENTIAL POWER

Cristiano Ronaldo dos Santos Aveiro got his second name because his father was a great fan of US President Ronald Reagan. Born on 5 February 1985, Cristiano grew up as a Benfica fan, but began his career with arch-rivals Sporting Lisbon before securing a move to Manchester United in 2003. His best season with United, in 2008, not only brought him the Golden Boot as well as Premier League and Champions League titles, but also helped him become only the second Portuguese player (after Luis Figo) to be named FIFA World Player of the Year. Spanish giants Real Madrid paid 93.9 million to make him the most expensive footballer in history the following year. His club record 60 goals in 2011–12 steered them to the La Liga title, before he hit three for Portugal at the 2012 UEFA European Championship – the fifth major international tournament at which he has scored. Only France's Thierry Henry, Sweden's Henrik Larsson and Germany's Rudi Voller have also scored in five, though Germany's Jurgen Klinsmann managed six.

THE FAMOUS FIVE

Eusebio, Mario Coluna, Jose Augusto, Antonio Simoes, and Jose Torres were the "Fabulous Five" in Benfica's 1960s Dream Team, who made up the spine of the Portuguese national side at the 1966 FIFA World Cup. Coluna (the "Sacred Monster"), scored the vital third goal in the 1961 European Cup final and captained the national side in 1966. Jose Augusto, who scored two goals in the opening game against Hungary, went on to manage the national side and later the Portuguese women's team. Antonio Simoes (the "Giant Gnome" – just 1.58 metres/5ft 3in tall) made his debut for Portugal and Benfica in 1962, aged just 18. Jose Torres – the only one of the five not to win the European Cup (though he played in the defeats in both 1963 and 1968) – scored the winner against Russia in the 1966 third-place match, and went on to manage the national side to their next appearance at the FIFA World Cup finals in 1986.

WAY TO GOMES

Portugal have provided three of the seven players to score at three different UEFA European Championships: Nuno Gomes (2000, 2004 and 2008) and Cristiano Ronaldo and **Helder Postiga** (both 2004, 2008 and 2012). Gomes scored four at Euro 2000, the first of which – in a 3-2 victory over England – was actually the first of his 29 goals for Portugal, despite the fact he had made his international debut four years earlier. He was named in the official UEFA team of the tournament for the 2000 event, despite ending it in disgrace: he pushed referee Gunter Benko following Portugal's semi-final defeat to France and was handed a lengthy international ban.

CLOUD NINE

Scoring nine goals in one match against Leca, eight goals in one match against Boavista, six goals in a game three times, five goals in a game 12 times and four goals in a game 17 times, Fernando Baptista Peyroteo is one of the most prolific goalscorers in world football history. He scored an astonishing 330 goals in 197 Portuguese league games (1.68 goals a game) between 1937 and 1949, and 15 goals in just 20 games for the national side.

REP. OF IRELAND

It took a combination of astute management and endless searching through ancestral records before the Republic of Ireland finally qualified for the finals of a major tournament, at the 20th time of asking. But ever since Jack Charlton took the team to UEFA Euro 88, Ireland have remained one of Europe's most dangerous opponents.

KEANE CARRY-ON

Roy Keane stormed out of Ireland's preparation for the 2002 FIFA World Cup in Japan and Korea, heading home before the tournament had even started. Keane's career with Ireland began against Chile on 22 May 1991. He played in all four of Ireland's matches at the 1994 FIFA World Cup in the United States, including the shock 1-0 defeat of Italy. Originally appointed captain by Mick McCarthy, Keane returned to the Irish set-up after McCarthy resigned – but announced his international retirement after Ireland failed to qualify for the 2006 FIFA World Cup. His final game was a 1-0 defeat to France on 7 September 2005.

CHAMPION CHARLTON

Jack Charlton became a hero after he took Ireland to their first major finals in 1988, defeating England 1-0 in their first game at the UEFA European Championship. Things got even better at their first FIFA World Cup finals two years later, where the unfancied Irish lost out only to hosts Italy in the quarter-finals.

KILBANE KEEPS ON AND ON

Only England's Billy Wright, with 70, has played more consecutive internationals than **Kevin Kilbane**, whose 109th Republic of Ireland cap against Macedonia in March 2011 was also his 65th in a row, covering 11 years and five months. The versatile left-sider – nicknamed "Zinedine Kilbane" by fans – was given a rest for Ireland's next game three days later, though, a friendly against Uruguay.

ROBBIE KEEN

The Republic of Ireland's all-time scoring record was taken over by much-travelled striker **Robbie Keane** in October 2004 and he has been adding to it ever since – not least with last-minute equalizers against both Germany and Spain at the 2006 FIFA World Cup. He marked the final game at the old Lansdowne Road with a hat-trick against San Marino in November 2006 – then, four years later, marked the inaugural game at the revamped replacement ground, now known as the Aviva Stadium, with his 100th cap against Argentina. Ireland's 2-1 win over Macedonia in March 2011 was Keane's 41st appearance as captain – equalling the record set in the 1980s and '90s by Andy Townsend. He followed this up with two more matches as skipper, as Ireland beat Northern Ireland and Scotland in the British-based Carling Nations Cup – scoring three goals across the two games, taking his overall tally to 49, before his brace against Macedonia in June 2011 took him to 51. These made him the first player from the British Isles to score a half-century of international goals, and past England's 49-goal top scorer Bobby Charlton.

DON GIOVANNI

Italian coach Giovanni Trapattoni took over as Republic of Ireland coach in 2008 and, after narrowly missing out in the play-offs on a place at the 2010 FIFA World Cup, led the Republic of Ireland to their first UEFA European Championship in 24 years two years later. "Il Trap" also became the oldest man to lead a side at a UEFA European Championship, aged 73 years and 93 days, when he faced his homeland Italy in Ireland's final game. The previous record-holder was Croatia's Otto Baric, who was 71 years and 2 days old at the 2004 tournament.

IT'S A GIVEN

The Republic of Ireland's second-most-capped player, goalkeeper Shay Given, bowed out of international football at the 2012 UEFA European Championship finals – the first major tournament his country had reached since the 1994 FIFA World Cup, when Given was also first-choice in goal. Despite going into UEFA Euro 2012 on a 14-game unbeaten run, the Irish lost all three games, to Croatia, Spain and Italy. The team's final match saw the captain's armband given to winger **Damien Duff**, as he became the fifth man to win a century of caps for Ireland. UEFA president Michel Platini praised the country's boisterous travelling fans and promised them a special award for their enthusiasm. Given, who gave all his international match fees to charity, announced his international retirement in the summer of 2012, following 55 clean sheets in 125 appearances, though he did suggest in January 2013 that he could be available for a comeback. One of his rivals has been Millwall goalkeeper David Forde, who was 33 when he faced Sweden in a FIFA World Cup qualifier in March 2013 – older than any other Ireland debutant in a competitive international.

MORE FOR MOORE

Paddy Moore was the first player ever to score four goals in a FIFA World Cup qualifier when Ireland came from behind to draw 4-4 with Belgium on 25 February 1934. Don Givens became the only Irishman to equal Moore's feat when he scored all four as Ireland beat Turkey 4-0 in October 1975.

CAPTAIN ALL-ROUND

Johnny Carey not only captained Matt Busby's Manchester United to the English league title in 1952, he also captained both Northern Ireland (nine caps) and later the Republic of Ireland (27 caps). He went on to manage the Republic of Ireland between 1955 and 1967.

HOORAY FOR RAY

Ray Houghton may have been born in Glasgow and spoke with a Scottish accent, but he scored two of Ireland's most famous goals. A header gave the Republic a shock 1-0 win over England at UEFA Euro 88 in West Germany and, six years later, his long-range strike was the only goal of the game against eventual finalists Italy, in the first round of the 1994 FIFA World Cup in the USA. It was exactly 18 years to the day from that 1994 shock that Ireland – now managed by Italian Giovanni Trapattoni – lost 2-0 to Italy in their third and final Group C match of the 2012 UEFA European Championship. Playing for Ireland that day was defender John O'Shea, who had previously been part of the Irish team that beat Italy 2-1 in the final of the 1998 UEFA European U-16s Championship final in Scotland. The Republic's only other continental title was the UEFA European U-19s Championship trophy they lifted by beating Germany, also in 1998.

CROSSING THE CODES

Cornelius "Con" Martin was a Gaelic footballer whose passion for soccer resulted in his expulsion from the Gaelic Athletic Association. His versatility meant he was as good at centre-half as he was in goal, both for club (Aston Villa) and country. He played both in goal and outfield for the fledgling Irish national team, scoring a penalty in the 2-0 victory over England at Goodison Park in 1949 – in what was England's first home defeat to a non-British opponent.

TOP CAPS

1	Robbie Keane	127
2	Shay Given	125
3	Kevin Kilbane	110
4	Steve Staunton	102
5	Damien Duff	100
6	Niall Quinn	91
7	John O'Shea	89
8	Tony Cascarino	88
9	Paul McGrath	83
10	Packie Bonner	80

TOP SCORERS

1	Robbie Keane	59
2	Niall Quinn	21
3	Frank Stapleton	20
4	John Aldridge	19
=	Tony Cascarino	19
=	Don Givens	19
7	Noel Cantwell	14
8	Gerry Daly	13
=	Jimmy Dunne	13
10	Kevin Doyle	12

ROMANIA

The history of Romanian football is littered with a series of bright moments – they were one of four countries (with Brazil, France and Belgium) to appear in the first three editions of the FIFA World Cup – followed by significant spells in the doldrums – since 1938 they have qualified for the finals of the tournament only four times in 14 attempts. The country's football highlight came in 1994 when, inspired by Gheorghe Hagi, they reached the quarter-finals of the FIFA World Cup.

TOP CAPS

1	Dorinel Munteanu	134
2	Gheorghe Hagi	125
3	Gheorghe Popescu	115
4	Ladislau Boloni	102
5	Dan Petrescu	95
6	Bogdan Stelea	91
7	Michael Klein	89
=	Razvan Rat	89
9	Marius Lacatus	83
=	Bogdan Lobont	83
=	Mircea Rednic	83

TERRIFIC TRIO

Gheorghe Hagi, **Florin Raducioiu** and Ilie Dumitrescu lit up the FIFA World Cup in the United States in 1994. Together they scored nine of Romania's ten goals (Raducioiu four, Hagi three, Dumitrescu two). All three successfully converted their penalties in the quarter-final shoot-out against Sweden, but misses from Dan Petrescu and Miodrag Belodedici sent the Romanians crashing out. All three made big-money moves for the following 1994–95 season: Hagi went from Brescia to Barcelona, Dumitrescu from Steaua Bucharest to Tottenham Hotspur and Raducioiu went from warming the bench at Milan to the first team at Espanyol.

THE "HERO OF SEVILLE"

Helmuth Duckadam, the "Hero of Seville", will always be remembered for saving four consecutive penalties as Steaua Bucharest became the first Eastern European side to win the European Cup, beating Barcelona in a shoot-out in 1986. A rare blood disease forced him to retire from the game in 1991, after which he became a stopper of a different kind as a major in the Romanian Border Police.

BORDER CROSSING

Some 14 footballers played for both Romania, during the 1930s, and Hungary, during the 1940s – the most prolific being striker Iuliu Bodola, who scored 31 goals in 48 games for Romania, including appearances at the 1934 and 1938 FIFA World Cups, and four in 13 matches for his adopted homeland Hungary.

YELLOW PERIL

Despite topping Group G ahead of England, Colombia and Tunisia at the 1998 FIFA World Cup, Romania's players of that tournament might perhaps be best remembered for their collective decision to dye their hair blond ahead of their final first-round game. The **newly bleached Romanians** struggled to a 1-1 draw against Tunisia, before being knocked out by Croatia in the second round, 1-0.

TOP SCORERS

1	Gheorghe Hagi	35
=	Adrian Mutu	35
3	Iuliu Bodola	31
4	Viorel Moldovan	25
5	Ladislau Boloni	23
6	Rodion Camataru	21
=	Dudu Georgescu	21
=	Anghel Iordanescu	21
=	Ciprian Marica	21
=	Florin Raducioiu	21

CEMETERY SENTRY

It was second time luckier for former international striker Victor Piturca when he coached Romania at the 2008 UEFA European Championship in Austria and Switzerland, even though they were eliminated in the first round. He had previously been manager when the country qualified for the 2000 UEFA European Championship, but was forced out of the job before the tournament started following arguments with big-name players such as Gheorghe Hagi. Piturca's cousin Florin Piturca was also a professional footballer but died aged only 27 in 1978. Florin's father and Victor's uncle Maximilian, a cobbler, not only built a mausoleum for Florin but also slept at night in the cemetery until his own death in 1994.

BROUGHT TO BUCHAREST

Romania's new national stadium in the capital Bucharest became the first in the country ever to stage a major European final, when it hosted the 2012 UEFA Europa League final in which Atletico Madrid beat fellow Spanish side Athletic Bilbao. The 55,200-capacity Arena Nationala was opened in September 2011, when Romania drew 0-0 with France. It has also been used by Steaua Bucharest and Dinamo Bucharest for league matches, Otelul Galati for UEFA Champions League games, and both Steaua and Rapid Bucharest for UEFA Europa League fixtures. The venue stands on the site of the old Stadionul National, built in 1953 and demolished 54 years later.

CENTURY MAN

Gheorghe Hagi, Romania's "Player of the [twentieth] Century", scored three goals and was named in the Team of the Tournament at the 1994 FIFA World Cup in the United States, at which Romania lost out on penalties to Sweden after a 2-2 draw in the quarter-finals. Hagi made his international debut in 1983, aged just 18, scored his first goal aged 19 (in a 3-2 defeat to Northern Ireland) and remains Romania's joint-top goalscorer with 35 goals in 125 games. Despite retiring from international football after the 1998 FIFA World Cup, Hagi couldn't resist answering his country's call to play in UEFA Euro 2000. Sadly, two yellow-card offences in six minutes in the quarter-final against Italy meant Hagi's final bow on the international stage saw him receive a red card – and leave the field to take an early bath. Farul Constanta, in Hagi's hometown, named their stadium after him in 2000 – but fans stopped referring to it as such after he took the manager's job at rivals Timisoara.

TEENAGE NIGHTMARES

Second-tier club CS Buftea suffered the biggest defeat in the country's history when going down 31-0 in a Romanian Cup tie in September 2012, having decided to field a team of under-19s. Their conquerors, ACS Berceni, were from the division below and even the victors' club president admitted when interviewed afterwards: "I'm ashamed to tell you the score."

ADRIAN'S AID

Romania have only lost once when **Adrian Mutu** has scored – a fact made all the better for them since, with 35 goals, he is (with Gheorghe Hagi) his country's all-time leading goalscorer. Mutu drew level with Hagi with a FIFA World Cup qualifying game equalizer against Hungary in March 2013, though this was his first international goal in 21 months. Unfortunately for Romania, controversy has followed their finest player of the 21st century: he has been banned twice for failed drugs tests. The first came after a test carried out by his club employers Chelsea in September 2004 showed traces of cocaine and brought about his dismissal. After a seven-month ban he rehabilitated his career in Italy, first with Juventus and then Fiorentina, before receiving a nine-month suspension after he tested positive for a banned anti-obesity drug in January 2010. He did score against Italy at the 2008 UEFA European Championship, Romania's only goal at the last major tournament for which they qualified.

RUSSIA

Before the break-up of the Soviet Union (USSR) in 1992, the team was a world football powerhouse, winning the first UEFA European Championship in 1960, gold at the 1956 and 1988 Olympic Games and qualifying for the FIFA World Cup on seven occasions. Playing as Russia since August 1992, the good times have eluded them – they were UEFA Euro 2008 semi-finalists, but then failed to advance from the qualifying play-offs to reach the 2010 FIFA World Cup. Yet Russia has now been chosen as Eastern Europe's first-ever FIFA World Cup host country, staging the tournament in 2018.

TOP SCORERS
(Russia only)

1	Vladimir Beschastnykh	26
2	Aleksandr Kerzhakov	22
3	Roman Pavlyuchenko	21
4	Andrei Arshavin	17
=	Valeri Karpin	17
6	Dmitri Sychev	15
7	Igor Kolyvanov	12
8	Roman Shorokov	11
9	Sergei Kiryakov	10
=	Aleksandr Mostovoi	10

TWINS SETTLED

Twin brothers **Vasili** and **Aleksei Berezutskiy** have been playing for CSKA Moscow and Russia since 2003, though Aleksei made his CSKA debut in 2001 – a year before Vasili. The twins, both defenders, were UEFA Cup winners with their club in 2005 and UEFA European Championship runners-up with their country three years later – though Vasili missed Euro 2012 through injury. The pair have otherwise been mainstays in the Russian defence for the past decade, alongside CSKA team-mate Sergei Ignashevich, who made his international debut a year earlier.

YOUNG PROMISE

Igor Akinfeev became post-Soviet Russia's youngest international footballer when he made his debut in a friendly against Norway on 28 April 2004. The CSKA Moscow goalkeeper was just 18 years and 20 days old. The following season would be perhaps just as memorable for him, clinching a domestic league and cup double with his club while also lifting the UEFA Cup as CSKA Moscow became post-Soviet Russia's first side to win a UEFA club trophy. The youngest Soviet-era debutant was Eduard Streltsov, who hit a hat-trick on his debut against Sweden in June 1956, at the age of 17 years and 340 days and then scored another treble in his second game, against India.

MONEY MAN

Roman Abramovich, the commodities billionaire behind Chelsea's 21st-century success, has also been instrumental in the resurgence of Russian football at all levels – including being heavily involved in the appointment of Dutchman Guus Hiddink as manager of the national side. In 2008, Hiddink took Russia to the semi-finals of the UEFA European Championship (their best post-Soviet performance), where they lost 3-0 to eventual winners Spain. Abramovich also sponsors the "National Academy of Football" in Russia, which helps build training facilities and pitches to support youth football throughout the country.

PUTTING ON THE STYLE

As a professional footballer who has a diploma in fashion design, perhaps it is no surprise **Andrey Arshavin** could strut across the pitch with a certain élan as the most skilful of Russia's 21st-century players. Even after missing the first two games of the 2008 UEFA European Championship through suspension, the Russia captain dazzled with his performances in his team's next two matches – especially a 3-1 quarter-final triumph over the Netherlands. Just a month earlier, Arshavin had been central as Zenit St Petersburg lifted the UEFA Cup, although his later spell with English club Arsenal proved patchier before his release in summer 2013. Arshavin's image back home was tainted a little when he argued with fans after their Euro 2012 first-round exit – and he then lost the captaincy under new coach Fabio Capello. Yet, on his day, this natty man with an eye for an outfit could prove a cut above.

TOP CAPS

(Russia only)

1	Viktor Onopko	109
2	Sergei Ignashevich	87
3	Aleksandr Anyukov	76
4	Andrei Arshavin	75
5	Valeri Karpin	72
=	Aleksandr Kerzhakov	72
7	Vladimir Beschastnykh	71
8	Vasili Berezutskiy	70
9	Sergei Semak	65
10	Igor Akinfeev	59

PAV A GO HERO

Roman Pavlyuchenko's thumping strike as a substitute to wrap up a 4-1 victory over the Czech Republic in Russia's opening game of the 2012 UEFA European Championship took him to within five goals of Vladimir Beschastnykh's post-Soviet scoring record. Pavlyuchenko also scored Russia's first goal of Euro 2008, this time in a 4-1 defeat at the hands of eventual champions Spain. Despite the loss, Russia still managed to reach the semi-finals that year; in 2012 they failed to make it beyond the group stages. Pavlyuchenko is Russia's top scorer in UEFA European Championships, with four overall – three in 2008 and one in 2012.

SUPER STOPPER

FIFA declared **Lev Yashin** to be the finest goalkeeper of the 20th century – naturally, he made it into their Century XI team, too. In a career spanning 20 years, Yashin played 326 league games for Dynamo Moscow – the only club side he ever played for – and won 78 caps for the Soviet Union, conceding on average less than a goal a game (only 70 in total). With Dynamo, he won five Soviet championships and three Soviet cups, the last of which came in his final full season in 1970. He saved around 150 penalties in his long career, and kept four clean sheets in his 12 FIFA World Cup matches. Such was Yashin's worldwide reputation, Chilean international Eladio Rojas was so excited at scoring past the legendary Yashin in the 1962 FIFA World Cup that he gave the surprised keeper a big hug with the ball still sitting in the back of the net. Yashin was nicknamed the "Black Spider" for his distinctive black jersey and his uncanny ability to get a hand, arm, leg or foot in the way of shots and headers of all kinds. In 1963, Yashin became the first, and so far only, keeper to be named European Footballer of the Year, the same year in which he won his fifth Soviet championship and starred for the Rest of the World XI in the English FA's Centenary Match at Wembley.

CAPPING IT ALL

Viktor Onopko, despite being born in the Ukraine, played all his career for the CIS and Russian national football teams. The first of Onopko's 113 international caps (the first four for the CIS) came in a 2-2 draw against England in Moscow on 29 April 1992. He played in the 1994 and 1998 FIFA World Cups, as well as the UEFA European Championship in 1996. He was due to join the squad for the UEFA European Championship in 2004 but missed out through injury. Onopko's club career, spanning 19 years, took him to Shakhtar Donetsk, Spartak Moscow, Real Oviedo, Rayo Vallecano, Alania Vladikavkaz and FC Saturn. He was Russian footballer of the year in 1993 and 1994.

GOLDEN BOY

Igor Netto captained the USSR national side to their greatest successes: gold at the 1956 Olympics in Melbourne and victory in the first-ever UEFA European Championship in France in 1960. Born in Moscow in 1930, Netto was awarded the Order of Lenin in 1957 and became an ice hockey coach after retiring from football.

SCOTLAND

A country with a vibrant domestic league and a rich football tradition – it played host to the first-ever international football match, against England, in November 1872 – Scotland have never put in the performances on the international stage to match their lofty ambitions. There have been moments of triumph, such as an unexpected victory over Holland at the 1978 FIFA World Cup, but far too many moments of despair. Scotland have not qualified for the finals of a major tournament since 1998.

TOP SCORERS

1	Kenny Dalglish	30
=	Denis Law	30
3	Hughie Gallacher	23
4	Lawrie Reilly	22
5	Ally McCoist	19
6	Kenny Miller	17
7	Robert Hamilton	15
=	James McFadden	15
9	Maurice Johnston	14
10	Bob McColl	13
=	Andrew Wilson	13

KING KENNY

Kenny Dalglish is Scotland's joint-top international goalscorer (with Denis Law) and remains the only player to have won more than a century of caps for the national side, with 102 in total – 11 more than the next highest cap-winner, goalkeeper Jim Leighton. Despite growing up a Rangers fan (he was born in Glasgow on 4 March 1951), Dalglish made his name spear-heading Celtic's domestic dominance in the 1970s, winning four league titles, four Scottish Cups and one League Cup. He then went on to become a legend at Liverpool, winning a hat-trick of European Cups (1978, 1981 and 1984) and leading the side as player-manager to their first-ever league and cup double in 1986. He later joined Herbert Chapman and Brian Clough as one of the few managers to lead two different sides to the league title – guiding Blackburn Rovers to the summit of English football in 1994–95. For Scotland, Dalglish scored at both the 1978 and 1982 FIFA World Cup finals, netting the first goal in the famous 3-2 victory over eventual runners-up Holland in the 1978 group stages. He played his last international in 1986.

THE LAWMAN

Denis Law is joint top scorer for Scotland with Kenny Dalglish, scoring 30 goals in only 55 games compared to the 102 it took Dalglish to do the same. Law twice scored four goals in a match for Scotland. First against Northern Ireland on 7 November 1962, helping win the British Home Championships. He repeated the feat against Norway in a friendly on 7 November 1963. Law clearly enjoyed playing against Norway, having grabbed a hat-trick in Bergen just five months earlier.

DON'T COME HOME TOO SOON

Scotland's 2-0 defeat to Serbia in March 2013 gave them the unenviable record of being the first European country eliminated from the 2014 FIFA World Cup – denying them the attempt to get beyond the first round of the finals for the first time. **Gordon Strachan**, who scored five goals in 50 games for Scotland in midfield between 1980 and 1992, had replaced the sacked Craig Levein in January 2013.

ROOM FOR ONE MORE?

Hampden Park, Scotland's national stadium, boasts the record for the highest-ever football attendance in Europe. The crowd was so huge no one can be quite sure how many squeezed in to watch Scotland v England in 1937, though the official figure is usually quoted as 149,415. Scotland won the British Home Championship tie 3-1, though they ended runners-up to Wales in the overall tournament. Since being redeveloped in 1999, Hampden Park has hosted all but one of Scotland's home internationals. The only exception was a 2008 UEFA European Championship qualifier against the Faroe Islands in September 2006, when Celtic Park in Glasgow was used instead – Hampden having been pre-booked for a concert by pop star Robbie Williams.

LONG WAIT FOR A TREBLE

Some 29 Scottish internationals have scored a total of 36 hat-tricks for the country – yet the last one was way back in 1969, when striker Colin Stein hit four goals in an 8-0 demolition of Cyprus. While Denis Law is the only man with two four-goal hauls for Scotland, he shares the record for most hat-tricks (three) with Bob McColl and Hughie Gallacher.

WEIR ON THE BALL

Rugged Rangers centre-back David Weir became Scotland's oldest international footballer when he faced Lithuania in a 2012 UEFA European Championship qualifier on 3 September 2010, aged 40 years and 111 days, for his 66th appearance. He was still representing his country three caps and 39 days later, against reigning world and European champions Spain.

TOP CAPS

1	Kenny Dalglish	102
2	Jim Leighton	91
3	Alex McLeish	77
4	Paul McStay	76
5	Tom Boyd	72
6	David Weir	69
7	Kenny Miller	68
8	Christian Dailly	67
9	Willie Miller	65
10	Danny McGrain	62

I HAVEN'T FELT THIS GOOD SINCE ARCHIE GEMMILL SCORED AGAINST HOLLAND

Archie Gemmill scored Scotland's greatest goal on the world stage in the surprise 3-2 victory over Holland at the 1978 FIFA World Cup. He jinked past three defenders before chipping the ball neatly over Dutch goalkeeper Jan Jongbloed. Amazingly, in 2008, this magical moment was turned into a dance in the English National Ballet's "The Beautiful Game".

ONE TEAM IN TALLINN

When Scotland travelled to Estonia for a FIFA World Cup qualifier in October 1996, there was only one team in it – literally. The hosts refused to play in protest at kick-off time being brought forward by almost four hours, following a Scottish complaint about the floodlights. At the newly scheduled time, Scotland sent 11 men onto the field at the Kadrioru Stadium in Tallinn, even though there were no opponents. FIFA later ordered the game to be replayed in neutral Monaco. It ended goalless, and Scotland went on to reach the 1998 FIFA World Cup finals in France.

FERGIE TIME

Arguably the greatest British football manager of all time bowed out in May 2013: **Sir Alex Ferguson** retired at the age of 71, 11 years after postponing his previous departure plans. He signed off after 27 years in charge at Manchester United, a glory-laden stint that brought 13 English league titles, two UEFA Champions League triumphs and 38 trophies in all. Before moving south of the border to Old Trafford, he had enjoyed success at Aberdeen – including a victory over Real Madrid in the 1983 UEFA European Cup Winners' Cup final. Ferguson, knighted after United's last-gasp win over Bayern Munich in the 1999 UEFA Champions League final, had also served a brief spell as Scotland manager. He led his country at the 1986 FIFA World Cup, standing in as caretaker manager after witnessing his predecessor Jock Stein die at the climax of a crucial qualifying match against Wales the previous year.

UNOFFICIAL WORLD CHAMPIONS

One of the victories most cherished by Scotland fans is the **3-2 triumph** over arch-rivals and reigning world champions England in April 1967 at Wembley – the first time Sir Alf Ramsey's team had lost since clinching the 1966 FIFA World Cup. Scotland's man of the match that day was ball-juggling left-half/midfielder Jim Baxter, while it was also the first game in charge for Scotland's first full-time manager, Bobby Brown. Less fondly recalled is Scotland's 9-3 trouncing by the same opposition at the same stadium in April 1961, which made unfortunate goalkeeper Frank Haffey the butt of a popular joke that did the rounds across the border in England: "What's the time? Nearly 10 past Haffey." The game was Haffey's second – and last – for Scotland.

SERBIA

The former Yugoslavia was one of the strongest football nations in eastern Europe. They reached the FIFA World Cup semi-finals in 1930 and 1962, they were also runners-up in the UEFA European Championships of 1960 and 1968. In addition, Yugoslavia's leading club, Red Star Belgrade, remain the only team from eastern Europe to win the European Cup, when they beat Marseille on penalties in the 1991 final.

MAGIC DRAGAN

Yugoslavia's greatest player was Red Star left winger **Dragan Dzajic**, who later went on to become the club's president. He made his international debut at 18, won a national record 85 caps and scored 23 goals. The most important was his last-minute winner against world champions England in the 1968 UEFA European Championship semi-final in Florence, which took Yugoslavia to the final against Italy. Pele said of Dzajic: "He's a real wizard. I'm sorry he's not Brazilian."

TOP CAPS

1	Savo Milosevic	102
=	Dejan Stankovic	102
3	Dragan Stojkovic	84
4	Predrag Mijatovic	73
5	Slavisa Jokanovic	64
6	Sinisa Mihajlovic	63
7	Branislav Ivanovic	61
8	Mladen Krstajic	59
=	Zoran Mirkovic	59
10	Darko Kovacevic	58

SAVICEVIC STRIKES

Dejan Savicevic is Serbia's greatest player of the modern era. The attacking midfielder was a key member of **Red Star Belgrade**'s 1991 European Cup-winning team. He also inspired them to three consecutive championships. He moved on to Milan and starred as his new club beat Barcelona 4-0 in the 1994 European Cup final. He created the opening goal, then crashed home a 35-yard volley. Savicevic later became a prominent supporter of the drive for Montenegrin independence from Serbia and has been credited with playing an influential role in the referendum vote on 21 May 2006 that led to the establishment of a separate Montenegrin state.

YUGOSLAVIA HIT BY BOYCOTT

The rivalry between Serbia and Croatia was apparent even in the early days of the old federation. Yugoslavia reached the last four of the inaugural FIFA World Cup in 1930, but they did so without any Croat players, who boycotted the squad for the finals in protest at the new federal association headquarters being located in the Serb capital, Belgrade.

TOP SCORERS

1	Savo Milosevic	37
2	Predrag Mijatovic	28
3	Nikola Zigic	20
4	Dejan Savicevic	19
5	Mateja Kezman	17
6	Dejan Stankovic	15
=	Dragan Stojkovic	15
8	Milan Jovanovic	11
=	Danko Lazovic	11
10	Slavisa Jokanovic	10
=	Darko Kovacevic	10
=	Marko Pantelic	10

STAN'S THE MAN

Internazionale midfielder **Dejan Stankovic** is the only footballer to have represented three different countries at separate FIFA World Cups, playing for Yugoslavia in 2002, Serbia and Montenegro in 2006, and Serbia in 2010. His pragmatic comment on his achievement was: "I'm happy with the record, but I'd rather win. It's OK to have been in three World Cups, but I would have liked to have better results." Stankovic, Serbia's joint most capped player, scored twice on his international debut for Yugoslavia in 1998. He has also twice scored memorable volleyed goals from virtually on the halfway line – once for Inter against Genoa in 2009–10, with a first-time shot from the opposing goalkeeper's clearance, and an almost identical finish against German club FC Schalke 04 in the UEFA Champions League the following season.

TURMOIL ON AND OFF THE FIELD

Serbia's failed qualifying campaign for the 2012 UEFA European Championship cost two coaches their jobs: first Radomir Antic, then Vladimir Petrovic. The nadir came in October 2010 when Serbian fans threw missiles and fireworks onto the pitch during their away tie with Italy. The match was abandoned after six minutes, Italy were awarded a 3-0 victory and Serbia were forced to play their next home game behind closed doors. Former player Sinisa Mihajlovic took over from Petrovic, but admitted he would likely leave in October 2013, at the end of his contract, after being unable to reach the 2014 FIFA World Cup. Mihajlovic, a free-kick specialist in his playing days despite being a defender, had been a key member of Red Star Belgrade's 1991 UEFA European Champions Cup-winning side.

MILORAD'S MILESTONE

The first man to captain and then coach his country at the FIFA World Cup was Milorad Arsenijevic, who captained Yugoslavia to the semi-finals at the inaugural tournament in Uruguay in 1930 and then managed their squad in Brazil 20 years later.

BRAN POWER

Versatile Chelsea defender and Serbia captain **Branislav Ivanovic** has enjoyed scoring significant late goals against Portuguese opposition. His first goal for his country was an 88th-minute equalizer in a UEFA European Championship qualifier away to Portugal in September 2007. His stoppage-time header gave Chelsea victory over Benfica in the final of the 2013 UEFA Europa League, a year after suspension ruled him out of the club's UEFA Champions League triumph over Bayern Munich.

GOING IT ALONE

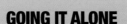

After Serbia and Montenegro competed at the 2006 FIFA World Cup, the 2010 tournament was the first featuring Serbia alone following Montenegro's independence. Topping their qualifying group ahead of France, Radomir Antic's Serbian side failed to make it through to the knockout stages in South Africa, despite a single-goal victory over Group D rivals Germany. A Serbian working for an opposing team was partly to blame – Milovan Rajevac was coach of the Ghana side that beat Serbia 1-0 in their opening first-round match. A mainstay in the Serbian defence was dominating centre-back **Nemanja Vidic**, a 2008 UEFA Champions League-winner and hero at Manchester United – but he announced his retirement from international football in October 2011.

SLOVAKIA

Slovakia have finally begun claiming bragging rights over their neighbours, the Czech Republic. A Slovak team did play games during the Second World War but then had to wait until post-war Czechoslovakia divided into Slovakia and the Czech Republic in 1993 before their next match. They returned to competitive action in qualifiers for the 1996 UEFA European Championship, finishing a promising third in their group. Continuing gradual progress culminated in qualification for their first FIFA World Cup, in 2010, at which they upset defending champions Italy 3-2 and reached the second round.

VLAD ALL OVER

Three relatives named Vladimir Weiss – different generations of the same family – have represented their country in international football, with two of them featuring at the 2010 FIFA World Cup. The first Vladimir won a footballing silver medal with Czechoslovakia at the 1964 Olympics, before his son Vladimir played for the same country at the 1990 FIFA World Cup. This second Vladimir then led Slovakia to the 2010 tournament as coach, picking his Manchester City winger son – yet another Vladimir – for three of the team's four matches. The first Vladimir made three appearances for Czechoslovakia, including the 1964 Olympics final in which he scored an own goal as Hungary triumphed 2-1. The second Vladimir won 19 caps for Czechoslavakia and 12 for Slovakia, and the third, still aged only 20, ended the 2010 FIFA World Cup with 12. The coach described their 3-2 victory over holders Italy at the 2010 FIFA World Cup as the second happiest day of his life – only beaten by the day his son was born. He stepped down as boss after failing to qualify for the 2012 UEFA European Championship.

HOMEMADE MARIAN

Marian Masny holds the international appearances record for Slovak-born footballers who played for the united Czechoslovakia, earning 75 caps between 1974 and 1982. Masny, from Rybany, was also the second-highest-scoring Slovak during the united Czechoslovakia era. His 18 goals were only bettered by the 22 in 36 matches struck by Vrutky-born Adolf Scherer from 1958 to 1964. Scherer's tally included three at the 1962 FIFA World Cup, when Czechoslovakia finished runners-up. Scherer scored the winner against Hungary in the quarter-finals and Czechoslovakia's final goal in their 3-1 semi-final victory over Yugoslavia.

TOP SCORERS

1	Robert Vittek	23
2	Szilard Nemeth	22
3	Miroslav Karhan	14
=	Marek Mintal	14
5	Peter Dubovsky	12
6	Stanislav Sestak	11
7	Marek Hamsik	10
8	Tibor Jancula	9
=	Lubomir Reiter	9
10	Filip Holosko	7
=	Martin Jakubko	7
=	Filip Sebo	7
=	Jaroslav Timko	7
=	Dusan Tittel	7

BROKEN-DOWN KARHAN

Slovakia's defensive midfielder Miroslav Karhan helped his country qualify for the 2010 FIFA World Cup, taking his appearances tally to a national-record 95. But an Achilles tendon injury meant the team captain was ruled out of the tournament itself. After returning to action later in 2010, Karhan became the first Slovakia player to pass 100 caps.

CZECH EIGHT

Eight Slovakia players played in Czechoslovakia's triumphant 1976 UEFA European Championship final against West Germany, including captain Anton Ondrus and both their scorers in the 2-2 draw: Jan Svehlik and Karol Dobias. Three of the team's successful penalty-takers in their 5-3 shoot-out win were Slovak-born: Marian Masny, Ondrus and substitute Ladislav Jurkemik. The other Slovaks to feature were Jan Pivarnik, Jozef Capkovic and Jozef Moder. Defender Koloman Gogh was born in what is now the Czech Republic, but had Slovak family ties and played most of his club football for Slovan Bratislava in the Slovak capital.

TOP CAPS

1	Miroslav Karhan	107
2	Robert Vittek	80
3	Marek Hamsik	64
4	Filip Holosko	62
5	Martin Skrtel	61
6	Szilard Nemeth	59
7	Jan Durica	57
=	Radoslav Zabavnik	57
9	Stanislav Varga	54
10	Marek Cech	52
=	Robert Tomaschek	52

SKRTEL'S A CERT

Slovakia captain and centre-back **Martin Skrtel** has won his country's Footballer of the Year award more times than any other Slovak player, since it was introduced in 1993. He collected the prize in 2007, 2008, 2011 and 2012 – with national team-mate Marek Hamsik the winner in 2009 and 2010, both years in which Skrtel suffered serious injuries while playing for English club Liverpool. The only man named Slovak Footballer of the Year three years in a row was defender Dusan Tittel – in 1993, 1994 and 1995.

ROBERT THE HERO

Slovakia's **Robert Vittek** became only the fourth player from a country making their FIFA World Cup debut to score as many as four goals in one tournament, at the 2010 event in South Africa. He hit one against New Zealand, two against defending champions Italy, and a late penalty in a second-round defeat to Holland. The previous three players to have done so were Portugal's Eusebio in 1966, Denmark's Preben Elkjaer Larsen in 1986 and Croatia's Davor Suker in 1998. Vittek's last-minute penalty against Holland made him Slovakia's all-time leading scorer with 23 goals, overtaking former Sparta Prague and Middlesbrough striker Szilard Nemeth. His 2010 FIFA World Cup form was all the more striking since he had failed to score at all in the qualifiers.

CUTTING EDGE HAMSIK

Playmaker Marek Hamsik was just 17 when he left Slovakia – after only six games for Slovan Bratislava – and moved to Italy in 2004, first joining Brescia and then, three years later, Napoli. After helping the Naples club win the 2012 Coppa Italia, he fulfilled an earlier promise to shave off his Mohawk hairstyle. Hamsik captained Slovakia at the 2010 FIFA World Cup, where he helped eliminate Italy in the opening round.

CARRY ON DOCTOR

All 10 of Slovakia's managers since their return to international football as an independent nation have been homegrown – including the current incumbents, joint coaches Michal Hipp and Stanislav Griga, who took charge together in 2012. Griga scored eight goals in 44 games for Czechoslovakia between 1983 and 1990; Hipp won five caps for Czechoslovakia in 1990 and 1991 and then another five for Slovakia in 1994. Slovakia's first coach was **Dr Josef Venglos**, who led the team between 1993 and 1995. Venglos had earlier been assistant coach when Czechoslovakia won the 1976 UEFA European Championship, and manager when the team finished third at the 1980 UEFA European Championship. He was later the first non-British- or Irish-born boss in England's top division when he took over at Aston Villa in 1990.

SWEDEN

Eleven appearances at the FIFA World Cup finals (with a best result of second, as tournament hosts, in 1958) and three Olympic medals (including gold in London in 1948), bear testament to Sweden's rich history on the world football stage. Recent success has been harder to find, however, with semi-final appearances at the 1992 UEFA European Championship (again as hosts) and the 1994 FIFA World Cup the country's best performances in recent years.

GRE-NO-LI OLYMPIC AND ITALIAN GLORY

Having conquered the world by leading Sweden to gold in the 1948 Olympics in London, Gunnar Gren, Gunnar Nordahl and **Nils Liedholm** were snapped up by AC Milan. Their three-pronged "Gre-No-Li" forward line led the Italian giants to their 1951 scudetto win. Nordahl, who topped the Serie A scoring charts five times between 1950 and 1955, remains Milan's all-time top scorer with 221 goals in 268 games. Gren and Liedholm went on to appear for the Swedish national team in the 1958 FIFA World Cup – where they finished runners-up.

TOP CAPS

1	Thomas Ravelli	143
2	Anders Svensson	141
3	Olof Mellberg	117
4	Roland Nilsson	116
5	Bjorn Nordqvist	115
6	Niclas Alexandersson	109
7	Andreas Isaksson	106
=	Henrik Larsson	106
9	Kim Kallstrom	103
10	Patrik Andersson	96

ONE MORE ENCORE, AGAIN!

One of the most famous and decorated Swedish footballers of modern times, **Henrik Larsson** (a star on the club scene with both Celtic and Barcelona) quit international football after the 2002 FIFA World Cup ... and again after the 2006 FIFA World Cup in Germany. He then made a further comeback in the 2010 FIFA World Cup qualifiers. With 37 goals in his 106 appearances, including five in his three FIFA World Cups, fans and officials clamoured for his return each time he tried to walk away. Sweden's failure to qualify for the tournament in 1998 meant a record-equalling 12 years elapsed between Larsson's first FIFA World Cup finals goal against Bulgaria in 1994 and his last, a dramatic late equalizer in a 2-2 group-stage draw with England in 2006. After finally retiring for good in 2009, he became manager of Swedish second-tier club Landskrona BoIS.

TOP-STOPPER RAVELLI

Thomas Ravelli kept goal for Sweden a record 143 times – conceding 143 goals. He saved two penalties in a shoot-out against Romania in the 1994 FIFA World Cup quarter-final to send Sweden into the last four, where they lost 1-0 to Brazil. Sweden went on to finish third, and were also the tournament's highest scorers with 15 goals in all – four more than eventual champions Brazil. Sweden's tally included five for Kennet Andersson, four for Martin Dahlin and three for Tomas Brolin.

IBRA–CADABRA

Few footballers these days can claim such consistent success – nor boast such an ego – as Swedish forward **Zlatan Ibrahimovic**. His proclamations have included "There's only one Zlatan", "I am like Muhammad Ali" and – in response to criticism from Norway's John Carew – "What Carew does with a football, I can do with an orange." Yet his clubs, including Ajax Amsterdam in the Netherlands, Juventus, Internazionale and AC Milan in Italy, Barcelona in Spain and Paris Saint-Germain in France, have all benefited from his presence: Ibra has collected 10 league titles since 2002. He christened the newly built Friends Arena in Solna with all four goals as Sweden beat England 4-2 in a November 2012 friendly – his final goal topping the lot, a 30-yard overhead kick. The haul made Ibrahimovic the first player in 915 matches to score four goals in one game against England. Other notable strikes include his back-heel volley against Italy at the 2004 UEFA European Championship and a long-range volley versus France at Euro 2012. Despite also qualifying for Bosnia and for Croatia through his family, Malmo-born Ibrahimovic made his Sweden debut in January 2001 and has scored 41 goals in 90 appearances.

ONE–MINUTE WONDERS

Sweden's Magnus Erlingmark can claim to have the shortest FIFA World Cup finals career – amounting to nothing more than his appearance as an 89th-minute substitute against Russia, in the first round of the 1994 tournament. His only rival for the unenviable record is Bulgaria's Petar Mikhtarski, another 89th-minute replacement that summer, in his country's second-round victory over Mexico.

TOP SCORERS

1	Sven Rydell	49
2	Gunnar Nordahl	43
3	Zlatan Ibrahimovic	41
4	Henrik Larsson	37
5	Gunnar Gren	32
6	Kennet Andersson	31
7	Marcus Allback	30
8	Martin Dahlin	29
9	Agne Simonsson	27
10	Tomas Brolin	26

MAGICAL MELL

Commanding centre-back **Olof Mellberg** became one of only seven players to appear at four different UEFA European Championship finals when he took part at Euro 2012 – and was the first Swede to achieve the feat. The 34-year-old also became Sweden's oldest UEFA European Championship goalscorer when he headed them into a 2-1 lead against England, ten minutes after his shot led to Glen Johnson scoring an own goal to draw the Swedes level. Unfortunately for Mellberg, and Sweden, however, England hit back to win 3-2. Mellberg's six previous goals for his country had all come in qualifying matches for either the UEFA European Championship or the FIFA World Cup.

FOUR SQUARE

In October 2012, Sweden became the first team to claw back a four-goal deficit against Germany, when they recovered from 4-0 down to finish 4-4 in a 2014 FIFA World Cup qualifier – thanks to second-half goals from Zlatan Ibrahimovic, Mikael Lustig, Johan Elmander and Rasmus Elm.

MANAGER SWAP

The most successful manager Sweden ever had was Englishman **George Raynor**, who led them to Olympic gold in London in 1948 and steered Sweden to third place and the runners-up spot in the 1950 and 1958 FIFA World Cups respectively. Raynor got one over on the country of his birth when Sweden became only the second foreign side to win at Wembley, with a 3-2 victory over England in 1959. Working in the opposite direction, in 2001 Sven-Goran Eriksson left Serie A side Lazio to become England's first foreign coach. He led the side to three consecutive quarter-finals – in the FIFA World Cups of 2002 and 2006 and, in between, the 2004 UEFA European Championship. Eriksson, however, failed to lead England to a win over his home country, recording three draws (1-1 in a 2001 friendly; 1-1 in a 2002 FIFA World Cup group game; 2-2 in a 2006 FIFA World Cup group game) and one defeat (0-1 in a 2004 friendly).

BROTHERS IN ARMS

The Nordahl brothers – Bertil, Knut and Gunnar – all won gold medals with Sweden in the 1948 Olympics football tournament. All three went on to play in Italy: Bertil with Atalanta, Knut with Roma, while Gunnar became a goalscoring legend at AC Milan before also turning out for Roma. Twins Thomas and Andreas Ravelli continued the brotherly tradition, winning 143 and 41 caps for Sweden respectively.

SWITZERLAND

Switzerland set a record in 2006 when they became the first side in FIFA World Cup finals history to depart the tournament without conceding a goal. It sums up the country's football history: despite three FIFA World Cup quarter-final appearances (in 1934, 1938 and 1954 – the latter as tournament hosts), Switzerland have failed to establish themselves on the international football stage. The country co-hosted the 2008 UEFA European Championship, with Austria, and is better known as being the home of both FIFA and UEFA.

CLEAN SHEET WIPE-OUT

The Swiss national team made history in 2006 by becoming the first – and to date only – team to exit the FIFA World Cup without conceding a single goal in regulation time. However, in the shoot-out defeat to Ukraine in the second round, following a goalless 120 minutes, they failed to score a single penalty and lost 3-0. Despite being beaten three times in the shoot-out, goalkeeper **Pascal Zuberbuhler**'s performances in Germany earned him a Swiss record for consecutive clean sheets at an international tournament.

DERDIYOK AT THE DOZEN

Nineteen-year-old striker **Eren Derdiyok** scored with his very first kick of the ball in international football after coming on as a substitute against England at Wembley in a February 2009 friendly. But England won 2-1. He scored three of Switzerland's goals in a thrilling 5-3 friendly victory over Germany in May 2012 – making him the first player to score a hat-trick against the Germans since England's Michael Owen almost 11 years earlier. He was playing his club football at the time for German side Hoffenheim – and all three of his goals were set up by another Bundesliga-based player, Bayer Leverkusen's Tranquillo Barnetta.

CHAMPION CHAPPI

Stephane "Chappi" Chapuisat – the third man to make 100 appearances for Switzerland – was the first Swiss player to win a UEFA Champions League medal when he led the line for Borussia Dortmund in their 3-1 victory over Juventus in 1997. But his most significant contribution in the final was to make way for Lars Ricken, whose goal with his first touch put the game beyond Juventus. Stephane's father, Pierre-Albert Chapuisat, was also a successful Swiss international – earning 34 caps for the national side in the 1970s and 1980s – but he failed to reach the heights of Stephane, who would later add both the Club World Cup and the Swiss super league (while playing for Grasshoppers) to his winners' medal collection.

TOP SCORERS

1	Alexander Frei	42
2	Max Abegglen III	34
=	Kubilay Turkyilmaz	34
4	Andre Abegglen II	29
5	Jacques Fatton	29
6	Adrian Knup	26
7	Josef Hugi II	23
8	Charles Antenen	22
9	Lauro Amado	21
=	Stephane Chapuisat	21

LLAMA FARMER FREI-ING HIGH

After being compared to a llama by an angry Swiss sports press for spitting at Steven Gerrard at UEFA Euro 2004, **Alexander Frei**, Switzerland's all-time top scorer, adopted a llama at Basel zoo as part of his apology to the nation. Frei appeared to abandon all hope of adding to his record Swiss goal tally of 42 in 84 games when he announced his retirement from international football in April 2011, blaming abuse from his own fans during recent matches. These included a goalless draw against minnows Malta, when both Frei and team-mate Gokhan Inler missed penalties. Frei was joined in international retirement by strike partner Marco Streller, who had scored 12 goals in 37 games.

OTT STUFF

One Swiss newspaper greeted Ottmar Hitzfeld as "The Messiah" when he was appointed manager in 2008 – though he got off to an unholy start with a humiliating defeat to Luxembourg at home in his first competitive international. Hitzfeld, a double UEFA Champions League-winning boss with Borussia Dortmund and Bayern Munich, recovered to steer the Swiss to the 2010 FIFA World Cup – even if his halo slipped a little again after they failed to reach Euro 2012. Despite being a German national, Hitzfeld spent much of his playing career in Switzerland – where he also held his first coaching roles, with SC Zug, FC Aarau and Grasshopper Club of Zurich.

TEENAGE RAMPAGE

Cristiano Ronaldo, Wayne Rooney, David Silva and Lukas Podolski were among the future world stars who featured at the 2002 UEFA U-17 European Championship – but it was surprise package Switzerland who took home the country's first international trophy, beating France on penalties after a goalless final. Future full internationals Tranquillo Barnetta and Reto Ziegler were among the spot-kick scorers.

YAK ATTACK

Brothers Murat and **Hakan Yakin** were both born in the Swiss city of Basel to Turkish parents and both opted to play for the country of their birth. Midfielder Murat, almost three years older than his brother, hit four goals and won 49 caps between 1994 and 2004, while Hakan – who played slightly further forward – made his international debut in 2000 and bowed out 11 years later. Hakan scored the opening goal of Switzerland's 2008 UEFA European Championship first-round 2-1 defeat to Turkey – in rain-sodden conditions and despite the ball sticking in the mud – but declined to celebrate. He ended his international career with 20 goals from 87 appearances.

"MERCI KOBI"

Former Swiss international player and manager, **Jakob "Kobi" Kuhn**, was left close to tears as his players unfurled a "thank you" banner at the end of his final game as Swiss national manager – the 2-0 victory over Portugal in the final group game of UEFA Euro 2008. How times have changed for Kuhn: while now a much-loved elder statesmen of the Swiss game, when he was just 22 years old, he was sent home from the 1966 FIFA World Cup for missing a curfew. He was then banned from the national side for a year. The shoe was on the other foot when Kuhn had to send Alexander Frei home from UEFA Euro 2004 after the centre-forward spat at England's Steven Gerrard. Kuhn spent most of his playing career, where he was described as playing "with honey in his boots", with FC Zurich, winning six league titles and five Swiss Cups. He played 63 times for the national side, scoring five goals. He then worked his way up through the ranks of the Swiss national team, leading first the Under-18s, then the Under-21s and finally the senior national team. He retired, aged 64, with a record of 32 victories, 18 draws and 23 defeats in 73 matches as Swiss coach.

TOP CAPS

1	Heinz Hermann	117
2	Alain Geiger	112
3	Stephane Chapuisat	103
4	Johann Vogel	94
5	Hakan Yakin	87
6	Alexander Frei	86
7	Patrick Muller	81
8	Severino Minelli	80
9	Andy Egli	79
=	Ciriaco Sforza	79

THE ORIGINAL BOLT

Karl Rappan did so much for Swiss football – including founding its first national football fan club – that it is often forgotten that he was Austrian. After a moderately successful career as a player and coach in Austria, Rappan achieved lasting fame as an innovative manager in Switzerland, leading the national side in the 1938 and 1954 FIFA World Cups, as well as securing league titles and cups as manager of Grasshopper Club, FC Servette and FC Zurich. He developed a flexible tactical system – which allowed players to switch positions depending on the situation and putting greater pressure on their opponents. This revolutionary new idea became known as the "Swiss bolt" and helped the unfancied hosts defeat Italy on the way to the quarter-finals of the 1954 FIFA World Cup, before losing out to Rappan's home country, Austria. An early advocate of a European league, Rappan eventually settled for the simpler knockout tournament, the Intertoto Cup, which he helped devise and launch in 1961. Rappan was, until Kobi Kuhn, Switzerland's longest-serving and statistically most successful manager, with 29 victories in 77 games in charge.

TURKEY

Galatasaray's penalty shoot-out success over Arsenal in the 2000 UEFA Cup final signalled a change in fortune for Turkish football. Prior to that night in Copenhagen, Turkey had qualified for the FIFA World Cup only twice (in 1950, when they withdrew, and 1954), and had consistently underachieved on the world stage. Since 2000, however, Turkish fans have had plenty to cheer about, including a third-place finish at the 2002 FIFA World Cup in Japan and South Korea, and a semi-final appearance at the 2008 UEFA European Championship.

MIXING UP THE MANAGERS

Only 26 of Turkey's 45 different managers have been homegrown – though the latest appointment, Abdullah Avci, marks a return to a Turkish-born boss after the failure of Dutchman Guus Hiddink to take the side to the 2012 UEFA European Championship. Avci was boss when Turkey won their second UEFA European U-17 Championship in 2005 – the first had been in 1994. A star of that 2005 side, now integral to the senior team, is German-born midfielder **Nuri Sahin**, whose goal on his international debut in October 2005 – aged 17, and against Germany – made him the youngest player both to play and score for Turkey. The country's first coach, back in 1923, was Turkish national Ali Semi Yen, who managed for just one game: a 2-2 draw with Romania. Overseas appointments that followed have included England's Pat Molloy, Scotland's Billy Hunter, Italy's Sandro Puppo and Germany's Sepp Piontek.

OLD GOLD

The last FIFA World Cup "golden goal" was scored by Turkey substitute Ilhan Mansiz, in the 94th minute of their 2002 quarter-final against Senegal – giving his side a 1-0 win on their way to finishing third overall. The "golden goal" rule was abandoned ahead of the 2006 FIFA World Cup, which went back to two guaranteed 15-minute periods of extra-time if a knockout fixture ended level after 90 minutes.

QUICK OFF THE MARK

Hakan Sukur scored the fastest-ever FIFA World Cup finals goal – taking only 11 seconds to score Turkey's first goal in their third-place play-off match against South Korea at the 2002 FIFA World Cup. Turkey went on to win the game 3-2 to claim third place, their finest-ever performance in the competition. His total of 51 goals (in 112 games) is more than double his nearest competitor in the national team ranking. His first goal came in only his second appearance, as Turkey beat Denmark 2-1 on 8 April 1992. He went on to score four goals in a single game twice – in the 6-4 win over Wales on 20 August 1997 and in the 5-0 crushing of Moldova on 11 October 2006.

GUESS WHO'S BACK?

Rustu Recber doesn't know the meaning of the word "quit". Less than a year after retiring from international football after UEFA Euro 2008, Turkey's most-capped player came out of retirement to join the national team once more in the qualifying campaign for the 2010 FIFA World Cup in South Africa. This was not his first international comeback – for UEFA Euro 2008, Rustu had been relegated to the bench, but played in the quarter-final against Croatia after first-choice keeper Volkan Demirel was sent off in the final group game. Rustu was the hero of the penalty shoot-out, saving from Mladen Petric to send Turkey through to their first-ever UEFA European Championship semi-final, in which they lost to Germany. Back in 1993, Rustu came back from an even more devastating set-back after he was seriously injured in a car crash that resulted in the death of a friend. The accident also scuppered a potential move to Besiktas, although he went on to star for Fenerbahce, winning five Turkish league titles in 12 years with them. With his distinctive pony-tail and charcoal-black war paint, Rustu has always stood out, but perhaps never more so than as a star performer in Turkey's third-place performance at the 2002 FIFA World Cup finals. He was elected into the Team of the Tournament and was named FIFA's Goalkeeper of the Year.

TWIN TURKS

Hamit Altintop (right) was born 10 minutes before identical twin brother **Halil** (left) – and he has been just about leading the way throughout their parallel professional footballing careers since their birth in the city of Gelsenkirchen, Germany, on 8 December 1982. Both began playing for German amateur side Wattenscheid, before defender-cum-midfielder Hamit signed for FC Schalke 04 in the summer of 2006 and striker Halil followed suit shortly afterwards. Hamit would stay just a season there, though, before being bought by Bayern Munich. Both helped Turkey reach the semi-finals of the 2008 UEFA European Championship – losing to adopted homeland Germany – though only Hamit was voted among UEFA's 23 best players of the tournament.

FATIH TERIM

Having coached Galatasaray to their UEFA Cup triumph in 2000, **Fatih Terim** put a disappointing year and a half in Italy (with Fiorentina and AC Milan) behind him to lead Turkey in their amazing run to the 2008 UEFA European Championship semi-finals. Defeat to Portugal in the opening game left the Turks with an uphill task, but stunning successive comebacks against Switzerland and the Czech Republic took them through to the quarter-finals. A 119th-minute goal seemed to have clinched the tie for Croatia, but, as the Croatian players celebrated, "Emperor" Fatih urged his players to get up, pick the ball out of the net and fight on to the very end. They did just that, and Semih Senturk's improbable equalizer took the match to penalties. The semi-final against Germany provided yet another rollercoaster ride, but this time there was no answer to the Germans' last-minute winner. When Fatih said "there is something special about this team" few could disagree.

TOP SCORERS

1	Hakan Sukur	51
2	Tuncay Sanli	22
3	Lefter Kucukandonyadis	21
4	Nihat Kahveci	19
=	Metin Oktay	19
=	Cemil Turan	19
7	Zeki Riza Sporel	15
8	Arda Turan	13
9	Arif Erdem	11
=	Ertugrul Saglam	11

TOP CAPS

1	Rustu Recber	120
2	Hakan Sukur	112
3	Bulent Korkmaz	102
4	Tugay Kerimoglu	94
5	Alpay Ozalan	90
6	Emre Belozoglu	90
7	Tuncay Sanli	80
8	Hamit Altintop	79
9	Ogun Temizkanoglu	76
10	Abdullah Ercan	71

500 MILESTONE

Turkey played their 500th match in international football on 14 November 2012, a friendly that ended in a 1-1 draw against Denmark. The game, played at Istanbul's Turk Telekom Arena, was preceded by pop star Hadise's performance and appearances by Turkish football legends. Turkey's first international match was also a draw in Istanbul: 2-2 against Romania on 26 October 1923.

WORK HARD, PLAY ARDA

Wing wizard **Arda Turan** is one of Turkish football's leading lights – and most prolific goalscorers – and also claimed the title of his country's most expensive player, when leaving boyhood club Galatasaray for Spain's Atletico Madrid in 2011. His time in Spain has brought him UEFA Europa League and UEFA Super Cup winners' medals. His initial 64 appearances and 13 goals for his country included two strikes at the 2008 UEFA European Championship, the first a stoppage-time winner against co-hosts Switzerland then Turkey's late opening goal as they beat the Czech Republic 3-2 in a first-round qualification decider. Off the field, Turan has survived a cardiac arrhythmia, a bout of swine flu and a car crash that left him merely cut and bruised.

UKRAINE

Ukraine has been a stronghold of football in eastern Europe for many years. A steady flow of talent from Ukrainian clubs with a rich European pedigree, such as Dynamo Kiev, provided the Soviet national team with many standout players in the years before independence. Since separating from the Soviet Union in 1991, Ukraine has become a football force in its own right, qualifying for the FIFA World Cup for the first time in 2006, reaching the quarter-finals.

MAJOR TOURNAMENTS

FIFA WORLD CUP: 1 appearance – quarter-finals (2006)
FIRST INTERNATIONAL: Ukraine 1 Hungary 3 (Uzhhorod, Ukraine, 29 April 1992)
BIGGEST WINS: Ukraine 6 Azerbaijan 0 (Kiev, Ukraine, 15 August 2006)
Andorra 0 Ukraine 6 (Andorra la Vella, Andorra, 14 October 2009)
BIGGEST DEFEATS: Croatia 4 Ukraine 0 (Zagreb, Croatia, 25 March 1995)
Spain 4 Ukraine 0 (Leipzig, Germany, 14 June 2006)

ROCKET MAN

Andriy Shevchenko beat team-mate **Anatoliy Timoshchuk**  to become the first Ukrainian footballer to reach a century of international appearances, but the defensive midfielder later overtook the striker to become the country's most-capped player with 128 appearances. He also enjoyed the rare honour of seeing his name in space, when Ukrainian cosmonaut Yuri Malenchenko launched into orbit wearing a Zenit St Petersburg shirt with "Tymoshchuk" on the back in 2007. After leaving Zenit in 2009 for Bayern Munich, he won the 2013 UEFA Champions League with the German club before announcing his return to his previous St Petersburg side.

YURI-KA MOMENT

Denys Harmash and Dmytro Korkishko scored the goals against England that gave Ukraine their first major international footballing title, in the final of the 2009 UEFA Under-19 European Championship. The coach was Yuri Kalitvintsev, later assistant to Oleg Blokhin with the senior international side.

HARD START

With the newly independent Ukraine unable to register with FIFA in time for the qualifying rounds for the 1994 FIFA World Cup, many of their stars opted to play for Russia and went to the finals in the United States representing that country. Andrei Kanchelskis, Viktor Onopko, Sergei Yuran and Oleg Salenko could all have played for the new Ukraine side, but decided not to. Ukraine then failed to qualify for an international tournament until the **2006 FIFA World Cup** in Germany, where they lost 3-0 in the quarter-finals to eventual winners Italy.

SUPER SHEVA

In 2004, **Andriy Shevchenko** became the third Ukrainian to win the Ballon D'Or. The first to do so, in 1975, was his 2006 FIFA World Cup coach Oleg Blokhin (second was Igor Belanov in 1986), but he was the first to win the award since Ukraine's independence from the Soviet Union. Born on 29 September 1976, Shevchenko was a promising boxer as a youngster, before deciding to focus on football full-time. He has won trophies at every club he's played for, including five titles in a row with Dynamo Kiev, the Serie A and the Champions League with AC Milan, and even two cups in his "disappointing" time at Chelsea. Shevchenko is Ukraine's second most-capped player and leading goalscorer, with 48 goals in 111 games. This includes two at the 2006 FIFA World Cup, where he captained his country in their first-ever major finals appearance, and a double to secure a 2-1 comeback win over Sweden in Ukraine's first match co-hosting the 2012 UEFA European Championship.

LEADING FROM THE FRONT

Oleg Blokhin, Ukraine's manager on their first appearance at the FIFA World Cup finals in 2006, made his name as a star striker with his hometown club Dynamo Kiev. Born on 5 November 1952, in the days when Ukraine was part of the Soviet Union, Blokhin scored a record 211 goals in another record 432 appearances in the USSR national league. He also holds the caps and goals records for the USSR, with 42 goals in 112 games. He led Kiev to two triumphs in the European Cup-Winners' Cup in 1975 and 1986, scoring in both finals, and winning the European Footballer of the Year trophy for his exploits in 1975. Always an over-achiever, Blokhin became the first manager to lead Ukraine to the finals of an international tournament, at the 2006 FIFA World Cup in Germany, where they lost out to eventual winners Italy 3-0 in the quarter-finals after knocking out Switzerland in the second round – also on penalties. Blokhin was renowned for his speed – when Olympic gold medallist Valeriy Borzov trained the Kiev squad in the 1970s, Blokhin recorded a 100 metres time of 11 seconds, just 0.46 seconds slower than Borzov's own 1972 medal-winning run. Blokhin quit as Ukraine manager in December 2007, but returned to the job in April 2011.

REBROV REBORN

Serhiy Rebrov, who retired in 2009, was Andriy Shevchenko's dynamic strike partner for both club and country. The forward pair starred for Dynamo Kiev in the late 1990s before making big-money moves across Europe. Like Shevchenko at Chelsea, Rebrov struggled in London, first at Tottenham Hotspur and then at West Ham United. But after returning to Ukraine in 2005, he earned a late-career recall to the international team – and scored a memorable long-range strike against Saudi Arabia at the 2006 FIFA World Cup. Having dropped back into midfield, he then crossed the border and helped outsiders Rubin Kazan win their first Russian league title in 2008. But Rebrov, a keen amateur radio "ham", remains the Ukrainian Premier League's all-time leading scorer, with 125 goals in 268 games.

TOP SCORERS

1	Andriy Shevchenko	48
2	Serhiy Rebrov	15
3	Oleh Husyev	13
4	Serhiy Nazarenko	12
5	Andriy Yarmolenko	11
6	Andriy Husin	9
=	Andriy Vorobey	9
8	Tymerlan Huseynov	8
=	Artem Milevskiy	8
=	Andriy Voronin	8

HUS WHO

Ukraine's first appearance at a FIFA World Cup, in 2006, took them to the quarter-finals, when they lost only to eventual champions Italy. Their second-round breakthrough came courtesy of a winning penalty against Switzerland in a shoot-out, scored by versatile right-sider **Oleh Husyev**. He was an ever-present for Ukraine that tournament, as he also was at the 2012 UEFA European Championship – and is now his nation's fourth-most-capped footballer, with 83 appearances yielding 13 goals. Husyev, who has spent almost all his career with Dynamo Kiev, is closing in on third-placed Oleksandr Shovkovskiy, the goalkeeper who saved two Swiss penalties in that 2006 shoot-out, but who missed out on Euro 2012 through injury.

TOP CAPS

1	Anatoliy Tymoshchuk	128
2	Andriy Shevchenko	111
3	Oleksandr Shovkovskiy	92
4	Oleh Husyev	83
5	Serhiy Rebrov	75
6	Andriy Voronin	74
7	Andriy Husin	71
8	Ruslan Rotan	68
=	Andriy Vorobey	68
10	Andriy Nesmachniy	67

WALES

In a land where rugby union remains the national obsession, Wales have struggled to impose themselves on the world of international football. Despite having produced a number of hugely talented players, Wales have only ever played once in the finals of a major tournament – at the 1958 FIFA World Cup finals in Sweden.

GOOD ON RAMSEY

Arsenal midfielder **Aaron Ramsey** became Wales's youngest captain when appointed to the role in March 2011 by new manager Gary Speed. Ramsey was 20 years 90 days old when he led the side out for the first time at Cardiff's Millennium Stadium in a 2012 UEFA European Championship qualifier that ended in a 2-0 win for England. The record had previously been held by centre-back Mike England, who was 22 years 135 days old when skipper against Northern Ireland in April 1964. Ramsey had not long returned to full fitness after a potentially career-threatening broken leg suffered while playing for Arsenal against Stoke City in February 2010.

WHERE'S OUR GOLDEN BOY?

One of the most skilful and successful players never to appear at the FIFA World Cup, **Ryan Giggs** somehow missed 18 consecutive friendlies for Wales. Giggs made his Manchester United debut in 1990 and was still playing in 2013, when he made his 1000th competitive appearance in a 2-1 UEFA Champions League defeat to Real Madrid. His tally by then included 932 club matches, 64 for Wales and four for Great Britain at the London 2012 Summer Olympics.

HAT-TRICK HERO

Welsh striker Robert Earnshaw holds the remarkable record of having scored hat-tricks in all four divisions of English football, the FA Cup, the League Cup, as well as scoring three for the national team against Scotland on 18 February 2004.

BRICKS TO BRILLIANCE

Goalkeeper **Neville Southall** made the first of his record 92 appearances for Wales in a 3-2 win over Northern Ireland on 27 May 1982. The former hod-carrier and bin man kept 34 clean sheets in 15 years playing for Wales and won the English Football Writers' Player of the Year in 1985 thanks to his performances alongside Welsh captain Kevin Ratcliffe at Everton. In his final match for Wales, on 20 August 1997, he was substituted halfway through a 6-4 defeat against Turkey in Istanbul.

RUSH FOR GOAL

Ian Rush is Wales's leading goalscorer, with 28 goals in 73 games. His first came in a 3-0 win over Northern Ireland on 27 May 1982; he scored the 28th and final goal in a 2-1 win over Estonia in Tallinn in 1994.

TOP CAPS

1	Neville Southall	92
2	Gary Speed	85
3	Dean Saunders	75
4	Craig Bellamy	73
=	Peter Nicholas	73
=	Ian Rush	73
7	Mark Hughes	72
=	Joey Jones	72
9	Ivor Allchurch	68
10	Brian Flynn	66

TOP SCORERS

1	Ian Rush	28
2	Ivor Allchurch	23
=	Trevor Ford	23
4	Dean Saunders	22
5	Craig Bellamy	19
6	Robert Earnshaw	16
=	Mark Hughes	16
=	Cliff Jones	16
9	John Charles	15
10	John Hartson	14

CAUGHT ON CAMERA

Pioneer movie-makers Sagar Mitchell and James Kenyon captured Wales v Ireland in March 1906, making it the first filmed international football match.

KEEPING UP WITH THE JONESES

Cliff Jones, left-winger for Wales at the 1958 FIFA World Cup and for Tottenham Hotspur's league and cup "Double" winners in 1961, was part of a Welsh footballing dynasty. His father Ivor Jones had previously played for Wales, as did Ivor's brother Bryn. Cliff's cousin Ken, a goalkeeper, was another member of the 1958 FIFA World Cup squad, but never actually played for his country.

SHOCK LOSS OF A MODEL PROFESSIONAL

Welsh and world football were united in shock and grief at the sudden death of Wales manager **Gary Speed** in November 2011. Former Leeds United, Everton, Newcastle United and Bolton Wanderers midfielder Speed, the country's most-capped outfield player, was found at his home in Cheshire, England. The 42-year-old had been manager for 11 months, overseeing a series of encouraging performances that saw a rise in the world rankings from 116th to 48th and a prize for FIFA's "Best Movers" of 2011. An official memorial game was played in Cardiff in February 2012 between Wales and Costa Rica – the country against whom he had made his international debut in May 1990. Among the tributes paid to Speed was one from FIFA president Sepp Blatter, who called him "a model professional and a fantastic ambassador for the game". Former Wales centre-back Chris Coleman was appointed as Speed's successor.

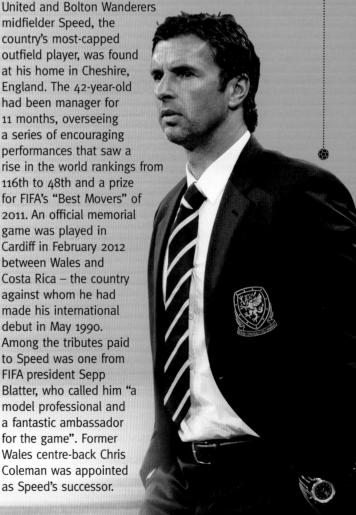

ALL HAIL BALE

One of the hottest properties in world football is **Gareth Bale**, even if his Welsh nationality has – so far – hampered his chances of playing on the highest international stages, at a FIFA World Cup or UEFA European Championship. He began his career at Southampton as a left-back, then flourished as a dynamic left-winger at Tottenham Hotspur before flourishing as an all-round forward. He was named English football's player of the year in 2011 and 2013 – voted so by both the Premier League's footballers and the nation's journalists – thanks to dazzling performances and strikes for both Spurs and Wales. Bale had first come to wider global attention with a hat-trick against Internazionale in the Stadio Meazza in the San Siro in October 2010. But by then he had already become Wales's youngest international, making his debut as a substitute against Trinidad and Tobago in May 2006 aged 16 years 315 days. His position, performances and club allegiances have prompted comparisons with another "Welsh wing wizard", Cliff Jones, who won the English league and FA cup double with Tottenham in 1961 and scored 16 goals in 59 games for his country. Jones played all five games the only time Wales qualified for a FIFA World Cup, in 1958.

OTHER TEAMS EUROPE

For the major European football powers, a qualifying campaign for one of the game's major international tournaments would not be the same without an awkward trip to one of the former Eastern Bloc countries or the chance of a goal-fest against the likes of San Marino or Luxembourg. For these countries' players, the thrill of representing their nation is more important than harbouring dreams of world domination.

SELVA SERVICE

San Marino, with a population of under 30,000, is the smallest country to be a member of UEFA. Striker **Andy Selva** is not only San Marino's top scorer with eight goals and for a long time was the country's only player to score twice – until midfielder Manuel Marani followed up his February 2007 goal against the Republic of Ireland with another, against Malta, in August 2012.

MOSQUITO STINGS

Malta ended a 20-year wait for an away win in a competitive international when they shocked Armenia 1-0 in a 2014 FIFA World Cup qualifier in June 2013. Appropriately enough, yhe decisive strike came from veteran forward **Michael Mifsud** – his country's captain and all-time leading scorer, who made his international debut in February 2000 and made his name in Germany with Kaiserslautern and in England with Coventry City. Nicknamed "Mosquito", the 1.65m-tall player's international exploits include five goals in the 7-1 trouncing of Liechtenstein in March 2008 – including a hat-trick within the first 21 minutes. Before Armenia, the last time Malta won a FIFA World Cup or UEFA European Championship away qualifier had been a 1-0 success in Estonia in May 1993.

UNDERDOGS HAVE THEIR DAY

Slovenia were the only unseeded team to win a UEFA qualifying play-off for the 2010 FIFA World Cup, beating Russia on away goals. Slovenia lost 2-1 in Moscow, thanks to substitute Nejc Pecnik's crucial away goal late in the first leg and Ztlatko Dedic scored the only goal in Maribor to give Slovenia victory. With a population of two million and just 429 registered professional players, Slovenia were the smallest nation in the finals.

LIT'S A KNOCK-OUT

Perhaps it's not be too surprising that **Jari Litmanen** should have become a football star – both his parents played for the Lahti-based club Reipas while Litmanen's father Olavi also won five caps for the national team. But Jari's skills and achievements far outstripped them both – and, arguably, any other player the country has produced. It was fitting that Litmanen became the first Finnish player to get his hands on the UEFA European Cup – or Champions League trophy – when his Ajax Amsterdam side beat AC Milan in 1995. Litmanen had left Finland at the age of 21 to make his name and mark with the legendary Dutch club Ajax, inheriting the great Dennis Bergkamp's support-striker role – and number 10 shirt. Litmanen scored in the 1996 UEFA Champions League final, though Ajax lost on penalties to Juventus. He remains the Dutch club's record scorer in European competition, with 24 goals in 44 games. Litmanen joined Barcelona in 1999 and then Liverpool two years later, though his time in England was hampered by a wrist injury he suffered on international duty and he returned to Ajax in 2002. Despite a series of injuries, he remained dedicated to his country, captaining the side between 1996 and 2008, and was still playing and scoring for Finland in 2010 at the age of 39 – having notched up more international goals and games than any other Finn, scoring 32 times in 137 appearances.

GIVING IT UP

Lithuania and Estonia did not bother playing their final group game against each other in the 1934 FIFA World Cup qualifying competition. Sweden had already guaranteed themselves top spot, and the sole finals place available, by beating Lithuania 2-0 and Estonia 6-2.

BEYOND THE IRON CURTAIN

The break-up of the Soviet Union in 1990 led to 15 new footballing nations, though initially Russia played on at the 1992 UEFA European Championship as CIS, or the Commonwealth of Independent States – without the involvement of Estonia, Latvia and Lithuania. In the coming years, UEFA and FIFA approved the creation of separate teams for Russia, Armenia, Azerbaijan, Belarus, Estonia, Georgia, Kazakhstan, Kyrgyzstan, Latvia, Lithuania, Moldova, Tajikstan, Turkmenistan, Ukraine and Uzbekistan. Upheavals in the early 1990s would also fragment the former Yugoslavia into Croatia, Serbia, Bosnia-Herzegovina, Macedonia, Slovenia and Montenegro, while Czechoslovakia split into Slovakia and the Czech Republic.

YEAR AFFILIATED TO FIFA

Albania	1932
Andorra	1996
Austria	1905
Belarus	1992
Bosnia-Herzegovina	1996
Cyprus	1948
Estonia	1923
Faroe Islands	1988
Finland	1908
Georgia	1992
Greece	1927
Iceland	1947
Israel	1929
Kazakhstan	1994
Latvia	1922
Liechtenstein	1974
Luxembourg	1910
Macedonia	1994
Malta	1959
Moldova	1994
Montenegro	2007
San Marino	1988
Slovenia	1992

FORLORN BOURG

If at first you don't succeed, try and try again – but poor Luxembourg have valiantly tried and failed to qualify for 19 consecutive FIFA World Cup finals. The only time they were not involved was the very first in 1930, when there was no qualification tournament and Luxembourg were not invited to the finals. The country has had only three victories in FIFA World Cup qualifiers: 4-2 at home to Portugal in October 1961, 2-0 at home to Turkey in October 1972, and 2-1 away to Switzerland in September 2008, when **Alphonse Leweck** scored a late winner.

THE FULL MONTY AND THE FULL MONTY

Estonia may have lost their June 2012 friendly against France 4-0, despite the presence up-front of all-time top scorer **Andres Oper**, but they did make history that night, becoming the first country to play all 52 fellow UEFA nations. The 52nd addition to the UEFA family was Montenegro, who became a FIFA member in 2007, a year after competing as part of Serbia and Montenegro in the 2006 FIFA World Cup. Both Estonia and Montenegro came their closest to a major tournament in their own right by reaching the play-offs for places at the 2012 UEFA European Championship, only to lose over two legs to the Republic of Ireland and the Czech Republic respectively.

TRAVELLING MEN

Israel looked like qualifying for the 1958 FIFA World Cup without kicking a ball, because scheduled opponents Turkey, Indonesia and Sudan refused to play them. But FIFA ordered them into a two-legged play-off against a European side – which Israel lost 4-0 on aggregate to Wales. Israel were unfortunate again in the 2006 FIFA World Cup qualifiers, ending the campaign unbeaten – yet failing even to make the play-offs, finishing third in their group behind France and Switzerland. Coach Avram Grant later went on to manage Chelsea, losing the 2008 UEFA Champions League final on penalties to Manchester United. Israel hosted, and won, the 1964 Asian Nations Cup, and qualified for the 1970 FIFA World Cup through a combined Asia/Oceania qualifying competition, but are now members of the European Federation.

SLO STARTERS

The only country to beat Italy on their way to winning the 2006 FIFA World Cup were Slovenia, who triumphed 1-0 in an October 2004 qualifier, thanks to a late goal by centre-back Bostjan Cesar. However, Slovenia still missed out on the finals.

AD ENOUGH

Temuri Ketsbaia scored 16 times for Georgia, more than anyone other than 26-goal Shota Arveladze, and was also the first coach to lead a Cypriot side – Anorthosis Famagusta – into the UEFA Champions League before taking over as Georgia's national coach in 2009. Yet to many fans – those in England especially – he might be best remembered for his bizarre celebration after scoring a last-minute winner for Newcastle United against Bolton Wanderers in January 1998, when instead of looking pleased he flung off his shirt and furiously kicked out at pitchside advertising hoardings. After receiving the ball when the game kicked off again, he instantly booted it high into the crowd.

MORE SIND AGAINST

Austria's star player **Matthias Sindelar** refused to play for a new, merged national team when Germany annexed Austria in 1938. Sindelar, born in modern-day Hungary in February 1903, was the inspirational leader of Austria's so-called Wunderteam of the 1930s. He scored 27 goals in 43 games for Austria, who went 14 internationals unbeaten between April 1931 and December 1932, won the 1932 Central European International Cup and silver at the 1936 Olympics. During a special reunification match between the Austrian and German teams in Vienna in April 1938, Sindelar disobeyed orders and scored a spectacular solo goal. Austria went on to win 2-0 in a game which might have been expected to end in a diplomatic draw. Sindelar was mysteriously found dead from carbon monoxide poisoning in his Vienna apartment in January 1939.

TWIN PEAKS

Austria's all-time leading marksman Toni Polster has two claims to fame: as a football goalscorer and as a musician with his band Achtung Liebe. His nickname was "Twin-pack Polster" for his habit of scoring twice in games. His 44 international goals included four braces and two hat-tricks, helping him finish ten goals ahead of compatriot Hans Krankl. Polster and Krankl won the Golden Shoe award as Europe's top scorer: Krankl in 1978 with Rapid Wien, Polster nine years later with city rivals FK Austria.

THE GUD SON

Iceland striker **Eidur Gudjohnsen** made history on his international debut away to Estonia in April 1996, by coming on as a substitute for his own father, Arnor Gudjohnsen. Eidur was 17 at the time, his father 34 – though both were disappointed they did not get to play on the pitch at the same time. The Icelandic Football Association thought they would get a chance to do so in Iceland's next home game, but Eidur was ruled out by an ankle injury and the opportunity never arose again.

REIM AND REASONING

Before being overtaken by Latvia's **Vitalijs Astafjevs**, the European record for most international appearances was held by another Baltic veteran – Estonian holding midfielder Martin Reim scored 14 goals in 157 games for his country between June 1992 and June 2009. Yet he could even have closed in on an unprecedented double-century of international appearances, had he not missed 40 games following a dispute with Latvia's Dutch manager Jelle Goes between 2004 and 2007. He retired from international football after matching the 150-cap record of Germany's Lothar Matthaus in February 2007, but was persuaded to return by new national boss Viggo Jensen. His 157th and final match, a testimonial played in his honour, came against Equatorial Guinea on 6 June 2009, a day that was also said to mark the centenary of football in Estonia.

VITAL VITALIJS

Midfielder Vitalijs Astafjevs put Latvia on the map when he became the most-capped European footballer of all time, with 167 appearances for his country – including three at the 2004 UEFA European Championship. He also scored 16 goals for Latvia. Astafjevs made his international debut in 1992, the year the Latvian football team was revived after independence following the break-up of the Soviet Union. He was still playing for his country at the age of 38 in November 2009, when his appearance in a friendly against Honduras saw him to overtake Estonian Martin Reim's record for most European caps.

MOST INTERNATIONAL APPEARANCES

Albania	Altin Lala	79
Andorra	Oscar Sonejee	92
Austria	Andreas Herzog	103
Belarus	Alyaksandr Kulchy	102
Bosnia-Herz.	Zvejzdan Misimovic	73
Cyprus	Ioannis Okkas	106
Estonia	Martin Reim	157
Faroe Islands	Oli Johannesen	83
Finland	Jari Litmanen	137
Georgia	Levan Kobiashvili	100
Iceland	Runar Kristinsson	104
Israel	Arik Benado	94
Kazakhstan	Ruslan Baltiev	73
Latvia	Vitalijs Astafjevs	167
Liechtenstein	Mario Frick	109
Luxembourg	Jeff Strasser	98
Macedonia	Goce Sedloski	100
Malta	David Carabott	121
Moldova	Radu Rabeja	74
Montenegro	Simon Vukcevic	41
San Marino	Damiano Vannucci	68
Slovenia	Zlatko Zahovic	80

ED BOY

Edin Dzeko became Bosnia-Herzegovina's all-time leading scorer with a second-half hat-trick in an 8-1 2014 FIFA World Cup qualifier victory over Liechtenstein in September 2012. The goals not only took him past previous record-holder Elvir Bolic, but also ahead of Dzeko's international team-mate Zvejdan Misimovic whose brace earlier in the game had briefly put him in the lead. Midfielder Misimovic drew level again with Dzeko in the following game, scoring twice in a 4-1 win, before Dzeko's last-minute strike put him ahead again. Not bad for a forward sold by Bosnian club Zeljeznicar to the Czech Republic's FK Teplice for a cut-price 25,000 in 2005 – six years before English club Manchester City handed over 32million to sign him from Germany's VfL Wolfsburg. Dzeko's off-field activities include a role as a UNICEF ambassador – and he donated almost 25,000 in 2012 towards the care of a 17-year-old Bosnian boy fighting bone marrow disease.

DARK ERA

Macedonian striker **Darko Pancev** had to wait 15 years to receive his European Golden Boot award for the 1990–91 season, when he scored 34 goals for European Cup winners Red Star Belgrade. Organizers originally suspended the competition between 1991 and 1996 due to disagreements about goal tallies in Cyprus – but eventually agreed to hand Pancev his prize in August 2006. The unlucky European top scorers from 1992 to 1996 were Scotland's Ally McCoist (twice), Welshman David Taylor, Armenian Arsen Avetisyan and Georgian Zviad Endeladze.

LAT'S ENTERTAINMENT

The 1938 FIFA World Cup went ahead with 15 instead of 16 teams after qualifiers Austria found themselves annexed by Germany – to the frustration of Latvia, who had finished runners-up in the Austrians' qualification group. Latvia was subsumed by the Soviet Union between 1940 and 1991, but qualified for their first major finals by beating Turkey in a play-off to reach the 2004 UEFA European Championship. Their team at that tournament featured all-time leading scorer Maris Verpakovskis, still playing for Latvia in 2013, and their most-capped player Vitalijs Astafjevs.

BASKET CASE

Captain **Rashad Sadygov** not only secured Azerbaijan's biggest win in their history when he scored the only goal against Turkey in a UEFA Euro 2012 qualifier in October 2010 – he was also delivering a blow against the country in which he was making his living. Having previously played for Turkish top-flight side Kayserispor, he had since moved on to rivals Eskisehirspor. Not every transfer has worked out well for Sadygov: he missed the transfer deadline when signing for Azeri side PFC Neftchi in 2006, so he decided to play basketball for a season to keep himself fit until allowed to resume football.

MOST INTERNATIONAL GOALS

Albania	Erjon Bogdani	19
Andorra	Ildefons Lima	7
Austria	Toni Polster	44
Belarus	Maksim Romashenko	20
Bosnia-Herz.	Edin Dzeko	29
Cyprus	Michalis Konstantinou	32
Estonia	Andres Oper	38
Faroe Islands	Rogvi Jacobsen	10
Finland	Jari Litmanen	32
Georgia	Shota Arveladze	26
Iceland	Eidur Gudjohnsen	24
Israel	Mordechai Spiegler	33
Kazakhstan	Ruslan Baltiev	13
Latvia	Maris Verpakovskis	29
Liechtenstein	Mario Frick	16
Luxembourg	Leon Mart	16
Macedonia	Goran Pandev	26
Malta	Michael Mifsud	37
Moldova	Serghei Clescenco	11
Montenegro	Mirko Vucinic	14
San Marino	Andy Selva	8
Slovenia	Zlatko Zahovic	35

TU-WHIT TWO-NIL

Finland's adopted lucky mascot is an eagle owl called "Bubi" that occasionally swoops down on the Helsinki Olympic Stadium during international matches – making his debut during a 2-0 UEFA European Championship qualifier win over Belgium in June 2007 and holding up the game for several minutes as he flew about the pitch and perched on goalposts. The eagle owl was later voted the Finnish capital's "Resident of the Year".

HIGH LIFE

At 64°09'N, Reykjavik, in Iceland, is the northernmost city to host a FIFA World Cup match – though so far only in qualifiers. The northernmost FIFA World Cup finals venue is Sandviken in Sweden, at 60°37'N – while Christchurch in New Zealand (43°32'S) holds the record for southernmost FIFA World Cup venue, with the finals record held by Mar del Plata in Argentina (38°01'S). Iceland's 9,800-seater national stadium, the Laugardalsvollur, was opened in 1958 and then renovated 39 years later.

BOHEMIAN RHAPSODY

Striker **Josef "Pepi" Bican** is, for many Austrian fans, the most prolific goalscorer of all time. Some authorities put his total tally in officially recognized matches at 805 goals, higher in the rankings than Romario, Pele and Gerd Muller. Bican played for Austrian clubs Rapid Vienna and Admira in the 1930s, but the bulk of his strikes came for Czech-based Slavia Prague between 1937 and 1948. He also scored 19 goals in 19 games for Austria from 1933 to 1936, before switching citizenship and hitting 21 in 14 matches for Czechoslovakia between 1938 and 1949. Although he reached the semi-finals of the 1934 FIFA World Cup with Austria, an administrative error meant he was not registered with his new country in time for the 1938 tournament. He also played one international match for a representative Bohemia and Moravia side in 1939, scoring a hat-trick.

PRISTINA CONDITION

Tough-tackling Albania captain Lorik Cana was born in Pristina, Kosovo, and family connections meant he had the choice of playing for Albania, France or Switzerland when he began his international career after impressive performances for Paris Saint-Germain. Cana, who later played club football for Marseille, Sunderland and Galatasaray, opted to represent Albania – as did his father Agim Cana, who won Albanian caps in the 1980s while also playing for FK Pristina, Dinamo Zagreb and Lausanne-Sport.

LIVING HAND TO FOOT

The part-time international footballers of the Faroe Islands have a motley collection of day jobs – and other sporting achievements. Bobble hat-wearing goalkeeper **Jens Martin Knudsen,** man of the match in their shock 1-0 win over Austria in 1989, made his living as a forklift truck driver – while also winning a national gymnastics title and playing handball. Team-mates who have also played both football and handball include journalist/musician Uni Arge, the Faroes' fourth-top-scorer, and third-placed John Petersen.

SIZE ISN'T EVERYTHING

Originally members of the AFC, Kazakhstan joined UEFA in 2002. It is UEFA's second largest member state by area, behind only Russia, but ranks only 16th by population.

A SEQUEL TO HAMLET

Striker **Hamlet Mkhitaryan** played twice for post-Soviet state Armenia in 1994, then died just two years later from a brain tumour at the age of just 33. His son Henrikh, seven when his father died, has gone on to become one of the country's leading stars – and one who often dedicates his achievements to his late parent. The younger Mkhitaryan became Armenia's joint top scorer, alongside Artur Petrosyan, when his 11th goal for his country helped pull off a stunning 4-0 away win in Denmark in a June 2013 qualifier that ended their host's hopes of reaching the 2014 FIFA World Cup. Petrosyan's goals came in 69 games, Mkhitaryan's in 39. The shock victory in Copenhagen came just five days after Armenia's embarrassing 1-0 home defeat to minnows Malta. Henrikh Mkhitaryan made his Armenia debut in 2007, meaning his international career overlapped with an unrelated player who was also named Hamlet Mkhitaryan – a midfielder who won 56 caps between 1994 and 2008.

RECORD WINS

Albania	5-0	v Vietnam (A, December 2003);
	6-1	v Cyprus (H, August 2009)
Andorra	2-0	v Belarus (H, April 2000);
	2-0	v Albania (H, April 2002)
Austria	9-0	v Malta (H, April 1977)
Belarus	5-0	v Lithuania (H, June 1998)
Bosnia-Herzegovina	7-0	v Estonia (H, September 2008)
Cyprus	5-0	v Andorra (H, November 2000)
Estonia	6-0	v Lithuana (H, July 1928)
Faroe Islands	3-0	v San Marino (H, May 1995)
Finland	10-2	v Estonia (H, August 1922)
Georgia	7-0	v Armenia (H, March 1997)
Iceland	9-0	v Faroe Islands (H, July 1985)
Israel	9-0	v Chinese Taipei (A, March 1988)
Kazakhstan	7-0	v Pakistan (H, June 1997)
Latvia	8-1	v Estonia (A, August 1942)
Liechtenstein	4-0	v Luxembourg (A, October 2004)
Luxembourg	6-0	v Afghanistan (A, July 1948)
Macedonia	11-1	v Liechtenstein (A, November 1996)
Malta	7-1	v Liechtenstein (H, March 2008)
Moldova	5-0	v Pakistan (A, August 1992)
Montenegro	3-0	v Kazakhstan (H, May 2008)
San Marino	1-0	v Liechtenstein (H, April 2004)
Slovenia	7-0	v Oman (A, February 1999)

RECORD DEFEATS

Albania	0-12	v Hungary (A, September 1950)
Andorra	1-8	v Czech Republic (A, June 2005);
	0-7	v Croatia (A, October 2006)
Austria	1-11	v England (H, June 1908)
Belarus	0-5	v Austria (A, June 2003)
Bosnia-Herzegovina	0-5	v Argentina (A, May 1998)
Cyprus	0-12	v West Germany (A, May 1969)
Estonia	2-10	v Finland (A, August 1922)
Faroe Islands	0-7	v Yugoslavia (A, May 1991);
	0-7	v Romania (A, May 1992);
	0-7	v Norway (H, August 1993);
	1-8	v Yugoslavia (H, October 1996)
Finland	0-13	v Germany (A, September 1940)
Georgia	0-5	v Romania (A, April 1996);
	1-6	v Denmark (A, September 2005)
Iceland	2-14	v Denmark (A, August 1967)
Israel*	1-7	v Egypt (A, March 1934)
Kazakhstan	0-6	v Turkey (H, June 2006);
	0-6	v Russia (A, May 2008)
Latvia	0-12	v Sweden (A, May 1927)
Liechtenstein	1-11	v Macedonia (H, November 1996)
Luxembourg	0-9	v England (H, October 1960);
	0-9	v England (A, December 1982)
Macedonia	0-5	v Belgium (H, June 1995)
Malta	1-12	v Spain (A, December 1983)
Moldova	0-6	v Sweden (A, June 2001)
Montenegro	0-4	v Romania (A, May 2008)
San Marino	0-13	v Germany (H, September 2006)
Slovenia	0-5	v France (A, October 2002)

* Played under the British Mandate of Palestine.

KULCHY COUP

Midfielder **Alyaksandr Kulchy** became the first player to win 100 caps for Belarus, skippering the side against Lithuania in a June 2012 friendly. He also ended ex-Arsenal and Barcelona playmaker Alexander Hleb's run of four successive Belarus footballer of the year awards by claiming the prize in 2009. Hleb, whose younger brother Vyacheslav has also played for Belarus, had previously won the accolade in 2002 and 2003 as well, only for Belarus's all-time top scorer Maksim Romashenko to take it in 2004.

NO-SCORE ANDORRA

Since playing their first international on New Year's Day 1996 – a 6-1 home defeat to Estonia – Andorra have won only three matches, two of them friendlies. Their only competitive triumph was a 1-0 success over Macedonia in an October 2004 FIFA World Cup qualifying match, when left-back Marc Bernaus struck the only goal of the game. Perhaps their lack of strength should come as no surprise – the principality is the sixth-smallest country in Europe, with a population of just 71,822 and they have played their most high-profile games, against England, across the Spanish border in Barcelona.

CAUGHT SHORT

If Montenegro are scoring, then fans can "put their shirt" on captain and all-time leading scorer **Mirko Vucinic** being among the goals. He celebrated scoring the winner against Switzerland in a UEFA Euro 2012 qualifier by removing not his top, but his shorts – and wearing them on his head, antics that earned him a yellow card. Vucinic had previously celebrated a goal for his Italian club side by taking off both his shorts and his shirt, revealing another AS Roma shirt underneath.

MASSIMO BETTER BLUES

Massimo Bonini was unable to inspire a win or even a draw as San Marino manager between 1996 and 1998. But his own playing career was far more effective, including seven years, 192 matches and three Serie A league titles at Italian giants Juventus during the 1980s. Bonini played all 90 minutes of Juventus's 1-0 victory over Liverpool in the 1985 UEFA European Cup final – making him the only San Marino footballer to lift the trophy, or even feature at such a high-flown footballing occasion.

SARG'S 20–YEAR SERVICE

Armenia's first international was a goalless draw at home to Moldova on 14 October 1992. In their starting line-up that day was centre-back Sargis Hovsepyan, who went on to win a record 132 caps for the country before his international retirement in November 2012. He was then appointed the Armenian national team's football director.

SOUTH AMERICA

The FIFA World Cup returns to Brazil in 2014, 84 years after the tournament was held on South American soil, in Uruguay, for the first time. The 2014 hosts will be among the favourites to win, hoping to keep the trophy in South America for the tenth time – following five Brazilian triumphs and two apiece for Uruguay and Argentina. The latter two, the first FIFA World Cup finalists back in 1930, are among the leading contenders to host the centenary FIFA World Cup in 2030.

New Brazilian golden boy Neymar gave the 2013 FIFA Confederations Cup in his homeland a spectacular start with an early, long-range goal against Japan in the tournament opener.

ARGENTINA

Copa America champions on 14 occasions, FIFA Confederations Cup winners in 1992, Olympic gold medallists in 2004 and 2008 and, most treasured of all, FIFA World Cup winners in 1978 and 1986: few countries have won as many international titles as Argentina. The country has a long and rich football history (the first Argentine league was contested in 1891) and has produced some of the greatest footballers ever to have played the game.

LONGEST-SERVING MANAGERS

Guillermo Stabile	1939–60
Cesar Luis Menotti	1974–83
Carlos Bilardo	1983–90
Alfio Basile	1990–94
	2006–08
Marcelo Bielsa	1998–2004
Jose Maria Minella	1964–68
Daniel Passarella	1994–98
Manuel Seoane	1934–37
Juan Jose Pizzuti	1969–72

CLASS OF '86

Argentina's failure to go beyond the quarter-finals of the 2011 Copa America they hosted cost manager Sergio Batista his job – and the end of his 12-month reign meant he was Argentina's shortest-serving coach since Vladislao Cap took charge for the 1974 FIFA World Cup. Batista, who coached Argentina to Olympic gold in 2008, had taken over as senior coach in 2010 from Diego Maradona. The two men had been team-mates when Argentina won the 1986 FIFA World Cup. Yet the man succeeding Batista was **Alejandro "Alex" Sabella**, an international midfielder who was left out of that 1986 squad. Sabella's playing career also had a link to Maradona – he was signed by Sheffield United in 1978 after the English club bid for, yet were unable to afford, Maradona.

FRINGE PLAYERS

Daniel Passarella was a demanding captain when he led his country to glory at the 1978 FIFA World Cup. He was the same as coach. After taking over the national side in 1994, he refused to pick anyone unless they had their hair cut short – and ordered striker Claudio Caniggia to get rid of his "girl's hair".

BOTTOMS UP

Perhaps the most predictable thing about Diego Maradona's spell as Argentina's coach was its unpredictability. He was banned from football for two months for his foul-mouthed criticism of journalists after his side finally clinched a place at the 2010 FIFA World Cup. The prospect of being abused did not deter hordes of journalists from flocking to his press conferences in South Africa, meaning attendance had to be made ticket-only. Eccentric elements of his squad's FIFA World Cup training sessions included Maradona puffing on cigars while issuing instructions – or bending over and inviting players to aim shots at his backside.

WORTH WAITING FOR

Argentina's national stadium, "El Monumental" in Buenos Aires, hosted its first game in 1938. But the original design was not completed until 20 years later – largely thanks to the £97,000 River Plate received for a transfer fee from Juventus for **Omar Sivori**. The stadium is a must-see stop on the itinerary of many global football tourists for the "Superclasico" derby between hosts River Plate and cross-city rivals Boca Juniors.

NUMBERS GAME

Argentina's FIFA World Cup squads of 1978 and 1982 were given numbers based on alphabetical order rather than positions, which meant the No. 1 shirt was worn by midfielders Norberto Alonso in 1978 and Osvaldo Ardiles in 1982. The only member of the 1982 squad whose shirt number broke the alphabetical order was No. 10, Diego Maradona.

BEGINNER'S LUCK

Aged just 27 years and 267 days old, Juan Jose Tramutola became the FIFA World Cup's youngest-ever coach when Argentina opened their 1930 campaign by beating France 1-0. Argentina went on to reach the final, only to lose 4-2 to Uruguay. Top-scorer at the 1930 FIFA World Cup was Argentina's Guillermo Stabile, with eight goals in four games – the only internationals he played. He later won six Copa America titles as his country's longest-serving coach between 1939 and 1960.

DO YOU COME HERE OFTEN?

Argentina and Uruguay have played each other more often than any other two nations, beginning with the Argentines' 3-2 victory in Uruguay's capital Montevideo in 1901 – the very first international staged outside the United Kingdom. The two teams have clashed 183 times since then, with Argentina winning 84, Uruguay 58 and 42 draws.

TARNISHED GOLD

Despite winning Olympics football gold in 2004 and 2008 – with **Javier Mascherano** becoming the first male footballer since 1928 to collect two Olympic golds – Argentina surprisingly failed to qualify for the 2012 tournament in London. South America's two places went instead to Brazil and Uruguay, based on performances at the 2011 South American Youth Championship staged in Peru. Argentina had finished third in the final group of six.

A ROUND DOZEN

Argentina were responsible for the biggest win in Copa America history, when five goals by Jose Manuel Moreno helped them thrash Ecuador 12-0 in 1942. The much-travelled Moreno won domestic league titles in Argentina, Mexico, Chile and Colombia.

CHINA IN YOUR HAND

In an unusual move, the two 2008 Olympics football finalists Argentina and Nigeria were allowed to take two drinks breaks during the match, which was watched by 89,102 spectators. The game was played in stifling heat in Chinese host city Beijing. Angel Di Maria scored the only goal for Argentina, allowing them to retain the title they won in Athens – for the first time – four years earlier.

MAJOR TOURNAMENTS

FIFA WORLD CUP Winners (2)	15 appearances – 1978, 1986
COPA AMERICA Winners (14)	39 appearances – 1921, 1925, 1927, 1929, 1937, 1941, 1945, 1946, 1947, 1955, 1957, 1959, 1991, 1993
CONFEDERATIONS CUP Winners (1)	Three appearances – 1992
FIRST INTERNATIONAL	Uruguay 2 Argentina 3 (Montevideo, Uruguay, 16 May 1901)
BIGGEST WIN	Argentina 12 Ecuador 0 (Montevideo, Uruguay, 22 January 1942)
BIGGEST DEFEAT	Czechoslovakia 6 Argentina 1 (Helsingborg, Sweden, 15 June 1958); Bolivia 6 Argentina 1 (La Paz, Bolivia, 1 April 2009)

THE KIDS ARE ALL RIGHT

Sergio Aguero struck in the final, and ended the tournament as six-goal top scorer, when Argentina won the FIFA World U-20 Championship for a record sixth time in 2007, in Canada, beating the Czech Republic 2-1. Two years later, Aguero married Giannina Maradona – the youngest daughter of Argentina legend Diego – and in February 2009 she gave birth to Diego's first grandchild, Benjamin. Sergio Aguero is widely known by his nickname of "Kun", after a cartoon character he was said to resemble as a child.

YELLOW GOODBYE

Some 20 years before France were forced to wear local Argentine club Atletico Kimberly's kit at the 1978 FIFA World Cup, Argentina themselves faced similar embarrassment for their first-round match against West Germany. The Argentines had neglected to bring along a second kit and a colour-clash with their opponents meant borrowing the yellow shirts of Swedish side IFK Malmo. Despite taking a third-minute lead, Argentina lost 3-1 and departed the tournament bottom of Group A.

PEOPLE'S FAVOURITE

Lionel Messi may be acclaimed as the finest footballer in the world – and one of the best of all-time – yet back home in Argentina the real hero for many fans is three-time South American Footballer of the Year **Carlos Tevez**. When Argentina staged the 2011 Copa America, team line-up announcements in stadia described Messi as "the best in the world" but Tevez as "the player of the people". Tevez grew up in poverty in Buenos Aires' tough "Fuerte Apache" neighbourhood and still bears scars on his neck from when boiling water was spilled on him as a child. Yet he ended the 2011 Copa America as a villain – his missed penalty gave Uruguay shoot-out victory in the quarter-final. Tevez then endured a turbulent 2011–12 season with English club Manchester City, apparently refusing to come on as a substitute in one game and then going AWOL in Argentina for five months – before returning to the side just in time to help them clinch the English Premier League title.

SPOT-KICK FLOP

If at first you don't succeed, try and try again – unfortunately Martin Palermo missed all three penalties he took during Argentina's 1999 Copa America clash with Colombia. The first hit the crossbar, the second flew over the bar and the third was saved. Colombia won the match 3-0.

WINNING TOUCH

Midfielder Marcelo Trobbiani played just two minutes of FIFA World Cup football – the last two minutes of the 1986 final, after replacing winning goalscorer Jorge Burruchaga. Trobbiani touched the ball once, a backheel. The former Boca star ended his international career with 15 caps and one goal to his name.

TOP SCORERS

#	Player	Goals
1	Gabriel Batistuta	56
2	Hernan Crespo	35
=	Lionel Messi	35
4	Diego Maradona	34
5	Luis Artime	24
6	Leopoldo Luque	22
=	Daniel Passarella	22
8	Herminio Masantonio	21
=	Jose Sanfilippo	21
10	Gonzalo Higuain	20
=	Mario Kempes	20

SECOND TIME LUCKY

Luisito Monti is the only man to play in the the FIFA World Cup final for two different countries. The centre-half, born in Buenos Aires on 15 May 1901 but with Italian family origins, was highly influential in Argentina's run to the 1930 final. They lost the game 4-2 to Uruguay – after Monti allegedly received mysterious pre-match death threats. Following a transfer to Juventus the following year, he was allowed to play for Italy and was on the winning side when the *Azzurri* beat Czechoslovakia in the 1934 final. Another member of the 1934 team was Raimundo Orsi, who had also played for Argentina before switching countries in 1929.

DIVINE DIEGO

To many people **Diego Armando Maradona** is the greatest footballer the world has ever seen, better even than Pele. The Argentine legend, born in Lanus on 30 October 1960, first became famous as a ball-juggling child during half-time intervals at Argentinos Juniors matches. He was distraught to be left out of Argentina's 1978 FIFA World Cup squad and was then sent off for retaliation at the 1982 tournament. Maradona, as triumphant Argentina captain in Mexico in 1986, scored the notorious "Hand of God" goal and then a spectacular individual strike within five minutes of each other in a quarter-final win over England. He again captained Argentina to the final in 1990, in Italy – the country where he inspired Napoli to Serie A and UEFA Cup success. He was thrown out of the 1994 FIFA World Cup finals in disgrace after failing a drugs test. Maradona captained Argentina 16 times in FIFA World Cup matches, a record, and was surprisingly appointed national coach in 2008, despite scant previous experience as a manager.

FITTER, JAVIER

Javier Zanetti is Argentina's most-capped player, with 145 international appearances – despite being surprisingly left out of squads for both the 2006 and 2010 FIFA World Cups. Zanetti, who can play at full-back or in midfield, has also played more Serie A matches than any other non-Italian – and all for Internazionale of Milan, with whom he won the treble of Italian league, Italian Cup and UEFA Champions League in 2009–10. Despite those achievements, he and Inter team-mate Esteban Cambiasso failed to make Diego Maradona's squad for the 2010 FIFA World Cup – but Zanetti returned to the fold under Maradona's successor Sergio Batista and captained his country at the 2011 Copa America. Zanetti made his 600th appearance in Italy's Serie A in March 2013.

SUPER MARIO

Mario Kempes, who scored twice in the 1978 FIFA World Cup final and won the Golden Boot, was the only member of Cesar Menotti's squad who played for a non-Argentine club. Playing for Valencia, he had been the Spanish league's top scorer for the previous two seasons.

THE ANGEL GABRIEL

Gabriel Batistuta, nicknamed "Batigol" and Argentina's all-time leading scorer, is the only man to have scored hat-tricks in two separate FIFA World Cups. He scored the first against Greece in 1994 and the second against Jamaica four years later. Hungary's Sandor Kocsis, France's Just Fontaine and Germany's Gerd Muller each scored two hat-tricks in the same FIFA World Cup. Batistuta, born in Reconquista on 1 February 1969, also set an Italian league record during his time with Fiorentina, by scoring in 11 consecutive Serie A matches at the start of the 1994–95 season.

LEO BRAVO

Arguments now rage over whether **Lionel Messi** could be as good as – even better than – his Argentine forerunner Diego Maradona. Barcelona star Messi has not yet won a FIFA World Cup, unlike Maradona, but he has now passed "El Diego" in the scoring stakes for his country – a June 2013 hat-trick against Guatemala took Messi to 35 goals in 82 international appearances, compared to Maradona's 34 in 91. Maradona was the manager who made Messi Argentina's youngest-ever captain, against Greece in their final first-round group-game at the 2010 FIFA World Cup. Maradona had complained of Messi before the tournament: "He is more difficult to get hold of than US President Barack Obama." Messi scored an astonishing 91 goals in the calendar year in 2012, six more than West Germany's Gerd Muller hit in 1971 – and the Argentine's 2012–13 tally included goals in 19 consecutive Spanish La Liga matches taking in every other club in the division.

TOP CAPS

1	Javier Zanetti	145
2	Roberto Ayala	115
3	Diego Simeone	106
4	Oscar Ruggeri	97
5	Javier Mascherano	92
6	Diego Maradona	91
7	Ariel Ortega	87
8	Lionel Messi	82
9	Gabriel Batistuta	78
10	Juan Pablo Sorin	76

SAINTED PALERMO

Veteran striker Martin Palermo waited 10 years between international appearances before being called up again by his former Boca Juniors team-mate Diego Maradona in 2009. He justified the surprise recall with a stoppage-time winner in the penultimate qualifier against Peru, prompting Maradona to take a celebratory dive in rain-sodden mud on the touchline and then hail it as "the miracle of St Palermo". Palermo also became his country's oldest-ever FIFA World Cup scorer, at the 2010 tournament in South Africa. He was 36 years and 227 days old when he came on as a substitute in the first round against Greece and completed the scoring in a 2-0 victory – a year and 358 days older than Maradona had been when scoring against the same country 16 years earlier.

BRAZIL

No country has captured the soul of the game to the same extent as Brazil. The country's distinctive yellow-shirted and blue-shorted players have thrilled generations of football fans and produced some of the game's greatest moments. No FIFA World Cup tournament would be the same without Brazil – the nation that gave birth to Pele, Garrincha, Zico, Ronaldo and Kaka. The only nation to have appeared in the finals of every FIFA World Cup – they have won the competition a record-breaking five times – in 2014, Brazil will welcome the world for a second time.

FIERCEST RIVALS

Brazil's oldest club classic is Fluminense versus Botafogo in Rio de Janeiro. The clubs faced each other for the first time on 22 October 1905, when Fluminense won 6-0. One particular match stirred a controversy that lasted 89 years. The two teams disagreed on the result of the 1907 championship, whose title was disputed up to 1996 ... when they finally decided to share it.

CLOSE ENCOUNTERS

Brazil have been involved in many memorable games. Their 3-2 defeat to Italy in 1982 is regarded as one of the classic games in FIFA World Cup finals history. Paolo Rossi scored all three of Italy's goals with Brazil coach Tele Santana much criticized for going all out in attack when only a 2-2 draw was needed. Brazil's 1982 squad, with players such as **Socrates**, Zico and **Falcao**, is considered one of the greatest teams never to win the tournament. In 1994, a 3-2 win over the Netherlands in the quarter-finals – their first competitive meeting in 20 years – was just as thrilling, with all the goals coming in the second half. Socrates – a qualified medical doctor, as well as elder brother to 1994 FIFA World Cup-winner Rai – was mourned across the globe when he died at the age of 57 in December 2011.

TAKING AIM WITH NEYMAR

Brazil's triumph in the 2013 FIFA Confederations Cup, a record third in a row, was some consolation for their failure in 2012 to break their Olympic Games hoodoo. This remains the only FIFA-approved prize Brazil have yet to win though they will fancy their chances as hosts in Rio de Janeiro in 2016. Brazil lost the 2012 final at London 2012 to Mexico even though **Neymar** was nine-goal top scorer. Neymar was later voted South American Footballer of the Year for the second successive year and was then official best player in the FIFA Confederations Cup. That was his last domestic appearance before he completed a lucrative transfer from Santos to Spanish champions Barcelona.

BRAZIL'S RECORD

FIFA WORLD CUP	19 appearances (every finals)
Matches (97)	W67, D15, L15, GF210, GA88
Winners (5)	1958, 1962, 1970, 1994, 2002
Runners-up (2)	1950, 1998
Third place (2)	1938, 1978
Fourth place (1)	1974
COPA AMERICA	33 appearances
Winners (8)	1919, 1922, 1949, 1989, 1997, 1999, 2004, 2007
CONFEDERATIONS CUP	Seven appearances
Winners (4)	1997, 2005, 2009, 2013
FIRST INTERNATIONAL	Argentina 3 Brazil 0 (Buenos Aires, 20 September 1914)
BIGGEST WIN	Brazil 10 Bolivia 1 (Sao Paulo, 10 April 1949)
HEAVIEST DEFEAT	Uruguay 6 Brazil 0 (Chile, 18 September 1920)

LAND OF FOOTBALL

No country is more deeply identified with football success than Brazil, who have won the FIFA World Cup a record five times – in 1958, 1962, 1970, 1994 and 2002. They are also the only team never to have missed a FIFA World Cup finals and are favourites virtually every time the competition is staged. After winning the trophy for a third time in Mexico in 1970, Brazil kept the **Jules Rimet Trophy** permanently. Sadly, it was stolen from the federation's headquarters in 1983 and was never recovered. Brazilians often refer to their country as "o país do futebol" ("the country of football"). It is the favourite pastime of youngsters, while general elections are often held in the same year as the FIFA World Cup, with critics arguing that political parties try to take advantage of the nationalistic surge created by football and bring it into politics. Charles Miller, the son of a Scottish engineer, is credited with bringing football to Brazil in 1894. Yet the sport would only truly become Brazilian when blacks were able to play at the top level in 1933. At first, because of the game's European origin, it was the sport of Brazil's urban white elite. However, it quickly spread among the urban poor as Brazilians realized the only thing they needed to play was a ball, which could be substituted inexpensively with a bundle of socks, an orange, or even a cloth filled with paper.

CAPTAIN TO COACH

Brazil's 1994 FIFA World Cup-winning captain **Dunga** was appointed national coach in 2006 despite having no previous management experience. He led the team to 2007 Copa America and 2009 FIFA Confederations Cup success. But he lost his job after Brazil were knocked out of the 2010 FIFA World Cup in a 2-1 quarter-final defeat to the Netherlands. Dunga – real name Carlos Caetano Bledorn Verri, but widely known by the Portuguese for "Dopey" – had already faced criticism back home for his team's defensive style and decisions not to take Ronaldinho, Adriano or Alexandre Pato to South Africa.

CUP FLOPS DROPPED

Only four players from Brazil's 2010 FIFA World Cup squad made the cut when new coach **Mano Menezes** picked 23 men for the first game of his reign, the August 2010 match against the USA. Brazil won 3–0, captained by Robinho – one of the few survivors from the South Africa tournament, along with Daniel Alves, Ramires and Thiago Silva.

MESSAGE TO MANDELA

Before Brazil's 2013 FIFA Confederations Cup final against Spain on 30 June 2013, a signed Brazil shirt was presented to South African government minister Tokyo Sexwale to pass on to the critically ill Nelson Mandela.

INFLICTING PAIN ON SPAIN

Brazil's 3-0 trounding of Spain in the 2013 FIFA Confederations Cup final at Rio's Maracana was the first competitive clash between the nations since Brazil won 6-1 also as hosts and also in Maracana in the 1950 World Cup finals. The latest meeting was its 102nd Brazil international.

EYE FOR GOAL

Centre-forward **Tostao** – full name Eduardo Goncalves de Andrade – was one of the stars of Brazil's legendary 1970 FIFA World Cup-winning team but almost did not make the tournament. He had suffered a detached retina when hit in the face by a football the previous year, prompting some doctors' warnings that he should be left out. Tostao eventually retired at the age of 26 in 1973, after another eye injury, and went to work as a doctor instead. His 1970 team-mate Pele also experienced failing eyesight.

TOP CAPS

1	Cafu	142
2	Roberto Carlos	125
3	Lucio	105
4	Claudio Taffarel	101
5	Djalma Santos	98
=	Ronaldo	98
=	Ronaldinho	98
7	Gilmar	94
9	Gilberto Silva	93
10	Pele	92
=	Rivelino	92

TOP SCORERS

1	Pele	77
2	Ronaldo	62
3	Romario	55
4	Zico	52
5	Bebeto	39
6	Rivaldo	34
7	Jairzinho	33
=	Ronaldinho	33
9	Ademir	32
=	Tostao	32

JOY OF THE PEOPLE

Garrincha, one of Brazil's greatest legends, was really Manuel Francisco dos Santos at birth but his nickname meant 'Little Bird' – inspired by his slender, bent legs. Despite the legacy of childhood illness, he was a star right-winger at Botafogo from 1953 to 1965. He and Pele were explosively decisive newcomers for Brazil at the 1958 FIFA World Cup finals. In 1962 Garrincha was voted player of the tournament four years later. He died in January 1983 at just 49. His epitaph was the title often bestowed on him in life: "The Joy of the People."

THE KING

Pele is considered by many as the greatest player of all time, a sporting icon *par excellence* and not only for his exploits on the pitch. When, for instance, he scored his 1,000th goal, Pele dedicated it to the poor children of Brazil. He began playing for Santos at the age of 15 and won his first FIFA World Cup two years later, scoring twice in the final. Despite numerous offers from European clubs, the economic conditions and Brazilian football regulations at the time allowed Santos to keep hold of their prized asset for almost two decades, until 1974. All-time leading scorer of the Brazilian national team, he is the only footballer to be a member of three FIFA World Cup-winning teams. Despite being in the Brazilian squad at the start of the 1962 tournament, an injury suffered in the second match meant he was not able to play on and, initially, he missed out on a winner's medal. However, FIFA announced in November 2007 that he would be awarded a medal retrospectively. After the disastrous 1966 tournament, when Brazil fell in the first round, Pele said he did not wish to play in the FIFA World Cup again. He was finally talked round and ended up, in 1970, playing a key role in what is widely considered as one of the greatest sides ever. Since his retirement in 1977, Pele has been a worldwide ambassador for football, as well undertaking various acting roles and commercial ventures.

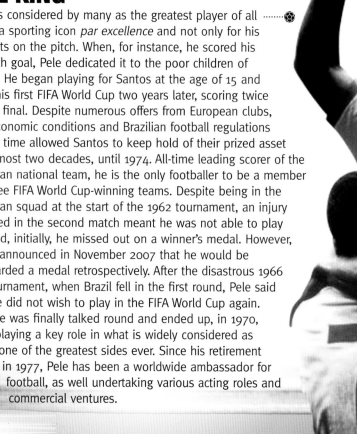

PARTY ANIMAL

Brazil's captain when they played Argentina (twice), Costa Rica and Mexico in autumn 2011 was a man many had not even expected to be in the international side again – former two-time FIFA World Footballer of the Year, Ronaldinho. Having amazed the world with his fancy footwork and prolific goalscoring for Paris Saint-Germain in France, Barcelona in Spain and AC Milan in Italy, he returned to his homeland with Flamengo in 2011 – but was widely accused of being more interested in partying than playing. But a return to form won him a recall under Mano Menezes. That appearance against Mexico took him to 33 goals, level with 1970 FIFA World Cup winner Jairzinho, then his next match – his 94th for Brazil – equalled the caps tally of 1958 and 1962 FIFA World Cup champion goalkeeper Gilmar. Ronaldinho himself became a FIFA World Cup winner in 2002, aged 22, when his long-range goal against England gave Brazil victory in the quarter-finals – though he was sent off seven minutes later and had to sit out the semi-final, before returning for the final.

WHITHER RONALDO?

Only one person knows exactly what happened to **Ronaldo** in the hours before the 1998 FIFA World Cup final – the man himself. He sparked one of the biggest mysteries in FIFA World Cup history when his name was left off the teamsheet before the game, only for it to reappear just in time for kick-off. It was initially reported that Ronaldo had an ankle injury, and then a upset stomach. Finally team doctor Lidio Toledo revealed the striker had been rushed to hospital after suffering a convulsion in his sleep, but that he had been cleared to play after neurological and cardiac tests. The most dramatic account came from Ronaldo's roommate Roberto Carlos. "Ronaldo was scared about what lay ahead. The pressure had got to him and he couldn't stop crying," said the legendary full-back. "At about four o'clock, he became ill. That's when I called the team doctor and told him to get over to our room as fast as he could."

TWO NAMES, TWO COUNTRIES

Playing competitively for two countries is no longer allowed, but **Jose Altafini**, the third-highest scorer in the history of Italy's Serie A who had dual nationality, played international football for both Brazil and Italy. In Brazil he was nicknamed "Mazzola" for his striking resemblance to the former Torino forward Valentino Mazzola. He played in the 1958 FIFA World Cup for Brazil, though not in the latter stages of the tournament, and then switched to Italy for the 1962 event. The Italians preferred to call him by his real name.

THAT'S MY BOY

When Bebeto scored for Brazil against the Netherlands in their 1994 FIFA World Cup quarter-final, he and strike partner Romario celebrated with a "cradling the baby" dance that would be much-imitated for years to come. Bebeto's wife had just given birth to their son Matheus – who would grow up to become a footballer himself, joining Flamengo's youth set-up in 2011. By this time, both **Bebeto** (middle) and **Romario** (right, Mazinho is left) were in tandem again – as elected politicians in Brazil.

RIGHT SAID FRED!

Fred finished joint top scorer at the 2013 FIFA Confederations Cup, his five goals matching the tally of Spain's Fernando Torres. The Brazilian was denied the Golden Boot, however, because Torres's goals came in fewer games. But Fred collected the main prize, his brace in the final against Spain helping Brazil to a 3-0 victory – and the trophy. Fred – full name Frederico Chaves Guedes – made his international debut in 2005 but played no Brazil games between 2007 and 2011 before a recall by then-manager Mario Menezes. His two goals against Uruguay in the FIFA Confederations Cup semi-final was his first double for Brazil, eight years after his debut.

BRAZIL'S YOUNGEST PLAYERS

1 Pele, 16 years and 257 days
   (v Argentina, 7 July 1958)
2 Ronaldo, 17 years and 182 days
   (v Argentina, 24 March 1994)
3 Adriano, 17 years and 272 days
   (v Australia, 17 November 1999)
4 Toninho, 17 years and 343 days
   (v Uruguay, 28 April 1976)
5 Carvalho Leite, 18 years and 26 days
   (v Bolivia, 22 July 1930)
6 Diego, 18 years and 60 days
   (v Mexico, 30 April 2003)
7 Marcelo, 18 years and 115 days
   (v Wales, 5 September 2006)
8 Philippe Coutinho, 18 years and 116 days
   (v Iran, 7 October 2010)
9 Doria, 18 years and 149 days
   (v Bolivia, 6 April 2013)
10 Neymar, 18 years and 186 days
   (v USA, 10 August 2010)

ROLLING RIVA

Brazilian legend **Rivaldo** was still playing into his 40s – a decade after the highlight of his career, helping Brazil win the 2002 FIFA World Cup. He scored 34 goals in 74 matches for his country between 1993 and 2003, including three goals at the 1998 FIFA World Cup and five more in Japan and South Korea four years later. His 2002 FIFA World Cup was marred only by blatant play–acting that helped get Turkey's Hakan Unsal sent off and earned Rivaldo a fine. Rivaldo - full name Rivaldo Vitor Borba Ferreira – became one of the world's finest footballers despite suffering malnourishment in a poverty-stricken childhood. His individual achievements including FIFA World Footballer of the Year and European Footballer of the Year prizes in 1999 while playing for Spanish giants Barcelona. His later clubs included AC Milan in Italy, Olympiacos and AEK Athens in Greece, Bunyodkor in Uzbekistan, Kabuscorp in Angola and – in 2013, at the age of 40, Brazilian second division side Sao Caetano.

WORLD–BEATING SAINTS

Right-back **Djalma Santos** is one of only two players to be voted into the official all-star team of a FIFA World Cup on three different occasions. He was honoured for his performances at the 1954, 1958 and 1958 finals – even though his only appearance in 1958 was in the final. West Germany's Franz Beckenbauer was the other, chosen in 1966, 1970 and 1974. On the opposite flank to Djalma Santos was the left-back Nilton Santos – no relation – who also played in 1954, 1958 and 1962 and had also been a member of Brazil's runners-up squad on home turf in 1950.

ON THE SLIDE?

In July 2012, Brazil fell out of the FIFA World Rankings top 10, to 11th, for the first time since the rankings began in 1993. Five months later, they were at a new low of 18th. Part of the reason is that Brazil, as 2014 FIFA World Cup hosts, had played few competitive matches.

YELLOW FEVER

The world-renowned yellow and blue kit now worn by Brazil was not adopted until 1954, as a replacement for their former all-white strip. The *Correio da Manha* newspaper organised a design competition which was won by 19-year-old Aldyr Garcia Schlee and the new colours were worn for the first time in March 1954 against Chile. Schlee was from Pelotas, close to Brazil's border with Uruguay and actually supported Uruguayan sides against Brazil.

GRAND ACHIEVEMENT

Brazil played their 1,000th match on 14 November 2012, with Neymar's second-half equaliser securing a 1-1 draw against Colombia in New Jersey, United States. Brazil's first match is considered generally to have been a 2-0 victory over visiting English club Exeter City on 21 July 1914, at the Estadio das Laranjeiras in Rio – still used by Fluminense. Brazil won that day despite star striker Arthur Friedenreich losing two teeth in a collision. Brazil's first international against another country was a 3-0 defeat to Argentina on 20 September 1914.

THE OLD RIVALS: BRAZIL V ARGENTINA

Matches played: 95
Brazil wins: 35
Argentina wins: 36
Draws: 24
Brazil goals: 145
Argentina goals: 151
First match: Argentina 3 Brazil 0 (20 September 1914)
Latest match: Argentina 2 Brazil 1 (21 November 2012)
Biggest Brazil win: Brazil 6 Argentina 2 (20 December 1945)
Biggest Argentina win: Argentina 6 Brazil 1 (5 March 1940)

THE FAME GAME

As of 2012, some 25 men had been inducted into the Brazilian Football Museum Hall of Fame, opened in September 2008 at Corinthians' old ground, the Estadio do Pacaembu. The 25 inductees are: Bebeto, Carlos Alberto, Didi, Djalma Santos, Falcao, Garrincha, Gerson, Gilmar, Jairzinho, Julinho, Nilton Santos, Pele, Rivaldo, Rivelino, Roberto Carlos, Romario, Ronaldinho, Ronaldo, Socrates, Claudio Taffarel, Tostao, Vava, **Mario Zagallo**, Zico and Zizinho.

BRAZIL'S 2014 WORLD CUP STADIA

1. Maracana, Rio de Janeiro (76,804)
2. Brasilia, Estadio Nacional Mane Garrincha (70,064)
3. Mineirao, Belo Horizonte (62,547, Atletico Mineiro and Cruzeiro)
4. Arena Corinthians, Sao Paulo (65,807)
5. Estadio Castelao, Fortaleza (64,846)
6. Estadio Beira-Rio, Porto Alegre (48,849)
7. Arena Fonte Neva, Salvador (48,747)
8. Arena Pernambuco, Recife (46,000)
9. Arena Pantanal, Cuiaba (42,968)
10. Arena da Amazonia, Manaus (42,374)
11. Arena das Dunas, Natal (42,086)
12. Arena da Baixaba, Curitiba (41,456)

BIG PHIL'S BACK

Luiz Felipe Scolari – popularly known as *Felipao* or "Big Phil" – became the latest Brazilian FIFA World Cup-winning coach to return for a second spell as manager, when he replaced the sacked Mano Menezes in November 2012. Scolari was in charge when Brazil when they became world champions in 2002. The former defender's other tastes of international management included spells in charge of Kuwait and Portugal, whom he took to the 2004 UEFA European Championship final and fourth place in the 2006 FIFA World Cup. Other world champion managers to return to the reins include Carlos Alberto Parreira, who won the 1994 tournament but could only reach the 2006 quarter-finals. Parreira's assistant in 1994 and then successor for the next four years was Mario Zagallo, who had previously won the FIFA World Cup as a player in 1958 and 1962 and as manager in 1970.

LETTING LUCIO

Elegant centre-back **Lucio** set a FIFA World Cup record during the 2006 tournament by playing for 386 minutes without conceding a foul – only ending in Brazil's 1-0 quarter-final defeat to France. While mostly noted for leadership and control at the back, he also had an eye for goal – heading the late winner that gave Brazil a 3-2 triumph over the USA in the 2009 FIFA Confederations Cup final. The following year he was part of Italian club Internazionale's treble success, clinching the Italian league and cup as well as the UEFA Champions League.

SUPER–POWERS' POWER CUT

A new addition to the annual international calendar is the Superclasico de los Americas, an annual two-legged event between Argentina and Brazil. The inaugural Superclasico was in 2011, and it was won by Brazil, thanks to a goalless draw followed by a 2-0 win. They retained the crown in 2012, though not without drama and delay. Brazil won the first leg at home, 2-1, but the return game at the Estadio Centariou Resistencia in Chaco was postponed afer a power cut – which might have been the result of Brazil's team bus colliding with an electricity trailer. The rearranged game ended 2-1 to Argentina, but the Brazilians won 4-3 on penalties, their goal being scored by Fred, while strike partner Neymar netted the winning spot-kick. For Brazil's coach Mano Menezes, however, his "reward" was the sack.

CHILE

Chile were one of four founding members of CONMEBOL, South America's football confederation, in 1916. They played in the first match at a South American football championship – losing the opener of the unofficial 1910 tournament 3-0 to Uruguay – and they played in the first official Copa America, in 1916. Never winners, they have been runners-up on four occasions, in 1955, 1956, 1979 and 1987. Their greatest glory was hosting – and taking third place at – the 1962 FIFA World Cup.

TOP SCORERS

1	Marcelo Salas	37
2	Ivan Zamorano	34
3	Carlos Caszely	29
4	Leonel Sanchez	23
5	Jorge Aravena	22
6	Humberto Suazo	21
7	Juan Carlos Letelier	18
8	Enrique Hormazabal	17
9	Alexis Sanchez	15
10	Matias Fernandez	14

BRAVO, BEAUSEJOUR

Chile went precisely 48 years between victories at a FIFA World Cup, finally ending a lengthy wait when Jean Beausejour scored the only goal of the game in their 2010 first-round match against Honduras in South Africa. Captain that day was **Claudio Bravo**, Chile's third-most-capped player and skipper since the retirement of Marcelo Salas in 2007. The win against Honduras, on 16 June 2010, came 48 years to the day since Chile's previous FIFA World Cup victory, on home turf, when they won their third-place play-off against Yugoslavia. The score then was also 1-0, thanks to a goal by Eladio Rojas. Seven defeats and six draws followed in FIFA World Cups.

CENTRE-BACK'S HAT-TRICK

The first player to be named South American Footballer of the Year three times was not Pele, Garrincha or Diego Maradona but Chilean centre-back **Elias Figueroa**, who took the prize in three consecutive years from 1974 to 1976 while playing for Brazilian club Internacional. The only players to emulate such a hat-trick were Brazil's Zico, in 1977, 1981 and 1982, and Argentina forward Carlos Tevez, in 2003, 2004 and 2005. Two more Chileans have won the award: Marcelo Salas in 1997 and Matias Fernandez in 2006. Outside of Brazil and Argentina, the most winners of the prize have come from Chile and Paraguay, with five apiece. Although Figueroa started and ended his playing career in Chile, he also played for clubs in Brazil, Uruguay and the US, while also representing his country for 16 years from 1966 to 1982 – including FIFA World Cup appearances in 1966, 1974 and 1982.

ALEXIS IS YOUNGEST

Chile's youngest-ever international is also now their most exciting star, winger **Alexis Sanchez**. He was just 17 years and four months old when he made his debut against New Zealand in April 2006, the month before he left South America to sign for Italy's Udinese. He did spend loan spells back in Chile and Argentina before making his breakthrough in Serie A with some eye-catching displays that helped earn a move to Barcelona in summer 2011, making him the Spanish club's first Chilean player. Sanchez is already among the all-time top ten scorers for Chile, his tally including three goals that helped them reach the 2010 FIFA World Cup. Chile reached the second round and won many admirers with their attacking instincts. Though their tougher edge could be detected in the nicknames for other star players, such as defender Gary "The Pitbull" Medel and Arturo "The Warrior" Vidal. Sanchez showed more tender emotions after scoring Chile's final goal, in a 4-0 friendly victory over Estonia in June 2011, by revealing a T-shirt bearing a photo of his adoptive father Jose Delaigue, who had died days earlier.

TOP CAPS

1	Leonel Sanchez	84
2	Nelson Tapia	74
3	Claudio Bravo	71
4	Alberto Fouilloux	70
=	Marcelo Salas	70
6	Fabian Estay	69
=	Ivan Zamorano	69
8	Pablo Contreras	67
9	Javier Margas	63
10	Miguel Ramirez	62

SALAS DAYS

Chile's all-time leading scorer **Marcelo Salas** formed a much-feared striking partnership with Ivan Zamorano during the late 1990s and early 21st century. Salas scored four goals as Chile reached the second round of the 1998 FIFA World Cup in France despite not winning a game. The Temuco-born striker later spent two years in international retirement, from 2005 to 2007, but returned for the first four games of qualification for the 2010 FIFA World Cup. His contribution included both Chile goals in a 2-2 draw with Uruguay on 18 November 2007, but his international career ended for good three days later, following a 3-0 defeat to Paraguay.

SURFACE APPEAL

Football helped keep up the spirits of 33 Chilean miners trapped underground for 69 days after an explosion at a mine in the Atacama desert on 5 August 2010. The men were initially given up for dead, but after news of their survival emerged, supplies sent underground included footage of Chile's 2-1 defeat to Ukraine in a friendly on 7 September. Some of the rescued miners played "keepy-uppies" with footballs on finally emerging into daylight at the surface and, two weeks later, played an exhibition match against their rescuers. The miners lost 3-2 in the 40-minute friendly, when the opposition's goalscorers included the president of Chile, Sebastian Pinera. Football clubs from across the world sent souvenirs and messages of support, and miners were invited as guests at games staged at Manchester United's Old Trafford in England and Real Madrid's Estadio Bernabeu in Spain.

LUCKY LEO

Leonel Sanchez holds the Chilean record for international appearances, scoring 23 goals in 84 games. But he was lucky to remain on the pitch for one of them. Sanchez escaped an early bath despite punching Italy's Humberto Maschio in the face during their so-called "Battle of Santiago" clash at the 1962 FIFA World Cup, when English referee Ken Aston could have sent off more than just the two players he did dismiss. Sanchez, a left-winger born in Santiago on 25 April 1936, finished the tournament as one of its six four-goal leading scorers – along with Brazilians Garrincha and Vava, Russian Valentin Ivanov, Yugoslav Drazan Jerkovic and Hungarian Florian Albert.

URUGUAY

Uruguay was the first country to win a FIFA World Cup, in 1930, and with a population of under four million, they remain the smallest to do so. They claimed the game's greatest prize for a second time in 1950, having already won Olympic gold in 1924 and 1928. Recent years were less productive, until a fourth-place finish at the 2010 FIFA World Cup and a record-breaking 15th Copa America triumph the following year.

FORLAN HERO

Diego Forlan was the stand-out Uruguayan star of the 2010 FIFA World Cup. He scored five goals – including three from outside the penalty area, the first player to achieve that feat at a FIFA World Cup since Germany's Lothar Matthaus in 1990. He also hit the crossbar with a long-range free-kick, the final touch of Uruguay's 3-2 defeat to Germany in the third-place play-off. Forlan went into the 2010 tournament having scored a late winner for Atletico Madrid, against Fulham, in the 2009–10 UEFA Europa League final. Uruguay's fourth-place finish in South Africa meant Diego fared better than his father Pablo, who had played in the Uruguay team that was knocked out in the first round of the 1974 FIFA World Cup. Diego became Uruguay's most-capped player during the 2011 Copa America, and his goal against Paraguay in the final equalled Hector Scarone's all-time scoring record. Forlan then took top spot in the scoring charts with a goal against Paraguay in October 2011, but has since been overtaken by Luis Suarez.

TOP SCORERS

1	Luis Suarez	35
2	Diego Forlan	34
3	Hector Scarone	31
4	Angel Romano	28
5	Oscar Miguez	27
6	Sebastian Abreu	26
7	Pedro Petrone	24
8	Carlos Aguilera	22
=	Fernando Morena	22
10	Jose Piendibene	20

DIFFERENT BALL GAME

Uruguay were the inaugural hosts – and the first winners – of the FIFA World Cup in 1930, having won football gold at the Olympics of 1924 in Paris and 1928 in Amsterdam. Among the players who won all three of those titles was forward Hector Scarone, who remains Uruguay's second-highest scorer with 31 goals in 52 internationals. Uruguay beat arch-rivals Argentina 4-2 in the 1930 final, in a game which used two different footballs – Argentina's choice in the first half, in which they led 2-1, before Uruguay's was used for their second-half comeback.

HAPPY ANNIVERSARY

A so-called "Mundialito", or "Little World Cup", was staged in December 1980 and January 1981 to mark the 50th anniversary of the FIFA World Cup – and, as in 1930, Uruguay emerged triumphant. The tournament was meant to involve all six countries who had previously won the tournament, though 1966 champions England turned down the invitation and were replaced by 1978 runners-up Holland. Uruguay beat Brazil 2-1 in the final, a repeat of the scoreline from the two teams' final match of the 1950 FIFA World Cup. The Mundialito-winning Uruguay side was captained by goalkeeper **Rodolfo Rodriguez** and coached by Roque Maspoli, who had played in goal in that 1950 final.

TOP CAPS

1	Diego Forlan	102
2	Diego Perez	86
3	Diego Lugano	85
4	Maxi Pereira	80
5	Rodolfo Rodriguez	78
6	Fabian Carini	74
7	Enzo Francescoli	73
8	Sebastian Abreu	70
9	Diego Godin	69
=	Alvaro Recoba	69
=	Angel Romano	69
=	Luis Suarez	69

CAV FAITH

It took just three minutes for **Edinson Cavani** to score his first international goal, after coming on as a substitute for his Uruguay debut against Colombia in February 2008. Since then, he has not only helped his country finish fourth at the 2010 FIFA World Cup and win a record 15th Copa America the following year, but with his scoring exploits for Italian club Napoli also established himself as one of the finest strikers in the world today. Cavani, a devout Christian, received high praise from the Archbishop of Naples, Crescenzio Sepe, who said: "God serves himself by having Cavani score goals." The forward was given his Uruguay debut by Oscar Tabarez, a former schoolteacher known as "The Maestro", whose second spell as international boss began in 2006. Cavani was aged just three when Tabarez led Uruguay at their most recent FIFA World Cup before 2010, reaching the second round in 1990.

LUCKY LUIS

Striker **Luis Suarez** made dramatic contributions at both the 2010 FIFA World Cup and the 2011 Copa America. In the closing seconds of extra-time in Uruguay's 2010 FIFA World Cup quarter-final against Ghana, he dived to punch the ball away on his own goal-line and prevent what would have been a match-winning goal. He was shown a straight red card, but danced exuberantly on the touchline when Ghana's Asamoah Gyan missed the resulting penalty. Suarez proved decisive at the other end of the pitch when Uruguay won the 2011 Copa America, scoring four times – including the opener in a 3-0 victory over Paraguay in the final – and was named player of the tournament. More controversy marred the Liverpool striker's career in 2011–12 and 2012–13: he was given an eight-match suspension for racially abusing Manchester United's Patrice Evra and then received a 10-match ban for inexplicably biting the arm of Chelsea's Branislav Ivanovic. He has enjoyed happier times on the international stage though and became his country's all-time leading goalscorer at the 2013 FIFA Confederations Cup.

BOYS IN BLUE

Uruguay's 3-2 home loss to Argentina, in Montevideo on 16 May 1901, was the first international match staged outside the UK. The second, on 20 July 1902, ended 6-0 to Argentina – still the *Celeste*'s heaviest loss. They have played each other another 176 times in official internationals – a world record – with Uruguay winning 53, Argentina 80, and 43 draws. Before an agreed kit-swap in 1910, Uruguay often wore vertical light-blue and white stripes and arch-rivals Argentina would don pale-blue shirts.

OLE, FRANCESCOLI

Until Diego Forlan passed him in 2011, no outfield player had represented Uruguay more often than **Enzo Francescoli** (73 caps) – and few can have taken the field quite so gracefully as the playmaker whose club career included stints with River Plate in Argentina, Racing and Marseille in France and Cagliari and Torino in Italy. His international swansong for Uruguay brought Copa America glory in 1995, when he starred as both midfielder and emergency striker and also scored one of Uruguay's spot-kicks in their penalty shoot-out final victory over Brazil. Among Francescoli's high-profile fans was Zinedine Zidane, who later named his first-born son Enzo, in honour of the Uruguayan maestro.

TRAVEL SICKNESS

Despite winning the 1930 FIFA World Cup, Uruguay turned down the chance to defend their crown four years later, when the tournament was held in Italy. Uruguayan football authorities were unhappy that only four European countries had made the effort to travel to Uruguay and take part in 1930.

OTHER TEAMS SOUTH AMERICA

GOING CARACAS FOR FOOTBALL

Baseball and boxing may have held more sway with Venezuelans in recent decades but football fever has been on the rise in the twenty-first century – given a big boost by the country staging its first Copa America in 2007. This not only saw extravagant investment in new stadia but also Venezuela's first Copa America victory since 1967 – and unprecedented progress into the knock-out stages. **Juan Arango,** a popular success in Spain with La Liga club RCD Mallorca, scored Venezuela's goal in the 4–1 quarter-final defeat to Uruguay. Venezuela followed this relative breakthrough by finishing eighth out of 10 in South America's qualification campaign for the 2010 FIFA World Cup, above Bolivia and Peru.

NATIONAL STADIUMS

Bolivia:
Estadio Hernando Siles,
La Paz (45,000 capacity)

Chile:
Estadio Nacional,
Santiago (63,379)

Colombia:
Estadio El Campin,
Bogota (48,600)

Ecuador:
Estadio Olimpico Atahualpa,
Quito (40,948)

Paraguay:
Estadio Defensores del Chaco,
Asuncion (36,000)

Peru:
Estadio Nacional,
Lima (45,574)

Venezuela:
Estadio Polideportivo
de Pueblo Nuevo,
San Cristobal (38,755)

BOLIVIA LEAVE IT LATE

Bolivia have only ever won the Copa America once, but did so in dramatic and memorable style when playing host in 1963. They were the only team to finish the competition unbeaten in all six matches, topping the league table. But they almost threw away glory on the competition's final day, twice squandering two-goal leads against Brazil. Bolivia led 2-0 before being pegged back to 2-2, then saw a 4-2 advantage turn to 4-4, before Maximo Alcocer scored what proved to be Bolivia's winning goal with four minutes remaining.

SIX AND OUT

Bolivia and El Salvador have both played the most FIFA World Cup finals matches without managing to win even once – six each. At least Bolivia did achieve a goalless draw against South Korea in 1994. But they went a record five successive FIFA World Cup finals matches without scoring a goal, across the 1930 and 1994 tournaments, before **Erwin Sanchez** put an end to their barren spell during a 3-1 defeat to Spain in their final 1994 fixture. The unwanted record was equalled at the 2010 FIFA World Cup, by both Honduras and New Zealand. Honduras drew twice and lost once in 1982, then drew once and lost twice in 2010. New Zealand lost all three matches in 1982 then drew all three in 2010.

ALVAREZ OUT

Colombia's two most-capped internationals are **Carlos Valderrama** (111 appearances) and Leonel Alvarez (101) – and Valderrama led the criticism when his former team-mate was fired after just three games and three months as national coach in 2011. Alvarez oversaw a victory over Bolivia, a draw with Venezuela and a loss to Argentina in the 2014 FIFA World Cup qualifiers before being replaced by former Argentina boss Jose Pekerman. "What a mess we're in," Valderrama said. The pair had played together when Colombia won their only Copa America ten years earlier.

VALUABLE VALENCIA

Luis Antonio Valencia had big boots to step into when Manchester United signed him from Wigan Athletic as a replacement for Real Madrid-bound world record transfer Cristiano Ronaldo in summer 2009, but 12 months later he had become the first Ecuadorian to pick up an English Premier League winners' medal. Valencia was one of the stars of Ecuador's progress to the second round of the 2006 FIFA World Cup and was nominated as one of tournament's six best-performing young players, alongside Ronaldo and eventual prize-winner Lukas Podolski. Valencia had already served notice of his talents during qualifying, scoring twice on his Ecuador debut in March 2005 in a 5-2 trouncing of Paraguay.

BIGGEST WINS

Bolivia 7 Venezuela 0
(22 August 1993)

Argentina 0 Colombia 5
(5 September 1993)

Colombia 5 Uruguay 0
(6 June 2004)

Colombia 5 Peru 0
(4 June 2006)

Ecuador 6 Peru 0
(22 June 1975)

Paraguay 7 Bolivia 0
(30 April 1949)

Hong Kong 0 Paraguay 7
(17 November 2010)

Peru 9 Ecuador 1
(11 August 1938)

Venezuela 6 Puerto Rico 0
(26 December 1946)

ABOVE–PAR PARAGUAY

In their eighth appearance at a FIFA World Cup, Paraguay topped their first-round group for the first time in 2010. Not only that, they went on to reach a later stage of the tournament than ever before, the quarter-finals, before narrowly losing 1-0 to Spain. Their penalty shoot-out victory over Japan in the second round (Oscar Cardozo converting the decisive kick) meant four South American countries made the quarter-finals – outnumbering the three European nations – for the first time. That said, there were no quarter-finals in 1930, 1950, 1974, 1978 or 1982. Paraguay followed up their impressive FIFA World Cup display by reaching the final of the following year's Copa America, only losing in the end to Uruguay (3-0).

TIM'S TIME

Peru were coached at the 1982 FIFA World Cup by Tim, who had been waiting an unprecedented 44 years to return to the FIFA World Cup finals – after playing once as striker for his native Brazil in the 1938 tournament.

HIGH LIFE

Bolivia and Ecuador play their home internationals at higher altitudes than any other teams on earth. Bolivia's showpiece Estadio Hernando Siles stadium, in the capital La Paz, is 3,637 metres (11,932ft) above sea level, while Ecuador's main Estadio Olimpico Atahualpa, in Quito, sits 2,800 metres (9,185ft) above sea level. Opposing teams have complained that the rarefied nature of the air makes it difficult to breathe, let alone play, but a FIFA ban on playing competitive internationals at least 2,500 metres (8,200ft) above sea level, first introduced in May 2007, was amended a month later – adjusting the limit to 3,000 metres (9,840ft) and allowing Estadio Hernando Siles to be used as a special case. The altitude ban was suspended entirely in May 2008. FIFA had changed its mind after protests by Bolivia, Ecuador and other affected nations Colombia and Peru. Other campaigners to overturn the law included Argentina legend Diego Maradona. He may have regretted his decision. In March 2009 Bolivia scored a 6-1 home win against Argentina in a FIFA World Cup qualifier. The Argentina coach was ... Maradona.

STUDYING THE FORM

Peru captain **Claudio Pizarro** is the highest-scoring foreign-born footballer in Germany's Bundesliga, his successful spells – two apiece – with Werder Bremen and Bayern Munich bringing him 166 goals in 353 league games, as well as a 2012–13 UEFA Champions League winners' medal with Bayern. His international career has been patchier, hampered by a fractured skull suffered against Venezuela at the 2004 Copa America and a three-month ban for joining a hotel party while on international duty in 2007. But he did score Peru's fastest international goal, after 18 seconds of their 3-1 friendly victory over Mexico in August 2003. He has also enjoyed success off the football field and on the racing track, as co-owner – with English footballer Joey Barton – of a racehorse named Crying Lightning, after a song by the rock band the Arctic Monkeys.

BIGGEST DEFEATS

Brazil 10 Bolivia 1
(10 April 1949)

Brazil 9 Colombia 0
(24 March 1997)

Argentina 12 Ecuador 0
(22 January 1942)

Argentina 8 Paraguay 0
(20 October 1926)

Brazil 7 Peru 0
(26 June 1997)

Argentina 11 Venezuela 0
(10 August 1975)

BOTERO'S ERA

Bolivia failed to reach the 2010 FIFA World Cup but did pull off one of the most eye-catching results of the qualifying campaign – a 6–1 thrashing of Argentina, who had previously been unbeaten under new coach Diego Maradona. The 1 April 2009 game in La Paz made an April fool of Maradona but a national icon of striker **Joaquin Botero,** who hit a hat-trick. But the 31-year-old announced his international retirement just a month later, bowing out after 48 caps with a Bolivian-record 20 goals.

ETCHEVERRY BRIEF APPEARANCE

Marco Etcheverry – nicknamed "El Diablo" – went from saint to sinner during Bolivia's 1994 FIFA World Cup adventure. His goals proved crucial in helping the country qualify for only their second FIFA World Cup, their first since 1950 – most notably in a 2–0 victory over eventual champions Brazil and a 3–1 win over Uruguay. But he began the tournament itself as a substitute, due to a niggling injury, and then lasted just three minutes of the opening match against Germany before being sent off for kicking Lothar Matthaus.

ELITE CUB

Peru forward Teofilo Cubillas became the first player to twice end a FIFA World Cup finals with at least five goals – he scored five apiece in 1970 and 1978, though failed to win the Golden Boot on either occasion. Germany's Miroslav Klose emulated the achievement by scoring five in 2002 and the same tally four years later, the same year he picked up the Golden Boot award.

COOL DUDAMEL

Venezuela suffered a series of hefty beatings during qualifiers for the 1998 FIFA World Cup – ending up with no wins and 13 defeats in 16 games, scoring 13 and conceding 41 goals. Their losses included 4–1 to Peru, 6–1 against Bolivia and 6–0 versus Chile, for whom Ivan Zamorano scored five. But Venezuelan goalkeeper Rafael Dudamel did enjoy a moment of joy against Argentina in October 1996, scoring direct from a free-kick with three minutes left. His side still lost the match 5–2.

MOST INTERNATIONAL CAPS

Bolivia	Luis Cristaldo	93
	Marco Sandy	93
Colombia	Carlos Valderrama	111
Ecuador	Ivan Hurtado	167
Paraguay	Paulo Da Silva	112
Peru	Roberto Palacio	127
Venezuela	Jose Manuel Rey	115

FALCAO TAKES FLIGHT

Radamel Falcao was named after Falcao, the skilful Brazilian midfielder of the 1980s who was among the favourites of his father Radamel Garcia, a professional footballer in Colombia. But the younger Falcao has gone on to become both a Colombian hero and one of the most-feared strikers in the world. His surge into Colombia's top-scoring ranks included an unbeaten first ten appearances for his country, scoring 11 goals himself. He also proved a lucky omen in the UEFA Europa League, winning and scoring in both the 2011 and 2012 finals – securing victories for Portugal's FC Porto in 2011 and for Spain's Atletico Madrid 12 months later. He followed the second success with a hat-trick against reigning UEFA Champions League champions Chelsea as Atletico won the UEFA Super Cup 4-1. He scored 17 UEFA Europa League goals in 2010–11 – two more than the previous record set by Germany's Jurgen Klinsmann – then a further 13 in 2011–12. Falcao left Spain for France in summer 2013, signed by promoted Monaco for 60 million euros.

FIVE–STAR PARAGUAY

The South American Footballer of the Year award dates back to 1971 and has been dominated by players from Brazil and Argentina. However, five Paraguayan players have won the award, all since 1985 – and the honours have come roughly every five years. The first was attacking midfielder Romerito (Julio Cesar Romero) – the only Paraguayan named in Pele's top 125 living players in 2004 – who claimed the prize in 1985. Five years later, it went to Raul Vicente Amarilla who, although Paraguayan, did not win a cap for his country (he had won two Spanish Under-21 caps when playing club football over there). Prolific goalscoring goalkeeper Jose Luis Chilavert won the award in 1996 and he was followed by two strikers, Jose Cardozo, in 2002, and Salvador Cabanas, in 2007.

IVAN THE ADMIRABLE

Ecuador defender Ivan Hurtado is South America's most-capped footballer, playing 167 games after making his debut in 1992 – including five goals. He was one of Ecuador's most influential players at their first FIFA World Cup finals, in 2002, and captained them as they reached the second round of the competition four years later.

MEDELLIN MURDER

Tragic Colombian defender Andres Escobar, 27, was shot dead outside a Medellin bar ten days after scoring an own goal in a 1994 FIFA World Cup first-round match against the United States. Colombia lost the game 2-1 and were eliminated from a tournament some observers – including Pele – had tipped them to win.

MARKSMAN SPENCER

Ecuador's greatest player of all time is arguably prolific striker **Alberto Spencer,** even though he played much of his club football in Uruguay. Spencer holds the record for most goals in South America's Copa Libertadores club championship, scoring 54 times between 1960 and 1972 and lifting the trophy three times with Uruguay's Penarol. He also scored four goals in 11 games for Ecuador and once in four appearances for Uruguay. Spencer was nicknamed "Magic Head" and was even praised as a better header of the ball than Pele – the tribute coming from Pele himself.

MOST INTERNATIONAL GOALS

Bolivia	Joaquin Botero	20
Colombia	Adolfo Valencia	31
Ecuador	Arnoldo Iguarin	25
Paraguay	Roque Santa Cruz	26
Peru	Teofilo Cubillas	26
Venezuela	Giancarlo Maldonado	22

SAFE HANDS OSCAR

Keeping clean sheets for Colombia all the way through the 2001 Copa America was **Oscar Cordoba**, who went on to become his country's most-capped goalkeeper – with 73 appearances between 1993 and 2006.

HIGHS AND LOWS FOR LOLO

Teodoro "Lolo" Fernandez scored six goals in two games for Peru at the 1936 Summer Olympics, including five in a 7–3 defeat of Finland and another in a 4–2 victory over Austria. But Peru were outraged when the Austrians claimed that fans had been invading the pitch and were even more upset when officials ordered the match to be replayed. Peru withdrew from the tournament in protest, while Austria went on to claim silver. But Fernandez and his team-mates had a happier ending at the Copa America three years later, with Peru crowned champions and Fernandez finishing as top scorer with seven goals. Only Teofilo Cubillas, with 26 goals in 81 games, has scored more for Peru than Fernandez's 24 from 32 appearances.

CANIZA CAN DO

Centre-back and captain Denis Caniza, 36, became the first Paraguayan to play at four different FIFA World Cups, with his one appearance against New Zealand during the 2010 tournament. The same event brought a milestone for team-mate Roque Santa Cruz – his goal in the first-round game against Brazil equalled Jose Saturnino Cardozo's all-time Paraguayan scoring record of 25. Fellow striker Salvador Cabanas missed out on the tournament after being shot in the head with a gun in a nightclub five months earlier – though he did recover well enough to return to professional football in 2012.

AFRICA

Even before African teams began to reach the closing stages of FIFA World Cups, the continent had been giving the world some of its most skilful and powerful players. While footballers from across Africa now star in the biggest league and cup competitions, the continent became the sustained focus of attention in 2010 when South Africa hosted the FIFA World Cup. A new name was inscribed on the Africa Cup of Nations trophy in 2012 when Zambia overcame the Ivory Coast, only for newly resurgent Nigeria to lift the trophy a year later by beating Burkina Faso.

Yaya Toure (19) has enjoyed much success in European club football, but not in the Africa Cup of Nations, a run which continued in 2013 as the Ivory Coast lost in the quarter-final.

NORTH AFRICA FIFA WORLD CUP RECORDS

FAWZI'S FIRST

Abdelrahman Fawzi became the first African footballer to score at a FIFA World Cup, when he pulled a goal back for Egypt against Hungary in the first round of the 1934 tournament – then scored an equalizer eight minutes later, to make it 2-2 at half-time. Egypt went on to lose the match 4-2, and would not return to the finals for another 56 years.

PLAY-OFF PIQUE

Morocco's qualification for the 1970 FIFA World Cup ended a 36-year African exile from the finals. No African countries played at the 1966 FIFA World Cup in Africa, with 16 possible candidate countries all boycotting the event because FIFA wanted the top African team to face a side from Asia or Oceania in a qualification play-off.

SUDDEN DEATH IN SUDAN

As if the North African rivalry between Algeria and Egypt were not intense enough, qualifiers for the 2010 FIFA World Cup pitted them against one another not once, not twice – but three times. A 2-0 win for Egypt against Algeria – including a stoppage-minute goal by Emad Moteab – in their scheduled second qualifier meant they ended the final African phase level on points, goal difference and goals scored. A one-off play-off match, hosted in neutral Sudan, was held – and Algeria's **Antar Yahia** (right) scored the only goal of the game, taking Algeria to the finals for the first time in 24 years. Both countries' governments felt compelled to call for calm, amid allegations that the Algerian team bus and Egyptian fans had come under attack ahead of the crucial matches.

AGELESS ALI

Tunisian goalkeeper **Ali Boumnijel** played in all three of his country's games at the 2006 FIFA World Cup – making him the oldest player to feature in Germany that summer, as well as only the fifth man over the age of 40 to play at a FIFA World Cup. Boumnijel conceded six goals in those three matches, against Saudi Arabia (two, in a 2-2 draw), Spain (three, in a 3-1 defeat) and Ukraine (one, in a 1-0 loss).

REDS IN A ROW

When Antar Yahia was sent off for a second bookable offence, three minutes into stoppage-time of Algeria's 1-0 defeat to the USA at the 2010 FIFA World Cup, it was not only the latest red card shown in any World Cup game not featuring extra-time. It also meant at least one player had been sent off on eight consecutive days of the 2010 tournament – a record run for any FIFA World Cup.

ANTAR THE STAR

Antar Yahia had been the hero of Algeria's 2010 FIFA World Cup qualifying campaign, scoring the winning goal in a play-off against arch-rivals Egypt. The defender was actually born in France, in 1982, and played for the French under-18s before switching to Algeria in 2004, scoring on his debut for the country's under-23s.

MOROCCAN ROLL

Morocco remain the only North African country to reach the second round of a FIFA World Cup, though they were knocked out, 1-0, by eventual finalists West Germany. It was in Mexico in 1986 that Morocco were the first African team to top a FIFA World Cup group, finishing above England, Poland and Portugal. Crucial was their 3-1 victory over Portugal in their final group game, following goalless draws against the other two teams – including an England side who lost captain Bryan Robson to a dislocated shoulder and vice-captain Ray Wilkins to a red card. **Abderrazak Khairi** scored two of the goals against Portugal, while Lothar Matthaus's winning strike for Germany came with just three minutes remaining.

NORTH AFRICAN COUNTRIES' BEST FIFA WORLD CUP PERFORMANCES

ALGERIA: First round 1982, 1986, 2010
EGYPT: First round 1934, 1990
MOROCCO: Second round 2006
TUNISIA: First round 1978, 1998, 2002, 2006

NORTH AFRICAN COUNTRIES' FIFA WORLD CUP QUALIFICATIONS

ALGERIA: 3 (1982, 1986, 2010)
EGYPT: 2 (1934, 1990)
MOROCCO: 4 (1970, 1986, 1994, 1998)
TUNISIA: 4 (1978, 1998, 2002, 2006)

NORTH AFRICA: TOP FIFA WORLD CUP GOALSCORERS

Salah Assad (Algeria) 2
Salaheddine Bassir (Morocco) 2
Abdelrahman Fawzi (Egypt) 2
Abdeljalil Hadda (Morocco) 2
Abderrazak Khairi (Morocco) 2

NO WAITING GAME

Morocco's 2-1 defeat to Saudi Arabia in 1994 was one of the last two games to be played simultaneously at a FIFA World Cup, without falling on a final match-day of a group. Belgium were beating Holland 1-0 at the same time, with every team in Group F having still one game to play. At later tournaments, every match has been played separately until the climactic two fixtures of any group.

HOMEGROWN HERO

Of the six African countries at the 2010 FIFA World Cup, Algeria's was the only squad with an African coach – **Rabah Saadane**, in his fifth separate stint in charge since 1981. He previously led his country to the 1986 FIFA World Cup in Mexico, where they were also eliminated in the first round. Along with Honduras, the Algeria team of 2010 were one of only two countries failing to score a single goal. However, they did concede just twice in their three games: 1-0 defeats to Slovakia and the USA, and a surprise goalless draw with England – Algeria's first-ever FIFA World Cup clean sheet.

MOKHTAR RUNS AMOK

Egypt had to play only two matches to qualify for the 1934 FIFA World Cup, becoming the first African representatives at the tournament. Both games were against a Palestine side under the British mandate – and the Egyptians won both games handsomely, 7-1 in Cairo and 4-1 in Palestine. Captain and striker Mahmoud Mokhtar scored a hat-trick in the first leg, a brace in the second. Turkey were also meant to contest qualifiers against the two sides, but withdrew, leaving the path to the finals free for Egypt.

TUNISIA IN TUNE

Tunisia became the first African team to win a match at a FIFA World Cup finals, when they beat Mexico 3-1 in Rosario, Argentina, in 1978 – thanks to goals from Ali Kaabi, Nejib Ghommidh and Mokhtar Dhouib. While they share with Morocco the North African record of reaching four different FIFA World Cups, they are the only nation from that part of the continent to qualify for three finals in a row – in 1998, 2002 and 2006. Among the players to feature in all three tournaments were 2006 captain Riadh Bouazizi, Hatem Trabelsi and **Radhi Jaidi**.

THANKS, PAL

Hungarian Pal Titkos became the first foreign coach to win the Africa Cup of Nations when he led Egypt to their second triumph in 1959. One Briton has achieved the feat: English-born former Wales manager **Mike Smith** coached Egypt to the title in 1986.

ABOUD AWAKENING

After the political upheaval in Libya in 2011, little was expected of the country's footballers at the 2012 Africa Cup of Nations. Yet they brought some joy to supporters with a surprise 2-1 victory over Senegal in their final first-round match – the first time Libya had ever won an Africa Cup of Nations match outside their own country. Their kit bore the new flag of the country's National Transitional Council. Among the star performers were Ihaab al Boussefi – scorer of both goals against Senegal – and goalkeeper and captain **Samir Aboud**, at 39 the oldest player at the tournament. Libya played their first competitive home game in the capital Tripoli since 2010 when they hosted the Democratic Republic of Congo in a 2014 FIFA World Cup qualifier in June 2013, the game ending in a 0-0 draw.

OFFICIAL INFLUENCE

The first African to referee a FIFA World Cup final was Morocco's **Said Belqola**, who controlled the 1998 climax in which hosts France beat Brazil 3-0. Perhaps his most notable moment was sending off France's **Marcel Desailly** in the 68th minute – brandishing only the third red card to be shown in a FIFA World Cup final. Belqola was 41 at the time. He died from cancer just under four years later.

FOUNDING FATHERS

The Confederation of African Football was officially established at a meeting in the Sudanese capital Khartoum, in the city's Grand Hotel on 7 February 1957 – three days before the first Africa Cup of Nations kicked off in the same city. Representatives of Sudan, South Africa, Ethiopia and Egypt were present at the first assembly, and Egypt's Abdel Aziz Salem became CAF's first president.

SUDAN IMPACT

After two second-place and one third-place finishes, Sudan became the third and last of the Africa Cup of Nations founders to lift the trophy, when they beat Ghana in the 1970 final. Hosts Sudan left it late to reach the final, with two goals from El-Issed – the second 12 minutes into extra-time – seeing off Egypt. The same player scored the only goal of the final, after 12 minutes.

NORTH AFRICA: SELECTED TOP GOALSCORERS

ALGERIA: Abdelhafid Tasfaout	34	
EGYPT: Hossam Hassan	69	
LIBYA: Tarik El Taib	23	
MOROCCO: Ahmed Faras	42	
SUDAN: Haytham Tambal	26	
TUNISIA: Issam Jemaa	34	

THE BLACK EAGLES HAVE LANDED

The Confederation of African Football welcomed a new and 54th member state on 10 February 2012, when the newly-independent nation of South Sudan created a new team and football association. The "Black Eagles" were not admitted in time to take part in qualifiers for the 2013 Africa Cup of Nations but hope to take part in future events – and win FIFA membership as well. Football association president Oliver Benjamin said: "We are a country that has just come out of war. We lack even the balls and the T-shirts – we don't have these in our country. Some of our players use their socks, put clothes in them, wrap them up and play with them. That is our love of football."

SALAH DAYS

Egypt have a rising star in **Mohamed Salah,** who has scored 14 goals in 22 senior appearances since making his debut, aged 18, against Sierra Leone in September 2011. His first goal came a month later in a 3-0 defeat of Niger. Salah played in all four matches at the London 2012 Olympic Games, scoring in each of the first-round ties, before Japan won 3-0 in the quarter-final. In June 2013, a week before he turned 21, he grabbed a hat-trick as Zimbabwe were beaten 4-2 in a FIFA World Cup 2014 qualifier. His performances at London 2012 earned Salah the African Football Confederation's Most Promising Talent of the Year award.

HEAD–TO–HEAD

The international career of Algeria's leading scorer **Abdelhafid Tasfaout** came to an end at the 2002 Africa Cup of Nations – though it could have been a lot worse. Tasfaout was knocked out by a collision with Mali defender Boubacar Diarra which caused him to swallow his tongue, prompting fears he might not even survive – though, thankfully, he did recover. Tasfaout, who played French league football for six years, scored 34 goals in 62 games for Algeria between 1990 and 2002.

SORE LOSERS

Libya could claim the record for highest-scoring victory by an African side, having racked up a 21-0 lead over Oman during the Arab Nations Cup in April 1966. But the Oman players walked off with 10 minutes remaining, in protest at Libya being awarded a penalty, and played no further part in the competition.

NORTH AFRICA: SELECTED TOP APPEARANCES

ALGERIA: Lakhdar Belloumi	101
EGYPT: Ahmed Hassan	184
LIBYA: Tarik El Taib	77
MOROCCO: Abdelmajid Dolmy	140
SUDAN: Haitham Mustafa	124
TUNISIA: Sadok Sassi	110

STRIKING RIVALS

A homegrown hero is back at the top of Tunisia's scoring ranks after Gabes-born **Issam Jemaa** overtook Francileudo Santos and now has 34 goals from 73 appearances since his debut in 2005. Jemma began his career with Esperance but since 2005 has played his club football in France, for Lens and Auxerre. Brazil-born Santos, by contrast, did not visit Tunisia until his late teens and only accepted citizenship at the age of 24 in 2004. Within weeks he was helping his new nation not only to host but win the 2004 Africa Cup of Nations, scoring four goals including the opener in the final against Morocco. Both Jemaa and Santos were hampered by injury ahead of the 2006 FIFA World Cup – Santos played only 11 minutes at the tournament, while Jemaa missed out all together. He has recovered to continue scoring ever since, including the winner against Niger at the 2012 Africa Cup of Nations.

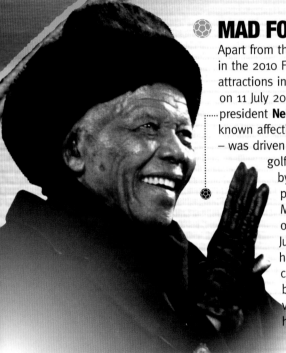

MAD FOR 'MADIBA'

Apart from the Dutch and Spanish sides competing in the 2010 FIFA World Cup final, one of the star attractions in Johannesburg's Soccer City stadium on 11 July 2010 was South Africa's legendary former president **Nelson Mandela**. The frail 91-year-old – known affectionately by his tribal name of "Madiba" – was driven on to the pitch before the game in a golf cart and given a rapturous reception by the crowd. It marked his one and only public appearance at the tournament. Mandela had hoped to attend the opening ceremony and game on 11 June, but was mourning the death of his 13-year-old great-granddaughter in a car crash the previous evening. He had been a high-profile presence at the FIFA vote in 2004 which awarded South Africa hosting rights for 2010.

GOING FOR A SONG

Two players have been sent off at two separate FIFA World Cups: Cameroon's Rigobert Song, against Brazil in 1994 and Chile four years later, and France's Zinedine Zidane – red-carded against Saudi Arabia in 1998 and against Italy in the 2006 final. Song's red card against Brazil made him the youngest player to be dismissed at a FIFA World Cup – he was just 17 years and 358 days old. Song, born in Nkanglikock on 1 July 1976, is Cameroon's most-capped player, with 137 appearances – including winning displays in the 2000 and 2002 finals of the Africa Cup of Nations. He has been joined in the national team by his nephew, Arsenal utility player Alexandre Song Billong.

LIONS TAMED

Cameroon's third and final game at the 2010 FIFA World Cup, a 2-1 defeat to Holland, made them the first African country to play as many as 20 FIFA World Cup matches. But there was little to celebrate this time around – the "Indomitable Lions", coached by Frenchman Paul Le Guen, had already become the first team eliminated from the 2010 competition.

JOLLY ROGER

Cameroon striker **Roger Milla**, famous for dancing around corner flags after each goal, became the FIFA World Cup's oldest scorer against Russia in 1994 – aged 42 years and 39 days. He came on as substitute during that tournament with his surname handwritten, rather than printed, on the back of his shirt. Milla, born in Yaounde on 20 May 1952, had retired from professional football for a year before Cameroon's president, Paul Biya, persuaded him to join the 1990 FIFA World Cup squad. His goals in that tournament helped him win the African Footballer of the Year award for an unprecedented second time – 14 years after he had first received the trophy. He finally ended his international career after the 1994 FIFA World Cup in the United States, finishing with 102 caps and 28 goals to his name.

SUB–SAHARAN AFRICAN COUNTRIES' BEST FIFA WORLD CUP PERFORMANCES

ANGOLA: First round 2006
CAMEROON: Quarter-finals 1990
GHANA: Quarter-finals 2010
IVORY COAST: First round 2006, 2010
NIGERIA: Second round 1994, 1998
SENEGAL: Quarter-finals 2002
SOUTH AFRICA: First round 1998, 2002, 2010
TOGO: First round 2006
ZAIRE/CONGO DR: First round 1974

SUB–SAHARAN AFRICAN COUNTRIES' FIFA WORLD CUP QUALIFICATIONS

CAMEROON: 6 (1982, 1990, 1994, 1998, 2002, 2010)
NIGERIA: 4 (1994, 1998, 2002, 2010)
SOUTH AFRICA: 3 (1998, 2002, 2010)
GHANA: 2 (2006, 2010)
IVORY COAST: 2 (2006, 2010)
ANGOLA: 1 (2006)
SENEGAL: 1 (2002)
TOGO: 1 (2006)
ZAIRE/CONGO DR: 1 (1974)

HENRI AND IVORY

The Ivory Coast were widely considered unfortunate to go out in the first round of their first FIFA World Cup, in 2006, having been drawn in the "group of death" alongside Argentina and Holland. A side starring **Didier Drogba**, Didier Zokora and brothers Kolo and Yaya Toure was managed by Frenchman Henri Michel, who was coaching at a fourth FIFA World Cup with a fourth different country. He had previously led France in 1986, Cameroon in 1994 and Morocco in 1998. Only Bora Milutinovic and Carlos Alberto Parreira have taken more different teams to FIFA World Cups. The same "group of death" nickname was given to the Ivory Coast's group in 2010, when they faced Brazil, Portugal and North Korea, and again finished third.

RATOMIR GETS IT RIGHT

Ghana went through four different managers during qualifiers for the 2006 FIFA World Cup, with Serbian coach Ratomir Dujkovic finally clinching the country a place at the finals for the very first time. He led them through the whole of 2005 unbeaten, winning a FIFA prize for being the most-improved team of the year. Ghana were the only African country to make it through the first round of both the 2006 and 2010 FIFA World Cups, despite having the youngest average age of any squad each time. They were again coached by a Serb in 2010, this time Milovan Rajevac.

BROTHERS AT ARMS

Two Boateng brothers were on the pitch at the same time when Germany played Ghana at the 2010 FIFA World Cup – but on opposing sides, a FIFA World Cup first. Jerome was playing left-back for Germany, while elder half-brother **Kevin-Prince** was in the Ghana midfield – having officially switched nationality just a month before the tournament. Both were born in the German capital Berlin, and have the same German mother but different Ghanaian fathers. Kevin-Prince had an extra effect on the 2010 FIFA World Cup in South Africa, through his tackle on German captain Michael Ballack in the May 2010 FA Cup final in England. Ballack was so badly injured that he had to be substituted and missed the World Cup altogether.

SUB–SAHARAN AFRICAN COUNTRIES: TOP FIFA WORLD CUP GOALSCORERS

Roger Milla (Cameroon) 5
Asamoah Gyan (Ghana) 4
Papa Bouba Diop (Senegal) 3
Samuel Eto'o (Cameroon) 3
Daniel Amokachi (Nigeria) 2
Emmanuel Amunike (Nigeria) 2
Shaun Bartlett (South Africa) 2
Henri Camara (Senegal) 2
Aruna Dindane (Ivory Coast) 2
Didier Drogba (Ivory Coast) 2
Patrick Mboma (Cameroon) 2
Benni McCarthy (South Africa) 2
Sulley Muntari (Ghana) 2
Francois Omam-Biyik (Cameroon) 2

HORN OF AFRICA

Colombian pop star Shakira sang the official 2010 FIFA World Cup anthem, which she performed at both an official tournament-opening concert and the closing ceremony. But perhaps an even more distinctive sound that summer was the din of the vuvuzelas – the plastic horns that have been a feature of South African football matches since the 1980s and were a must-have for many fans attending FIFA World Cup fixtures. Some players – including Argentina's Lionel Messi and Portugal's Cristiano Ronaldo – complained that the constant drone was distracting, though others such as England's Jamie Carragher and Holland's Wesley Sneijder spoke up in the horns' defence. FIFA and the South African tournament organizers resisted calls for the instruments to be banned, while some television channels made technical arrangements to turn down the vuvuzelas' volume.

'BAFANA BAFANA' BACK 'BAGHANA BAGHANA'

Despite missing injured midfielder Michael Essien, Ghana were the only African side to survive the first round of the 2010 FIFA World Cup – and received exuberant support from home fans in South Africa as they reached the quarter-finals. Ghana's footballers, traditionally known as the "Black Stars", were renamed "Africa's Stars" by some – or "BaGhana BaGhana", playing on South Africa's nickname "Bafana Bafana", which means "The Boys, The Boys".

SUB-SAHARAN AFRICA NATIONAL RECORDS

HOT DROG

Didier Drogba may have been raised in France but he was born in Ivory Coast and remains one of the African country's favourite sons for his actions both on and off the pitch. The Ivory Coast captain has a record 60 goals in 95 appearances for the Elephants. He has been credited with influence off the pitch, too, when he called for a ceasefire in the civil war-torn nation. He also pushed for an Africa Cup of Nations qualifier against Madagascar in June 2007 to be moved from the capital Abidjan to rebel army stronghold Bouake, in an effort to encourage reconciliation. Drogba, a two-time CAF African Footballer of the Year, captained the Ivory Coast team at the two FIFA World Cups they have reached, in 2006 and 2010.

SUB–SAHARAN AFRICA: SELECTED TOP GOALSCORERS

Country	Player	Goals
ANGOLA:	Akwa	36
BOTSWANA:	Dipsy Selolwane	16
CAMEROON:	Samuel Eto'o	55
GHANA:	Asamoah Gyan	35
IVORY COAST:	Didier Drogba	60
NIGERIA:	Rashidi Yekini	37
SENEGAL:	Henri Camara	29
SOUTH AFRICA:	Benni McCarthy	32
TOGO:	Emmanuel Adabayor	27
ZAMBIA:	Godfrey Chitalu	78
ZIMBABWE:	Peter Ndlovu	38

KNOCKED OUT ON PENALTIES

Botswana goalkeeper and captain Modiri Marumo was sent off in the middle of a penalty shoot-out against Malawi in May 2003, after punching the opposing goalkeeper Philip Nyasulu in the face. Botswana defender Michael Mogaladi had to go in goal for the rest of the shoot-out, which Malawi won 4-1.

FIFTEEN LOVE

Fifteen-year-old Samuel Kuffour became the youngest footballer to win an Olympic medal when Ghana took bronze at the 1992 Olympics in Barcelona – 27 days before his 16th birthday.

EAGLETS SOAR

The first African country to win an official FIFA tournament was Nigeria, when their "Golden Eaglets" beat Germany 2-0 in the final of the 1985 World Under-17 Championships.

SO LONG, PITSO

South Africa went through four different foreign coaches – in five separate spells – between 2004 and 2010 before the top job went to South African Pitso Mosimane. He had previously won four caps as a player, then assisted Brazilian Carlos Alberto Parreira at the 2010 FIFA World Cup. Mosimane's first nine games in charge brought six wins, two draws and just one defeat, but he lost the post in 2012 after a winless nine-game streak cost South Africa the chance of competing at the 2014 FIFA World Cup and was replaced by Gordon Igesund.

GENEROUS GEORGE

In 1995 Liberia's George Weah became the first African to be named FIFA World Player of the Year, an award that recognized his prolific goalscoring exploits for Paris Saint-Germain and AC Milan. That same year he added the European Footballer of the Year and African Footballer of the Year prizes to his collection. Weah not only captained his country, but often funded the team's travels – though he remains the only FIFA World Player of the Year whose country has never qualified for a FIFA World Cup. After retiring in 2003 after 60 caps and 22 international goals, he moved into politics and ran unsuccessfully for the Liberian presidency in 2005.

SUPER FRED

In 2007, **Frederic Kanoute** became the first non-African-born player to be named African Footballer of the Year. The striker was born in Lyon, France, and played for France U-21s. But the son of a French mother and Malian father opted to play for Mali in 2004, scoring 23 goals in 37 appearances before retiring from international football after the 2010 Africa Cup of Nations. As well as going down in history as one of Mali's greatest-ever players, he is also a hero to fans of Spanish side CF Sevilla, for whom he scored 143 goals, winning two UEFA Cups along the way. Only three men have scored more goals for the club.

SUB–SAHARAN AFRICA: SELECTED TOP APPEARANCES

ANGOLA: Akwa	80
BOTSWANA: Dipsy Selolwane	42
CAMEROON: Rigobert Song	137
GHANA: Richard Kingson	90
IVORY COAST: Didier Zokora	113
NIGERIA: Joseph Yobo	95
SENEGAL: Henri Camara	99
SOUTH AFRICA: Aaron Mokoena	107
TOGO: Dare Nibombe	71
ZAMBIA: David Chabala	108
ZIMBABWE: Peter Ndlovu	100

DRAMATIC TURNAROUNDS

Ghana managed to concede three goals in a minute to world champions Germany in an April 1993 friendly. Ghana had been 1-0 up with 20 minutes left, before losing the game 6-1. In the 1989 FIFA World Youth Championships, Nigeria were 4-0 down with 25 minutes left in their quarter-final against the Soviet Union, but hit back to draw 4-4 before winning 5-3 on penalties.

QUICKFIRE KONATE

Senegal forward **Pape Moussa Konate** scored five goals in four appearances at the 2012 Summer Olympics in London – at a rate of one goal every 76 minutes – as his team reached the quarter-finals. The 19-year-old became the first man to score in his opening four Olympic football matches since the Soviet Union's Fyodor Cherenkov in Moscow in 1980.

ASIA & OCEANIA

Asia carved out a major place in footballing history in 2002 when South Korea and Japan became the first co-hosts of a FIFA World Cup – and the South Koreans marked the moment by also becoming Asia's first semi-finalists, losing to Germany, then to Turkey in the third-place play-off. There have been further good showings since then, not only by South Korea and Japan, but also by North Korea and Australia. Surprisingly, the billion-plus populations of India and China have yet to make a lasting mark, and neither will feature at Brazil 2014.

Keisuke Honda scored the goal that made Japan the first country – aside from hosts Brazil – to qualify for the 2014 FIFA World Cup, amid rising hopes for both his own nation and Asia as a whole.

AUSTRALIA

Victims, perhaps, of an overcomplicated qualifying system that has limited the country's FIFA World Cup finals appearances, and hampered by its geographical isolation that, in the early years, saw other sports prosper in the country at football's expense, it has taken many years for Australia to establish itself on the world football map. However, driven by a new generation of players, many based with top European clubs, the Socceroos delivered for the first time at the 2006 FIFA World Cup and are now the No. 1 ranked team in Asia.

NATIVE HERO

Harry Williams holds a proud place in Australian football history as the first Aboriginal player to represent the country in internationals. He made his debut in 1970 and was part of the first Australian squad to compete at a FIFA World Cup finals, in West Germany in 1974.

MOMENTOUS MORI

Damian Mori's Australian record tally of 29 goals, in just 45 internationals, included no fewer than five hat-tricks: trebles against Fiji and Tahiti, four-goal hauls against the Cook Islands and Tonga, and five in Australia's 13-0 trouncing of the Solomon Islands in a 1998 FIFA World Cup qualifier. His international career spanned from 1992 to 2002, but he never played in a FIFA World Cup finals as Australia didn't qualify. He did, though, claim a world record for scoring the fastest goal – after just 3.69 seconds for his club side Adelaide City against Sydney United in 1996.

AUSTRALIA RECORDS

Honours: Oceania champions 1980, 1996, 2000, 2004
First international: v New Zealand (lost 3-1), Auckland, 17 June 1922
Biggest win: 31-0 v American Samoa, Coffs Harbour, 11 April 2001
Biggest defeat: 7-0 v Croatia, Zagreb, 6 June 1998

NEILL APPEAL

Tough-tackling Australia veteran **Lucas Neill** had to wait until his 91st international appearance before scoring his first goal for his country: the final strike in a 4-0 victory over Jordan in June 2013 that boosted their chances of reaching the 2014 FIFA World Cup. Qualification was clinched in the next game, thanks to a lone goal by Josh Kennedy to defeat Iraq – making Australia the third team, after hosts Brazil and Japan, to secure a place at the finals. Former Blackburn Rovers, West Ham United and Galatasary defender Neill made his Australia debut in October 1996, becoming the country's third-youngest international. His scoring record, though, pales alongside that of fellow centre-back Robbie Cornthwaite, his goal against Romania in February 2013 was his third in his first six games for Australia.

TOP CAPS

1	Mark Schwarzer	108
2	Brett Emerton	95
3	Lucas Neill	92
4	Alex Tobin	87
5	Paul Wade	84
6	Luke Wilkshire	78
7	Tony Vidmar	76
8	Mark Bresciano	69
9	Scott Chipperfield	68
10	Peter Wilson	64

CAHILL MAKES HISTORY

Tim Cahill netted Australia's first-ever FIFA World Cup finals goal when he scored an 84th-minute equalizer against Japan in Kaiserslautern on 12 June 2006. Cahill added another five minutes later and John Aloisi struck in stoppage time to give the Socceroos a 3-1 win – their only victory in the finals. Australia later lost 2-0 to Brazil and drew 2-2 with Croatia to qualify from their group. Cahill found the net three times in 2014 FIFA World Cup qualifiers, taking him only one behind Damien Mori in Australia's all-time goalscoring list.

AUSTRALIA'S SHOOT-OUT RECORD

Australia are the only team to reach the FIFA World Cup finals via a penalty shoot-out – in the final qualifying play-off in November 2005. They had lost the first leg 1-0 to Uruguay in Montevideo. Mark Bresciano's goal levelled the aggregate score, which remained 1-1 after extra-time. Goalkeeper **Mark Schwarzer** made two crucial saves as Australia won the shoot-out 4-2, with John Aloisi scoring the winning spot-kick. Schwarzer passed Alex Tobin to become Australia's most-capped footballer with his 88th appearance, in January 2011, in the AFC Asian Cup final defeat to Japan. Tobin had been in defence when Schwarzer made his Australia debut against Canada in 1993.

COME TO A LAND DOWN UNDER

After reaching the quarter-finals of their first AFC Asian Cup in 2007 and finishing runners-up to Japan four years later, Australia will want to make it third time lucky at the 2015 tournament – especially as this time the country will be playing host. Australia was the only country to bid for staging rights.

THREE-CARD TRICK

Graham Poll, in 2006, was not the first referee at a FIFA World Cup to show the same player three yellow cards. It happened in another game involving Australia, when their English-born midfielder Ray Richards was belatedly sent off against Chile at the 1974 FIFA World Cup. Reserve official Clive Thomas, from Wales, informed Iranian referee Jafar Namdar he had booked Richards three times without dismissing him. Richards played four unwarranted minutes before eventually receiving his marching orders.

PRECEDENT KENNEDY

Australian newspapers acclaimed a player nicknamed "Jesus" as their "saviour" when Josh Kennedy's 83rd-minute goal against Iraq in June 2013 clinched a place at the 2014 FIFA World Cup for his country – ensuring a third consecutive appearance at the finals. Lofty striker Kennedy, given the nickname for his former styling of long hair and a beard, had entered the field just six minutes earlier as a replacement for Tim Cahill. It was his 16th – and most significant – goal in 30 appearances for Australia.

BET ON BRETT

Brett Holman's goal against Ghana, in a 1-1 draw at the 2010 tournament, made him Australia's youngest marksman at a FIFA World Cup. He was 26 years 84 days old at the time, 105 days younger than Tim Cahill had been when striking against Japan in 2006. Holman added to his tally five days later, when Australia beat Serbia 2-1. Cahill himself was also on the scoresheet, though goal difference meant Australia failed to reach the second round.

TOP SCORERS

1	Damian Mori	29
2	Tim Cahill	28
=	Archie Thompson	28
4	John Aloisi	27
5	Attila Abonyi	25
=	John Kosima	25
7	Brett Emerton	20
=	David Zdrilic	20
9	Graham Arnold	19
10	Ray Baartz	18

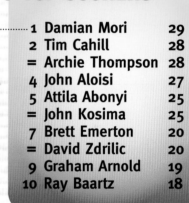

KEWELL THE TOPS

Harry Kewell (born on 22 September 1978) is widely regarded as Australia's best-ever player. The left winger has scored 13 goals in 39 international appearances, including the equalizer against Croatia that took Australia to the last 16 of the 2006 FIFA World Cup finals. Kewell has enjoyed a successful club career with Leeds United, Liverpool and Galatasaray. He is also the only Australian-born player to gain a Champions League winner's medal, with Liverpool in 2005. He endured an unhappier time at the 2010 FIFA World Cup, when he lasted just 22 minutes before being red-carded for handball against Ghana – the 150th sending-off in the history of the finals.

JAPAN

The past two decades have seen great breakthroughs for Japanese football. Until the first professional league was introduced in 1993, clubs had been amateur and football was overshadowed in Japan's affections by other sports such as baseball, martial arts, table tennis and golf. Even more significantly, Japan co-hosted the 2002 FIFA World Cup – where the team reached the second round for the first time. And AFC Asian Cup wins in 1992, 2000, 2004 and 2011 were celebrated keenly as proof of surging standards.

TOP SCORERS

1	Kunishige Kamamoto	55
=	Kazuyoshi Miura	55
3	Hiromi Hara	37
4	Shinji Okazaki	35
5	Takuya Takagi	27
6	Kazushi Kimura	26
7	Shunsuke Nakamura	24
8	Naohiro Takahara	23
9	Masashi Nakayama	21
10	Teruki Miyamoto	18

NAKATA BLAZES THE TRAIL

Hidetoshi Nakata ranks among Japan's best-ever players. The midfielder set up all three goals in a 3-2 FIFA World Cup qualifying play-off win over Iran in November 1997. Nakata moved to Perugia in Italy after the 1998 finals, becoming the first Japanese player to star in Europe, and won a Serie A championship medal with Roma in 2001. He was followed abroad by international team-mates such as Shinji Ono, who joined Feyenoord in the Netherlands, and midfielder Shunsuke Nakamura, whose European employers included Reggina in Italy, Celtic in Scotland and Espanyol in Spain. Nakata started in three FIFA World Cup finals tournaments, making ten appearances and scoring one goal – the second in a 2-0 win over Tunisia that took Japan to the last 16 in 2002. Nakata won 77 caps and scored 11 goals, before surprisingly retiring from all forms of football after the 2006 FIFA World Cup, aged just 29.

POLITICAL FOOTBALL

Japan were surprise bronze medallists in the football tournament at the 1968 summer Olympics in Mexico City, and star striker **Kunishige Kamamoto** finished top scorer overall with seven goals. He remains Japan's all-time leading scorer, with 76 goals in 75 matches. Since retirement, he has combined coaching with being elected to Japan's parliament and serving as vice-president of the country's football association.

HONDA INSPIRES

After hosts Brazil, Japan were the first country to qualify for the 2014 FIFA World Cup, after Keisuke Honda's stoppage-time penalty secured a 1-1 draw with Australia in June 2013. CSKA forward Honda had previously won two man-of-the-match awards at the 2010 FIFA World Cup and was named player of the tournament when Japan won the 2011 AFC Asian Cup. Since 2010, Japan have been coached by Alberto Zaccheroni. The veteran Italian succeeded Takeshi Okada, who had spoken of wanting to leave football behind to become a farmer, declaring: "When it rains, I'll read a book, and when it's fine, I'll work on the farm."

TOP CAPS

1	Yasuhito Endo	133
2	Masami Ihara	122
3	Yoshikatsu Kawaguchi	116
4	Yuji Nakazawa	110
5	Shunsuke Nakamura	98
6	Kazuyoshi Miura	89
7	Junichi Inamoto	82
=	Alessandro Santos	82
9	Satoshi Tsunami	78
10	Hidetoshi Nakata	77
=	Seigo Narazaki	77

YOU'RE BARRED

Japan achieved their first-ever FIFA World Cup victory on foreign soil at the 2010 tournament in South Africa, and reached the knock-out stages for the first time away from home as well. Their penalty shoot-out against Paraguay in the second round was the first in FIFA World Cup history that did not feature at least one European country. The shoot-out was the first of the 2010 tournament and the 21st overall. Paraguay won 5-3 on penalties after the match had ended goalless after extra-time. Japanese full-back Yuichi Komano was the only taker to miss, hitting the bar with his spot-kick.

THREE AND IN

Japan's 3-1 Group E victory over Denmark in Bloemfontein at the 2010 FIFA World Cup made them the first Asian side to score three times in one FIFA World Cup match since North Korea's 5-3 defeat to Portugal in their 1966 quarter-final. Japan's goals came from Keisuke Honda, Yasuhito Endo and Shinji Okazaki. Honda and Endo both scored directly from free-kicks, the first time a team has managed such a double in one FIFA World Cup game since Yugoslavia hit three when beating Zaire 9-0 in 1974. Endo has gone on to become Japan's most-capped player, surpassing Masami Ihara's tally by appearing in an October 2012 friendly against Brazil.

SHINJI BENEFITS

Playmaker **Shinji Kagawa** became the first Japanese footballer to be part of an English league championship-winning side, when securing the Premier League title with Manchester United in 2012–13 – 12 months after helping his former club Borussia Dortmund win the Bundesliga in Germany. Kagawa was named 2012 AFC International Player of the Year. Yet he suffered for his art during Japan's triumphant 2011 AFC Asian Cup campaign, scoring twice in their victorious quarter-final but breaking his foot in the next game and thus missing the final.

TA–DA, TADANARI

The goalscoring hero whose extra-time strike clinched a record fourth AFC Asian Cup for Japan in 2011 was a man who had not even played for his country before the tournament began. Striker **Tadanari Lee** made his international debut in the first-round match against Jordan – and conjured perfect timing for his first Japan goal, with 11 minutes of extra-time left in the final against Australia. His midfield team-mate Kaisuke Honda took the prize for the event's most valuable player, while forward Shinji Okazaki's first-round hat-trick against Saudi Arabia helped earn him a place in the team of the tournament.

JAPANESE GOAL GLUT

No team have scored more goals in one AFC Asian Cup tournament than Japan's 21 in six games on their way to winning the title for the second time, in Lebanon in 2000 – though the final against Saudi Arabia was settled with just a single goal, by Shigeyoshi Mochizuki. Nine different players scored for Japan during the tournament – including Akinori Nishizawa and Naohiro Takahara, who each managed five – while their team-mate Ryuzo Morioka scored once in his own net. Japan's most emphatic victory of the tournament came in the first round, 8-1 against Uzbekistan, with both Nishizawa and Takahara hitting hat-tricks.

SOUTH KOREA

"Be the Reds!" was the rallying cry of South Korea's fervent fans as they co-hosted the 2002 FIFA World Cup – and saw their energetic team become the first Asian side to reach the semi-finals, ultimately finishing fourth. South Korea also won the AFC Asian Cup the first two times it was staged (in 1956 and 1960). South Korea could well claim to be the continent's leading football side, even if AFC Asian Cup triumphs have been thin on the ground since then. The country's professional K-League is making progress and South Korean teams have won the Asian club championship 10 times.

HIDDINK THE SOUTH KOREAN HERO

Dutchman **Guus Hiddink** is Asia's most successful national coach. The former PSV Eindhoven and Holland coach took charge of South Korea in late 2000. He changed the team approach, and experimented in friendlies because, as co-hosts, they had automatically qualified for the 2002 FIFA World Cup. Home fans and media hoped South Korea might make it out of the first round for the first time ever. Their team did far better than that: topping their group, eliminating Italy in the second round and reaching the semi-finals with a shoot-out win over Spain, where they lost 1-0 to Germany and then went down 3-2 in the third-place play-off against Turkey. Fourth place was still the best-ever finish for an Asian team. Hiddink was rewarded by becoming the first foreigner to be made an honorary South Korean citizen, and the stadium at Gwangju was renamed in his honour.

HWANG'S THE MAN

A rare veteran among South Korea's young guns at the 2002 FIFA World Cup was 33-year-old **Hwang Sun-Hong**, after Cha Bum-Kun the only other player to score a half-century of goals for the country. His 50th goal came in the 2-0 win over Poland that clinched South Korea's place in the second round. Hwang had also played in the 1990 and 1994 FIFA World Cups, but missed the 1998 event through injury. Eight of Hwang's goals came in one game, an 11-0 crushing of Nepal in October 1994. South Korea's record victory was also against poor Nepal, in September 2003 – this time ending 16-0, with five for Park Jin-Sub and three apiece for Woo Sung-Yong and Kim Do-Hoon.

SPIDER CATCHER

Goalkeeper **Lee Woon-Jae** – nicknamed "Spider Hands" – made himself a national hero by making the crucial penalty save that took co-hosts South Korea into the semi-finals of the 2002 FIFA World Cup. He blocked Spain's fourth spot-kick, taken by winger Joaquin, in a quarter-final shoot-out. Lee, who also played in the 1994, 2006 and 2010 FIFA World Cups, provided more penalty saves at the 2007 AFC Asian Cup – stopping three spot-kicks in shoot-outs on South Korea's way to third place. Lee's form restricted his frequent back-up, Kim Byung-Ji, to just 62 international appearances. But Kim did at least set a new South Korean top-flight landmark of 200 clean sheets in June 2012, at the age of 42.

PARK LIFE

The tirelessly-energetic midfielder **Park Ji-Sung** can claim to be the most successful Asian footballer of all time. He became the first Asian player to lift the UEFA Champions League trophy when his club Manchester United beat Chelsea in 2008, despite missing the final. He also became the first Asian footballer to score at three successive FIFA World Cups – beginning on home turf in 2002, when his goal broke the deadlock in a first-round game against Portugal, putting South Korea through to the knock-out stages for the first time ever. International team-mate Ahn Jung-Hwan and Saudi Arabia's Sami Al-Jaber are the only other Asian footballers to have scored three FIFA World Cup goals. Park became the eighth South Korean to reach a century of caps when he captained the side in their 2011 AFC Asian Cup semi-final defeat to Japan, before announcing his international retirement to allow a younger generation to emerge.

TOP CAPS

1	Hong Myung-Bo	136
2	Lee Woon-Jae	132
3	Lee Young-Pyo	127
4	Yoo Sang-Chul	122
5	Cha Bum-Kun	121
6	Kim Tae-Young	105
7	Hwang Sun-Hong	103
8	Park Ji-Sung	100
9	Kim Nam-Il	97
=	Lee Dong-Gook	97

TOP SCORERS

1	Cha Bum-Kun	55
2	Hwang Sun-Hong	50
3	Park Lee-Chun	36
4	Kim Jae-Han	33
5	Kim Do-Hoon	30
=	Lee Dong-Gook	30
=	Choi Soon-Ho	30
8	Huh Jung-Moo	29
9	Choi Yong-Soo	27
10	Park Chu-Young	23

HONG SETS FIFA WORLD CUP RECORD

South Korea defender **Hong Myung-Bo** was the first Asian footballer to appear in four consecutive FIFA World Cup finals tournaments. He played all three games as South Korea lost to Belgium, Spain and Uruguay in 1990. He scored twice in three appearances in 1994 – his goal against Spain sparking a Korean fightback from 2-0 down to draw 2-2. In 1998 he started all three group games as South Korea were eliminated at the group stage. Four years later, on home soil, he captained South Korea to fourth place in the finals and was voted third-best player of the tournament. Hong coached South Korea's U-23 side to Olympic bronze at the 2012 Summer Games – beating Japan 2-0 in the medal play-off – and was put in charge of South Korea's senior team in June 2013. The goals against Japan were scored by Arsenal's Park Chu-Young and WfL Wolfsburg Koo Ja-Cheol, but midfielder Park Jong-Woo was barred from the prize ceremony after parading a provocative political banner after the match – and only received his bronze medal in February 2013.

CHA BOOM AND BUST

Even before South Korea made their FIFA World Cup breakthrough under Guus Hiddink, the country had a homegrown hero of world renown – thunderous striker **Cha Bum-Kun**, known for his fierce shots and suitable nickname "Cha Boom". He helped pave the way for more Asian players to make their name in Europe by signing for German club Eintracht Frankfurt in 1979 and later played for Bundesliga rivals Bayer Leverkusen. His achievements in Germany included two UEFA Cup triumphs – with Frankfurt in 1980 and with Leverkusen eight years later – while his performances helped make him a childhood idol for future German internationals such as Jurgen Klinsmann and Michael Ballack. His record 55 goals for the national team, in 121 appearances, included a seven-minute hat-trick against Malaysia in the 1977 Park's Cup tournament – levelling the score after South Korea had been trailing 4-1. "Cha Boom" later served as national coach, winning 22, losing 11 and drawing eight during his time in charge between January 1997 and June 1998 – but there was an unhappy ending when he was sacked two games into the 1998 FIFA World Cup, after South Korea's 5-0 defeat to the Netherlands.

OTHER ASIAN COUNTRIES

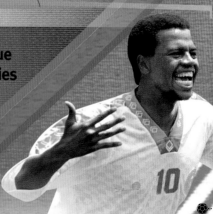

The lesser-known Asian footballing nations represent the true backwaters of world football. These may well be the countries in which true football obsession has yet to take hold, but competition between, and achievements by, these teams are no less vibrant. The regions are the home to many of the game's record-breakers – from the most goals in a single game to the most career appearances – and some of these records may never be broken.

SAUDIS MAKE FLYING START

Saudi Arabia reached the last 16 in their first FIFA World Cup finals appearance in 1994. **Saeed Owairan**'s winner against Belgium enabled them to finish level on points with the Netherlands in Group F. After the Saudis lost their opening game 2-1 to the Dutch, Sami Al-Jaber and Fuad Amin then scored in a 2-1 win over Morocco before they lost 3-1 to Sweden in the last 16. Substitute Fahad Al-Ghesheyan scored in the 85th minute after the Swedes led 2-0. Kennet Andersson grabbed Sweden's decisive third goal three minutes later. The Saudis have failed to advance beyond the group stages in their three subsequent appearances.

IRAN TOP SCORERS

1	Ali Daei	109
2	Karim Bagheri	50
3	Ali Karimi	38
4	Javad Nekounam	36
5	Gholam Hossein Mazloomi	37
6	Farshad Pious	19
7	Ali Asghar Modir Roosta	18
8	Vahid Hashemian	15
9	Alireza Vahedi Nikbakht	14
10	Mehdi Mahdavikia	13
=	Ali Parvin	13
=	Hassan Rowshan	13

NEK'S THE NEXT IN LINE

Iran's current captain Javad Nekounam has moved into second place in not only the list of Iran's most-capped players, but also of that showing who has worn their skipper's armband most often. The skilful midfielder's 132 appearances since 2000 have included 39 as captain, one more than Ahmad Reza Abedzadeh between 1988 and 1998 but still short of Ali Daei's 80 captain appearances out of 149 caps.

IRAN'S WINNING RUN

Iran won all 13 matches across their hat-trick of AFC Asian Cup triumphs in 1968, 1972 and 1976 – and their 8-0 win over South Yemen in 1976 remains a tournament record. Among the players who enjoyed repeat success was Homayoun Behzadi, who scored in all four games in 1968 and was again on the winning side four years later. Iran's manager in 1976 was Heshmat Mohajerani, who also led the team to the quarter-finals of that year's Summer Olympics in Montreal before steering Iran to their first-ever FIFA World Cup appearance in 1978. Iran's captain at the tournament in Argentina was midfielder Ali Parvin – who had scored the only goal of the 1976 AFC Asian Cup final against Kuwait.

RANK OUTSIDERS

North Korea only narrowly lost their first game of the 2010 FIFA World Cup, 2-1 to Brazil – **Ji Yun-Nam** scoring late on for the Koreans. The match was between the tournament's highest- and lowest-ranked qualifying teams. Brazil were in first place in the FIFA rankings, while North Korea were 105th.

IRAN TOP CAPS

#	Name	Caps
1	Ali Daei	149
2	Javad Nekounam	132
3	Ali Karimi	127
4	Mehdi Mahdavikia	111
5	Hossein Kaebi	89
6	Karim Bagheri	87
7	Mohammad Nosrati	83
8	Hamid Reza Estili	82
9	Javad Zarincheh	80
10	Ahmad Reza Abedzadeh	79
=	Jalal Hosseini	79

APPEARANCES IN THE FIFA WORLD CUP FINALS

Saudi Arabia	4	(1994, 1998, 2002, 2006)
Iran	3	(1978, 1998, 2006)
New Zealand	2	(1982*, 2010*)
North Korea	2	(1966, 2010)
China	1	(2002)
Indonesia**	1	(1938)
Iraq	1	(1986)
Israel	1	(1970)
Kuwait	1	(1982)
United Arab Emirates	1	(1990)

* Qualified for FIFA World Cup as Oceania Confederation member
** Played in the 1938 FIFA World Cup as Dutch East Indies

SHAKEN SHEIKH

Kuwait have qualified for the FIFA World Cup just once, in 1982 – though they made a memorable appearance when they almost walked off the field in protest at a decision. Kuwait's chief Olympic official, Sheikh Fahad Al-Ahmed, even stomped on to the pitch in Valladolid, Spain, when France's Alain Giresse scored a goal that would have given les Bleus a 4-1 lead. The Kuwaitis claimed they had heard a whistle and stopped playing and ultimately convinced referee Myroslav Stupar to disallow the strike. The game still finished 4-1 to France, though, and Kuwait were eliminated in the first round.

IRAN STOP AT 19

Iran hold the record for the highest score in an Asian zone FIFA World Cup qualifier. They thrashed Guam 19-0 in Tabriz on 24 November 2000. Karim Bagheri scored six goals and Ali Karimi four. Future national coach Ali Daei and Farhad Majidi both netted three. This was two goals better than Iran's previous highest qualifying win – 17-0 against the Maldives on 2 June 1997, during which Bagheri scored seven times. Two days after their 19-goal thrashing, Guam crashed 16-0 to Tajikistan.

PALESTINE THE PIONEERS

Palestine, then under British rule, were the first Asian team to enter the FIFA World Cup qualifiers. They lost 7-1 away to Egypt on 16 March 1934. They lost the return match at home on 6 April, 4-1. Four years later, they were eliminated by Greece, who won 3-1 in Tel Aviv and 1-0 at home.

CHINA YET TO REALIZE POTENTIAL

China, the world's most populous nation, have qualified just once for the FIFA World Cup finals, in 2002. They topped their final qualifying group by eight points from the United Arab Emirates, but coach Bora Milutinovic's team slumped in the finals, failing to score a goal in defeats by Costa Rica (2-0), Brazil (4-0) and Turkey (3-0). Their 2002 side included record caps-holder Zi Feng (114 appearances) and all-time leading scorer **Hao Haidong** (37 goals).

WORLD'S WORST

On the same day that Brazil and Germany contested the FIFA World Cup final on 30 June 2002, the two lowest-ranked FIFA countries were also taking each other on. Asian side Bhutan ran out 4-0 winners over CONCACAF's Montserrat, in a match staged in the Bhutan capital Thimphu. The winning side's captain, striker Wangay Dorji, scored a hat-trick.

IRAQ AND ROLL

One of the greatest – and most heart-warming – surprises of recent international football was Iraq's unexpected triumph at the 2007 AFC Asian Cup, barely a year after the end of the war that ravaged the country and forced them to play "home" games elsewhere. Despite disrupted preparations, they eliminated Vietnam and South Korea on the way to the 2007 final in which captain **Younis Mahmoud**'s goal proved decisive against Saudi Arabia. They were unable to retain their title four years later, losing to Australia in the quarter-finals. Mahmoud retired from international football in June 2013, after 47 goals in 116 games for his country. He is second in Iraq's most-capped and top-scoring lists, both times behind Hussein Saeed, who scored 61 goals in 126 appearances between 1977 and 1990.

AI–DEAYEA CAPS THEM ALL

Saudi goalkeeper Mohamed Al-Deayea had to choose between football and handball as a youngster. He was persuaded by his elder brother Abdullah to pick football and he went on to make 181 appearances for his country: the first coming against Bangladesh in 1990 and the last against Belgium in May 2006. He also appeared in the FIFA World Cup finals tournaments of 1994, 1998 and 2002. He played his last finals game in a 3-0 defeat by the Republic of Ireland on 11 June 2002 and was recalled to the squad for the 2006 finals, although he did not play.

HAPPY DAEI

Iran striker **Ali Daei** became the first footballer to score a century of international goals, when  his four in a 7-0 defeat of Laos on 17 November 2004 took him to 102. He ended his career having scored 109 times for Iran in 149 internationals between 1993 and 2006 – though none of his goals came during FIFA World Cup appearances in 1998 and 2006. He is also the all-time leading scorer in the AFC Asian Cup, with 14 goals, despite failing ever to win the tournament. His time as national coach was less auspicious – he lasted only a year from March 2008 to March 2009 before being fired, as Iran struggled in qualifiers for the 2010 FIFA World Cup.

BARCA'S BEST

The first Asian footballer ever to play for a European club remains the all-time leading scorer for Spanish giants Barcelona – the best part of a century on. Paulino Alcantara, from the Philippines, scored 357 goals in 357 matches for Barcelona between 1912 and 1927, having made his debut aged just 15 – another club record. Alcantara, who was born in the Philippines but had a Spanish father, played internationals for Catalonia, Spain and his native Philippines – for whom he featured in a record 15-2 trouncing of Japan in 1917. Alcantara became a doctor after retiring from football at the age of 31, though he did briefly manage Spain in 1951.

KUWAIT IN GOLD

Kuwait's one and only AFC Asian Cup triumph came in 1980, when they also hosted the tournament. They beat South Korea 3-0 in the final – having lost by the same scoreline, to the same opponents, in a first-round group game. Faisal Al-Dakhil was Kuwait's hero in the final, scoring two of their goals, his fourth and fifth of the tournament. He had also struck what proved to be the winner in a 2-1 semi-final victory over Iran.

THE JONG TURNING

North Korea's star striker at the 2010 FIFA World Cup, Jong Tae-Se, sobbed when their anthem was played before the first game against Brazil, but he had never actually visited the country he was playing for. Jong was born in Japan, where he continues to play his club football for Kawasaki Frontale, and has parents who are South Korean citizens. But he chose to pursue his family right to a North Korean passport.

SURPRISE SEVEN

The top scorer in the Asian qualification campaign for the 2014 FIFA World Cup was Japan's eight-goal Shinji Okazaki, but he was followed by players from outside the Asian Confederation's traditional superpowers. Tied on seven goals apiece were Iraq's Younis Mahmoud, Jordan's Ahmad Hayel and Hassan Abdel- Fattah and Vietnam's **Le Cong Vinh**, whose strikes helped him to an all-time national record of 31. Jordan had never reached the fourth and final round of AFC qualifiers before and did so this time coached by Adnan Hamad, who had previously served five different stints as manager of his native Iraq.

AFC ASIAN CUP ALL-TIME TOP SCORERS

1	Ali Daei (Iran)	14
2	Lee Dong-Gook (South Korea)	10
3	Naohiro Takahara (Japan)	9
4	Jassem Al-Houwaidi (Kuwait)	8
5	Behtash Fariba (Iran)	7
=	Hossein Kalani (Iran)	7
=	Choi Soon-Ho (South Korea)	7
=	Faisal Al-Dakhil (Kuwait)	7
9	Yasser Al-Qahtani (Saudi Arabia)	6
=	Alexander Geynrikh (Uzbekistan)	6

PAK STRIKE MAKES HISTORY

North Korea's **Pak Doo Ik** earned legendary status by scoring the goal that eliminated Italy from the 1966 FIFA World Cup finals. The shockwaves caused by the victory were comparable to those caused by the United States' 1-0 win over England in 1950. Pak netted the only goal of the game in the 42nd minute at Middlesbrough on 19 July. North Korea thus became the first Asian team to reach the quarter-finals. Pak, an army corporal, was promoted to sergeant after the victory and later became a gymnastics coach.

ASIAN FOOTBALLER OF THE YEAR

Year	Player	Country
1988	Ahmed Radhi	Iraq
1989	Kim Joo-Sung	South Korea
1990	Kim Joo-Sung	South Korea
1991	Kim Joo-Sung	South Korea
1992	not awarded	
1993	Kazuyoshi Miura	Japan
1994	Saeed Owarain	Saudi Arabia
1995	Masami Ihara	Japan
1996	Khodadad Azizi	Iran
1997	Hidetoshi Nakata	Japan
1998	Hidetoshi Nakata	Japan
1999	Ali Daei	Iran
2000	Nawaf Al Temyat	Saudi Arabia
2001	Fan Zhiyi	China
2002	Shinji Ono	Japan
2003	Mehdi Mahdavikia	Iran
2004	Ali Karimi	Iran
2005	Hamad Al-Montashari	Saudi Arabia
2006	Khalfan Ibrahim	Qatar
2007	Yasser Al-Qahtani	Saudi Arabia
2008	Server Djeparov	Uzbekistan
2009	Yasuhito Endo	Japan
2010	Sasa Ognenovski	Australia
2011	Server Djeparov	Uzbekistan
2012	Lee Keun-Ho	South Korea

SO NEAR AND SO FAR

The Asian Confederation's September 2013 two-legged tie to discover who would face a South American team in the final play-off for a place in Brazil in 2014 was between two teams still waiting for their first FIFA World Cup finals: Uzbekistan and Jordan. The Uzbeks finished their final group level on points with automatic qualifiers South Korea but with an inferior goal difference – by one. This was despite ending with a 5-1 victory over Qatar, including a Basodir Nasimov equalizer just 18 seconds after he came on as substitute.

AFC ASIAN CUP–WINNING COACHES

1956	**Lee Yoo-Hyung** (South Korea)
1960	**Wi Hye-Deok** (South Korea)
1964	**Gyula Mandl** (Israel)
1968	**Mahmoud Bayati** (Iran)
1972	**Mohammad Ranjbar** (Iran)
1976	**Heshmat Mohajerani** (Iran)
1980	**Carlos Alberto Parreira** (Kuwait)
1984	**Khalil Al-Zayani** (Saudi Arabia)
1988	**Carlos Alberto Parreira** (Saudi Arabia)
1992	**Hans Ooft** (Japan)
1996	**Nelo Vingada** (Saudi Arabia)
2000	**Philippe Troussier** (Japan)
2004	**Zico** (Japan)
2007	**Jorvan Vieira** (Iraq)
2011	**Alberto Zaccheroni** (Japan)

AL-JABER TO THE FORE

Sami Al-Jaber (born on 11 December 1972 in Riyadh) became only the second Asian player to appear in four FIFA World Cup finals tournaments when he started against Tunisia in Munich on 14 June 2006. He scored in a 2-2 draw, his third goal in nine appearances at the finals. Al-Jaber played only one game in 1998 before he was rushed to hospital with a burst appendix, which ruled him out of the competition. He became Saudi Arabia's record scorer, with 44 goals in 163 matches.

A LONG JOURNEY FOR A BEATING

The first Asian country to play in a FIFA World Cup finals was Indonesia, who played in France in 1938 as the Dutch East Indies. The tournament was a straight knockout and, on 5 June in Reims, Hungary beat them 6-0, with goals from Gyorgy Sarosi, Gyula Zsengeller (two each), Vilmos Kohut and Geza Toldi.

QATAR HERO

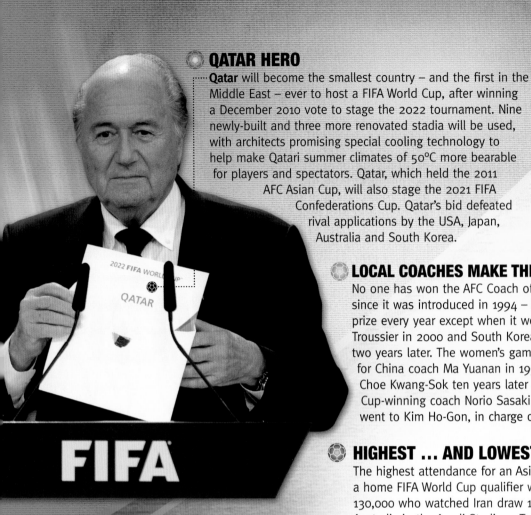

Qatar will become the smallest country – and the first in the Middle East – ever to host a FIFA World Cup, after winning a December 2010 vote to stage the 2022 tournament. Nine newly-built and three more renovated stadia will be used, with architects promising special cooling technology to help make Qatari summer climates of 50°C more bearable for players and spectators. Qatar, which held the 2011 AFC Asian Cup, will also stage the 2021 FIFA Confederations Cup. Qatar's bid defeated rival applications by the USA, Japan, Australia and South Korea.

FOREIGN DOUBLE AGENT

Brazilian Carlos Alberto Parreira is the only coach to win the AFC Asian Cup twice – and he did so with two different countries. His Kuwait side won in 1980 and he got his hands on the trophy again eight years later, this time in charge of Saudi Arabia.

LOCAL COACHES MAKE THEIR MARK

No one has won the AFC Coach of the Year award more than once since it was introduced in 1994 – though Asians have claimed the prize every year except when it went to Japan's French boss Philipppe Troussier in 2000 and South Korea's Dutch manager Guus Hiddink two years later. The women's game was recognized with triumphs for China coach Ma Yuanan in 1996, North Korea's U-20 manager Choe Kwang-Sok ten years later and Japan's FIFA Women's World Cup-winning coach Norio Sasaki in 2011. The award 12 months later went to Kim Ho-Gon, in charge of South Korean club Ulsan Hyundai.

HIGHEST ... AND LOWEST

The highest attendance for an Asian team in a home FIFA World Cup qualifier was the 130,000 who watched Iran draw 1-1 with Australia in the Azadi Stadium, Tehran, on 22 November 1997. The game was the first leg of a final playoff for the last place in the 1998 finals. Iran advanced on away goals after drawing the second leg 2-2 in Melbourne. The lowest attendance was the "crowd" of 20 that turned out for Turkmenistan's 1-0 win over Taiwan, played in Amman, Jordan, on 7 May 2001.

HUGE FOLLOWING FOR FOOTBALL IN CHINA

China's national team boasts a massive fan base – as was demonstrated when they reached the FIFA World Cup finals for the only time in 2002. Between their qualification on 19 October 2001 and their opening game of the finals against Costa Rica on 4 June 2002, an estimated 170 million new TV sets were sold throughout China. TV audiences for the team's three matches regularly topped 300 million, even though China lost all three matches and failed to score a goal.

DESERVING SERVER

Uzbekistan's four most-capped internationals are all still playing: midfielders **Timur Kapadze** (107 appearances) and two-time Asian Footballer of the Year Server Djeparov (94), striker Alexander Geynrikh (83) and goalkeeper Ignatiy Nesterov (82). Striker Maksim Shatskikh leads the country's scoring list, with 34 goals in 60 games, and has also enjoyed success in the Ukraine with several sides including Dynamo Kiev – with whom he became the second Uzbek, after Mirjalol Qosimov, to score in UEFA club competitions. Qosimov, who managed 31 goals for his country, is now Uzbekistan's manager.

CHINA'S 4X4

Four teams carry the name of China. The China national team receives the most attention, but Hong Kong (a former British colony) and Macau (a former Portuguese colony) both retain their autonomous status for football – as Hong Kong China and Macau China respectively. Meanwhile, the independent island state of Taiwan competes in the FIFA World Cup and other competitions as Chinese Taipei.

UAE KO ZAGALLO

Brazilian great Mario Zagallo, who won the FIFA World Cup as both player and manager, coached the United Arab Emirates when they qualified for their one and only FIFA World Cup finals in 1990. But despite his success in the Asian qualifiers, he was sacked on the eve of the FIFA World Cup itself. Zagallo was replaced by Polish coach Bernard Blaut, whose UAE team lost all three matches at Italia 90. Other big names to have managed the UAE over the years include Brazil's Carlos Alberto Parreira (another FIFA World Cup winner with Brazil), England's Don Revie and Roy Hodgson, Ukraine's Valery Lobanovsky and Portugal's Carlos Queiroz.

SOVIET REPUBLICS FIND NEW HOME

The break-up of the former Soviet Union swelled the ranks of the Asian Confederation in the early 1990s. Former Soviet republics Kazakhstan, Kyrgyzstan, Tajikistan, Turkmenistan and Uzbekistan all joined in 1994, though the Kazaks switched to UEFA in 2002. **Uzbekistan** have been the most successful, reaching the quarter-finals in 2004 and 2007 and finishing fourth in 2011. Australia became the AFC's 46th – and newest – member, entering the Confederation on 1 January 2006, a few months after East Timor had become the 45th.

ASIAN CUP WINNERS

The Asian Cup is Asia's continental championship

Year	Winners
1956	South Korea
1960	South Korea
1964	Israel
1968	Iran
1972	Iran
1976	Iran
1980	Kuwait
1984	Saudi Arabia
1988	Saudi Arabia
1992	Japan
1996	Saudi Arabia
2000	Japan
2004	Japan
2007	Iraq
2011	Japan

DOUBLE AGENT

Although North Korea's Kim Myong-Won usually plays as a striker, he was named as one of three goalkeepers in the country's 23-man squad for the 2010 FIFA World Cup. FIFA told North Korea he would only be able to play in goal, rather than outfield, though he failed to make it on to the pitch in any form during his country's three Group G matches.

THE ISRAEL ISSUE

Israel is, geographically, an Asian nation. It hosted – and won – the Asian Cup in 1964. But, over the years, many Asian confederation countries refused to play Israel on political grounds. When Israel reached the 1970 FIFA World Cup finals they came through a qualifying tournament involving two Asian nations – Japan and South Korea – and two from Oceania – Australia and New Zealand. In 1989, Israel topped the Oceania group, but lost a final play-off to Colombia for a place in the 1990 finals. They switched to the European zone qualifiers in 1992 and have been a full member of the European federation, UEFA, since 1994.

FROZEN OUT

Mongolia went 38 years without playing a single international between 1960 and 1998 and the country still barely stages any action, international or domestic, due to below-freezing conditions between October and June.

OCEANIA

Football in Oceania can claim some of the most eye-catching football statistics – though not necessarily in a way many there would welcome, especially the long-suffering goalkeepers from minnow islands on the end of cricket-style scorelines. The departure to the Asian Football Confederation of Australia, seeking more testing competition, was a morale blow – but benefited New Zealand out on the pitch. The finals tournament of the 2010 FIFA World Cup was the first to feature both Australia and New Zealand.

KAREMBEU THE FIFA WORLD CUP WINNER

Christian Karembeu, born in New Caledonia, is the only FIFA World Cup winner to come from the Oceania region. He started for France in their 3-0 final victory over Brazil on 12 July 1998. The defensive midfielder had earlier begun against Denmark (group), Italy (quarter-finals) and Croatia (semi-finals). He played 53 times for France, scoring one goal, and was also a double European Champions League Cup winner with Real Madrid in 1998 in 2000.

RYAN'S SISTER

New Zealand's captain **Ryan Nelsen** flew back from Blackburn in England to his native city of Christchurch in March 2011 after the city was devastated by an earthquake. Nelsen was worried for the safety of his family, especially his pregnant sister Stephanie Martin – but after being "knocked down" by the 6.3-magnitude quake, she safely gave birth to a healthy baby boy.

PAIA FIRE IN VAIN

No team from Oceania other than Australia or New Zealand has ever qualified for the men's football tournament at the Summer Olympics – but Fiji came close to reaching the 2012 event, only losing 1-0 to New Zealand in the final of the qualifying competition. The top scorers were the Solomon Islands, but they didn't make it out of their opening group. They recorded a best first-round goal difference of +12 – thanks to a 16-1 destruction of American Samoa, including seven goals by Ian Paia. However, defeats by Fiji and Vanuatu left them third in the four-team section.

TOP CAPS: NEW ZEALAND

1	Ivan Vicelich	86
2	Simon Elliott	69
3	Vaughan Coveney	64
4	Ricki Herbert	61
5	Chris Jackson	60
6	Brian Turner	59
7	Duncan Cole	58
=	Steve Sumner	58
9	Chris Zoricich	57
10	Ceri Evans	56

TOP SCORERS: NEW ZEALAND

1	Vaughan Coveney	28
2	Shane Smeltz	23
3	Steve Sumner	22
4	Brian Turner	21
5	Jock Newall	17
6	Keith Nelson	16
7	Chris Killen	15
=	Grant Turner	15
9	Darren McClennan	12
=	Michael McGarry	12
=	Wynton Rufer	12

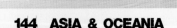

RETURNING RICKI

Ricki Herbert is the only footballer from New Zealand to reach a FIFA World Cup twice – he played left-back at the 1982 tournament in Spain, then coached the country to their second World Cup appearance, in 2010. Qualification second time around came courtesy of a play-off win over Asian Football Confederation representatives Bahrain – though the New Zealand football authorities have been pondering whether to follow Australia in defecting from Oceania and joining the AFC. Herbert, born in Auckland in 1961, combined qualifying for the 2010 FIFA World Cup with coaching New Zealand-based club Wellington Phoenix, who play in Australia's A-League.

TEHAU ABOUT THAT?

The Pacific Island underdogs of Tahiti finally broke the stranglehold Australia and New Zealand had over the OFC Nations Cup by winning the tournament when it was held for the ninth time in 2012, following four previous triumphs for Australia and four for New Zealand. Tahiti scored 20 goals in their five games at the event in the Solomon Islands – 15 of which came from the Tehau family: brothers Lorenzo (five), Alvin and **Jonathan Tehau** (four each) and their cousin Teaonui (two). Steevy Chong Hue scored the only goal of the final, against New Caledonia, to give the team managed by Eddy Etaeta not only the trophy but a place at the 2013 FIFA Confederations Cup in Brazil.

PIERRE'S PERFECT START

The very first goal of the 2010 FIFA World Cup was scored, in qualifying, by New Caledonia's Pierre Wajoka – the only strike of an August 2007 match against Tahiti, the country of his birth.

BAD LUCK OF THE DRAW

Despite featuring at only their second-ever FIFA World Cup – and their first since 1982 – New Zealand did not lose a game in South Africa in 2010. They drew all three first-round matches, against Slovakia, Italy and Paraguay. The three points were not enough to secure a top-two finish in Group F, but third-placed New Zealand did finish above defending world champions Italy. The only other three teams to have gone out despite going unbeaten in their three first-round group games were Scotland (1974), Cameroon (1982) and Belgium (1998).

LAUGHING ALL THE WAY TO THE BANK

New Zealand went to the 2010 FIFA World Cup with four amateur players in their 23-man squad. Midfielder **Andy Barron**, who works as an investment adviser at a bank in Wellington, even made it on to the pitch as a stoppage-time substitute against reigning world champions Italy.

BUSY NICKY

Nicky Salapu was the unfortunate goalkeeper who conceded an international-record 31 times, as his American Samoa team lost 31-0 to Australia in April 2001. Just two days earlier, Australia had crushed Tonga 22-0. Passport problems meant American Samoa were denied several of their best players for the Australia game and included three 15-year-olds in a line-up that had an average age of just 18. Despite this, they managed to keep the game goalless ... for the first 10 minutes. In his eight international appearances, Salapu conceded 91 goals – with just one in his opposite number's net, scored by Natia Natia, in a 9-1 defeat to Vanuatu in May 2004. Midfielder Natia's goal was American Samoa's first in a FIFA World Cup qualifier. But their long wait for a win finally ended in November 2011, when goals by Ramin Ott and Shamin Luani clinched a 2-1 victory over Tonga in a 2014 FIFA World Cup qualifier. This came after 30 consecutive defeats – and was followed with a 1-1 draw against the Cook Islands. Luani found the net again in this game, taking him alongside Ott as American Samoa's joint leading scorers – on two goals apiece.

THE WHITE STUFF

New Zealand's national football team is known as the "All-Whites" – not just a recognition of their kit colours, but also a counterpoint to the "All-Blacks" nickname of the country's more famous and successful rugby union side.

CONCACAF

Mexico's fans provide colour and the Wave, the USA offers pizzazz and Caribbean nations provide joyous vibrancy. All in all, football fans in the CONCACAF region, covering the Caribbean, Central and North America, now follow the game as keenly as anywhere in the world. Mexico's love of the FIFA World Cup dates back to the first tournament in 1930 and the country was the first two-time host, in 1970 and 1986. The question is: how far will a CONCACAF team go in 2014?

Combative midfielder Gerardo Torrado, a junior squad member when Mexico won the 1999 FIFA Confederations Cup, was back in action for his country at the 2013 edition.

MEXICO

Mexico may well be the powerhouse of the CONCACAF region and are regular qualifiers for the FIFA World Cup – they did not play in the finals of the tournament on just three occasions (1934, 1974 and 1982) – but they have always struggled to impose themselves on the international stage. Two FIFA World Cup quarter-final appearances (both times as tournament hosts, in 1970 and 1986) represent their best performances to date. A football-mad nation expects more.

TOP SCORERS

1	Jared Borghetti	46
2	Cuauhtemoc Blanco	39
3	Carlos Hermosillo	35
=	Javier Hernandez	35
=	Luis Hernandez	35
6	Enrique Borja	31
7	Luis Roberto Alves	30
8	Luis Flores	29
=	Benjamin Galindo	29
=	Luis Garcia	29
=	Hugo Sanchez	29

VICTOR HUGO

Jared Borgetti may hold the record as Mexico's all-time leading scorer, but perhaps the country's most inspirational striker remains **Hugo Sanchez,** famed for his acrobatic bicycle-kick finishes and somersaulting celebrations. Sanchez played for Mexico at the 1978, 1986 and 1994 FIFA World Cups and would surely have done so had they qualified in 1982 and 1990. During spells in Spain with Atletico Madrid and Real Madrid he finished as La Liga's top scorer five years out of six between 1985 and 1990. The highlight of his disappointing term as Mexico coach, from 2006 to 2008, was finishing third at the 2007 Copa America.

MAKING HIS MARQUEZ

Rafael Marquez set a FIFA World Cup appearance record for Mexico when playing in the 2010 second-round defeat to Argentina. That game took him to 12 games in the competition, one more than former goalkeeper Antonio Carbajal and also two other members of the 2010 squad – forward Cuauhtemoc Blanco and midfielder Gerardo Torrado.

PRECOCIOUS PEREZ

Mexico's youngest international remains midfielder **Luis Ernesto Perez,** who won the first of his 69 caps at the age of 17 years and 308 days, against El Salvador on 17 November 1998. Less impressive was his red card in Mexico's third first-round match against Portugal at the 2006 FIFA World Cup. Hugo Sanchez was the nation's oldest player, 39 years and 251 days old for his final international, against Paraguay on 19 March 1998 – though this was a farewell game for Sanchez, four years after his previous Mexico appearance, and he was replaced in the first minute by Luis Garcia.

TOP CAPS

1	Claudio Suarez	178
2	Pavel Pardo	148
3	Gerardo Torrado	144
4	Jorge Campos	130
5	Cuauhtemoc Blanco	121
=	Ramon Ramirez	121
7	Carlos Salcido	116
8	Rafael Marquez	111
9	Alberto Garcia-Aspe	109
10	Oswaldo Sanchez	99

LITTLE PEA FROM A POD

When Javier Hernandez appeared for Mexico against South Africa on 11 June 2010, he became the third generation of his family to play at a FIFA World Cup. Hernandez – nicknamed "Chicharito", or "Little Pea" – is the son of Javier Hernandez who reached the quarter-finals with Mexico in 1986 and the grandson of Tomas Balcazar, a member of the country's 1954 squad. Another Mexican pair were the first grandfather-grandson pairing to each play at the finals. Luis Perez represented Mexico in 1930 in Uruguay. His grandson Mario Perez played for Mexico, on home turf, 40 years later. Hernandez scored all three of Mexico's goals at the 2013 FIFA Confederations Cup – in a 2-1 defeat to Italy and a 2-1 win over Japan – taking him to joint-third in his country's scoring ranks, alongside Carlos Hermosillo and Luis Hernandez. Chicharito reached the tally in 53 games, compared to Hermosillo's 90 and Luis Hernandez's 85.

FAMILY SPLIT

Winger **Giovani dos Santos** was distraught when Mexico's 30-man preliminary squad was reduced to 23 for the 2010 FIFA World Cup – though not for the obvious reason. He actually made the cut, and played in all four of Mexico's matches, but his brother Jonathan dos Santos was left out by coach Javier Aguirre.

MEXICO RECORDS

First international:
won 3-2 v Guatemala,
Guatemala City,
1 January 1923
Biggest win:
13-0 v Bahamas,
Toluca, 28 April 1987
Biggest defeat: 8-0 v
England, Wembley,
10 May 1961
CONCACAF champions:
1965, 1971, 1977, 1993,
1996, 1998, 2003, 2009, 2011
Confederations Cup winners: 1999

MEXICO BEATS EARTHQUAKE

Mexico stepped in to host the 1986 FIFA World Cup finals after the original choice, Colombia, pulled out in November 1982. FIFA chose Mexico as the replacement venue because of its stadiums and infrastructure, still in place from the 1970 finals. The governing body turned down rival bids from Canada and the United States. Mexico had to work overtime to be ready for the finals, after the earthquake of 19 September 1985, which killed an estimated 10,000 people in central Mexico and destroyed many buildings in Mexico City.

SUAREZ SETS OUTFIELD RECORD

Only Egypt's Ahmed Hassan and Saudia Arabia's Mohamed Al-Deayea have played more internationals than Mexico defender **Claudio Suarez**, who has 178 caps. Suarez – nicknamed "The Emperor" – played in all of Mexico's four games at the 1994 and the 1998 FIFA World Cups, though missed the 2002 finals because of a broken leg. He did travel as part of the squad for the 2006 tournament but did not play.

ROSAS NETS HISTORIC PENALTY

Mexico's Manuel Rosas scored the first penalty ever awarded in the FIFA World Cup finals when he converted a 42nd-minute spot-kick in his country's match against Argentina in 1930. Rosas scored again in the 65th minute, but it was too little too late for the Mexicans: they crashed to a 6-3 defeat.

MEXI–GOLD

The continental CONCACAF championship, now known as the CONCACAF Gold Cup, has had the same two finalists at the last three tournaments. The USA defeated Mexico 2-1 in 2007, but the tables have been turned twice since. Mexico trounced their arch rivals 5-0 in 2009, then fought back from 2-0 goals down to win 4-2 in 2011 – with starring performances by Giovani dos Santos and seven-goal tournament top scorer **Javier Hernandez**. Mexico have been CONCACAF Gold Cup winners six times, followed by the USA on four occasions and Canada once. The pre-1991 CONCACAF Championship was won three times each by Mexico and Costa Rica, and once apiece by Guatemala, Haiti, Honduras and Canada.

UNITED STATES

Some of the game's biggest names – from Pele to David Beckham – may well have graced the United States' domestic league over the years, and the country may well be one of only 15 countries to have been granted the honour of hosting a FIFA World Cup, but football is still very much a minority sport in the world's most powerful country. However, following a series of impressive performances on the world stage, the expectation is that the situation will soon change.

TOP CAPS

1	Cobi Jones	164
2	Landon Donovan	144
3	Jeff Agoos	134
4	Marcelo Balboa	128
5	Claudio Reyna	112
6	Carlos Bocanegra	110
=	Paul Caligiuri	110
8	Eric Wynalda	106
9	DaMarcus Beasley	103
10	Kasey Keller	102

ALTIDORE OPENS THE FLOODGATES

Jozy Altidore became the United States' youngest scorer of an international hat-trick in a 3-0 victory over Trinidad and Tobado on 1 April 2009, aged 19 years and 146 days. But he endured a 15-month barren spell for his country between November 2011 and June 2013, when he scored the opener in a dramatic 4-3 victory over Germany in a Washington DC friendly marking America's Centennial. He then found the net in the following games against Jamaica, Panama and Honduras, equalling a national record of scoring four games in a row previously shared by William Lubb, Eric Wynalda, Eddie Johnson, **Brian McBride** and Landon Donovan. Altidore's scoring spree came in a 2012–13 season in which he also set a US record for goals in a European club league, with 31 strikes for Dutch club AZ Alkmaar.

CALIGIURI'S SHOT MAKES HISTORY

The US's FIFA World Cup qualifying win in Trinidad, on 19 November 1989, is regarded as a turning point in the country's football history. The team included just one full-time professional, Paul Caligiuri, of (West) German second division club Meppen. He scored the only goal of the game with a looping shot after 31 minutes to take the US to their first finals for 40 years. Trinidad's goalkeeper, Michael Maurice, claimed to have been blinded by the sun, but the win raised the profile of the US team hugely, despite a first-round elimination in the 1990 FIFA World Cup.

LANDON HOPE AND GLORY

The US's all-time leading scorer **Landon Donovan** was the undoubted star of their 2010 FIFA World Cup campaign. He scored three goals in four matches, including a stoppage-time winner against Algeria that meant his side finished top of Group C. His four displays at the tournament meant he has now featured in 13 FIFA World Cup matches for the USA, two ahead of compatriots Earnie Stewart and Cobi Jones. His successful penalty in a second-round defeat to Ghana also made him the USA's all-time top scorer in the competition, with five goals – one more than 1930 hat-trick hero Bert Patenaude. He remains the only man to score more than one hat-trick for the US, having hit four goals against Cuba in July 2003 then trebles versus Ecuador in March 2007 and Scotland in May 2012. Nine others have scored individual hat-tricks.

KLIN SWEEP

After Serbian coach Bora Milutinovic was followed by Americans Steve Sampson, Bruce Arena and finally Bob Bradley, the USA ended a 16-year devotion to homegrown managers by appointing German legend and long-time Los Angeles resident **Jurgen Klinsmann** in July 2011. Among his early successes was a first-ever US victory over Italy, in February 2012 – Clint Dempsey's only goal of the game in Genoa ended the US's ten-match run without a win against the Italians that dates back all the way to 1934.

BOB'S YOUR FATHER

Coach Bob Bradley's US team were surprise winners of Group C at the 2010 FIFA World Cup, a place above seeded favourites England. This was the first time the country had topped their first-round group since the very first FIFA World Cup in 1930. Bradley picked his son Michael for all four of the US's games at the 2010 tournament, and the midfielder rewarded his father's faith by scoring a late equalizer in the 2-2 Group C draw with Slovenia. The US achieved their best FIFA World Cup finish under Bradley's predecessor Bruce Arena when they reached the 2002 quarter-finals, only losing to eventual finalists Germany.

DEMPSEY'S DOUBLE

Clint Dempsey became only the second US international to score at two different FIFA World Cups when his long-range shot was fumbled into the net by England goalkeeper Robert Green in their 1-1 draw in Rustenburg at the 2010 tournament. Dempsey had previously scored in a 2-1 defeat to Ghana, in the first round in Germany four years earlier. The first American to achieve the feat was striker Brian McBride, who netted against Iran in 1998 and winners against Portugal and Mexico in 2002. Dempsey's feat was emulated by Landon Donovan – a goalscorer against Poland and Mexico in 2002 and against Slovenia, Algeria and Ghana in 2010.

TOP SCORERS

1	Landon Donovan	49
2	Clint Dempsey	35
3	Eric Wynalda	34
4	Brian McBride	30
5	Joe-Max Moore	24
6	Bruce Murray	21
7	Jozy Altidore	17
=	DaMarcus Beasley	17
=	Earnie Stewart	17
10	Eddie Johnson	15
=	Cobi Jones	15

ENGLAND STUNNED BY GAETJENS

The US's 1-0 win over England on 29 June 1950 ranks among the biggest surprises in FIFA World Cup history. England, along with hosts Brazil, were joint favourites to win the trophy. The US had lost their last seven matches, scoring just two goals. Joe Gaetjens scored the only goal, in the 37th minute, diving to head Walter Bahr's cross past goalkeeper Bert Williams. England dominated the game, but US keeper Frank Borghi made save after save. Defeats by Chile and Spain eliminated the US at the group stage, but their victory over England remains the greatest result in the country's football history.

"OLD MAN" HAHNEMANN

Goalkeeper Marcus Hahnemann became the US's oldest international when he faced Paraguay on 29 March 2011 at the age of 38 years and 286 days. That was the last of his nine caps, testament to the US's strength in depth when it comes to goalkeepers in recent years – Kasey Keller (101 caps), Tim Howard (90) and Brad Friedel (82) were among the competition. Hahnemann's debut was in 1994, followed by two more appearances that year, but he then had to wait until 2004 for his next international action.

KEEPING UP WITH JONES

His dreadlocked hair helped catch the attention, but **Cobi Jones**'s raiding runs down the wing also made him one of the host country's most high-profile performers at the 1994 FIFA World Cup. Jones went on to become the US's most-capped player, with 164 international appearances between 1992 and 2004. When he finally retired from all forms of the game in 2007, his number 13 shirt was officially "retired" by the Los Angeles Galaxy – the first time a Major League Soccer club had honoured a player in such a way. Jones had been with the Galaxy since the MLS was launched in 1996 and later served the club as assistant coach and caretaker manager.

CONCACAF OTHER TEAMS

Mexico and the United States (with 23 FIFA World Cup finals appearances between them) are undoubtedly the powerhouses of the CONCACAF region. Of the other teams to make up the football nations in North and Central America and the Caribbean, only three countries (Costa Rica in 1990, 2002 and 2006), El Salvador (1970 and 1982) and Honduras (1982 and 2010) have qualified for the FIFA World Cup finals on more than one occasion.

PAVON ... AND ON ... AND ON

Striker **Carlos Pavon**, on 101, is one of only three Hondurans to achieve a century of caps – third behind goalkeeper Noel Valladares (111) and midfielder Amado Guevara (138), who was captain at the 2010 FIFA World Cup before retiring. Pavon scored seven goals in the qualifiers to reach that tournament, Honduras' first FIFA World Cup since 1982. Yet the veteran, then aged 36, played just 60 minutes of the tournament itself. Pavon, nicknamed "The Shadow", has played club football in seven different countries: Honduras, Mexico, Spain, Italy, Colombia, Guatemala and the United States, where he starred alongside David Beckham for the Los Angeles Galaxy.

COSTA RICA KEEP BATTLING

Costa Rica, spearheaded by **Paulo Wanchope**, have been the most successful of Mexico's Central American neighbours at the FIFA World Cup finals. They qualified in 1990, 2002 and 2006, and reached the last 16 at that first attempt, beating Scotland 1-0 and Sweden 2-1 in their group. They were knocked out by Czechoslovakia, 4-1. In 2002, they beat China 2-0 and drew 1-1 with Turkey but went home after losing 5-2 to Brazil. They again departed at the group stage in 2006, losing all three matches. El Salvador qualified twice, in 1970 and 1982 – but lost all six of their matches, including a 10-1 defeat by Hungary in 1982. Honduras have also qualified twice but gone out in the first round both times. In 1982, they drew 1-1 with Spain and Northern Ireland, but lost 1-0 to Yugoslavia. They didn't score a goal in 2010, losing to Chile and Spain before drawing with Switzerland.

WAITING GAMES

Patience is the watchword for many of Central America's smaller nations when it comes to footballing achievement – or even participation. International matches are rare in Montserrat due to the risk of volcanic activity on the 5,000-population Caribbean island. The team has played just 15 international matches in the 21st century, none between November 2004 and March 2008. More positively, Puerto Rico finally ended a 14-year wait for a win when they beat Bermuda 2-0 in January 2008, before reaching the second round of CONCACAF's qualifiers for the 2010 FIFA World Cup. The British Virgin Islands were eliminated from those qualifiers despite not losing a game – their two-legged first-round tie against the Bahamas ended 5-5 on aggregate, with the British Virgin Islands knocked out on away goals.

COSTA RICA WIN WITHOUT A CROWD

The lowest-ever attendance for a CONCACAF FIFA World Cup qualifier was for the Costa Rica–Panama game on 26 March 2005. FIFA ordered the game, staged at the Saprissa Stadium in San Jose, to be played behind closed doors after missiles were thrown at visiting players and the match officials when Mexico won there 2-1 on 9 February. The game was known as "the ghost match". Costa Rica beat Panama 2-1, thanks to a **Roy Myrie** goal in the first minute of stoppage time.

CONCACAF TEAMS IN THE FIFA WORLD CUP FINALS

Appearances made by teams from the CONCACAF region at the FIFA World Cup finals

1	Mexico	14
2	US	9
3	Costa Rica	3
4	El Salvador	2
=	Honduras	2
6	Canada	1
=	Cuba	1
=	Haiti	1
=	Jamaica	1
=	Trinidad & Tobago	1

PROUD RECORD

The CONCACAF confederation can boast of having had at least one representative in every FIFA World Cup finals. Mexico and the United States entered the first finals in 1930 – and the US reached the semi-finals before losing to Argentina. Since then, these two have dominated the qualifying competition. Mexico have played in a total of 14 finals tournaments; the USA in nine, and all of the last six. Other countries have challenged them recently. Costa Rica's third appearance and Trinidad & Tobago's debut at the 2006 FIFA World Cup gave CONCACAF a record four representatives at one tournament. And, at the 2010 FIFA World Cup, Honduras made their second finals appearance.

REGGAE BOYZ STEP UP

In 1998, Jamaica became the first team from the English-speaking Caribbean to reach the FIFA World Cup finals. The "Reggae Boyz", as they were nicknamed, included several players based in England. They were eliminated at the group stage, despite beating Japan 2-1 in their final game thanks to two goals by **Theodore Whitmore**. They had earlier lost 3-1 to Croatia and 5-0 against Argentina.

BROTHERS IN ARMS

Honduras became the first team to field not one, not two, but three siblings at a FIFA World Cup, when they picked defender Johnny, midfielder Wilson and striker Jerry Palacios in the 2010 squad. Jerry was a last-minute call-up, as a replacement for injured Julio Cesar de Leon. Stoke City defensive midfielder Wilson Palacios was perhaps the most famous and acclaimed player in the first Honduras side to reach a FIFA World Cup in 28 years. Like the 1982 side, though, Reinaldo Rueda's men went three games without a win or even a goal. An older brother, Milton Palacios, played 14 times as a defender for Honduras between 2003 and 2006 but was not in the running for the 2010 squad.

CUBA SHOW THE WAY

In 1938, Cuba became the first island state of the CONCACAF region to reach the FIFA World Cup quarter-finals. They drew 3-3 with Romania after extra-time in the first round, then won the replay 2-1 with goals by Hector Socorro and Carlos Oliveira after trailing at half-time. They were thrashed 8-0 by Sweden in the last eight. Haiti were the next Caribbean island to play in the finals, in 1974. They lost all three group games, 3-1 to Italy, 7-0 against Poland and 4-1 to Argentina.

RUIZ ON TARGETS

Guatemala's all-time leading scorer **Carlos Ruiz** had double cause for celebration when scoring in their 3-3 draw with Paraguay in August 2012: the game gave him not only a century of international appearances, but a half-century of goals. The player nicknamed "Pescado", or "Fish", announced his international retirement two months later, finishing with a record of 104 matches and 55 goals.

STERN OPPOSITION

Only seven internationals have claimed more goals than the 70 in 114 matches scored by Trinidad and Tobago's **Stern John** between his debut in 1995 and his final game for his country in 2011. The former Columbus Crew, Nottingham Forest and Sunderland striker was Trinidad and Tobago's top scorer and second-highest appearance-maker, behind midfielder Angus Eve. John was part of the country's squad for the 2006 FIFA World Cup, though Eve missed out – prompting him to retire from international football after 117 appearances.

TRINIDAD'S FIRST TIME

Trinidad & Tobago reached the FIFA World Cup finals for the first time in 2006 after a marathon qualifying competition that ended with their 1-0 play-off victory in Bahrain. The team, nicknamed the "Socca Warriors", held Sweden 0-0 in their opening game, but lost 2-0 to England and 2-0 to Paraguay.

PART 2:
FIFA ALL-TIME RECORDS
WORLD CUP

Spain became only the eighth winners of the FIFA World Cup when they triumphed in South Africa in 2010. However, Brazil remain the record-holders, with five victories inspired by superstars from Pele and Garrincha to Ronaldo and Ronaldinho. Argentina and Uruguay are the other South American winners, with past champions from Europe being England, France, Germany and Italy.

OCEANIA ADVENTURES

After completing their qualification rounds in Oceania for the 2010 FIFA World Cup, **New Zealand** had to wait 11 months before finally taking on Bahrain – Asia's fifth-best-placed team – in a two-legged play-off for a place in South Africa. The "All Whites" triumphed 1-0 on aggregate in November 2009, but it was another Oceanian team that boasted the best goals-per-game ratio of any country taking part in 2010 qualifiers. The Solomon Islands scored an average of 3.8 times per match, their record boosted by a 12-1 win over American Samoa. England were the next most prolific, managing 3.4 goals per game – and, unlike the unfortunate Solomon Islands, they secured a berth at the finals to boot.

T&T AT FULL STRETCH

Trinidad and Tobago share the record for the most games played to qualify for a FIFA World Cup finals. They played 20 in reaching the 2006 finals, beginning with 2-0 away and 4-0 home wins over the Dominican Republic in the preliminaries. T&T then finished second behind Mexico at the four-team first group stage to reach the six-team final group. After finishing fourth, they had to play off against Bahrain and won 2-1 on aggregate. Uruguay matched that figure in 2010, with 18 South America group matches and a two-legged play-off.

UAE IN A SQUEEZE

The **United Arab Emirates** reached the finals in 1990 by recording just one win and scoring only four goals in the Asian final round. They drew four of their five matches, but beat China 2-1 to qualify in second place behind South Korea.

FIFA OPENS WORLD CUP TO THE WORLD

FIFA has enlarged the World Cup finals twice since 1978, to take account of the rising football nations of Africa and Asia. The rise in interest is reflected in the massive number of sides entering the qualifying competition – 204 for the 2010 event. Brazilian **João Havelange**, FIFA president from 1974 to 1998, enlarged the organization both to take advantage of commercial opportunities and to give smaller nations a chance. The number of teams in the finals was first increased from 16 to 24 for the 1982 finals in Spain, with an extra place given for Africa and Asia and a chance for a nation from Oceania to reach the finals. The number of finalists was further increased to 32 for the 1998 tournament in France. This decision offered five places to African teams, four to sides from Asia and Oceania and three from North/Central America and the Caribbean. The formula for the 2010 finals in South Africa offered 13 places to Europe, four to South America, five to Africa, plus the hosts; four to Asia, with another for the winners of an Asia v Oceania play-off, in which Oceania's New Zealand beat Asia's Bahrain. CONCACAF (the North and Central American and Caribbean federation) had three spots. The other place was decided by a play-off in which Uruguay, the fifth-placed South American team, saw off Costa Rica, the fourth-placed team in the CONCACAF qualifiers. The formula remains the same for Brazil 2014.

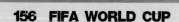

TAKING AIM

The 2014 FIFA World Cup will culminate in a final staged in Rio's Maracana Stadium. Some 203 nations have kicked off in qualifiers for that tournament – two fewer than the record 205 tilting at South Africa in 2010. The Bahamas and Mauritius subsequently later withdrew from the 2014 running, bringing the Brazil-bound contenders down to 201. Six more FIFA member states were missing, including the already-qualified hosts. New independent country South Sudan joined FIFA too late to compete, while four more nations opted not to take part this time: Bhutan, Brunei, Guam and Mauritania.

ALL–TIME QUALIFICATIONS BY REGIONAL CONFEDERATION

1	Europe	218
2	South America	74
3	North/Central America & Caribbean	35
4	Africa	34
5	Asia	28
6	Oceania	4

THE FIRST SHOOT–OUT

The first penalty shoot-out in qualifying history came on 9 January 1977 when Tunisia beat Morocco 4-2 on spot-kicks after a 1-1 draw in Tunis. The first game, in Casablanca, had also finished 1-1. Tunisia went on to qualify for the finals.

SPANISH INVINCIBLES

Several countries have qualified for a FIFA World Cup without losing or even drawing a single game. But the Spain side who cruised their way through to the 2010 tournament in South Africa were the first to do so while playing as many as 10 matches. Qualifying for the same finals from a smaller group, Holland won eight games out of eight. West Germany also went through eight matches without dropping a point in reaching the 1982 FIFA World Cup in Spain, and Brazil won six out of six in qualifying for the 1970 competition – at which Mario Zagallo's men won another six out of six on their way to lifting the trophy.

MOVING THE FINALS AROUND

After the 1954 and 1958 finals in Europe, FIFA decided that they would be staged alternately in South America and Europe. This lasted until the award of the 1994 tournament to the United States. Things have changed since then. Japan and South Korea were the first Asian hosts in 2002 and in 2010 South Africa were the first hosts from Africa.

THE GROWTH OF THE QUALIFYING COMPETITION

This charts the number of countries entering qualifiers for the FIFA World Cup finals. Some withdrew before playing.

World Cup	Teams entering
Uruguay 1930	-
Italy 1934	32
France 1938	37
Brazil 1950	34
Switzerland 1954	45
Sweden 1958	55
Chile 1962	56
England 1966	74
Mexico 1970	75
West Germany 1974	99
Argentina 1978	107
Spain 1982	109
Mexico 1986	121
Italy 1990	116
USA 1994	147
France 1998	174
Japan/South Korea 2002	199
Germany 2006	198
South Africa 2010	205
Brazil 2014	203

DEON AND ON AND ON

Belize striker **Deon McCaulay** scored the first goal of the 2014 FIFA World Cup qualifiers in his side's 5-2 victory over Montserrat in June 2011. He went on to strike another two that day, making him the 2014 qualification campaign's first scorer of a hat-trick. Belize won the two-legged tie 8-3, but were knocked out in the CONCACAF qualifiers' second round.

THE FASTEST SUBSTITUTION

The quickest-ever substitution in the history of FIFA World Cup qualifiers came on 30 December 1980, when North Korea's Chon Byong Ju was substituted in the first minute of his country's home game against Japan.

KOSTADINOV STUNS FRANCE

On 17 November 1993, in the last game of the Group Six schedule, Bulgaria's Emil Kostadinov scored one of the most dramatic goals in qualifying history to deny France a place at the 1994 finals. France seemed to be cruising with the score at 1-1 in stoppage time, but Kostadinov earned Bulgaria a shock victory after David Ginola had lost the ball. The Bulgarians reached the semi-finals of the tournament in the United States, losing 2-1 to Italy.

PALMER BEATS THE WHISTLE

Carl Erik Palmer's second goal in Sweden's 3-1 win over the Republic of Ireland in November 1949 was one of the most bizarre in qualifying history. The Irish defenders stopped, having heard a whistle, while Palmer ran on and put the ball in the net. The goal stood, because the whistle had come from someone in the crowd, not the referee. The 19-year-old forward went on to complete a hat-trick.

BWALYA LEAVES IT LATE

Zambia's **Kalusha Bwalya** is the oldest player to have scored a match-winning goal in a FIFA World Cup qualifying match. The 41-year-old netted the only goal against Liberia on 4 September 2004 after coming on as a substitute. He had also scored in his first qualifier, 20 years previously, in Zambia's 3-0 win over Uganda.

AUSTRALIA'S INCREDIBLE GOAL SPREE

Australia set a FIFA World Cup qualifying record in 2001, one that is unlikely to be beaten, as the Socceroos scored 53 goals in the space of two days. The details:

9 April 2001, Sydney: Australia 22, Tonga 0
Australia scorers: Scott Chipperfield 3, 83 mins; Damian Mori 13, 23, 40; John Aloisi 14, 24, 37, 45, 52, 63; **Kevin Muscat** (No. 2, right) 18, 30, 54, 58, 82; Tony Popovic 67; Tony Vidmar 74; David Zdrilic 78, 90; Archie Thompson 80; Con Boutsiania 87

11 April 2001, Sydney: Australia 31, American Samoa 0
Australia scorers: Boutsiania 10, 50, 84 mins; Thompson 12, 23, 27, 29, 32, 37, 42, 45, 56, 60, 65, 68, 88; Zdrilic 13, 21, 25, 33, 58, 66, 78, 89; Vidmar 14, 80; Popovic 17, 19; Simon Colosimo 51, 81; Fausto De Amicis 55

THOMPSON SETS UNLIKELY MARK

Archie Thompson eased past Iran striker Karim Bagheri's record for the number of goals in a single qualifying match (seven) as Australia thrashed American Samoa 31-0 on 11 April 2001. He netted 13 goals. David Zdrilic also beat Bagheri's total with eight goals. Two days earlier, Australia had previously smashed Iran's scoring record after completing a 22-0 victory over Tonga.

THE FASTEST GOAL

Davide Gualtieri, of minnows San Marino, scored the fastest goal in qualifying history when he netted after just nine seconds against England on 17 November 1993. England went on to win 7-1 but still failed to qualify.

MUNICH DISASTER HITS ENGLAND

England's 1958 FIFA World Cup hopes were wrecked by the Munich air disaster on 6 February 1958, which devastated champions Manchester United. Three United players – left-back Roger Byrne, left-half Duncan Edwards and centre-forward Tommy Taylor – had been outstanding in England's unbeaten qualification campaign, with each playing in all four matches. Nineteen-year-old Edwards netted twice and Taylor scored eight goals. Byrne and Taylor died in the crash; Edwards died 15 days later.

A REAL ALL–ROUNDER

West Indian cricket legend Sir Viv Richards can be acclaimed as an all-rounder in more than just the so-called "summer game" alone. He may have more famously helped his country win the cricket World Cup in 1975 and 1979, but he also played football for Antigua and Barbuda in qualifiers for the 1974 FIFA World Cup. Unfortunately, his football side lost all four of the qualifying matches they contested.

RECORD HAT–TRICK

Abdel Hamid Bassiouny of Egypt scored the fastest-ever hat-trick in qualifying history in their 8-2 win over Namibia on 13 July 2001. He netted three times in just 177 seconds between the 39th and 42nd minutes.

YOUNGEST AND OLDEST

The youngest player to appear in the FIFA World Cup qualifiers is Souleymane Mamam of Togo, who was 13 years 310 days when he played against Zambia on 6 May 2001. The oldest was MacDonald Taylor, who was 46 years, 180 days when he played for the Virgin Islands against St Kitts Nevis on 18 February 2004.

DAEI TOPS THE SCORERS

Iran's **Ali Daei** is the all-time top scorer in FIFA World Cup qualifiers. His nine goals in the 2006 qualifying campaign took his total to 30, nine ahead of the previous joint record-holder, Japan's Kazu Miura. Daei also scored seven goals in the 1994 qualifiers, four in the 1998 preliminaries and ten in 2002.

HORST THE FIRST TO GIVE WAY

The first player to be substituted during a FIFA World Cup qualifier was West Germany's **Horst Eckel,** when he was replaced by Richard Gottinger in their 3-0 victory over the short-lived protectorate of Saarland in October 1953. Eckel would go on to play on the right side of midfield in the side that beat Hungary in the 1954 FIFA World Cup final, while Gottinger's delayed appearance against Saarland was his first and last for his country. By the time of the 1958 FIFA World Cup qualifiers, Saarland had been integrated within West Germany.

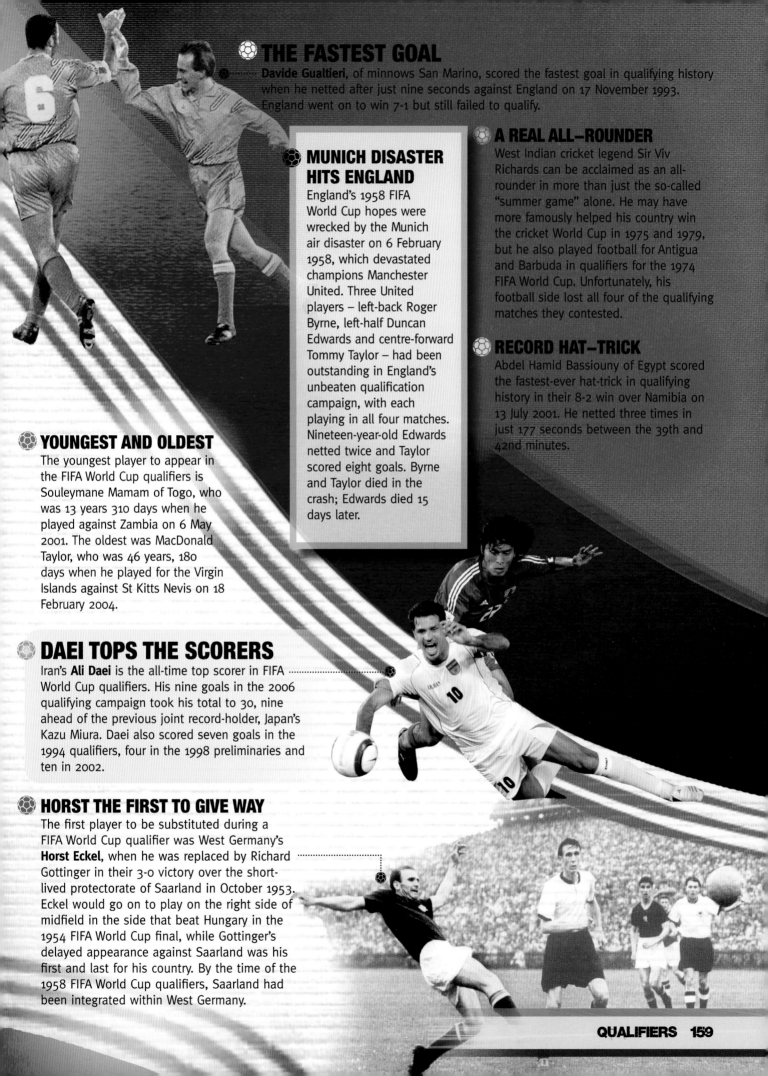

⚽ UNITED STATES LEAVE IT LATE

The latest of all qualifying play-offs took place in Rome on 24 May 1934, when the USA beat Mexico 4-2 to clinch the last slot in the FIFA World Cup finals. Three days later, the Americans were knocked out 7-1 by hosts Italy in the first round of the tournament.

⚽ ITALY FORCED TO QUALIFY

Italy are the only host country who have been required to qualify for their own tournament. The 1934 hosts beat Greece 4-0 to go through. FIFA decided that, for the 1938 finals, the holders and the hosts would qualify automatically. That decision was changed for the 2006 finals. Since then, only the hosts have been exempt from qualifying, though South Africa played in the second round of qualifying for 2010. This is because it doubled up as qualifiers for the 2010 Africa Cup of Nations.

⚽ TURKEY THROUGH ON LUCK OF THE DRAW

Turkey were the first team to qualify for the FIFA World Cup finals after the drawing of lots. Their play-off against Spain, in Rome on 17 March 1954, ended 2-2. Qualification was decided by a 14-year-old Roman boy, Luigi Franco Gemma. He was blindfolded to draw the lots – and pulled out Turkey, instead of much-fancied Spain.

⚽ THE "FOOTBALL WAR"

War broke out between El Salvador and Honduras after El Salvador beat Honduras 3-2 in a play-off on 26 June 1969 to qualify for the 1970 finals. Tension had been running high between the neighbours over a border dispute and there had been rioting at the match. On 14 July, the Salvador army invaded Honduras.

MOST SUCCESSFUL QUALIFYING ATTEMPTS

Italy	13
West Germany/Germany	12
Mexico	12
Spain	12
Argentina	12
Brazil	11
England	11
Belgium	10
Sweden	10
Yugoslavia/Serbia	10
Czechoslovakia/Czech Republic	9
Hungary	9

⚽ ENGLAND IN, SCOTLAND OUT

England, led by **Billy Wright**, took part in the FIFA World Cup finals for the first time in 1950. They won their all-British group ahead of Scotland. Both teams thus qualified, but the Scots refused to go to the finals in Brazil because they had only finished second. The Scots subsequently qualified eight times, but have never advanced beyond the first round of the finals and have not appeared at the FIFA World Cup finals since 1998.

THIERRY'S TRICKERY

France qualified for the 2010 FIFA World Cup finals thanks to one of the most controversial international goals of recent history. The second leg of their play-off against the Republic of Ireland in November 2009 was 14 minutes into extra-time when striker **Thierry Henry** clearly controlled the ball with his hand, before crossing to William Gallas who gave his side a decisive 2-1 aggregate lead. After Swedish referee Martin Hansson allowed the goal to stand, the Football Association of Ireland first called for the game to be replayed, then asked to be allowed into the finals as a 33rd country – but both requests proved in vain.

NICE ONE, SON

The latest goal of 2014 FIFA World Cup qualifiers was **Son Heung-Min**'s winner for South Korea, six minutes into stoppage-time of their crucial March 2013 match against Qatar. The strike not only secured a 2-1 win, but also South Korea's qualification for the finals in Brazil.

GOING UNDERCOVER

The Kingdome in Seattle, United States, hosted the first FIFA World Cup qualifier to be played indoors, when the US beat Canada 2-0 in October 1976 – just a few months after the same venue had staged its first rock concert, by Paul McCartney's post-Beatles band Wings, and a religious rally featuring evangelist Billy Graham and country singer Johnny Cash. Canada gained revenge by beating the US 3-0 in a play-off, hosted in Haiti, to reach the next stage of the CONCACAF qualifying round. But only Mexico would go on to represent the continent at the 1978 FIFA World Cup in Argentina.

WALES IN THROUGH THE BACK DOOR

Only once have all four British teams have reached the same FIFA World Cup finals, in 1958. England, Scotland and Northern Ireland all topped their groups, but Wales qualified by a roundabout route. They had been eliminated – then were offered a second chance. Israel had emerged unchallenged, for political reasons, from the Asian qualifying section. However, FIFA ruled that the Israelis could not qualify without having played a match and determined that they must play off against one of the second-placed European teams. Wales were drawn to meet them and qualified by winning both games 2-0.

ARGENTINA'S LONG BOYCOTT

Argentina boycotted the FIFA World Cup for nearly 20 years. They were Copa America holders in 1938, but refused to travel to France because they were upset at being passed over to host the finals. They were also unhappy at being paired with Brazil in a qualifier. They did not take part in the 1950 or 1954 competitions either, after Brazil were chosen to host the 1950 finals and did not return to FIFA World Cup competition until the qualifiers for the 1958 finals due to be held in Sweden.

FIFA WORLD CUP TEAM RECORDS

SPAIN GAIN

The FIFA World Cup trophy had a new name engraved on it for first time since 1998 when **Spain** beat the Netherlands 1-0 in the 2010 final, in Johannesburg's Soccer City stadium on 11 July. The match was the first final in 32 years to feature two teams who had never won the competition before. The only previous finals featuring two non-former winners were when Argentina beat the Dutch in 1978, Brazil beat Sweden in 1958, West Germany defeated Hungary in 1954, Italy beat Czechoslovakia in 1934 and, of course, Uruguay saw off Argentina in the inaugural 1930 tournament.

SHARING THE GOALS

France in 1982 and winners Italy, in 2006, supplied the most individual goalscorers during a FIFA World Cup finals tournament – ten. Gerard Soler, Bernard Genghini, Michel Platini, Didier Six, Maxime Bossis, Alain Giresse, Dominque Rocheteau, Marius Tresor, Rene Girard and Alain Couriol netted for France. Alessandro Del Piero, Alberto Gilardino, Fabio Grosso, Vincenzo Iaquinta, Luca Toni, Pippo Inzaghi, Marco Materazzi, Andrea Pirlo, Francesco Totti and Gianluca Zambrotta all scored for Italy, who went on to win the tournament.

BRAZIL COLOUR UP

Brazil's yellow shirts are famous throughout the world. But the national team wore **white shirts** for each of the first four World Cup tournaments. Brazil's 2-1 defeat by Uruguay, which cost them the 1950 World Cup, came as such a shock to the population that the national association decided to change the team's shirt colours, to try and wipe out the bitter memory.

SINGING THE BLUES

Spain's 2010 FIFA World Cup triumph – for whom **Xavi** was a star even in an unfamiliar all-blue kit – made them the first team to win the tournament while playing the final in their second kit since England in 1966.

ITALY KEEP IT TIGHT

Italy set the record for the longest run without conceding a goal at the FIFA World Cup finals. They went five games without conceding at the 1990 finals, starting with their 1-0 group win over Austria. Goalkeeper Walter Zenga was not beaten until Claudio Caniggia scored Argentina's equalizer in the semi-final. And a watertight defence did not bring Italy the glory it craved: Argentina reached the final by winning the penalty shoot-out 4-3.

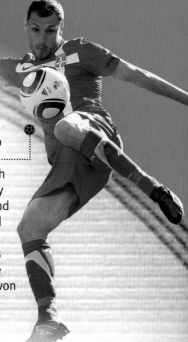

TODAY EUROPE, TOMORROW THE WORLD

Spain's 2010 trophy-lifting coach **Vicente del Bosque** became only the second manager to have won both the FIFA World Cup and the UEFA Champions League or its previous incarnation, the European Champions' Cup. Marcello Lippi won the UEFA prize with Juventus in 1996, 10 years before his Italy team became world champions. Del Bosque won the UEFA Champions League twice with Real Madrid, in 2000 and 2002, though he was sacked in summer 2003 for "only" winning the Spanish league title the previous season.

DO YOU COME HERE OFTEN?

Germany or West Germany have now played Yugoslavia/Serbia a record-equalling seven times at FIFA World Cup finals, after **Milan Jovanovic's** goal gave Serbia a 1–0 win in Port Elizabeth, South Africa, in the 2010 tournament. Germany enjoyed victories in 1954, 1958, 1974 and 1990, while Yugoslavia won in 1962 and the countries drew in 1998. There have also been seven FIFA World Cup clashes between Brazil and Sweden, though the latter have yet to taste success. Brazil won in 1938, 1950, 1958, 1990 and twice in 1994 – but drew in 1978.

MOST APPEARANCES IN THE FIFA WORLD CUP FINAL

1	Brazil	7
=	Germany/West Germany	7
3	Italy	6
4	Argentina	4
5	Netherlands	3
6	Czechoslovakia	2
=	France	2
=	Hungary	2
=	Uruguay	2
10	England	1
=	Spain	1
=	Sweden	1

BRAZIL PROFIT FROM RIMET'S VISION

Jules Rimet, president of FIFA from 1921 to 1954, was the driving force behind the first World Cup, in 1930. The tournament in Uruguay was not the high-profile event it is now, with only 13 nations taking part. The long sea journey kept most European teams away. Only four – Belgium, France, Romania and Yugoslavia – made the trip. Regardless, Rimet's dream had been realized and the FIFA World Cup grew and grew in popularity. Brazil have been the most successful team in the competition's history, winning the trophy five times. They have won more games in the FIFA World Cup finals (67) than any other country, though Germany have now played more games – 99 to Brazil's 97. Italy have won the FIFA World Cup four times and West Germany three. The original finalists, Uruguay and Argentina, have both lifted the trophy twice. England, in 1966, and France, in 1998, have won once, both as hosts, before Spain lifted their first FIFA World Cup in South Africa in 2010.

WHY THE BRITISH TEAMS STAYED OUT

England and Scotland are considered the homelands of football, but neither country entered the FIFA World Cup until the qualifiers for the 1950 finals. The four British associations – England, Scotland, Wales and Northern Ireland – quit FIFA in the 1920s over a row over broken-time (employment compensation) payments to amateurs. The British associations did not rejoin FIFA until 1946.

ONE-TIME WONDERS

Indonesia, then known as the Dutch East Indies, made one appearance in the finals, in the days when the tournament was a strictly knockout affair. On 5 June 1938, they lost 6-0 to Hungary in the first round, and have never qualified for the tournament since.

MOST APPEARANCES IN FIFA WORLD CUP FINALS TOURNAMENTS

1	Brazil	19
2	Germany/West Germany	17
=	Italy	17
4	Argentina	15
5	Mexico	14

FIFA WORLD CUP STOPS THE WORLD

The FIFA World Cup finals are the biggest sporting event in history. Television was in its infancy when the first finals were held in 1930. The tournament has since become the most popular TV sporting event of all. The 2006 finals were watched by a worldwide audience of 26.3 billion, 0.1 billion fewer than the 2002 finals. In addition to the estimated 700 million fans who watched the 2010 FIFA World Cup final at Soccer City, Johannesburg, between Spain and the Netherlands on televisions around the world, hundreds of thousands of others went to public squares and Fan Fests to watch the match on giant screens.

GOLDEN NARROWS

Before 2010, no country had won five consecutive FIFA World Cup matches by a one-goal margin – but **Arjen Robben** and the Netherlands and became the first, thanks to their 3-2 semi-final victory over Uruguay. Before then, the record rested with Italy, who managed four single-goal wins in a row across the 1934 and 1938 FIFA World Cups. Spain's 1-0 defeat of the Dutch in the 2010 FIFA World Cup was also their fifth consecutive single-goal victory and fourth in the knockout stages.

GERMANY'S GOAL BONANZA

West Germany conceded 14 goals in the 1954 finals, the most ever conceded by the FIFA World Cup winners. But they scored 25 – second most in FIFA World Cup history. Only their victims in the final – Hungary – scored more than the Germans: they netted 27.

EVER RED

England's victory in 1966 was not just the only time they have won the FIFA World Cup – it also now remains the only time the prize has been clinched by a side wearing red shirts in the final. Spain might have emulated England's fashion sense in 2010 but had to wear blue to avoid clashing with the Netherlands' bright orange – they did, however, change back into their usual red to receive the trophy from FIFA president **Joseph S. Blatter**.

THE FEWEST GOALS CONCEDED

FIFA World Cup winners France (1998), Italy (2006) and Spain (2010) hold the record for the fewest goals conceded on their way to victory. All three conceded just two. Spain also now hold the record for fewest goals scored by FIFA World Cup winners. They netted just eight in 2010, below the 11 scored by Italy in 1938, England in 1966 or Brazil in 1994.

SPONSORS MAKE THE FINALS PAY

The 2010 FIFA World Cup was the most lucrative ever, with world football's governing body FIFA pocketing $3.2 million in profits from the event in South Africa. A record 700m viewers tuned in to the final between Spain and the Netherlands – another all-time high.

FEWEST GOALS CONCEDED IN ONE TOURNAMENT:
Switzerland: 0, 2006

MOST GOALS SCORED IN ONE TOURNAMENT
Hungary: 27, 1954

MOST WINS IN ONE TOURNAMENT
Brazil: 7, 2002

MOST GOALS SCORED IN ONE TOURNAMENT
Just Fontaine (France): 13, 1958

MOST CONSECUTIVE MATCHES SCORING A GOAL AT FIFA WORLD CUP FINALS

18	Brazil	1930–58
18	Germany	1934–58, 1986–98
17	Hungary	1934–62
16	Uruguay	1930–62
15	Brazil	1978–90
15	France	1978–86

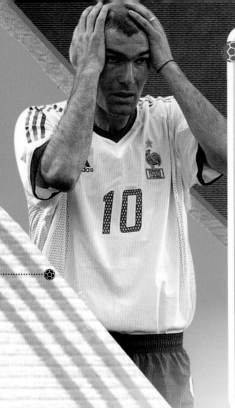

PERFORMANCES BY HOST NATION AT FIFA WORLD CUP FINALS

1930	Uruguay	Champions
1934	Italy	Champions
1938	France	Quarter-finals
1950	Brazil	Runners-up
1954	Switzerland	Quarter-finals
1958	Sweden	Runners-up
1962	Chile	Third place
1966	England	Champions
1970	Mexico	Quarter-finals
1974	West Germany	Champions
1978	Argentina	Champions
1982	Spain	Second round
1986	Mexico	Quarter-finals
1990	Italy	Third place
1994	United States	Second round
1998	France	Champions
2002	South Korea	Fourth place
	Japan	Second round
2006	Germany	Third place
2010	South Africa	First round

SAFE EUROPEAN HOME

Spain's triumph at the 2010 FIFA World Cup in South Africa made them the first European team to lift the trophy outside their own continent. After Italian glory in 2006, Spain's success four years later set another first – the first time the prize has gone to different European countries twice in succession. Furthermore, Europe has also now edged ahead of South America in FIFA World Cup wins – 10–9 up, since the inaugural tournament in 1930.

HOLDERS CRASH OUT

France produced the worst performance by a defending FIFA World Cup winner in Japan and South Korea in 2002: they lost their opening game 1-0 to Senegal, drew 0-0 against Uruguay and were eliminated after losing 1-0 to Denmark. They were the first defending champions to be knocked out without scoring a goal. In 2010 Italy emulated France by exiting at the first-round stage, and without winning a match – nor indeed ever taking the lead. At least Italy did achieve two draws – and scored four goals. They opened with a 1-1 draw against Paraguay, needed a penalty to force another 1-1 draw against minnows New Zealand, and they were on their way home after losing 3-2 to Slovakia.

THREE AND OUT

The Netherlands, coached by **Bert van Marwijk** in 2010, became the only country to have reached the final of three FIFA World Cups without managing to lift the trophy once. Their six victories en route to the 2010 final are also more than any other team has managed in one tournament without going on to claim the main prize.

BRAZIL LEAD THE WAY

Brazil scored the most victories in finals tournaments when they won all their seven games in 2002. They began with a 2-1 group win over Turkey and ended with a 2-0 final triumph over Germany. They scored 18 goals in their unbeaten run and conceded on only four occasions.

HOME DISCOMFORT

South Africa became the first host nation to fail to reach the second round of a FIFA World Cup, when staging the 2010 tournament – though their first-round record of one win, one draw and one defeat was only inferior on goal difference to the opening three games played by hosts Spain, in 1982, and the USA, in 1994, both of whom reached the second round. Uruguay's 3–0 victory over South Africa in Pretoria on 16 June 2010 equalled the highest losing margin suffered by a FIFA World Cup host, following Brazil's 5–2 win over Sweden in the 1958 final and Italy's 4–1 trouncing of Mexico in their 1970 quarter-final.

FINE HOST

Siphiwe Tshabalala's goal for South Africa at Soccer City, Johannesburg, in the opening match of the 2010 FIFA World Cup not only gave his team the lead against Mexico – it was also the fifth time the hosts had scored the first goal of a FIFA World Cup. Previous examples were: Ademir, for Brazil in a 4–0 win over Mexico in 1950; Agne Simonsson, for Sweden in a 3–0 win, also against Mexico, in 1958; Paul Breitner, West Germany's only and winning goal against Chile in 1974 (though it was the second game – Brazil and Yugoslavia having played out a goalless draw); and Philipp Lahm, for Germany in a 4–2 defeat of Costa Rica in 2006. Tshabalala's strike was also the fourth time Mexico had let in the opening goal of a FIFA World Cup. As well as Ademir and Simonsson, Mexico conceded the first-ever goal in a FIFA World Cup, scored by France's Lucien Laurent in 1930.

HIGHEST SCORES

The highest-scoring game in the FIFA World Cup finals was the quarter-final between Austria and Switzerland on 26 June 1954. Austria staged a remarkable comeback to win 7-5, with centre-forward **Theodor Wagner** scoring a hat-trick, after trailing 3-0 in the 19th minute. Three other games have produced 11 goals – Brazil's 6-5 win over Poland in the 1938 first round, Hungary's 8-3 win over West Germany in their 1954 group game and the Hungarians' 10-1 rout of El Salvador at the group stage in 1982.

LOW-SCORING SPAIN

Spain won the 2010 FIFA World Cup despite scoring just eight goals in seven games on their way to the title – fewer than any world champions in history, including 11-goal Italy in 1934, England in 1966 and Brazil in 1994. Vicente del Bosque's Spain were also the first team to win 1-0 in all four of their knockout matches. David Villa scored the decisive goal in two of those matches.

GENEROUS OPPONENTS

Germany were the first team to benefit from an opponent scoring an own goal at a FIFA World Cup – Switzerland's Ernst Loertscher put the ball into his own net during Germany's 4–2 win at the 1938 tournament. Germany, or West Germany, have been gifted a record-equalling four own goals in FIFA World Cup history – level with Italy. Mexico, Bulgaria, the Netherlands, Yugoslavia, Portugal and South Korea have all scored two FIFA World Cup own goals apiece – the most recent being perpetrated by Park Chu-Young, in South Korea's 4–1 defeat to Argentina in 2010, three days after Denmark's Daniel Agger gave the Netherlands the lead in another first-round match.

ZERO TOLERANCE

Paraguay's 0-0 draw and subsequent **penalty shoot-out win** over Japan in the second round at the 2010 FIFA World Cup made it seven goalless draws at the one tournament – equalling the stalemate record set in both 1982 and 2006. Andres Iniesta's late winner for Spain against the Netherlands in the 2010 final meant Brazil against Italy in 1994 is still the only FIFA World Cup final to remain goalless.

THE FASTEST GOAL

Turkey's **Hakan Sukur** holds the record for the quickest goal scored in the FIFA World Cup finals. He netted after 11 seconds against South Korea in the 2002 third-place play-off. Turkey went on to win 3-2. The previous record was held by Vaclav Masek of Czechoslovakia, who struck after 15 seconds against Mexico in 1962.

BIGGEST FIFA WORLD CUP FINALS WINS

Hungary 10, El Salvador 1 (15 June 1982)
Hungary 9, South Korea 0 (17 June 1954)
Yugoslavia 9, Zaire 0 (18 June 1974)
Sweden 8, Cuba 0 (12 June 1938)
Uruguay 8, Bolivia 0 (2 July 1950)
Germany 8, Saudi Arabia 0 (1 June 2002)

MOST GOALS IN ONE FIFA WORLD CUP

Goals	Country	Year
27	**Hungary**	**1954**
25	**West Germany**	**1954**
23	**France**	**1958**
22	**Brazil**	**1950**
19	**Brazil**	**1970**

MOST GOALS IN FIFA WORLD CUP FINALS (MINIMUM 100)

1	**Brazil**	**210**
2	**Germany/W Germany**	**206**
3	**Italy**	**126**
4	**Argentina**	**123**

MOST AND LEAST

The most goals scored in a single FIFA World Cup finals tournament is 171, in France in 1998, after FIFA extended the competition to 32 teams and 64 matches for the first time. The highest number of goals per match was recorded in the 1954 finals, with 140 goals in just 26 games at an average of 5.38 goals per game. The lowest average per game came in Italy in 1990, when 115 goals were scored in 52 matches, an average of 2.21 goals per game. The 2010 FIFA World Cup saw 145 goals – at an average of 2.26 per game.

YOUNGEST AND OLDEST

The youngest-ever scorer of a goal in FIFA World Cup finals history is **Pele**. He was 17 years and 239 days old when he notched Brazil's winner against Wales in the 1958 quarter-finals. Cameroon's **Roger Milla** – aged 42 years and 39 days – became the oldest scorer when he netted his country's only goal in a 6-1 defeat by Russia in 1994.

GOING FOR GOLD

Four different players were tied as top scorer at the 2010 FIFA World Cup, but for the first time, the adidas Golden Boot prize was awarded to only one after being decided on goals set up as well as goals scored. Uruguay's Diego Forlan, Spain's David Villa and the Netherlands' Wesley Sneijder missed out on the award, which went instead to Germany's 20-year-old **Thomas Muller.** Like them, he had scored five times, but had also contributed more assists – three, compared with one apiece for Villa, Sneijder and Forlan. Villa received the adidas Silver Boot, because he made his contributions in fewer minutes on the pitch (634) than adidas Bronze Boot recipient Sneijder (652) or Forlan (654).

COMING BACK FOR MORE

Seven footballers have scored goals at FIFA World Cup tournaments 12 years apart, the latest being Mexico's Cuauhtemoc Blanco. His successful penalty against France, in Polokwane in 2010, came a dozen years after his first FIFA World Cup goal, against Belgium, in 1998. Others to have scored across a similar time-span are Brazil's Pele (1958–1970), West Germany's Uwe Seeler (1958–1970), Argentina's Diego Maradona (1982–1994), Denmark's Michael Laudrup (1986–1998), Sweden's Henrik Larsson (1994–2006) and Saudi Arabia's Sami Al-Jaber (1994–2006).

HEAD FOR FIGURES

Arjen Robben's emphatic header against Uruguay, to put the Netherlands 3-1 up in their 3-2 semi-final win at the 2010 FIFA World Cup, was the 2,200th goal ever scored in the competition. **Andres Iniesta**'s winning goal for Spain in that summer's final took the overall FIFA World Cup tally to 2,208.

ROSSI THE ITALY HERO

Paolo Rossi turned from villain to hero as Italy won the 1982 FIFA World Cup. Coach Enzo Bearzot had picked Rossi even though he had only just completed a two-year suspension after a match-fixing scandal. Rossi was criticized for a lack of fitness in the early matches, but he scored a hat-trick against Brazil, two goals as Italy beat Poland in the semi-final, and the opener in their FIFA World Cup final victory over West Germany.

EUSEBIO THE STRIKE FORCE

Portugal's **Eusebio** was the striking star of the 1966 FIFA World Cup finals. Ironically, he would not be eligible to play for Portugal now. He was born in Mozambique, then a Portuguese colony, but now an independent country. He finished top scorer with nine goals, including two as Portugal eliminated champions Brazil and four as they beat North Korea 5-3 in the quarter-finals after trailing 3-0.

FIFA WORLD CUP FINALS
TOP SCORERS (1930–78)

Maximum 16 teams in finals

Year	Venue	Top Scorer	Country	Goals
1930	Uruguay	Guillermo Stabile	Argentina	8
1934	Italy	Oldrich Nejedly	Czechoslovakia	5
1938	France	Leonidas	Brazil	7
1950	Brazil	Ademir	Brazil	9
1954	Switzerland	Sandor Kocsis	Hungary	11
1958	Sweden	Just Fontaine	France	13
1962	Chile	Garrincha	Brazil	4
		Vava	Brazil	
		Leonel Sanchez	Chile	
		Florian Albert	Hungary	
		Valentin Ivanov	Soviet Union	
		Drazen Jerkovic	Yugoslavia	
1966	England	Eusebio	Portugal	9
1970	Mexico	Gerd Muller	West Germany	10
1974	West Germany	Grzegorz Lato	Poland	7
1978	Argentina	Mario Kempes	Argentina	6

KEMPES MAKES HIS MARK

Mario Kempes was Argentina's only foreign-based player in the hosts' squad at the 1978 finals. Twice top scorer in the Spanish league, Valencia's Kempes was crucial to Argentina's success. Coach Cesar Luis Menotti told him to shave off his moustache after he failed to score in the group games. Kempes then netted two against Peru, two more against Poland, and two decisive goals in the final against the Netherlands.

NO GUARANTEES FOR TOP SCORERS

Topping the FIFA World Cup finals scoring chart is a great honour for all strikers, but few have gained the ultimate prize and been leading scorer. Argentina's Guillermo Stabile started the luckless trend in 1930, topping the scoring charts but finishing up on the losing side in the final. The list of top scorers who have played in the winning side is small: Garrincha and Vava (joint top scorers in 1962), Mario Kempes (top scorer in 1978), Paolo Rossi (1982) and Ronaldo (2002). Gerd Muller, top scorer in 1970, gained his reward as West Germany's trophy winner four years later. Other top scorers, such as Sandor Kocsis, 1954, Just Fontaine, 1958, and Gary Lineker, 1986, have been disappointed in the final stages. Kocsis was the only one to reach the final – and Hungary were defeated. Four players finished tied on five goals at the 2010 FIFA World Cup and one – David Villa – collected a winner's medal, but the Golden Boot went to Germany's Thomas Muller.

STABILE MAKES AN IMPACT

Guillermo Stabile, top scorer in the 1930 FIFA World Cup finals, had never played for Argentina before the tournament. He made his debut – as a 25-year-old – against Mexico because first-choice Roberto Cherro had suffered a panic attack. He netted a hat-trick then scored twice against both Chile and the United States as Argentina reached the final. He struck one of his side's goals in the 4-2 defeat by Uruguay in the final.

SCORING SKIPPERS

Both captains scored when the Netherlands beat Uruguay in their Cape Town semi-final at the 2010 FIFA World Cup in South Africa – **Giovanni van Bronckhorst** for the Dutch, Diego Forlan for Uruguay. This had happened only four times before in FIFA World Cup history.

HURST MAKES HISTORY

England's **Geoff Hurst** became the first and to date only player to score a hat-trick in a FIFA World Cup final when he netted three in the hosts' 4-2 victory over West Germany in 1966. Hurst headed England level after the Germans took an early lead, then scored the decisive third goal with a shot that bounced down off the crossbar and just over the line, according to the Soviet linesman. Hurst hit his third in the last minute. The British TV commentator Kenneth Wolstenholme described Hurst's strike famously with the words: "Some people are on the pitch ... They think it's all over ... It is now!"

TWO OUT OF 10

Only two players wearing the iconic No. 10 shirt have won the Golden Boot at FIFA World Cup finals: Argentina's Mario Kempes in 1978 and England's Gary Lineker eight years later. Dutch No. 10 Wesley Sneijder was in the running for the prize in 2010, but finished second behind Germany's No. 13 Thomas Muller.

ANDRES THE GIANT

Spain's hero in the 2010 FIFA World Cup final was **Andres Iniesta** (right), whose 116th-minute goal was also the latest trophy-winning strike in the tournament's history – not counting penalty shoot-outs, that is.

FIFA WORLD CUP FINALS ALL–TIME LEADING GOALSCORERS

	Name	Country	Tournaments	Goals
1	Ronaldo	Brazil	1998, 2002, 2006	15
2	Gerd Muller	West Germany	1970, 1974	14
=	Miroslav Klose	Germany	2002, 2006, 2010	14
3	Just Fontaine	France	1958	13
4	Pele	Brazil	1958, 1962, 1966, 1970	12
5	Sandor Kocsis	Hungary	1954	11
=	Jurgen Klinsmann	W Germany/Germany	1990, 1994, 1998	11
7	Gabriel Batistuta	Argentina	1994, 1998, 2002	10
=	Teofilo Cubillas	Peru	1970, 1978	10
=	Gregorz Lato	Poland	1974, 1978, 1982	10
=	Gary Lineker	England	1986, 1990	10
=	Helmut Rahn	West Germany	1954, 1958	10

THE BRADLEY BUNCH

Michael Bradley's late equalizer for the United States, in their Group C 2-2 draw with Slovenia in June 2010, made him the first person to score a FIFA World Cup goal for a team coached by his own father – in this case, Bob Bradley.

THE GREAT GONZALO

Argentina striker **Gonzalo Higuain** ended an eight-year wait for a FIFA World Cup hat-trick when he scored three in his team's 4-1 victory over South Korea in the first round of the 2010 tournament. The 2006 FIFA World Cup was the only one without a single hat-trick, making Higuain's treble the first for eight years and seven days – since Pauleta scored three in Portugal's 4-0 trouncing of Poland at the 2002 tournament.

⚽ PELE SO UNLUCKY

Pele would surely have been the all-time FIFA World Cup top scorer but for injuries. He was sidelined early in the 1962 finals, and again four years later. He scored six goals in Brazil's 1958 triumph, including two in the 5-2 final victory over Sweden. He also netted Brazil's 100th FIFA World Cup goal as they beat Italy 4-1 in the 1970 final.

⚽ MULLER'S SCORING HABIT

West Germany's **Gerd Muller** had the knack of scoring in important games. He struck the winner against England in the 1970 quarter-final and his two goals in extra-time against Italy almost carried his side to the final. Four years later, Muller's goal against Poland ensured that West Germany reached the final on home soil. Then he scored the winning goal against the Netherlands in the FIFA World Cup final. He also had a goal disallowed for offside – wrongly, as TV replays proved.

⚽ RONALDO SO CONSISTENT

Ronaldo was a consistent scorer in the three FIFA World Cup finals tournaments he played in. He netted four times in 1998, when they were runners-up to France, eight as Brazil won the 2002 tournament – including both goals in the final – and three more in 2006. He became the all-time top scorer when netting Brazil's opener in a 3-0 win over Ghana in the last-16 round at Dortmund on 27 June 2006. As a teenager, Ronaldo had been a member of Brazil's FIFA World Cup winning squad in the United States in 1994, but did not play.

⚽ KLINSMANN'S CONTRIBUTION

Jurgen Klinsmann has been an influential force at the FIFA World Cup both as a player and a coach. He scored three goals when West Germany won the FIFA World Cup in 1990, five more – for a unified Germany – in the 1994 finals, and three in 1998. He then coached Germany to the semi-finals in 2006.

⚽ WHO SCORED THE FIRST HAT-TRICK?

For many years, Argentina's Guillermo Stabile was considered the first hat-trick scorer in the FIFA World Cup finals. He netted three in Argentina's 6-3 win over Mexico on 19 July 1930, but has since been superseded by Bert Patenaude of the United States. FIFA changed its records in November 2006, to acknowledge that Patenaude's treble two days earlier, in the Americans' 3-0 win over Paraguay, had been the tournament's first hat-trick.

⚽ THE POWER OF 73

The goals that proved to be decisive in both semi-finals at the 2010 FIFA World Cup were each scored in the 73rd minute: Arjen Robben's header in the Netherlands' 3–2 win over Uruguay, and **Carles Puyol's** header – the only goal of the game – for Spain against Germany the following evening.

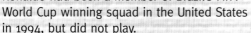
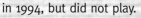

FIFA WORLD CUP APPEARANCES

Two players, Mexico's Antonio Carbajal and Germany's Lothar Matthaus, have appeared in a record five FIFA World Cup final tournaments, but for many players, appearing just once in football's ultimate event is cause enough for dreams. The following pages chart individual appearance records at football's premier competition, from the longest to the shortest, to the greatest time elapsed between FIFA World Cup appearances.

YOUNGEST AND OLDEST

Northern Ireland forward Norman Whiteside became the then youngest player to appear in the FIFA World Cup finals when he started against Yugoslavia in 1982, aged just 17 years and 41 days. The oldest player to feature in the tournament was Cameroon forward Roger Milla, who faced Russia in 1994 aged 42 years and 39 days.

THIS IS ENGLAND

England's Premier League (including Chelsea and England's **Frank Lampard**) was the best-represented domestic league at the 2010 FIFA World Cup, with 117 of the 32 squads' 736 players appearing in that competition. Germany's Bundesliga had 84 players, Italy's Serie A 80, Spain's Primera Liga 59, France's Ligue 1 45, the Netherlands' Eredivisie 34 and Japan's J-League 25.

MOST APPEARANCES IN FIFA WORLD CUP FINALS

25 Lothar Matthaus (West Germany/ Germany)
23 Paolo Maldini (Italy)
21 Diego Maradona (Argentina)
   Uwe Seeler (West Germany)
   Wladyslaw Zmuda (Poland)

DOUBLE WINNERS

Players who have played on the winning side in two FIFA World Cup finals:

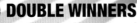

Giovanni Ferrari (Italy), 1934, 1938
Giuseppe Meazza (Italy), 1934, 1938
Pele (Brazil), 1958, 1970
Didi (Brazil), 1958, 1962
Djalma Santos (Brazil), 1958, 1962
Garrincha (Brazil), 1958, 1962
Gilmar (Brazil), 1958, 1962
Nilton Santos (Brazil), 1958, 1962
Vava (Brazil), 1958, 1962
Zagallo (Brazil), 1958, 1962
Zito (Brazil), 1958, 1962
Cafu (Brazil), 1994, 2002

THE "DOUBLE" CHAMPIONS

Franz Beckenbauer and Mario Zagallo are a unique duo. They have both won the FIFA World Cup as a player and a coach. Beckenbauer also had the distinction of captaining West Germany to victory on home soil in 1974. As coach, he steered them to the final in Mexico in 1986 and to victory over Argentina in Italy four years later. He was nicknamed "Der Kaiser" (The Emperor) both for his style and his achievements. Zagallo gained two winners' medals as a player. He was the left-winger in Brazil's triumphant march to the 1958 championship, before playing a deeper role in their 1962 victory. He took over from the controversial Joao Saldanha as Brazil coach three months before the 1970 finals and guided the side to victory in all six of its games, scoring 19 goals and routing Italy 4-1 in the final. Zagallo later filled the role of the team's technical director when Brazil won the FIFA World Cup for a fourth time in 1994.

MOST FIFA WORLD CUP FINALS TOURNAMENTS

These players all played in at least four FIFA World Cup finals tournaments.

5 **Antonio Carbajal** (Mexico) 1950, 1954, 1958, 1962, 1966
  Lothar Matthaus (West Germany/Germany) 1982, 1986, 1990, 1994, 1998
4 **Djalma Santos** (Brazil) 1954, 1958, 1962, 1966
  Pele (Brazil) 1958, 1962, 1966, 1970
  Uwe Seeler (West Germany) 1958, 1962, 1966, 1970
  Karl-Heinz Schnellinger (West Germany) 1958, 1962, 1966, 1970
  Gianni Rivera (Italy) 1962, 1966, 1970, 1974
  Pedro Rocha (Uruguay) 1962, 1966, 1970, 1974
  Wladyslaw Zmuda (Poland) 1974, 1978, 1982, 1986
  Giuseppe Bergomi (Italy) 1982, 1986, 1990, 1998
  Diego Maradona (Argentina) 1982, 1986, 1990, 1994
  Enzo Scifo (Belgium) 1986, 1990, 1994, 1998
  Franky van der Elst (Belgium) 1986, 1990, 1994, 1998
  Andoni Zubizarreta (Spain) 1986, 1990, 1994, 1998
  Paolo Maldini (Italy) 1990, 1994, 1998, 2002
  Hong Myung-Bo (South Korea) 1990, 1994, 1998, 2002
  Cafu (Brazil) 1994, 1998, 2002, 2006
  Sami Al-Jaber (Saudi Arabia) 1994, 1998, 2002, 2006
  Denis Caniza (Paraguay) 1998, 2002, 2006, 2010
  Fabio Cannavaro (Italy) 1998, 2002, 2006, 2010
  Thierry Henry (France) 1998, 2002, 2006, 2010
  Rigobert Song (Cameroon) 1994, 1998, 2002, 2010

HOME IS IN CATALONIA

Spanish champions **Barcelona** had more players at the 2010 FIFA World Cup than any other club, with 14 – eight for Spain, including new signing David Villa, with reserve goalkeeper Victor Valdes being the only one not to play. English clubs Chelsea and Liverpool had 12 players apiece in South Africa for the tournament, followed by 11 from Germany's Bayern Munich.

DOUBLE DUTCH, DOUBLE WHAMMY

Arjen Robben and Mark van Bommel suffered an unusual double whammy in the 2009–10 season: they ended on the losing side in both the UEFA Champions League final, for Bayern Munich against Internazionale, and the FIFA World Cup final, for the Netherlands against Spain. Others who have endured similar fates are Oliver Neuville, Bernd Schneider and Carsten Ramelow (for Bayer Leverkusen against Real Madrid, and Germany against Brazil, in 2002) and Thierry Henry (for Arsenal against Barcelona, and France against Italy, in 2006).

IT'S THE SAME OLD SONG

Cameroon's veteran defender **Rigobert Song** played just 17 minutes of the 2010 FIFA World Cup in South Africa, but it did make him the first African to play at four editions of the tournament – nine matches, stretching across 16 years and nine days. He featured in 1994, 1998, 2002 and 2010 – missing the 2006 event because Cameroon failed to qualify. Only three players have enjoyed longer FIFA World Cup careers: Mexicans Antonio Carbajal (spanning 16 years and 25 days) and Hugo Sanchez (16 years, 17 days) and Germany's Lothar Matthaus (16 years, 14 days). Other players for whom the 2010 tournament was their fourth FIFA World Cup were Italy's Fabio Cannavaro (taking his total appearances to 18), France's Thierry Henry (14) and Paraguay's Denis Caniza (10).

MOST FIFA WORLD CUP FINALS MATCHES (BY POSITION)

Goalkeeper: Claudio Taffarel (Brazil, 18 matches)
Defence: Cafu (Brazil, 20); Wladyslaw Zmuda (Poland, 21); Fabio Cannavaro (Italy, 18); Paolo Maldini (Italy, 23)
Midfielders: Grzegorz Lato (Poland, 20); Lothar Matthaus (West Germany/Germany, 25); Wolfgang Overath (West Germany, 19); Enzo Scifo (Belgium, 17)
Forwards: Diego Maradona (Argentina, 21); Uwe Seeler (West Germany, 21)

PROSINECKI'S SCORING RECORD

Robert Prosinecki is the only player to have scored for different countries in FIFA World Cup finals tournaments. He netted for Yugoslavia in their 4-1 win over the United Arab Emirates in the 1990 tournament. Eight years later, following the break-up of the old Yugoslavia, he scored for Croatia in their 3-0 group-game win over Jamaica, and then netted the first goal in his side's 2-1 third-place play-off victory over the Netherlands.

QUICKEST SUBSTITUTIONS

The three fastest substitutions in the history of the FIFA World Cup finals have all come in the fourth minute. In each case the player substituted was so seriously injured that he took no further part in the tournament: Steve Hodge came on for Bryan Robson in England's 0-0 draw with Morocco in 1986; Giuseppe Bergomi replaced Alessandro Nesta in Italy's 2-1 win over Austria in 1998; and Peter Crouch subbed for Michael Owen in England's 2-2 draw with Sweden in 2006.

UNHAPPY ENDINGS

For the second FIFA World Cup final in a row, the climactic match of the 2010 tournament featured a footballer not only playing his last international, but the final game of his career. Like Zinedine Zidane in 2006, **Giovanni van Bronckhorst** didn't complete the game four years later – though, unlike the Frenchman, he wasn't sent off but substituted, in the 105th minute. Dutch captain van Bronckhorst had scored a spectacular goal in the 2010 semi-final victory against Uruguay, but finished on the losing side in the final against Spain.

SIMUNIC'S THREE–CARD MATCH

Croatia's Josip Simunic shares (with Ray Richards of Australia in 1974) the record for collecting the most yellow cards in one match at the FIFA World Cup finals – three. He received three yellows against Australia in 2006 before he was sent off by English referee Graham Poll. When Poll showed Simunic his second yellow, he forgot he had already booked him.

LEADING CAPTAINS

Three players have each captained their teams in two FIFA World Cup finals – Diego Maradona of Argentina, Dunga of Brazil and West Germany's Karl-Heinz Rummenigge. Maradona lifted the trophy in 1986, but was a loser four years later. Dunga was the winning skipper in 1994, but was on the losing side in 1998. Rummenigge was a loser on both occasions, in 1982 and 1986. Maradona has made the most appearances as captain at the FIFA World Cup finals, leading out Argentina 16 times between 1986 and 1994.

FIRST ELEVEN

In an age of squad numbers, **Brazil** may have pleased some traditionalists when fielding players wearing shirt numbers one to 11 in the starting line-ups for their first two games of the 2010 FIFA World Cup, against North Korea and the Ivory Coast. Kicking off for coach Dunga on each occasion were: 1 Julio Cesar, 2 Maicon, 3 Lucio, 4 Juan, 5 Felipe Melo, 6 Michel Bastos, 7 Elano, 8 Gilberto Silva, 9 Luis Fabiano, 10 Kaka and 11 Robinho. **the Netherlands** managed a similar starting structure for not only their second-round tie against Slovakia, but the final against Spain: 1 Maarten Stekelenburg, 2 Gregory van der Wiel, 3 Johnny Heitinga, 4 Joris Mathijsen, 5 Giovanni van Bronckhorst, 6 Mark van Bommel, 7 Dirk Kuyt, 8 Nigel de Jong, 9 Robin van Persie, 10 Wesley Sneijder and 11 Arjen Robben. Both Brazil and the Netherlands came close to the same feat when they met in the quarter-finals, though both featured a number 13 – Brazil's Dani Alves, in place of 7 Elano, and the Netherlands' Andre Ooijer instead of 4 Joris Mathijsen (Elano and Mathijsen were unavailable through injury).

FASTEST RED CARDS IN THE FIFA WORLD CUP FINALS

1 min Jose Batista (Uruguay) v Scotland, 1986
8 min Giorgio Ferrini (Italy) v Chile, 1962
14 min Zeze Procopio (Brazil) v Czechoslovakia, 1938
19 min Mohammed Al Khlaiwi (Saudi Arabia) v France, 1998
Miguel Bossio (Uruguay) v Denmark, 1986
21 min Gianluca Pagliuca (Italy) v Rep of Ireland, 1994

FASTEST YELLOW CARDS IN THE FIFA WORLD CUP FINALS

1 min Sergei Gorlukovich (Russia) v Sweden, 1994
Giampiero Marini (Italy) v Poland, 1982
2 min Jesus Arellano (Mexico) v Italy, 2002
Henri Camara (Senegal) v Uruguay, 2002
Michael Emenalo (Nigeria) v Italy, 1994
Humberto Suazo (Chile) v Switzerland, 2010
Mark van Bommel (Netherlands) v Port., 2006

DENILSON STEPS UP FROM THE BENCH

Brazil winger **Denilson** has made the most substitute appearances at the FIFA World Cup finals – 11. He was involved in 12 of Brazil's games at the 1998 and 2002 finals, but started only one, against Norway in 1998. He was a half-time substitute for Leonardo in the 1998 final and came on for Ronaldo in stoppage time of the 2002 final (his last appearance in the finals), when Brazil beat Germany 2-0.

YOUNGEST PLAYERS IN FIFA WORLD CUP FINAL
Pele (Brazil) – 17 years, 249 days, in 1958
Giuseppe Bergomi (Italy) – 18 years, 201 days, in 1982
Ruben Moran (Uruguay) – 19 years, 344 days, in 1950

OLDEST PLAYERS IN FIFA WORLD CUP FINAL
Dino Zoff (Italy) – 40 years, 133 days, in 1982
Gunnar Gren (Sweden) – 37 years, 241 days, in 1958
Jan Jongbloed (Netherlands) – 37 years, 212 days, in 1978
Nilton Santos (Brazil) – 37 years, 32 days, in 1962

PUZACH THE FIRST SUB
The first substitute in FIFA World Cup finals history was Anatoli Puzach of the Soviet Union. He replaced Viktor Serebrianikov at half-time of the Soviets' o-o draw with hosts Mexico on 31 May 1970. The 1970 tournament was the first in which substitutes were allowed, with two permitted for each side. FIFA increased this to three per team for the 1998 finals.

FOUR AND OUT
The most players sent off in one FIFA World Cup finals game is four. Costinha and Deco of Portugal and Khalid Boulahrouz and Gio van Bronckhorst of the Netherlands were sent off by Russian referee Valentin Ivanov in their second-round match in Germany in 2006.

CANIGGIA – SENT OFF, WHILE ON THE BENCH...
Claudio Caniggia of Argentina became the first player to be sent off from the substitutes' bench, during the match against Sweden in 2002. Caniggia was dismissed in first-half stoppage time for dissent towards UAE referee Ali Bujsaim. Caniggia carried on protesting after the referee warned him to keep quiet, so Bujsaim showed him a red card.

MALDINI'S MINUTES RECORD
Lothar Matthaus of West Germany/Germany has started the most FIFA World Cup finals matches – 25. But Italy defender **Paolo Maldini** (left) has stayed on the field for longer, despite starting two games fewer. Maldini played for 2,220 minutes, Matthaus for 2,052. According to the stopwatch, the top four are completed by Uwe Seeler of West Germany, who played for 1,980 minutes, and Argentina's Diego Maradona, who played for 1,938.

SHOOT–OUT SAVIOURS
West Germany's Harald "Toni" Schumacher and Sergio Goycochea of Argentina hold the record for the most penalty shoot-out saves in the finals – four each. Schumacher's saves came over two tournaments – in 1982 and 1986, including the decisive stop in the 1982 semi-final against France. Goycochea made his crucial saves in 1990, first in Argentina's quarter-final win over Yugoslavia and then against Italy to take his team to the final. His four shoot-out saves in one tournament is also a record. The record for the most shoot-out saves in one game is held by Portugal goalkeeper Ricardo. He saved three times to knock out England in the quarter-finals of the 2006 FIFA World Cup.

UNBEATEN GOALKEEPERS IN THE FIFA WORLD CUP FINALS*

Walter Zenga (Italy)	517 minutes without conceding a goal, 1990
Peter Shilton (England)	502 minutes, 1986–90
Sepp Maier (W Germany)	475 minutes, 1974–78
Gianluigi Buffon (Italy)	460 minutes, 2006
Emerson Leao (Brazil)	458 minutes, 1978
Gordon Banks (England)	442 minutes, 1966

* Pascal Zuberbuhler did not concede a goal in all 390 minutes played by Switzerland in the 2006 FIFA World Cup. Iker Casillas of Spain completed 433 minutes without conceding a goal in 2010.

FIFA WORLD CUP GOALKEEPING

IKER'S REPEAT PERFORMANCE

Spain's **Iker Casillas** became only the third goalkeeper to save two FIFA World Cup penalties – aside from shoot-outs – and the first to spread them across different tournaments. First he pushed away Ian Harte's spot-kick in a second-round tie against the Republic of Ireland in 2002. Even more impressive was how he caught Paraguayan forward Oscar Cardozo's effort in their 2010 quarter-final. Spain went on to win both matches. The two goalkeepers who had enjoyed such double success before were Poland's Jan Tomaszewski in 1974 and the United States' Brad Friedel in 2002.

NOT THINKING OUTSIDE THE BOX

Italy's Gianluca Pagliuca was the first goalkeeper to be sent off at a FIFA World Cup match when he was dismissed for handball outside his penalty area after 21 minutes against Norway at Giants Stadium, New York, in 1994. Despite sacrificing playmaker Roberto Baggio for goalkeeper Luca Marchegiani, Italy still won 1-0.

ITALY'S ELDER STATESMAN

Dino Zoff became both the oldest player and oldest captain to win the FIFA World Cup when his Italian side lifted the trophy in Spain in 1982. He was 40 years and 133 days old at the time. Alongside him in the team was defender Giuseppe Bergomi, aged 18 years and 201 days, a difference of 21 years and 297 days.

FIVE-STAR CARBAJAL

Antonio Carbajal, of Mexico, is one of only two men to have appeared at five FIFA World Cup finals – the other was Germany's versatile Lothar Matthaus. Carbajal, who played in 1950, 1954, 1958, 1962 and 1966, conceded a record 25 goals in his 11 FIFA World Cup finals appearances – the same number let in by Saudi Arabia's Mohamed Al-Deayea across ten games in 1994, 1998 and 2002. Al-Deayea was a member of the Saudi squad for the 2006 tournament but did not play.

HUMBLE ORIGINS

As recently as 1978, English club Wigan Athletic were playing non-league football in the country's fifth tier. Yet by 2010 they were not only in the top-flight English Premier League, but had two of their players facing each other at that year's FIFA World Cup in South Africa. Even more unusually, Ghana's **Richard Kingson** and Serbia's **Vladimir Stojkovic** were both goalkeepers – and had both spent the season as reserves to Wigan's first-choice Chris Kirkland. Kingson emerged triumphant from the two countries' first-round clash, keeping a clean sheet as Ghana won 1–0.

NUMBER-ONE NUMBER ONES

The Lev Yashin Award was introduced in 1994 for the man voted best goalkeeper of the FIFA World Cup – though a goalkeeper has been picked for an all-star team at the end of every tournament dating back to 1930. The all-star team was expanded from 11 to 23 players in 1998, allowing room for more than one goalkeeper, but returned to 11 players in 2010. Players who were picked for the all-star teams but missed out on the Lev Yashin Award were Paraguay's Jose Luis Chilavert in 1998, Turkey's Rustu Recber in 2002, and Germany's Jens Lehmann and Portugal's Ricardo in 2006. The first Lev Yashin Award was presented to Belgium's Michel Preud'homme, even though he only played four games, conceding four goals, at the 1994 competition – his side were edged out 3-2 by Germany in the second round. Legendary Soviet goalkeeper Lev Yashin, after whom the trophy is named, played in the 1958, 1962 and 1966 FIFA World Cups and was a member of his country's 1970 squad as third-choice keeper and assistant coach – although he was never chosen for a FIFA World Cup team of the tournament. Yashin conceded the only FIFA World Cup finals goal scored directly from a corner-kick, taken by Colombia's Marcos Coll during a 4-4 draw in 1962.

OLIVER'S ARMS

Germany's **Oliver Kahn** is the only goalkeeper to have been voted FIFA's Player of the Tournament, winning the award at the 2002 FIFA World Cup – despite taking a share of the blame for Brazil's winning goals in the final.

RIGHT WAY FOR RICARDO

Spain's Ricardo Zamora became the first man to save a penalty in a FIFA World Cup finals match, stopping Valdemar de Brito's spot-kick for Brazil in 1934. Spain went on to win 3-1.

BROTHERS IN ARMS

Brothers Viktor and Viacheslav Chanov were two of the three goalkeepers in the Soviet Union's 1982 FIFA World Cup squad, but first-choice Rinat Dasayev was preferred to them both throughout. Viktor, eight years younger than Vyacheslav, did make one appearance at the 1986 FIFA World Cup four years later and ended his career with 21 caps. Vyacheslav had to wait until 1984 for his first and only international appearance.

LEADING FROM THE BACK

Iker Casillas became the third goalkeeper to captain his country to FIFA World Cup glory, when Spain became champions in South Africa in 2010. He emulated Italians Gianpiero Combi (in 1934) and Dino Zoff (1982). Casillas was also the first man to lift the trophy after his side had lost their opening match of the tournament.

UNLUCKY BREAK

Goalkeeper Frantisek Planicka broke his arm during Czechoslovakia's 1938 second-round clash against Brazil, but played on, even though the game went to extra-time before ending in a 1-1 draw. Not surprisingly, given the extent of his injury, Planicka missed the replay two days later, which the Czechs lost 2-1, and the goalkeeper of the 1938 FIFA World Cup never added to his tally of 73 caps.

PLAYERS VOTED BEST GOALKEEPER OF THE TOURNAMENT

1930 Enrique Ballestrero (Uruguay)	1978 Ubaldo Fillol (Argentina)
1934 Ricardo Zamora (Spain)	1982 Dino Zoff (Italy)
1938 Frantisek Planicka (Czechoslovakia)	1986 Harald Schumacher (West Germany)
1950 Roque Maspoli (Uruguay)	1990 Sergio Goycoechea (Argentina)
1954 Gyula Grosics (Hungary)	1994 Michel Preud'homme (Belgium)
1958 Harry Gregg (Northern Ireland)	1998 Fabien Barthez (France)
1962 Viliam Schrojf (Czechoslovakia)	2002 Oliver Kahn (Germany)
1966 Gordon Banks (England)	2006 Gianluigi Buffon (Italy)
1970 Ladislao Mazurkiewicz (Uruguay)	2010 Iker Casillas (Spain)
1974 Jan Tomaszewski (Poland)	

FIFA MANAGERS
WORLD CUP

PERSONAL EXPERIENCE

Eight managers at the 2010 FIFA World Cup had previous World Cup experience as a player: Mexico's Javier Aguirre, Brazil's **Dunga,** New Zealand's Ricki Herbert, Denmark's Morten Olsen, South Korea's Huh Jung-Moo, Argentina's **Diego Maradona,** Slovakia's former Czechoslovakia international Vladimir Weiss and England's Italian coach Fabio Capello. Both Maradona and Dunga had won the trophy, not just as players but as captains, while Maradona and Aguirre had both been red-carded at a FIFA World Cup – Maradona against Brazil in 1982, Aguirre against West Germany four years later.

YOUNG JUAN

Juan Jose Tramutola remains the youngest-ever FIFA World Cup coach, leading Argentina in the 1930 tournament at the age of 27 years and 267 days. Italian Cesare Maldini became the oldest in 2002, taking charge of Paraguay when aged 70 years and 131 days.

DREAM ELEVEN

Luiz Felipe Scolari managed a record 11 FIFA World Cup finals wins in a row, across the 2002 tournament, when he was in charge of Brazil, and 2006, when coach of Portugal. That winning run extends to 12 games if one counts Portugal's victory over England in the 2006 quarter-final, though that was on penalties after a goalless draw.

PUFF DADDIES

The coaches of the two sides appearing at the 1978 FIFA World Cup final were such prolific smokers that an oversized ashtray was produced for Argentina's Cesar Luis Menotti and the Netherlands's Ernst Happel so they could share it on the touchline.

SOCCER SIX

Only one man has gone to six FIFA World Cups as coach: Brazilian **Carlos Alberto Parreira,** whose greatest moment came when he guided Brazil to the trophy for the fourth time in 1994. His second stint as Brazil coach was less successful – they fell in the quarter-finals in 2006. Parreira also led Kuwait (1982), the United Arab Emirates (1990), Saudi Arabia (1998) and hosts South Africa (2010) at the finals. He had stepped down as South Africa coach in April 2008, for family reasons, but returned late the following year. Parreira was once sacked midway through a FIFA World Cup. In 1998 he led Saudi Arabia for the first two of their three games – losing 1-0 to Denmark and 4-0 to France – before receiving his marching orders.

ELDEST STATESMAN OTTO

Otto Rehhagel was not only the oldest coach at the 2010 FIFA World Cup, but the oldest in the competition's history. The German was 71 years 317 days old when his Greece team played their third and final game of the tournament, a 2-0 defeat to Argentina.

CRASHING BORA

Only one tournament behind record-holder Carlos Alberto Parreira, **Bora Milutinovic** has coached at five different FIFA World Cups – with a different country each time, two of them being the hosts. As well as Mexico in 1986 and the United States in 1994, he led Costa Rica in 1990, Nigeria in 1998 and China in 2002. He reached the knockout stages with every country except China – who failed to score a single goal.

DIVIDED LOYALTIES

No coach has won the FIFA World Cup in charge of a foreign country, but several have found themselves taking on their homelands in the FIFA World Cup. These include Brazilian 1958 FIFA World Cup-winning midfielder Didi, whose Peru side lost 4-2 to his home country in 1970. Sven-Goran Eriksson was England coach for their 1-1 draw against his native Sweden in 2002, the same year Frenchman Bruno Metsu led Senegal to a 1-0 opening-match win over France. Former Yugoslavia goalkeeper Blagoje Vidinic endured the most bittersweet moment – he coached Zaire to their first and only FIFA World Cup in 1974, and then had to watch his adopted players lose 9-0 to Yugoslavia.

FIFA WORLD CUP–WINNING COACHES

1930	Alberto Suppici
1934	Vittorio Pozzo
1938	Vittorio Pozzo
1950	Juan Lopez
1954	Sepp Herberger
1958	Vicente Feola
1962	Aymore Moreira
1966	Alf Ramsey
1970	Mario Zagallo
1974	Helmut Schon
1978	Cesar Luis Menotti
1982	Enzo Bearzot
1986	Carlos Bilardo
1990	Franz Beckenbauer
1994	Carlos Alberto Parreira
1998	Aime Jacquet
2002	Luiz Felipe Scolari
2006	Marcello Lippi
2010	Vicente del Bosque

SCHON SHINES

West Germany's **Helmut Schon** was coach for more FIFA World Cup matches than any other man – 25, across the 1966, 1970, 1974 and 1978 tournaments. He has also won the most games as a coach, 16 in all – including the 1974 final against the Netherlands. The 1974 tournament was third time lucky for Schon. He he had taken West Germany to second place in 1966 and to third in 1970. Before taking charge of the national side, Schon had worked as an assistant to Sepp Herberger, coach of West Germany's 1954 FIFA World Cup-winning team – Schon was coach of the then-independent Saarland regional side at the time. Dog-lover Schon, born in Dresden on 15 September 1915, scored 17 goals in 16 internationals for Germany between 1937 and 1941. He succeeded Herberger in 1964 and spent 14 years in charge of his country. He was the only coach to win both the FIFA World Cup (1974) and the European Championship (1972).

FIFA WORLD CUP DISCIPLINE

ADVANCE BOOKING

Two players have been booked within a minute of kick-off – Italy's Giampiero Marini, against Poland, in 1982, and Russia's Sergei Gorlukovich against Sweden 12 years later. But Uruguayan Jose Batista went one worse in a 1986 first-round match against Scotland, receiving a red card after just 56 seconds for a gruesome foul on Gordon Strachan. His team-mates held on for a goalless draw.

NOT LEADING BY EXAMPLE

The first man to be sent off at a FIFA World Cup was Peru's Placido Galindo, at the first tournament in 1930 during a 3-1 defeat to Romania. Chilean referee Alberto Warnken dismissed the Peruvian captain for fighting.

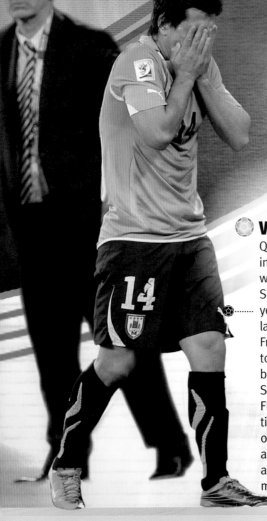

REPEAT OFFENDERS

France's **Zinedine Zidane** and Brazil's **Cafu** are both FIFA World Cup winners – and both notched up a record six FIFA World Cup cards, though Cafu escaped any reds, while Zidane was sent off twice. Most famously, Zidane was dismissed for headbutting Italy's Marco Materazzi in extra-time of the 2006 final in Berlin – the final match of the Frenchman's career. He had also been sent off during a first-round match against Saudi Arabia in 1998, but returned from suspension in time to help France win the trophy with a sensational two-goal performance in the final. The only other man to have been sent off twice at two different FIFA World Cups is Cameroon's Rigobert Song. When dismissed against Brazil in 1994, he became the FIFA World Cup's youngest red card offender – aged just 17 years and 358 days. He saw red for the second time against Chile in 1998.

VERY EARLY BATHS

Quickfire offenders at the 2010 FIFA World Cup included Algerian striker Abdelkader Ghezzal, booked within a minute of coming on as a substitute against Slovakia and sent off after 15 minutes for his second yellow. Uruguay's young playmaker **Nicolas Lodeiro** lasted just 16 minutes as a substitute against France before becoming the first dismissal of the tournament – receiving one booking for kicking the ball away and a second for a late lunge on Bacary Sagna. But it was Brazilian superstar Kaka – a former FIFA World Footballer of the Year – who left the least time between his first and second yellow cards in one match. He was first booked 85 minutes into a first-round match against the Ivory Coast, before a second yellow – and inevitable red – just three minutes later.

CARDS CLOSE TO CHEST

Only one group in FIFA World Cup finals history has featured no bookings at all – Group 4 in 1970, featuring West Germany, Peru, Bulgaria and Morocco. In contrast, the 2006 FIFA World Cup in Germany was the worst for both red and yellow cards, with 28 dismissals and 345 bookings in 64 matches.

FIFA WORLD CUP RED CARDS, BY TOURNAMENT

1930	1
1934	1
1938	4
1950	0
1954	3
1958	3
1962	6
1966	5
1970	0
1974	5
1978	3
1982	5
1986	8
1990	16
1994	15
1998	22
2002	17
2006	28
2010	17

FINAL COUNT

Before 14 yellow cards were shown in the 2010 FIFA World Cup final, the previous 18 finals had featured 40 bookings between them – an average of 2.2 per game. The 15 cards flourished by 2010 final referee Howard Webb – 14 yellows and one red – were nine more than those shown by previous record-holder Romualdo Arppi Filho, who "awarded" Argentina four and West Germany two yellows in the 1986 final.

SOLE CHANCE OF GLORY

India withdrew from the 1950 FIFA World Cup because some of their players wanted to play barefoot but FIFA insisted all players must wear football boots. India have not qualified for the tournament since.

BREAKING COVER

Zaire defender Mwepu Llunga was booked for running out of the wall and kicking the ball away as Brazil prepared to take a free-kick, at the 1974 FIFA World Cup. Romanian referee Nicolae Rainea ignored Llunga's pleas of innocence.

GOOD SON, BAD SON

Cameroon's Andre Kana-Biyik served two suspensions during the 1990 FIFA World Cup. The first came after he was sent off in the opening match against Argentina – six minutes before his brother Francois Omam-Biyik scored the only goal. His second ban came after yellow cards in the final group game against Russia and in the second-round defeat of Colombia.

YELLOW MELO'S RED MIST

Felipe Melo's red card for stamping on Arjen Robben, in Brazil's 2010 FIFA World Cup quarter-final defeat to the Netherlands, means Brazil have now had more players sent off in FIFA World Cup history than any other team – one more than Argentina. Melo was Brazil's 11th dismissal, after Kaka had become the 10th in a first-round victory over the Ivory Coast. Melo could also have gone down as the first player ever to score an own goal and be sent off in the same FIFA World Cup match, but the first Dutch goal was later officially awarded to their own playmaker Wesley Sneijder.

ALL'S FAIR

FIFA World Cup organizers hailed an improvement in fair play between the 2006 tournament in Germany and the event in South Africa four years later. Not only were red cards down from 28 to 17, but also injuries which could be blamed on fouls were reduced from 40 per cent to 16 per cent. There were 260 yellow cards shown in 2010 – down from the all-time record of 345 in 2006 – and eight of those were second yellow cards. Three of those eight (Aleksandar Lukovic of Serbia, **Kaka** of Brazil and Johnny Heitinga of the Netherlands) also received a yellow card in one other match they played.

ELBOWED OUT

Italian defender Mauro Tassotti was given an unprecedented eight-game ban for smashing Spain's Luis Enrique in the face with his elbow in 1994 – an offence missed by match referee Sandor Puhl. Spain lost 2-1 and were further enraged when the Hungarian official was then selected to referee the final.

FIFA WORLD CUP ATTENDANCES

CAPACITY PLANNING

If current plans are realized and every seat is occupied, the attendances at the final match of each of the next three FIFA World Cups will be 85,000 at the **Maracana** in Rio de Janeiro, Brazil, in 2014; 89,318 at the Luzhniki in Moscow, Russia, four years later; and 86,250 at the **Lusail Iconic Stadium** in Lusail, Qatar, in 2022. The smallest proposed capacities at the next three tournaments are 41,375 at Curitiba's Arena da Baixada in 2014, 43,702 at the Rostov-on-Don stadium in 2018 and 43,520 at the new Qatar University Stadium in Doha in 2022. FIFA regulations insist that any venue staging a FIFA World Cup match must have a capacity of at least 40,000.

TWO'S COMPANY, 300'S A CROWD

The 300 people who were recorded as watching Romania beat Peru 3-1 in 1930 formed the FIFA World Cup finals' smallest attendance, with plenty of room for manoeuvre inside the Estadio Pocitos in Montevideo. A day earlier, ten times as many people are thought to have been there to watch France's 4-1 win over Mexico.

SOUTH AFRICAN SUCCESS

The 2010 FIFA World Cup in South Africa was watched by a total of 3,178,856 spectators, across the 64 matches in 10 different stadiums – the third-highest aggregate attendance in the tournament's history, behind the United States in 1994 and Germany in 2006. The average attendance was 49,670 and though some concerns were raised about patches of empty seats at several games, organizers said they were happy that 92.9 per cent of places were filled.

CITY SLICKER

The capacity of South Africa's 2010 FIFA World Cup showpiece venue, **Soccer City** in Johannesburg, was increased from 78,000 to 84,490. The design of the newly revamped stadium was based on traditional African pottery and nicknamed the Calabash. Soccer City hosted both the opening game and the final – as well as four more first-round fixtures, a second-round clash and a quarter-final.

GENDER EQUALITY

Only two stadiums have hosted the finals of the FIFA World Cup for both men and women. The Rose Bowl, in Pasadena, California, was the venue for the men's final in 1994 – when Brazil beat Italy – and the women's showdown between the victorious US and China five years later, which was watched by 90,185 people. But Sweden's Rasunda Stadium, near Stockholm, just about got there first – though it endured a long wait between the men's final in 1958 and the women's in 1995. Both sets of American spectators got their money's worth, watching games that went into extra-time and which were settled on penalties.

FIFA WORLD CUP FINAL ATTENDANCES

Year	Attendance	Stadium	City
1930	93,000	Estadio Centenario	Montevideo
1934	45,000	Stadio Nazionale del PNF	Rome
1938	60,000	Stade Olympique de Colombes	Paris
1950	174,000	Estadio do Maracana	Rio de Janeiro
1954	60,000	Wankdorfstadion	Berne
1958	51,800	Rasunda Fotbollstadion	Solna
1962	68,679	Estadio Nacional	Santiago
1966	98,000	Wembley Stadium	London
1970	107,412	Estadio Azteca	Mexico City
1974	75,200	Olympiastadion	Munich
1978	71,483	Estadio Monumental	Buenos Aires
1982	90,000	Estadio Santiago Bernabeu	Madrid
1986	114,600	Estadio Azteca	Mexico City
1990	73,603	Stadio Olimpico	Rome
1994	94,194	Rose Bowl	Pasadena
1998	80,000	Stade de France	Paris
2002	69,029	International Stadium	Yokohama
2006	69,000	Olympiastadion	Berlin
2010	84,490	Soccer City	Johannesburg

TOURNAMENT ATTENDANCES

Year	Total	Average
1930	434,500	24,139
1934	358,000	21,059
1938	376,000	20,889
1950	1,043,500	47,432
1954	889,500	34,212
1958	919,580	26,274
1962	899,074	28,096
1966	1,635,000	51,094
1970	1,603,975	50,124
1974	1,768,152	46,530
1978	1,546,151	40,688
1982	2,109,723	40,572
1986	2,393,331	46,026
1990	2,516,348	48,391
1994	3,587,538	68,991
1998	2,785,100	43,517
2002	2,705,197	42,269
2006	3,359,439	52,491
2010	3,178,856	49,670
TOTAL	34,108,964	44,182

FAN FESTS FIND FAVOUR

After city centre **"Fan Fests"**, including giant TV screens and food stalls, proved popular at the 2006 FIFA World Cup in Germany, they were staged again in 2010 – not only across South African cities (such as **Durban**, below), but also elsewhere in the world including Rio in Brazil, Rome in Italy, Paris in France and Sydney in Australia. A total of 6,151,823 people visited the Fan Fests for the tournament's 64 games, including 2,634,018 across South Africa and 3,517,805 abroad. German capital Berlin attracted the biggest crowd, with 350,000 flocking to the Fan Fest there to watch Germany's semi-final defeat to Spain.

ABSENT FRIENDS

Only 2,823 spectators turned up at the Rasunda Stadium in Stockholm to see Wales play Hungary in a first-round play-off match during the 1958 FIFA World Cup. More than 15,000 had attended the first game between the two sides, but boycotted the replay in tribute to executed Hungarian uprising leader Imre Nagy.

MORBID MARACANA

The largest attendance for a FIFA World Cup match was at Rio de Janeiro's Maracana for the last clash of the 1950 tournament – though no one is quite sure how many were there. The final tally was officially given as 174,000, though some estimates suggest as many as 210,000 witnessed the host country's traumatic defeat. Tensions were so high at the final whistle, winning Uruguay captain Obdulio Varela was not awarded the trophy in a traditional manner, but had it surreptitiously nudged into his hands. FIFA president Jules Rimet described the crowd's overwhelming silence as "morbid, almost too difficult to bear". Uruguay's triumphant players barricaded themselves inside their dressing room for several hours before they judged it safe enough to emerge. Those spectators, however many there were, were the last to see Brazil play in an all-white kit – the unlucky colours were scrapped and, after a competition was held to find a new national strip, were replaced by the now-familiar yellow and blue.

BERLIN CALL

Despite later becoming the capital of a united Germany, then-divided Berlin only hosted three group games at the 1974 FIFA World Cup in West Germany – the host country's surprise loss to East Germany took place in Hamburg. An unexploded World War Two bomb was discovered beneath the seats at Berlin's Olympiastadion in 2002, by workers preparing the ground for the 2006 tournament. Germany, along with Brazil, had applied to host the tournament in 1942, before it was cancelled due to the outbreak of World War Two.

TWIN PEAKS

Five stadiums have the distinction of staging both the final of a FIFA World Cup and the Summer Olympics athletics: Berlin's Olympiastadion (1936 Olympics, 2006 FIFA World Cup); London's Wembley (1948 Olympics, 1966 FIFA World Cup); Rome's Stadio Olimpico (1960 Olympics, 1990 FIFA World Cup); Mexico City's Azteca (1968 Olympics, 1970 and 1986 FIFA World Cups); and Munich's Olympiastadion (1972 Olympics, 1974 FIFA World Cup). The Rose Bowl in Pasadena, California, hosted both the final of the 1994 FIFA World Cup and the 1984 Olympics football tournament, but not the main Olympics track-and-field events.

OLYMPIC NAMES

The stadium hosting the opening match of the 1930 FIFA World Cup had stands named after great Uruguayan footballing triumphs: Colombes, in honour of the 1924 Paris Olympics venue; Amsterdam, after the site where that title was retained four years later; and Montevideo, even though it would be another fortnight before the home team clinched the first FIFA World Cup in their own capital city.

RIO'S MARIO

Most people know Brazil's largest stadium as the Maracana, named after the Rio neighbourhood and a small nearby river. But, since the mid-1960s, the official title has actually been "Estadio Jornalista Mario Filho", after a Brazilian journalist who had helped in the campaign for the stadium to be built.

TERRITORIAL GAINS

History was made twice over when **FIFA** decided in December 2010 which countries would stage the 2018 and 2022 FIFA World Cups. The 2018 vote went in favour of Russia – ahead of Spain/Portugal, Belgium/Netherlands and England – meaning the first FIFA World Cup to be held in Eastern Europe. The tournament will then go to the Middle East for the first time in 2022, after Qatar emerged ahead of rival bids from the USA, Japan, South Korea and Australia.

MEXICAN SAVE

Mexico was not the original choice to host the 1986 FIFA World Cup, but stepped in when Colombia withdrew in 1982 due to financial problems. Mexico held on to the staging rights despite suffering from an earthquake in September 1985 that left approximately 10,000 people dead, but which left the stadiums unscathed. FIFA kept faith in the country, and the **Azteca Stadium** went on to become the first venue to host two FIFA World Cup final matches – and Mexico the first country to stage two FIFA World Cups. The Azteca – formally named the "Estadio Guillermo Canedo", after a Mexican football official – was built in 1960 using 100,000 tonnes of concrete, four times as much as was needed for the old Wembley.

ARCHITECTS' PREROGATIVE

Distinctive and creative elements were added to the stadiums built especially for the 2010 FIFA World Cup in South Africa, including the giraffe-shaped towers at **Nelspruit's Mbombela stadium**, the 350-metre-long arch with its mobile viewing platform soaring above **Durban's main arena**, and the white "petals" shrouding the Nelson Mandela Bay stadium in Port Elizabeth.

UNSUCCESSFUL HOSTING BIDS

1930	Hungary, Italy, Netherlands, Spain, Sweden
1934	Sweden
1938	Argentina, Germany
1950	None
1954	None
1958	None
1962	Argentina, West Germany
1966	Spain, West Germany
1970	Argentina
1974	Spain
1978	Mexico
1982	West Germany
1986	Colombia*, Canada, USA
1990	England, Greece, USSR
1994	Brazil, Morocco
1998	Morocco, Switzerland
2002	Mexico
2006	Brazil, England, Morocco, South Africa
2010	Egypt, Libya/Tunisia, Morocco
2014	None
2018	England, Netherlands/Belgium, Spain/Portugal
2022	Australia, Japan, South Korea, USA

* Colombia won hosting rights for 1986 but later withdrew.

MORE MARACANA

No other stadium was ever likely to get a look-in when it came to choosing the host venue for the 2014 FIFA World Cup final than the **Maracana** in Brazil's Rio de Janeiro. The iconic stadium will become the second to host its second FIFA World Cup final, following the Azteca in Mexico City. Up to 200,000 are thought to have crammed into the Maracana for the 1950 final between Brazil and Uruguay but the capacity this time will be an all-seated 85,000, when the stadium is reopened in 2013 following renovation. The Maracana was awarded protected status in 1998, protecting it from ever being demolished although a vast redevelopment is under way. Seven entirely new stadia will be among the other host venues in 2014, in the capital Brasilia, Cuiaba, Manaus, Natal, Recife, Salvador and Sao Paulo. The latter city will stage the tournament's opening game. The other four grounds used will have been specially upgraded, in Belo Horizonte, Curitiba, Fortaleza and Porto Alegre. Five more cities applied to be involved but were ruled out in 2009.

BREAKING THE CODE

Not all the stadiums at the 2010 FIFA World Cup were entirely new constructions – several were old-fashioned mainly rugby venues given enough of a facelift to cope with the new football-led demand. These included Johannesburg's Ellis Park and Pretoria's **Loftus Versfeld**. The Pretoria arena is the usual home ground of popular rugby team the Blue Bulls, though they did play a pre-FIFA World Cup game at Johannesburg's showpiece Soccer City stadium. Soccer City also staged an August 2010 rugby international between the Springboks of South Africa and the All-Blacks of New Zealand.

HOSTS WITH THE MOST

No other single-hosted FIFA World Cup has used as many venues as the 14 spread across Spain in 1982. The 2002 tournament was played at 20 different venues, but ten of these were in Japan and ten in co-host country South Korea.

FIFA WORLD CUP PENALTIES

FIFA WORLD CUP PENALTY SHOOT-OUTS

Year	Round	120-minute Score	Winners	Shoot-out Score
1982	Semi-final	West Germany 3 France 3	West Germany	5-4
1986	Quarter-final	West Germany 0 Mexico 0	West Germany	4-1
1986	Quarter-final	France 1 Brazil 1	France	4-3
1986	Quarter-final	Belgium 1 Spain 1	Belgium	5-4
1990	Second round	Republic of Ireland 0 Romania 0	Republic of Ireland	5-4
1990	Quarter-final	Argentina 0 Yugoslavia 0	Argentina	3-2
1990	Semi-final	Argentina 1 Italy 1	Argentina	4-3
1990	Semi-final	West Germany 1 England 1	West Germany	4-3
1994	Second round	Bulgaria 1 Mexico 1	Bulgaria	3-1
1994	Quarter-final	Sweden 2 Romania 2	Sweden	5-4
1994	Final	Brazil 0 Italy 0	Brazil	3-2
1998	Second round	Argentina 2 England 2	Argentina	4-3
1998	Quarter-final	France 0 Italy 0	France	4-3
1998	Semi-final	Brazil 1 Netherlands 1	Brazil	4-2
2002	Second round	Spain 1 Republic of Ireland 1	Spain	3-2
2002	Quarter-final	South Korea 0 Spain 0	South Korea	5-3
2006	Second round	Ukraine 0 Switzerland 0	Ukraine	3-0
2006	Quarter-final	Germany 1 Argentina 1	Germany	4-2
2006	Quarter-final	Portugal 0 England 0	Portugal	3-1
2006	Final	Italy 1 France 1	Italy	5-3
2010	Second round	Paraguay 0 Japan 0	Paraguay	5-3
2010	Quarter-final	Uruguay 1 Ghana 1	Uruguay	4-2

TAKING THE FIFTH

Paraguay's 5-3 victory on penalties over Japan, following a goalless draw in their 2010 second-round match, made them the seventh team to score as many as five spot-kicks in a FIFA World Cup shoot-out. They followed West Germany against France in 1982, Belgium against Spain in 1986, the Republic of Ireland against Romania in 1990, Sweden against Romania in 1994, South Korea against Spain in 2002 and Italy against France in the 2006 final. West Germany and Sweden also missed one apiece in their respective shoot-outs.

FIRST IS BEST

Paraguay's defeat of Japan and **Diego Forlan** and Uruguay's win against Ghana in 2010 mean seven straight FIFA World Cup penalty shoot-outs have been won by the team taking the first kick. The last side to go second and win was Spain, against the Republic of Ireland in 2002.

WOE FOR ASAMOAH

Ghana striker **Asamoah Gyan** is the only player to have missed two penalties during match-time at FIFA World Cups. He hit the post with a spot-kick against the Czech Republic during a group game at the 2006 tournament, then struck a shot against the bar with the final kick of extra-time in Ghana's 2010 quarter-final versus Uruguay. Had he scored then, Gyan would have given Ghana a 2–1 win – following Luis Suarez's goal-stopping handball on the goal-line – and a first African place in a FIFA World Cup semi-final. Despite such a traumatic miss, Gyan did then step up to take Ghana's first penalty in the shoot-out, again striking it high – but this time into the back of the net. His team still lost, though, 4–2 on penalties.

FRENCH KICKS

The first penalty shoot-out at a FIFA World Cup finals came in the 1982 semi-final in Seville between West Germany and France, when French takers Didier Six and **Maxime Bossis** were the unfortunate players to miss. The same two countries met in the semi-finals four years later – and West Germany again won, though in normal time, 2-0. The record for most shoot-outs is shared by the 1990 and 2006 tournaments, with four apiece. Both semi-finals in 1990 went to penalties, while the 2006 final was the second to be settled that manner – Italy beating France 5-3 after David Trezeguet struck the crossbar.

CLOSE SAVES

Just two minutes and three seconds separated the two penalties awarded by Guatemalan referee Carlos Batres in the second-round clash between Paraguay and Spain in 2010 – a FIFA World Cup record. Not only were the spot-kicks given at either end of the pitch in Johannesburg's Ellis Park stadium, but both were saved. First, Spanish goalkeeper Iker Casillas caught Oscar Cardozo's attempt, after the Paraguay striker was fouled by Gerard Pique. Then, after striker David Villa was brought down by Antolin Alcaraz, **Justo Villar** palmed away Xabi Alonso's penalty. Alonso actually scored with his attempt, but Batres ordered a retake due to Spanish encroachment in the area. Spain had scored all 14 of their FIFA World Cup penalties going into the 2010 tournament – excluding shoot-outs – but Alonso's miss came just 12 days after David Villa fired a spot-kick wide against Honduras.

THREE IN ONE

Argentina's stand-in goalkeeper Sergio Goycochea set a tournament record by saving four shoot-out penalties in 1990 – though West Germany's Harald Schumacher managed as many, across the 1982 and 1986 tournaments. Portugal's Ricardo achieved an unprecedented feat by keeping out three attempts in a single shoot-out, becoming an instant hero in his side's quarter-final win over England in 2006.

THE PLAYERS WHO MISSED IN SHOOT-OUTS

Argentina: Diego Maradona (1990), Pedro Troglio (1990), Hernan Crespo (1998), Roberto Ayala (2006), Esteban Cambiasso (2006)
Brazil: Socrates (1986), Julio Cesar (1986), Marcio Santos (1994)
Bulgaria: Krassimir Balakov (1994)
England: Stuart Pearce (1990), Chris Waddle (1990), Paul Ince (1998), David Batty (1998), Frank Lampard (2006), Steven Gerrard (2006), Jamie Carragher (2006)
France: Didier Six (1982), Maxime Bossis (1982), Michel Platini (1986), Bixente Lizarazu (1998), David Trezeguet (2006)
Germany/West Germany: Uli Stielike (1982)
Ghana: John Mensah (2010), Dominic Adiyiah (2010)
Italy: Roberto Donadoni (1990), Aldo Serena (1990), Franco Baresi (1994), Daniele Massaro (1994), Roberto Baggio (1994), Demetrio Albertini (1998), Luigi Di Biagio (1998)
Japan: Yuichi Komano (2010)
Mexico: Fernando Quirarte (1986), Raul Servin (1986), Alberto Garcia Aspe (1994), Marcelino Bernal (1994), Jorge Rodriguez (1994)
Netherlands: Phillip Cocu (1998), Ronald de Boer (1998)
Portugal: Hugo Viana (2006), Petit (2006)
Republic of Ireland: Matt Holland (2002), David Connolly (2002), Kevin Kilbane (2002)
Romania: Daniel Timofte (1990), Dan Petrescu (1994), Miodrag Belodedici (1994)
Spain: Eloy (1986), Juanfran (2002), Juan Carlos Valeron (2002), Joaquin (2002)
Sweden: Hakan Mild (1994)
Switzerland: Marco Streller (2006), Tranquillo Barnetta (2006), Ricardo Cabanas (2006)
Ukraine: Andriy Shevchenko (2006)
Uruguay: Maximiliano Pereira (2010)
Yugoslavia: Dragan Stojkovic (1990), Dragoljub Brnovic (1990), Faruk Hadzibegic (1990)

PENALTY SHOOT-OUTS BY COUNTRY

4 Germany/West Germany (4 wins)	**1** Belgium (1 win)
4 Argentina (3 wins, 1 defeat)	**1** Bulgaria (1 win)
4 France (2 wins, 2 defeats)	**1** Paraguay (1 win)
4 Italy (1 win, 3 defeats)	**1** Portugal (1 win)
3 Brazil (2 wins, 1 defeat)	**1** South Korea (1 win)
3 Spain (1 win, 2 defeats)	**1** Sweden (1 win)
3 England (3 defeats)	**1** Ukraine (1 win)
2 Republic of Ireland (1 win, 1 defeat)	**1** Uruguay (1 win)
2 Mexico (2 defeats)	**1** Yugoslavia (1 win)
2 Romania (2 defeats)	**1** Ghana (1 defeat)
	1 Netherlands (1 defeat)
	1 Japan (1 defeat)
	1 Switzerland (1 defeat)

GERMAN EFFICIENCY

Germany, or West Germany, have won all four of their FIFA World Cup penalty shoot-outs, more than any other team. Their run began with a semi-final victory over France in 1982, when goalkeeper Harald Schumacher was the matchwinner, despite being lucky to stay on the pitch for a vicious extra-time foul on France's Patrick Battiston. West Germany also reached the 1990 final thanks to their shoot-out expertise, this time proving superior to England – as they similarly did in the 1996 European Championships semi-final. Germany were better at spot-kicks than Argentina in their 2006 quarter-final, when goalkeeper **Jens Lehmann** consulted a note predicting the direction the Argentine players were likely to shoot towards. The vital information was scribbled on a scrap of hotel notepaper by Germany's chief scout Urs Siegenthaler. The only German national team to lose a major tournament penalty shoot-out were the West Germans, who contested the 1976 European Championships final against Czechoslovakia – their first shoot-out experience, and clearly an effective lesson, as they have not lost a shoot-out since.

PART 3: UEFA EUROPEAN CHAMPIONSHIP

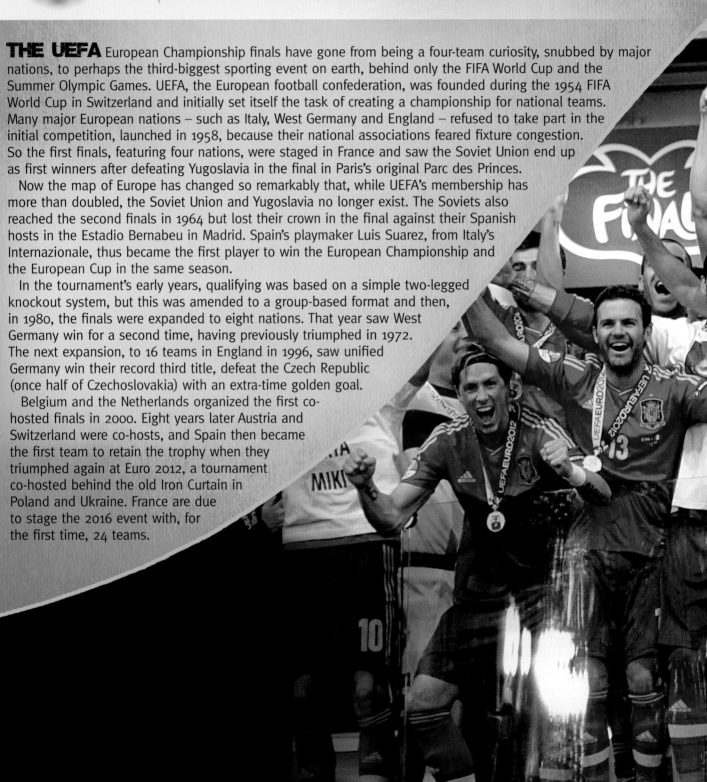

THE UEFA European Championship finals have gone from being a four-team curiosity, snubbed by major nations, to perhaps the third-biggest sporting event on earth, behind only the FIFA World Cup and the Summer Olympic Games. UEFA, the European football confederation, was founded during the 1954 FIFA World Cup in Switzerland and initially set itself the task of creating a championship for national teams. Many major European nations – such as Italy, West Germany and England – refused to take part in the initial competition, launched in 1958, because their national associations feared fixture congestion. So the first finals, featuring four nations, were staged in France and saw the Soviet Union end up as first winners after defeating Yugoslavia in the final in Paris's original Parc des Princes.

Now the map of Europe has changed so remarkably that, while UEFA's membership has more than doubled, the Soviet Union and Yugoslavia no longer exist. The Soviets also reached the second finals in 1964 but lost their crown in the final against their Spanish hosts in the Estadio Bernabeu in Madrid. Spain's playmaker Luis Suarez, from Italy's Internazionale, thus became the first player to win the European Championship and the European Cup in the same season.

In the tournament's early years, qualifying was based on a simple two-legged knockout system, but this was amended to a group-based format and then, in 1980, the finals were expanded to eight nations. That year saw West Germany win for a second time, having previously triumphed in 1972. The next expansion, to 16 teams in England in 1996, saw unified Germany win their record third title, defeat the Czech Republic (once half of Czechoslovakia) with an extra-time golden goal.

Belgium and the Netherlands organized the first co-hosted finals in 2000. Eight years later Austria and Switzerland were co-hosts, and Spain then became the first team to retain the trophy when they triumphed again at Euro 2012, a tournament co-hosted behind the old Iron Curtain in Poland and Ukraine. France are due to stage the 2016 event with, for the first time, 24 teams.

Goals from David Silva, Jordi Alba, Fernando Torres and Juan Mata meant Spain's goalkeeper-captain Iker Casillas lifted the Henri Delaunay Trophy, his third international cup in a row, at the climax of Euro 2012.

UEFA EUROPEAN CHAMPIONSHIP QUALIFIERS

The UEFA European Championship qualifying competition has become a huge event in its own right, with 50 teams having competed for places alongside hosts Austria and Switzerland at Euro 2008. How times have changed. There was one two-legged qualifying round for the 1960 competition, to reduce the 17 entrants to 16, and none for the 1964 tournament, which saw teams meet each other on a home-and-away basis in the first round. A full-scale qualifying competition was first launched for the 1968 finals, with eight groups of four and one group of three. The number of qualifiers increased in size again during the 1990s as several new associations joined UEFA after the break-ups of the Soviet Union and Yugoslavia and entered the championship for the first time.

QUICK TURNOVER

Germany's Joachim Low and Croatia's **Slaven Bilic**  were the only managers among the eight Euro 2008 quarter-finalists still in the same job when Euro 2012 qualifiers began. Spain's Luis Aragones, the Netherlands' Marco van Basten, Portugal's Luiz Felipe Scolari and Italy's Roberto Donadoni all left their jobs after the 2008 tournament. Turkey's Fatih Terim stepped down in October 2009, to be replaced by Guus Hiddink, who had managed Russia in 2008.

IRISH VICTORY NOT ENOUGH

West Germany's 1-0 defeat by Northern Ireland in Hamburg on 11 November 1983 was their first-ever home loss in the qualifying competition, but their 2-1 win over Albania in Saarbrucken four days later enabled them to pip Northern Ireland on goal difference for a place in the 1984 finals.

FONTAINE MAKES HISTORY JUST SO

Just Fontaine of France scored the first hat-trick in Euro history in the inaugural 1958-60 tournament. Fontaine, top scorer at the 1958 FIFA World Cup, hit three goals in France's 5-2 second-round win over Austria in Paris on 13 December 1959. France won the return 4-2 for a 9-4 aggregate win and went on to host the finals, at which they finished fourth.

GERMANS RUN UP 13

Germany's 13-0 win in San Marino on 6 September 2006 was the biggest victory margin in qualifying history. **Lukas Podolski**  (4), Miroslav Klose (2), Bastian Schweinsteiger (2), Thomas Hitzlsperger (2), Michael Ballack, Manuel Friedrich and Bernd Schneider scored the goals. The previous biggest win was Spain's 12-1 rout of Malta in 1983.

FIRST-TIMERS AND SECOND-CHANCERS

The play-offs for best group runners-up gave two countries the chance to qualify for the first major tournament and two separate chances for revenge. Sadly for Estonia and Montenegro, they are still waiting for their major breakthroughs, as Estonia lost 5-1 on aggregate to the Republic of Ireland and Montenegro went down 3-0 over two legs to the Czech Republic. Croatia's 3-0 triumph over Turkey gave them some vengeance over the country that knocked them out of the 2008 UEFA European Championship quarter-finals on penalties. Bosnia and Herzegovina, however, lost 6-2 on aggregate to Portugal – the same nation that beat them in a qualifying play-off for the 2010 FIFA World Cup. The format for qualifying groups – and possible play-offs – has not yet been decided for the 2016 UEFA European Championship, which will be staged in France and will be the first to feature 24 finalists.

GERMANY'S WEMBLEY WONDER NIGHT

West Germany's greatest-ever team announced their arrival at Wembley on 29 April 1972, when they beat England 3-1 in the first leg of the UEFA European Championship quarter-finals. Uli Hoeness, Gunter Netzer and Gerd Muller scored the goals. West Germany went on to win the trophy, beating the Soviet Union 3-0 in the final. Their team at Wembley was: Sepp Maier; Horst Hottges, Georg Schwarzenbeck, Franz Beckenbauer, Paul Breitner; Jurgen Grabowski, Herbert Wimmer, Gunter Netzer, Uli Hoeness; Sigi Held, Gerd Muller. Eight of them played in West Germany's 1974 FIFA World Cup final win over the Netherlands.

APPEARANCES IN THE FINALS TOURNAMENT

11	West Germany/Germany
10	Soviet Union/CIS/Russia
9	Netherlands
	Spain
8	Czechoslovakia/ Czech Republic
	Denmark
	England
	France
	Italy
6	Portugal
5	Sweden
	Yugoslavia
4	Belgium
	Croatia
	Greece
	Romania
3	Switzerland
	Turkey
2	Bulgaria
	Hungary
	Poland
	Republic of Ireland
	Scotland
1	Austria
	Latvia
	Norway
	Slovenia
	Ukraine

Includes appearances as hosts/co-hosts.

HEALY POSTS GOAL RECORD

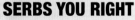
Northern Ireland forward **David Healy** (No.9 – born in Killyleagh on 5 August 1979) set a new scoring record with 13 goals in the Euro 2008 qualifiers. His tally included hat-tricks against Spain and Liechtenstein. Healy beat the previous record of 12 goals, netted by Croatia's Davor Suker in the qualifiers for UEFA Euro 96. Ole Madsen of Denmark scored 11 goals before the finals tournament in 1964, but qualifying groups were not introduced until two years later. Netherlands striker **Klaas-Jan Huntelaar** was the top scorer during Euro 2012 qualifiers, with 12 goals – three more than closest challenger, Germany's Miroslav Klose. The Dutch were also overall top scorers, with 37 goals from ten games – though they also conceded eight, more than any other group-winner.

SERBS YOU RIGHT

The UEFA Euro 2012 qualifier between Group C rivals Italy and Serbia on 12 October 2010 was abandoned after just six minute, following disturbances among Serbian supporters in Genoa's Stadio Luigi Ferraris. UEFA later awarded Italy a 3–0 win.

PANCEV FORCED TO MISS OUT

Yugoslavia's **Darko Pancev** (born in Skopje on 7 September 1965) was top scorer in the qualifiers for Euro 1992 with ten goals. Yugoslavia topped qualifying Group Four, but they were banned from the finals because of their country's war in Bosnia, so Pancev never had the chance to shine. After the break-up of the Yugoslav federation, he went on to become the star player for the new nation of Macedonia.

ANDORRA, SAN MARINO STRUGGLE

Minnows Andorra and San Marino each have yet to win a match in the qualifying competition. Andorra have lost all their 30 games, with a goal difference of six against 88. San Marino have lost all their 46 games, with a goal difference of six against 200!

DUTCH EDGE FIRST PLAY-OFF

The first-ever group qualifying play-off was held on 13 December 1995 at Liverpool's Anfield stadium when the Netherlands beat the Republic of Ireland 2-0 to clinch the final place at Euro 96. Patrick Kluivert scored both of the Dutch goals.

FANCY SEEING YOU AGAIN

When Spain and Italy met in the 2012 final it was the fourth time UEFA European Championship opponents had faced each other twice in the same tournament. Each time, it followed a first-round encounter. The Netherlands lost to the Soviet Union, then beat them in the final in 1988; Germany beat the Czech Republic twice at Euro 96, including the final; and Greece did the same to Portugal in 2004. Spain and Italy drew in Euro 2012's Group C, with Cesc Fabregas replying to Antonio Di Natale's opener for Italy. Their second showdown was rather less even.

THREE OFF AS CZECHS ADVANCE

Czechoslovakia's 3-1 semi-final win over the Netherlands in Zagreb, on 16 June 1976, featured a record three red cards. The Czechs' Jaroslav Pollak was dismissed for a second yellow card – a foul on Johan Neeskens – after an hour. Neeskens followed in the 76th minute for kicking Zdenek Nehoda. Wim van Hanegem became the second Dutchman dismissed, for dissent, after Nehoda scored the Czechs' second goal with six minutes of extra-time left.

DENMARK'S UNEXPECTED TRIUMPH

Denmark were unlikely winners of UEFA Euro 1992. They had not even expected to take part after finishing behind Yugoslavia in their qualifying group, but they were invited to complete the final eight when Yugoslavia were barred for security fears following the country's collapse. Goalkeeper **Peter Schmeichel** was their hero – in the semi-final shoot-out win over the Netherlands and again in the final against Germany, when goals by John Jensen and Kim Vilfort earned Denmark a 2-0 win.

GERMANS DOMINATE AS COMPETITION TAKES OFF

In 52 years, the UEFA European Championship has grown to become the most important international football tournament after the FIFA World Cup. Only 17 teams entered the first tournament, won by the Soviet Union in 1960, yet 51 took part in qualifying for the right to join co-hosts Poland and Ukraine at Euro 2012. Germany (formerly West Germany) and Spain have each won the competition three times, though the Germans have played and won more matches (43 and 23, respectively), as well as scoring and conceding more goals (63 and 45) than any other country. Defender Berti Vogts is the only man to win the tournament as a player (1972) and coach (1996), both with the Germans, the latter after unification. Some of Europe's most famous teams have under-achieved: Italy only claimed the title on home soil in 1968 and England have never reached the final, finishing third in 1968 and reaching the semi-finals in 1996.

DOMENGHINI RESCUES ITALY

The most controversial goal in the history of the final came on 8 June 1968. Hosts Italy were trailing 1-0 to Yugoslavia with ten minutes left. The Yugoslavs seemed still to be organizing their wall when Angelo Domenghini curled a free-kick past goalkeeper Ilja Pantelic for the equalizer. Yugoslavia protested but the goal was allowed to stand. Italy won the only replay in finals history 2-0, two days later, with goals from Gigi Riva and Pietro Anastasi.

FRANCE BOAST PERFECT RECORD

France, on home soil in 1984, are the only side to win all their matches since the finals expanded beyond four teams. They won them without any shoot-outs, too, beating Denmark 1-0, Belgium 5-0 and Yugoslavia 3-2 in their group, Portugal 3-2 after extra-time in the semi-finals and Spain 2-0 in the final.

CZECHS WIN LONGEST SHOOT-OUT

The longest penalty shoot-out in finals history came in the 1980 third-place play-off between hosts Italy and Czechoslovakia, in Naples on 21 June. The Czechs won 9-8, following a 1-1 draw. After eight successful spot-kicks each, Czech goalkeeper **Jaroslav Netolicka** saved Fulvio Collovati's kick.

FRANCE STRIKE, WITHOUT STRIKERS

France still hold the record for the most goals scored by one team in a finals tournament, 14 in 1984. Yet only one of those goals was netted by a recognized striker – Bruno Bellone, who hit the second in their 2-0 final win over Spain. France's inspirational captain, Michel Platini, supplied most of the French firepower, scoring an incredible nine goals in five appearances. He hit hat-tricks against Belgium and Denmark and a last-gasp winner in the semi-final against Portugal. Midfielders Alain Giresse and Luis Fernandez chipped in with goals in the 5-0 win over Belgium. Defender Jean-Francois Domergue gave France the lead against Portugal in the semi-finals, and added another in extra-time after Jordao had put Portugal 2-1 ahead.

SAME OLD SPAIN

Spain not only cruised their way to the largest winning margin of any UEFA European Championship final by trouncing Italy 4-0 in the climax to 2012 – they also became the first country to successfully defend the title. David Silva, **Jordi Alba** – with his first international goal – and substitutes Fernando Torres and Juan Mata got the goals in Kiev's Olympic Stadium on 1 July. Spain thus landed their third major trophy in a row, having won Euro 2008 and the 2010 FIFA World Cup.

TOP TEAM SCORERS IN THE FINALS

Year	Team	Goals
1960	Yugoslavia	6
1964	Spain, Soviet Union, Hungary	4
1968	Italy	4
1972	West Germany	5
1976	West Germany	6
1980	West Germany	6
1984	France	14
1988	Netherlands	8
1992	Germany	7
1996	Germany	10
2000	France, Netherlands	13
2004	Czech Republic	9
2008	Spain	12
2012	Spain	12

BIGGEST WINS IN THE FINALS

Netherlands 6, Yugoslavia 1, 2000
France 5, Belgium 0, 1984
Denmark 5, Yugoslavia 0, 1984
Sweden 5, Bulgaria 0, 2004

SPAIN REFUSE TO MEET SOVIETS

Political rivalries wrecked the planned clash between Spain and the Soviet Union in the 1960 quarter-finals. The fascist Spanish leader, General Francisco Franco, refused to allow Spain to go to the communist Soviet Union – and banned the Soviets from entering Spain. The Soviet Union were handed a walkover on the grounds that Spain had refused to play. Franco relented four years later, allowing the Soviets to come to Spain for the finals. He was spared the embarrassment of presenting the trophy to them, however, as Spain beat the Soviet Union 2-1 in the final.

TOSS FAVOURS HOSTS ITALY

Italy reached the 1968 final on home soil thanks to the toss of a coin. It was the only game in finals history decided in such fashion. Italy drew 0-0 against the Soviet Union after extra-time in Naples on 5 June 1968. The Soviet captain, Albert Shesternev, made the wrong call at the toss – so Italy reached the final where they beat Yugoslavia.

UEFA EUROPEAN CHAMPIONSHIP WINNERS

3 West Germany/Germany
  (1972, 1980, 1996)
  Spain
  (1964, 2008, 2012)
2 France (1984, 2000)
1 Soviet Union (1960)
  Czechoslovakia (1976)
  Italy (1968)
  Netherlands (1998)
  Denmark (1992)
  Greece (2004)

DELLAS TIMES IT RIGHT FOR GREECE

Greece scored the only "silver goal" victory in the history of the competition in the UEFA Euro 2004 semi-finals. (The silver goal rule meant that a team leading after the first period of extra-time won the match.) Traianos Dellas headed Greece's winner seconds before the end of the first period of extra-time against the Czech Republic in Porto on 1 July. Both golden goals and silver goals were abandoned for UEFA Euro 2008, and drawn knockout matches reverted to being decided over the full 30 minutes of extra-time, and penalties if necessary.

PLAYER RECORDS

SHEARER TALLY BOOSTS ENGLAND

Alan Shearer is the only Englishman to top the finals scoring chart. Shearer led the scorers with five goals as England went out on penalties to Germany in the Euro 96 semi-final at Wembley. He netted against Switzerland, Scotland and the Netherlands (2) in the group and gave England a third-minute lead against the Germans. Shearer added two more goals at Euro 2000, to stand second behind Michel Platini in the all-time scorers' list.

ILYIN GOAL MAKES HISTORY

Anatoly Ilyin of the Soviet Union scored the first goal in UEFA European Championship history when he netted after four minutes against Hungary on 29 September 1958. A crowd of 100,572 watched the Soviets win 3-1 in the Lenin Stadium, Moscow. The Soviet Union went on to win the first final, in 1960.

GOLDEN ONE–TOUCH

Spain striker **Fernando Torres** claimed the Golden Boot, despite scoring the same number of goals – three – as Italy's Mario Balotelli, Russia's Alan Dzagoev, Germany's Mario Gomez, Croatia's Mario Mandzukic and Portugal's Cristiano Ronaldo. The decision came down to number of assists – with Torres and Gomez level on one apiece – then amount of time played. The 92 minutes spent on the pitch by Torres, compared to Gomez, meant his contributions were deemed better value for the prize.

VONLANTHEN BEATS ROONEY RECORD

The youngest scorer in finals history was Switzerland midfielder **Johan Vonlanthen.** He was 18 years 141 days when he netted in their 3-1 defeat by France on 21 June 2004. He beat the record set by England forward Wayne Rooney four days earlier. Rooney was 18 years 229 days when he scored the first goal in England's 3-0 win over the Swiss. Vonlanthen retired from football at the age of 26 in May 2012 due to a knee injury.

KIRICHENKO NETS QUICKEST GOAL

The fastest goal in the history of the finals was scored by Russia forward Dmitri Kirichenko. He netted after just 67 seconds to give his side the lead against Greece on 20 June 2004. Russia won 2-1, but Greece still qualified for the quarter-finals – and went on to become shock winners. The fastest goal in the final was Spain midfielder Jesus Pereda's sixth-minute strike in 1964, when Spain beat the Soviet Union 2-1.

GROOM FOR SUCCESS

Spanish playmaker Andres Iniesta, scorer of the winner in the 2010 FIFA World Cup, followed that tournament in style by being named the best player of Euro 2012 – despite not appearing on the scoresheet in any of his team's six matches. Six days after the final against Italy, Iniesta had more cause for celebration. This time the occasion was back home in Spain, where he got married in a ceremony attended by international team-mates Cesc Fabregas and Sergio Busquets.

TOP SCORERS IN FINALS HISTORY

1	Michel Platini (France)	9
2	Alan Shearer (England)	7
3	Nuno Gomes (Portugal)	6
=	Thierry Henry (France)	
=	Patrick Kluivert (Netherlands)	
=	Zlatan Ibrahimovic (Sweden)	
=	Cristiano Ronaldo (Portugal)	
=	Ruud van Nistelrooy (Netherlands)	
9	Milan Baros (Czech Republic)	5
=	Jurgen Klinsmann (W Germany/Germany)	
=	Savo Milosevic (Yugoslavia)	
=	Wayne Rooney (England)	
=	Fernando Torres (Spain)	
=	Marco van Basten (Netherlands)	
=	Zinedine Zidane (France)	

BIERHOFF NETS FIRST "GOLDEN GOAL"

Germany's **Oliver Bierhoff** scored the first golden ⋯⋯⋯ goal in the history of the tournament when he hit the winner against the Czech Republic in the Euro 96 final at Wembley on 30 June. (The golden goal rule meant the first team to score in extra-time won the match.) Bierhoff netted in the fifth minute of extra-time. His shot from 20 yards deflected off defender Michal Hornak and slipped through goalkeeper Petr Kouba's fingers.

PONEDELNIK'S MONDAY MORNING FEELING

Striker Viktor Ponedelnik headed the Soviet Union's extra-time winner to beat Yugoslavia 2-1 in the first final on 10 July 1960 – and sparked some famous headlines in the Soviet media. The game in Paris kicked off at 10pm Moscow time on Sunday. It was running into Monday morning there by the time Ponedelnik – whose name means "Monday" in Russian – scored. He said: "When I scored, all the journalists wrote the headline 'Ponedelnik zabivayet v Ponedelnik' – 'Monday scores on Monday'."

MARCHING ORDERS

Only one man has ever been sent off in a UEFA European Championship final: France defender Yvon Le Roux, who received a second yellow card with five minutes remaining of his team's 2-0 triumph over Spain in 1984. The most red cards were shown at Euro 2000, when then ten dismissals included Romania's Gheorghe Hagi, Portugal's **Nuno Gomes**, Italy's Gianluca Zambrotta and the Czech ⋯⋯⋯⋯⋯ Republic's Radoslav Latal – an unprecedented second sending-off for Latal, who was also given his marching orders at Euro 96.

VASTIC THE OLDEST

The oldest scorer in finals history is Austria's Ivica Vastic. He was 38 years and 257 days old when he equalized in the 1-1 draw with Poland at UEFA Euro 2008.

TOP SCORERS IN THE FINALS

1960	Francois Heutte (France)	2
	Milan Galic (Yugoslavia)	
	Valentin Ivanov (Soviet Union)	
	Drazan Jerkovic (Yugoslavia)	
	Slava Metreveli (Soviet Union)	
	Viktor Ponedelnik (Soviet Union)	
1964	Ferenc Bene (Hungary)	2
	Dezso Novak (Hungary)	
	Jesus Pereda (Spain)	
1968	Dragan Dzajic (Yugoslavia)	2
1972	Gerd Muller (West Germany)	4
1976	Dieter Muller (West Germany)	4
1980	Klaus Allofs (West Germany)	3
1984	Michel Platini (France)	9
1988	Marco van Basten (Netherlands)	5
1992	Dennis Bergkamp (Netherlands)	3
	Tomas Brolin (Sweden)	
	Henrik Larsen (Denmark)	
	Karlheinz Riedle (Germany)	
1996	Alan Shearer (England)	5
2000	Patrick Kluivert (Netherlands)	5
	Savo Milosevic (Yugoslavia)	
2004	Milan Baros (Czech Republic)	5
2008	David Villa (Spain)	4
2012	Mario Balotelli (Italy)	3
	Alan Dzagoev (Russia)	
	Mario Gomez (Germany)	
	Mario Mandzukic (Croatia)	
	Cristiano Ronaldo (Portugal)	
	Fernando Torres (Spain)	

MATTHAUS MIRRORS TOURNAMENT GROWTH

The career of Lothar Matthaus straddles the growth of the European Championship. He appeared in four tournaments between 1980 and 2000. He missed Euro 92 because of injury and stayed at home for Euro 96 after falling out with coach Berti Vogts and skipper Jurgen Klinsmann. He had made his entry as a 19-year-old substitute for Bernd Dietz in West Germany's 3-2 group win over the Netherlands in Naples on 14 June 1980. That was the first tournament which involved eight teams and two groups rather than the previous four semi-finalists. He ended his association with the championship at the age of 39, playing for a reunited Germany as they were eliminated 3-0 by Portugal at Euro 2000. By now the tournament had expanded to include 16 teams in four groups. Despite featuring in four tournaments, Matthaus made only 11 appearances in total. He did, however, enter the tournament when it was taking its first steps to expansion and left it when the European Championship had become second only to the FIFA World Cup as football's most important international competition.

BROTHERS IN ARMS

Four pairs of brothers went to Euro 2000: Gary and Phil Neville (England), Frank and Ronald de Boer (Netherlands), Daniel and Patrik Andersson (Sweden) and Belgium's Emile and Mbo Mpenza.

BECKENBAUER'S 100th ENDS IN DEFEAT

West Germany legend Franz Beckenbauer won his 100th cap in the 1976 final against Czechoslovakia. After his side's shoot-out defeat, he played only three more games for his country before retiring from international football.

PORTUGAL TRIO BANNED FOR THE LONGEST

The longest suspensions in the history of the finals were handed out to three Portugal players after their Euro 2000 semi-final defeat by France. Zinedine Zidane's "Golden Goal" penalty infuriated the Portuguese, who surrounded referee Gunter Benko and assistant Igor Sramka. The three Portuguese players – **Abel Xavier**, Nuno Gomes and Paulo Bento – were banned for "physically and verbally intimidating" the officials. Xavier was suspended from European football for nine months. Gomes, who was also sent off, was banned for eight months. Bento received a six-month suspension.

CLEAN SHEETS FOR CASILLAS

Spain saw out the 2012 tournament conceding just one goal, emulating the achievement of Italy in 1980 and Norway in 2000 – neither of whom achieved what Spain did and lifted the trophy. That successful 2012 campaign took Spanish captain and goalkeeper Iker Casillas to nine clean sheets in UEFA European Championships, from 14 games – equalling the record held by the Netherlands' Edwin van der Sar, with his nine clean sheets from 16 matches.

MOST FINALS TOURNAMENTS PLAYED

Eight players have appeared in four finals tournaments:

Lothar Matthaus	(West Germany/Germany)	1980, 1984, 1988, 2000
Peter Schmeichel	(Denmark)	1988, 1992, 1996, 2000
Aron Winter	(Netherlands)	1988, 1992, 1996, 2000
Alessandro del Piero	(Italy)	1996, 2000, 2004, 2008
Edwin van der Sar	(Netherlands)	1996, 2000, 2004, 2008
Lilian Thuram	(France)	1996, 2000, 2004, 2008
Olof Mellberg	(Sweden)	2000, 2004, 2008, 2012
Iker Casillas	(Spain)	2000, 2004, 2008, 2012

MULLERY THE FIRST TO GO

Wing-half Alan Mullery became the first England player ever to be sent off when he was dismissed in the 89th minute of their 1-0 semi-final defeat by Yugoslavia in Florence on 5 June 1968. Mullery was sent off for a foul on Dobrivoje Trivic, three minutes after Dragan Dzajic had scored Yugoslavia's winner. His dismissal came in England's 424th official international match.

HAGI'S JOURNEY ENDS IN RED

Romania's greatest player, Gheorghe Hagi won the last of his 125 caps in a 2-0 UEFA Euro 2000 quarter-final defeat by Italy on 24 June. However, his international career would end in sad circumstances: he was sent off in the 59th minute for two yellow-card offences. Hagi had previously been booked against Germany and Portugal – and had missed Romania's 3-2 group win over England through suspension.

MOST MATCHES PLAYED IN THE FINALS

16	Edwin van der Sar (Netherlands)
	Lilian Thuram (France)
14	Iker Casillas (Spain)
	Luis Figo (Portugal)
	Nuno Gomes (Portugal)
	Philipp Lahm (Germany)
	Karel Poborsky (Czech Republic)
	Cristiano Ronaldo (Portugal)
	Zinedine Zidane (France)

BACK OF THE WRONG NET

Glen Johnson became only the fifth man to score an own goal at a UEFA European Championship, when the England right-back put through his own net against Sweden in their Euro 2012 first-round clash. The earlier unfortunates were Czechoslovakia's Anton Ondrus in 1976, Bulgaria's Dimitar Penev in 1996, Yugoslavia's Dejan Govedarica in 2000 and Portugal's Jorge Andrade in 2004.

ARAGONES THE VETERAN COACH

Luis Aragones, Spain's coach in 2008, is the oldest boss of a European champion team. Aragones (born in Madrid on 28 July 1938) was 29 days short of his 70th birthday when Spain beat Germany 1-0 in the final on 29 June. That was his last match in charge. He had taken over the national team after Euro 2004.

KADLEC FATHER AND SON

Czech defenders Miroslav and Michal Kadlec are the only father and son to have played in the finals. Miroslav (born on 22 June 1964 in Uherske Hradiste) captained the Czech Republic side that finished as runners-up to Germany at Euro 96. He also scored the winning penalty in the semi-final shoot-out against France. Michal (born on 13 December 1984 in Vyskov) made his first appearance as an 80th-minute substitute for Jaroslav Plasil in the Group A game against Turkey in Geneva on 15 June 2008.

SUAREZ GAINS FIRST DOUBLE

The first man to earn winners' medals in the European Championship and the European Cup in the same season was Spain's **Luis Suarez**. He helped Spain beat the Soviet Union 2-1 in the final on 21 June 1964. A few weeks earlier, Suarez had been in the Internazionale team that beat Real Madrid 3-1 in the European Cup final. Four players were in both PSV Eindhoven's 1988 European Cup final victory over Benfica and the Netherlands' UEFA Euro 88 final defeat of Russia. Nicolas Anelka won the Champions League with Real Madrid in 2000 and was in the France squad that won Euro 2000, but he did not appear in the final.

KARAGOUNIS A GONER

The yellow card shown to Greece's Giorgos Karagounis in their final first-round match of Euro 2012, against Russia, achieved even more than ruling him out of their quarter-final against Germany. It was also his eighth in UEFA European Championship history, a competition record. He had previously been able to play in the final of Euro 2004 after collecting two bookings beforehand.

MATTHAUS THE OLDEST

The oldest player to appear in a game at the UEFA European Championship finals was Germany's Lothar Matthaus. He was 39 years 91 days when he played in their 3-0 defeat by Portugal on 20 June 2000.

LOW CONQUERS ALMOST ALL

Germany coach Joachim Low claimed the record for most UEFA European Championship victories in charge, when his side beat Greece 4-2 in the Euro 2012 quarter-finals. This took him to eight wins from ten games, across Euro 2008 and Euro 2012. The semi-final defeat against Italy also equalled Berti Vogts's record of 11 UEFA European Championship games as a manager.

NAMES ON THEIR SHIRTS

Players wore their names as well as their numbers on the back of their shirts for the first time at Euro 92. They had previously been identified only by numbers.

REPEAT PROENCA

Portuguese official Pedro Proenca achieved the double feat of refereeing the 2012 UEFA Champions League final between Chelsea and Bayern Munich and the 2012 UEFA European Championship final between Spain and Italy. He also became the third man to referee four matches in one UEFA European Championship, after Sweden's Anders Frisk (2004) and Italy's Roberto Rosetti (2008). Frisk's eight matches overall is a UEFA European Championship record.

RECORD EURO GOAL DROUGHT

Between **Xabi Alonso**'s added-time penalty in Spain's 2-0 quarter-final defeat of France and Mario Balotelli's 20th-minute semi-final strike for Italy in their 2-1 victory against Germany, Euro 2012's goalless spell lasted 260 minutes – a UEFA European Championship record.

ITALY HOSTS TWICE

Italy were the first country to host the finals twice – in 1968 and 1980. They were awarded the finals in 1968 in recognition of the 60th anniversary of the Italian football federation. Belgium have also hosted the finals twice: first, alone, in 1972, and then in partnership with the Netherlands for Euro 2000.

ELLIS BLOWS THE WHISTLE

English referee **Arthur Ellis** took charge of the first UEFA European Championship final between the Soviet Union and Yugoslavia in 1960. Ellis had also refereed the first-ever European Cup final, between Real Madrid and Reims, four years earlier. After he retired from football, he became the "referee" on the British version of the Europe-wide game show *It's a Knock-out*.

GREEKS HAND ALBANIA WALKOVER

When Greece were drawn against Albania in the first round of the 1964 tournament, the Greeks immediately withdrew, handing Albania a 3-0 walkover win. The countries had technically been at war since 1940. The Greek government did not formally lift the state of war until 1987, although diplomatic relations were re-established in 1971.

FINALS HOSTS

1960	France
1964	Spain
1968	Italy
1972	Belgium
1976	Yugoslavia
1980	Italy
1984	France
1988	West Germany
1992	Sweden
1996	England
2000	Netherlands and Belgium
2004	Portugal
2008	Austria and Switzerland
2012	Poland and Ukraine

HOSTS WITH (ALMOST) THE MOST

In 2000, Belgium and the Netherlands began the trend for dual hosting the UEFA European Championship finals – it was the first time the tournament was staged in more than one country. The opening game was Belgium's 2-1 win over Sweden in Brussels on 10 June, with the final in Rotterdam. Austria and Switzerland co-hosted Euro 2008, starting in Basel and climaxing in Vienna, before Poland and Ukraine teamed up in 2012. Warsaw staged the opening match and Kiev was the host city for the final.

SINGING IN UKRAINE

The eight venues – four apiece – in Poland and Ukraine matched the number used when Belgium and the Netherlands shared hosting rights at Euro 2000 and when Austria and Switzerland did so eight years later. Only Euro 2004 in Portugal had more venues (10). Poland's 56,070-capacity National Stadium in Warsaw staged the opening game between Poland and Greece, while Kiev's 64,640-seater Olympic Stadium was the setting for the final. France will stage Euro 2016, while the final tournament in 2020 will be played – for the first time – in as many as 13 different cities across 13 different countries.

WELL DONE, WELBECK

Perhaps surprisingly, the biggest official attendance at Euro 2012 was not for the final but for a first-round Group D match, when 64,640 saw England beat Sweden 3-2 thanks to a late back-heeled winner by **Danny Welbeck**.

UEFA EUROPEAN CHAMPIONSHIP FINAL REFEREES

1960	Arthur Ellis (England)
1964	Arthur Holland (England)
1968	Gottfried Dienst (Switzerland)
	Replay: Jose Maria Ortiz de Mendibil (Spain)
1972	Ferdinand Marschall (Austria)
1976	Sergio Gonella (Italy)
1980	Nicolae Rainea (Romania)
1984	Vojtech Christov (Czechoslovakia)
1988	Michel Vautrot (France)
1992	Bruno Galler (Switzerland)
1996	Pierluigi Pairetto (Italy)
2000	Anders Frisk (Sweden)
2004	Markus Merk (Germany)
2008	Roberto Rosetti (Italy)
2012	Pedro Proenca (Portugal)

THE "ITALIAN JOB"

The 1968 finals in Italy were used as the backdrop to a famous English-language film – *The Italian Job*, starring Michael Caine – about a British gang who use the cover of the finals to stage a daring gold robbery in Turin. The film was released in England on 2 June 1969.

GOALS AREN'T EVERYTHING

Despite being widely praised for the quality of attacking football on display, Euro 2012 actually had the lowest average of goals per game for any UEFA European Championship since Euro 96 in England. The 76 goals across 31 matches in Poland and Ukraine was one fewer than was scored at each of the 2004 and 2008 tournaments, and meant an average of 2.45 goals per game. It was not until the fourth of the four quarter-finals that Euro 2012 witnessed its first goalless draw, between England and Italy – but this was followed by another stalemate in the next game, three days later, between Spain and Portugal in the first of the semi-finals.

KEEPING IT CLEAN

Only three red cards were shown during Euro 2012 – Greece's Sokratis Papastathopoulos and Poland's **Wojciech Szczesny** in the opening game, and Keith Andrews for the Republic of Ireland against Italy. This equalled the sendings-off total in the 2008 UEFA European Championship but was half the tally of Euro 2004.

PART 4: COPA AMERICA

THE WORLD'S OLDEST surviving international championship finds its rich history repeating itself even in a modern world much-transformed since the inaugural Copa America – with both the 1916 and 2011 tournaments being won by Uruguay. Their 15th Copa America triumph in 2011 made them the competition's most successful country – flying high on the football field once more.

More literal jet travel was missing, however, when they first hoisted the trophy – one of the factors that helped make a continental championship such a worthwhile idea for its South American founders. Before jet travel became commonplace in the last half-century, major footballing events were difficult to organize – and that played an influence in FIFA's founding membership in 1904 being entirely European. Although South American nations such as Brazil, Argentina and Uruguay were not slow in signing up, the opportunities available to them to play against their European cousins were scarce – open only to those willing to endure laborious journeys by sea.

The South Americans thus decided to organize their own international competitions, which led to the creation in 1916 of the South American Championship, now known as the Copa America. Communications not being what they are today, even then organization was far from simple – and many of the early championships are now considered unofficial. Further problems arose over scheduling which meant that countries could not secure the release of their best players who were under contract to European clubs. Argentina were champions in 1957 and considered favourites for the following year's FIFA World Cup. But they soon lost all their inspirational forward trio – Humberto Maschio, Antonio Valentin Angelillo and Enrique Omar Sivori – to Italian clubs.

Now, however, the club-versus-country issue has been largely resolved by FIFA's enforcement of a unified international calendar, recognizing the priority status of the Copa America.

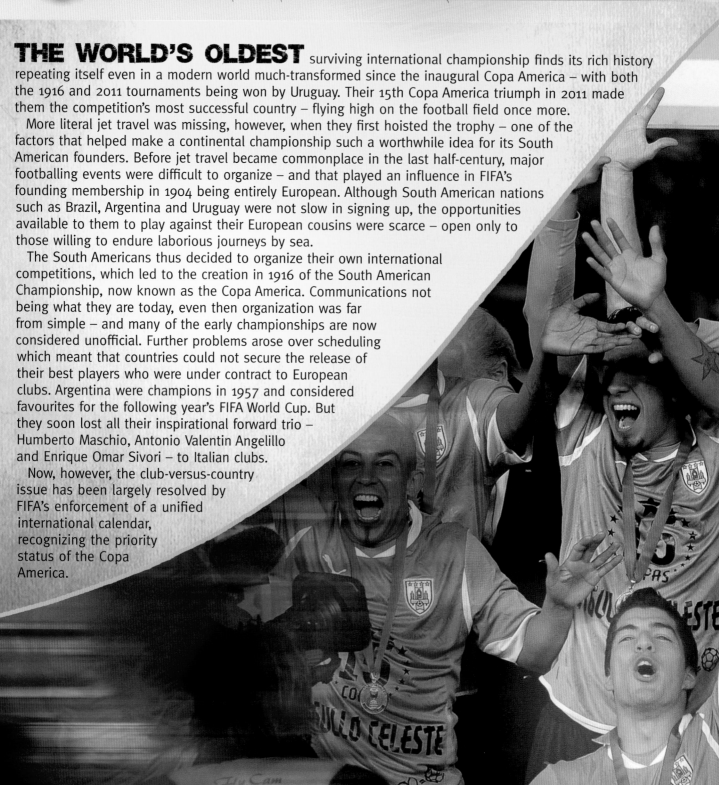

Uruguay might have been South America's most successful nation at the 2010 FIFA World Cup, but their 2011 Copa America triumph, in Argentina, was still considered a big surprise.

COPA AMERICA TEAM RECORDS

LITTLE NAPOLEON

In 1942, Ecuador and their goalkeeper Napoleon Medina conceded more goals in one tournament than any other team, when they let in 31 goals across six games – and six defeats. Three years later he and his team-mates finally managed to keep a clean sheet, in a goalless draw against Bolivia – but still managed to let in another 27 goals in their five other matches.

LUCK OF THE DRAW

Paraguay reached the 2011 final despite not winning a single game in normal play. Instead, they drew all three matches in the first-round group stage, then needed penalties to win their quarter-final against Brazil and semi-final versus Venezuela after both games ended goalless. Perhaps not surprisingly, their captain **Justo Villar** was voted the tournament's best goalkeeper.

COPA AMERICA WINNERS

1916	Uruguay (league format)
1917	Uruguay (league format)
1919	Brazil 1 Uruguay 0
1920	Uruguay (league format)
1921	Argentina (league format)
1922	Brazil 3 Paraguay 1
1923	Uruguay (league format)
1924	Uruguay (league format)
1925	Argentina (league format)
1926	Uruguay (league format)
1927	Argentina (league format)
1929	Argentina (league format)
1935	Uruguay (league format)
1937	Argentina 2 Brazil 0
1939	Peru (league format)
1941	Argentina (league format)
1942	Uruguay (league format)
1945	Argentina (league format)
1946	Argentina (league format)
1947	Argentina (league format)
1949	Brazil 7 Paraguay 0
1953	Paraguay 3 Brazil 2
1955	Argentina (league format)
1956	Uruguay (league format)
1957	Argentina (league format)
1959	Argentina (league format)
1959	Uruguay (league format)
1963	Bolivia (league format)
1967	Uruguay (league format)
1975	Peru 4 Colombia 1 (on aggregate, after three games)
1979	Paraguay 3 Chile 1 (on aggregate, after three games)
1983	Uruguay 3 Brazil 1 (on aggregate, after two games)
1987	Uruguay 1 Chile 0
1989	Brazil (league format)
1991	Argentina (league format)
1993	Argentina 2 Mexico 1
1995	Uruguay 1 Brazil 1 (Uruguay won 5-3 on penalties)
1997	Brazil 3 Bolivia 1
1999	Brazil 3 Uruguay 0
2001	Colombia 1 Mexico 0
2004	Brazil 2 Argentina 2 (Brazil won 4-2 on penalties)
2007	Brazil 3 Argentina 0
2011	Uruguay 3 Paraguay 0

HOSTING RIGHTS BY COUNTRY

Country		
Argentina	9	(1916, 1921, 1925, 1929, 1937, 1946, 1959, 1987, 2011)
Uruguay	7	(1917, 1923, 1924, 1942, 1956, 1967, 1995)
Chile	6	(1920, 1926, 1941, 1945, 1955, 1991)
Peru	6	(1927, 1935, 1939, 1953, 1957, 2004)
Brazil	4	(1919, 1922, 1949, 1989)
Ecuador	3	(1947, 1959, 1993)
Bolivia	2	(1963, 1997)
Paraguay	1	(1999)
Colombia	1	(2001)
Venezuela	1	(2007)

EXTRA TIME

The longest match in the history of the Copa America was the 1919 final between Brazil and Uruguay. It lasted 150 minutes, 90 minutes of regular time plus two extra-time periods of 30 minutes each.

HOW IT STARTED

The first South American "Championship of Nations", as it was then known, was held in Argentina from 2–17 July 1916, during the country's independence centenary commemorations. The tournament was won by Uruguay, who drew with Argentina in the last match of the tournament. It was an inauspicious beginning. The 16 July encounter had to be abandoned at 0-0 when fans invaded the pitch and set the wooden stands on fire. The match was continued at a different stadium the following day and still ended goalless ... but Uruguay ended up topping the mini-league table and were hailed the first champions. Isabelino Gradin was the inaugural tournament's top scorer. The event also saw the foundation of the South American federation CONMEBOL, which took place a week into the competition on 9 July 1916. From that point on the tournament was held every two years, though some tournaments are now considered to have been unofficial. There was, a three-year gap between the 2004 and 2007 tournaments, and the competition is now staged every four years instead.

SUB–STANDARD

During the 1953 Copa America, Peru were awarded a walkover win when Paraguay tried to make one more substitution than they were allowed. Would-be substitute Milner Ayala was so incensed, he kicked English referee Richard Maddison and was banned from football for three years. Yet Paraguay remained in the tournament and went on to beat Brazil in the final – minus, of course, the disgraced Ayala.

ROTATING RIGHTS

The Campeonato Sudamericano de Selecciones was rebaptized the Copa America from 1975. Between then and 1983 there was no host nation, before CONMEBOL adopted the policy of rotating the right to host the Copa America among the ten member confederations. The first rotation was complete after Venezuela hosted the 2007 edition, with Argentina lined up to play host for the ninth time in 2011.

HISTORY MEN

The Copa America is the world's oldest surviving international football tournament, having been launched in 1916 when the participating nations were Argentina, Bolivia, Brazil, Chile, Colombia, Ecuador, Paraguay, Peru, Uruguay and Venezuela. In 1910, an unofficial South American championship had been won by Argentina, who beat Uruguay 4-1 in the decider – though the final match had been delayed a day after rioting fans burnt down a stand at the Gimnasia stadium in Buenos Aires.

FALLEN ANGELS

Argentina's 1957 Copa America-winning forward trio of Humberto Maschio, Omar Sivori and Antonio Valentin Angelillo became known by the nickname "the angels with dirty faces". At least one of them scored in each of the side's six matches – Maschio finished with nine, Angelillo eight and Sivori three. Argentina's most convincing performance was an opening 8-2 win over Colombia, in which Argentina had scored four goals and missed a penalty within the first 25 minutes. The dazzling displays made Argentina, not eventual winners Brazil, favourites for the following year's FIFA World Cup. Before then, however, Maschio, Sivori and Angelillo had all been lured away to Europe by Italian clubs and the Argentine federation subsequently refused to pick them for the trip to Sweden for the FIFA World Cup. Sivori and Maschio ultimately made it to the FIFA World Cup, in 1962. However, to fury back home, they did so wearing not the light blue-and-white stripes of Argentina, but the Azzurri blue of their newly adopted Italy.

CONSISTENT COLOMBIANS

In 2001, Colombia, who went on to win the trophy for the first and only time in their history, became the only country to go through an entire Copa America campaign without conceding a single goal. They scored 11 goals themselves, more than half of them from six-goal tournament top scorer **Victor Aristazabal**. Keeping the clean sheets was goalkeeper Oscar Cordoba, who had previously spent much of his international career as back-up to the eccentric Rene Higuita. Just a month earlier, Cordoba had won the South American club championship, the Copa Libertadores, with Argentine side Boca Juniors.

TRIUMPHS BY COUNTRY

Uruguay 15 (1916, 1917, 1920, 1923, 1924, 1926, 1935, 1942, 1956, 1959, 1967, 1983, 1987, 1995, 2011)
Argentina 14 (1921, 1925, 1927, 1929, 1937, 1941, 1945, 1946, 1947, 1955, 1957, 1959, 1991, 1993)
Brazil 8 (1919, 1922, 1949, 1989, 1997, 1999, 2004, 2007)
Peru 2 (1939, 1975)
Paraguay 2 (1953, 1979)
Bolivia 1 (1963)
Colombia 1 (2001)

MORE FROM MORENO

Argentina were not only responsible for the Copa America's biggest win, but also the tournament's highest-scoring game, when they put 12 past Ecuador in 1942 – to no reply. Jose Manuel Moreno's five strikes in that game included the 500th goal in the competition's history. Moreno, born in Buenos Aires on 3 August 1916, ended that tournament as joint top scorer with team-mate Herminio Masantonio – hitting seven goals. Both men ended their international careers with 19 goals for their country, though Moreno did so in 34 appearances – compared to Masantonio's 21. Masantonio scored four in the Ecuador thrashing.

URUGUAY AGAIN

Uruguay, the first ever winners of the Copa America, once more became the competition's most successful side by claiming their 15th triumph in 2011 – pulling one clear of neighbours and rivals Argentina. What might have made the glory even sweeter was that it came on Argentine turf and included a quarter-final victory on penalties over their hosts. Argentina and Brazil had gone into the tournament as favourites, with many expecting them to contest the final for the third tournament running – but instead both were knocked out in the quarter-finals, producing an unlikely last four of Uruguay, Paraguay, Venezuela and Peru.

COPA AMERICA PLAYER RECORDS

FROG PRINCE

Chilean goalkeeper Sergio Livingstone holds the record for most Copa America appearances, with 34 games, across the 1941, 1942, 1945, 1947, 1949 and 1953 tournaments. Livingstone, nicknamed "The Frog", was voted player of the tournament in 1941 – becoming the first goalkeeper to win the award – and might have played even more Copa America matches had he not missed out on the 1946 competition. Livingstone, born in Santiago on 26 March 1920, spent almost his entire career in his home country – save for a season with Argentina's Racing Club in 1943–44. Overall, he made 52 appearances for Chile between 1941 and 1954, before retiring and becoming a popular TV journalist and commentator.

CHILE'S ILL FORTUNE

The first Copa America own goal was scored by Chile's Luis Garcia, giving Argentina a 1-0 win in 1917, in the second edition of the tournament. Even more unfortunately for Chile, Garcia's strike was the only goal by one of their players throughout the tournament – making Chile the first team to fail to score a single goal in a Copa America competition.

MOST GAMES PLAYED

1	Sergio Livingstone (Chile)	34
2	Zizinho (Brazil)	33
3	Leonel Alvarez (Colombia)	27
4	Carlos Valderrama (Colombia)	27
5	Alex Aguinaga (Ecuador)	25
6	Claudio Taffarel (Brazil)	25
7	Teodoro Fernandez (Peru)	24
8	Angel Romano (Uruguay)	23
9	Djalma Santos (Brazil)	22
10	Claudio Suarez (Mexico)	22

OVERALL TOP SCORERS

1	Norberto Mendez (Argentina)	17
=	Zizinho (Brazil)	17
3	Teodoro Fernandez (Peru)	15
=	Severino Varela (Uruguay)	15
5	Ademir (Brazil)	13
=	Jair da Rosa Pinto (Brazil)	13
=	Gabriel Batistuta (Argentina)	13
=	Jose Manuel Moreno (Argentina)	13
=	Hector Scarone (Uruguay)	13

REPEATING THE FEAT

Uruguay's Pedro Petrone (in 1923 and 1924) and **Gabriel Batistuta** of Argentina (in 1991 and 1995) are the only players to finish as top scorers in the Copa America on two occasions. Batistuta made his Argentina debut just a few days before the 1991 Copa America, in which his starring performances – including a decisive goal in the final – helped him win a transfer from Boca Juniors to Italy's Fiorentina.

LIKE GRANDFATHER, LIKE FATHER, LIKE SON

Diego Forlan's two goals in the 2011 Copa America final helped Uruguay to a 3-0 victory over Paraguay and their record 15th South American championship. They also ensured he followed in family footsteps in lifting the trophy – his father **Pablo** was part of the Uruguay side who won in 1967, when his grandfather Juan Carlos Corazzo was the triumphant coach. Corazzo had previously managed Uruguay's winning team in 1959. The brace against Paraguay put the youngest Forlan level with Hector Scarone as Uruguay's all-time leading scorer, with 31 goals. Yet it was Forlan's strike partner Luis Suarez – opening goal-scorer in the final – who was voted best player of the 2011 tournament.

MAGIC ALEX

When Alex Aguinaga lined up for Ecuador against Uruguay in his country's opening game at the 2004 event, he became only the second man to take part in eight different Copa Americas – joining legendary Uruguayan goalscorer Angel Romano. Aguinaga, a midfielder born in Ibarra on 9 July 1969, played a total of 109 times for his country – 25 of them in the Copa America, a competition that yielded four of his 23 international goals. His Copa America career certainly began well: Ecuador went undefeated for his first four appearances, at the 1987 and 1989 events, but his luck had ran out by the time his Ecuador career was coming to an end: he lost his final seven Copa America matches.

START TO FINISH

Colombia playmaker Carlos Valderrama and defensive midfielder **Leonel Alvarez** played in all 27 of their country's Copa America matches between 1987 and 1995, winning ten, drawing ten and losing seven – including third-place finishes in 1987, 1993 and 1995. Valderrama's two Copa America goals came in his first and final appearances in the competition – in a 2-0 victory over Bolivia in 1987 and a 4-1 thrashing of the United States eight years later.

GUERRERO'S RARE ACHIEVEMENT

Peru endured a disastrous qualification campaign for the 2010 FIFA World Cup, finishing bottom of the South American table – which made their third-place finish at the 2011 Copa America all the more remarkable. There was even more joy for striker **Paolo Guerrero,** whose five goals made him only the third Peruvian ever to finish top scorer at a Copa America – following Teodoro Fernandez in 1939 and Eduardo Malasquez in 1983. Guerrero's haul included a hat-trick in a 4-1 defeat of Venezuela in the third-place play-off.

FANTASTIC FIVES

Four players have scored five goals in one Copa America game: Hector Scarone in Uruguay's 6-0 win over Bolivia in 1926; Juan Marvezzi in Argentina's 6-1 win over Ecuador in 1941; Jose Manuel Moreno in Argentina's 12-0 win over Ecuador in 1942; and Evaristo de Macedo in Brazil's 9-0 win over Colombia in 1957.

LOW–KEY JOSE

The first-ever Copa America goal, in 1916, was scored by Jose Piendibene – setting Uruguay on the way to a 4-0 triumph over Chile. But he is not thought to have marked the moment with any great extravagance – Piendibene, renowned for his sense of fair play, made a point of not celebrating goals, to avoid offending his opponents.

PELE'S INSPIRATION

Brazilian forward **Zizinho** jointly holds the all-time goalscoring record for the Copa America, along with Argentina's Norberto Mendez. Both men struck 17 goals, Zizinho across six tournaments and Mendez three – including the 1945 and 1946 tournaments, which featured both men. Mendez was top scorer once and runner-up twice and won championship medals on all three occasions, while Zizinho's goals helped Brazil take the title only once, in 1949. Zizinho, Pele's footballing idol, would emerge from the 1950 FIFA World Cup as Brazil's top scorer and was also voted the tournament's best player – but was forever traumatized by the hosts' surprise defeat to Uruguay that cost Brazil the title.

COPA AMERICA OTHER RECORDS

SUCCESSFUL INVADERS

Only two foreign coaches have led a country to Copa America glory – Brazilian Danilo Alvim, whose Bolivian side won in 1963, and Englishman Jack Greenwell, Peru coach in 1939. Alvim, who won the tournament as a centre-half with Brazil in 1949, not only coached Bolivia to their one and only Copa America triumph – he did it by beating his native land 5-4 in the final match.

HOME COMFORTS

Uruguay have a unique record in remaining unbeaten in 38 Copa America games on home turf, all played in the country's capital Montevideo – comprising 31 wins, seven draws. The last tournament match they hosted was both a draw and a win – 1-1 against Brazil in 1995, with Uruguay emerging as champions, 5-3 on penalties after Fernando Alvez saved Tulio's penalty.

INVITED GUESTS

1993	Mexico (runners-up), United States
1995	Mexico, United States (fourth)
1997	Costa Rica, Mexico (third)
1999	Japan, Mexico (third)
2001	Costa Rica, Honduras (third), Mexico (runners-up)
2004	Costa Rica, Mexico
2007	Mexico (third), United States
2011	Costa Rica, Mexico

WRONG JUAN

It took 21 years, but Uruguay's Juan Emilio Piriz became the first Copa America player sent off, against Chile in 1937 – the first of 170 dismissals so far. Some 127 of those disgraced players have had a red card flourished in their face, since FIFA introduced the card system for referees in 1970.

MULTI-TASKING

Argentina's **Guillermo Stabile** not only holds the record for most Copa America triumphs as coach – he trounces all opposition. He led his country to the title on no fewer than six occasions – in 1941, 1945, 1946, 1947, 1955 and 1957. No other coach has lifted the trophy more than twice. Stabile coached Argentina from 1939 to 1960, having been appointed at the age of just 34. He lasted for 123 games in charge, winning 83 of them – and still managed to coach three clubs on the side at different times throughout his reign. He remained as Red Star Paris manager during his first year in the Argentina role, then led Argentine club Huracan for the next nine years – before leading domestic rivals Racing Club from 1949 to 1960. Stabile's Argentina may have, unusually, missed out on Copa America success in 1949, but that year brought the first of three Argentina league championships in a row for Stabile's Racing Club.

CAPTAIN CONSISTENT

Uruguay's 1930 World Cup-winning captain **Jose Nasazzi** is the only footballer to be voted player of the tournament at two different Copa America tournaments. Even more impressively, he achieved the feat 12 years apart – first taking the prize in 1923, then again in 1935. He was a Cup winner in 1923, 1924, 1926 and 1935. Nasazzi also captained Uruguay to victory in the 1924 and 1928 Olympic Games and in the 1930 World Cup.

TROPHY–WINNING COACHES

6 Guillermo Stabile (Argentina 1941, 1945, 1946, 1947, 1955, 1957)
2 Alfio Basile (Argentina 1991, 1993)
  Juan Carlos Corazzo (Uruguay 1959, 1967)
  Ernesto Figoli (Uruguay 1920, 1926)
1 Jorge Pacheco and Alfredo Foglino (Uruguay 1916)
  Ramon Platero (Uruguay 1917)
  Pedro Calomino (Argentina 1921)
  Lais (Brazil 1922)
  Leonardo De Lucca (Uruguay 1923)
  Ernesto Meliante (Uruguay 1924)
  Americo Tesoriere (Argentina 1925)
  Jose Lago Millon (Argentina 1927)
  Francisco Olazar (Argentina 1929)
  Raul V Blanco (Uruguay 1935)
  Manuel Seoane (Argentina 1937)
  Jack Greenwell (Peru 1939)
  Pedro Cea (Uruguay 1942)
  Flavio Costa (Brazil 1949)
  Manuel Fleitas Solich (Paraguay 1953)
  Hugo Bagnulo (Uruguay 1956)
  Victorio Spinetto (Argentina 1959)
  Danilo Alvim (Bolivia 1963)
  Marcos Calderon (Peru 1975)
  Ranulfo Miranda (Paraguay 1979)
  Omar Borras (Uruguay 1983)
  Roberto Fleitas (Uruguay 1987)
  Sebastiao Lazaroni (Brazil 1989)
  Hector Nunez (Uruguay 1995)
  Mario Zagallo (Brazil 1997)
  Wanderlei Luxemburgo (Brazil 1999)
  Francisco Maturana (Colombia 2001)
  Carlos Alberto Parreira (Brazil 2004)
  Dunga (Brazil 2007)
  Oscar Washington Tabarez (Uruguay 2011)

EXTENDED INVITE

Japan are the Copa America participants – as guests – who have featured in fewer games than any other nation, playing three matches at the 1999 competition. They were invited to take part in the 2011 tournament, but pulled out following the devastating 9.0 magnitude earthquake and tsunami that struck the country four months beforehand, and were replaced by Costa Rica – whose up-and-coming stars included striker **Joel Campbell**, who signed for English giants Arsenal just after the tournament.

GOALS AT A PREMIUM

In terms of goals per game, the 2011 Copa America was the second tightest of all time – with only 54 strikes hitting the back of the net in 26 matches, an average of 2.08 per game. Only the 1922 tournament, in Brazil, saw fewer – 22 goals in 11 games, an average of two. Both competitions were a far cry from the prolific 1927 event in Peru, where 37 goals across six games averaged out at 6.17.

SEEING RED

Brazil may have the worst FIFA World Cup disciplinary record, but neighbours Uruguay assume that unenviable position in the Copa America. Uruguayan players have been sent off 31 times, followed by Peru on 24 dismissals, Argentina (23), Brazil and Venezuela (20) apiece, Chile (17), Bolivia and Paraguay (13 each), Colombia, Ecuador and Mexico (nine each), and Costa Rica, Honduras and Japan (one apiece). Only the United States have, so far, made their way through Copa America participations with 11 men on the field throughout. Despite their overall record, however, Uruguay were given the Fair Play Award for the 2011 competition. Venezuela's Tomas Rincon, by contrast, suffered double disgrace – given not one but two straight red cards in matches that tournament.

MARKARIAN MAKES HIS MARK

The 2011 Copa America was not only a Uruguayan success story for the eventual champions, but also third-placed Peru's Uruguayan coach **Sergio Markarian**. Uruguay's winning manager Oscar Washington Tabarez had Markarian as his club coach at Bella Vista in the 1970s. Markarian could also claim some credit for Paraguay's runners-up finish, having been a successful and influential coach in that country during the 1980s, 1990s and early 21st century.

PART 5:
AFRICA CUP OF NATIONS

THE AFRICAN governing football confederation – Confederation Africaine de Football (or CAF) – is three years younger than UEFA, yet their cross-continental tournament, the Africa Cup of Nations, kicked off before the first European Championship. Formed on 8 February 1957, the CAF announced the first championship just three days later.

Egypt's ultimate triumph in that inaugural tournament set an appropriate pattern – the "Pharaohs" have won a record number of championships overall (seven) – but the competition has changed, and progressed, plenty since then.

Only three teams entered in 1957, but 47 nations vied for 15 qualification spots at the last event, in 2013, alongside already-qualified hosts South Africa who were replacing original choice Libya. The global prominence of the Africa Cup of Nations has also grown, especially as the spotlight falls on major African stars taking time off from European club duties every other January. There have been mounting calls for the competition to be moved to the middle of the year, to avoid disrupting European league seasons, but these have been rejected for climatic and seasonal reasons.

Whatever the place in the calendar, the trophy – now in its third physical incarnation – will always be contested with vivacious skills and fierce local pride. More different countries have won the ACN than any other continental championship, with glory being shared among 14 separate nations – including Africa's largest three countries Sudan, Algeria and Congo DR, as well as mid-sized entrants such as Cameroon, Morocco, the Ivory Coast, and early standard-setters Ghana, plus surprise 2012 champions Zambia.

And extra significance was achieved when the preliminary rounds for the 2010 event were integrated into Africa's FIFA World Cup 2010 qualification competition.

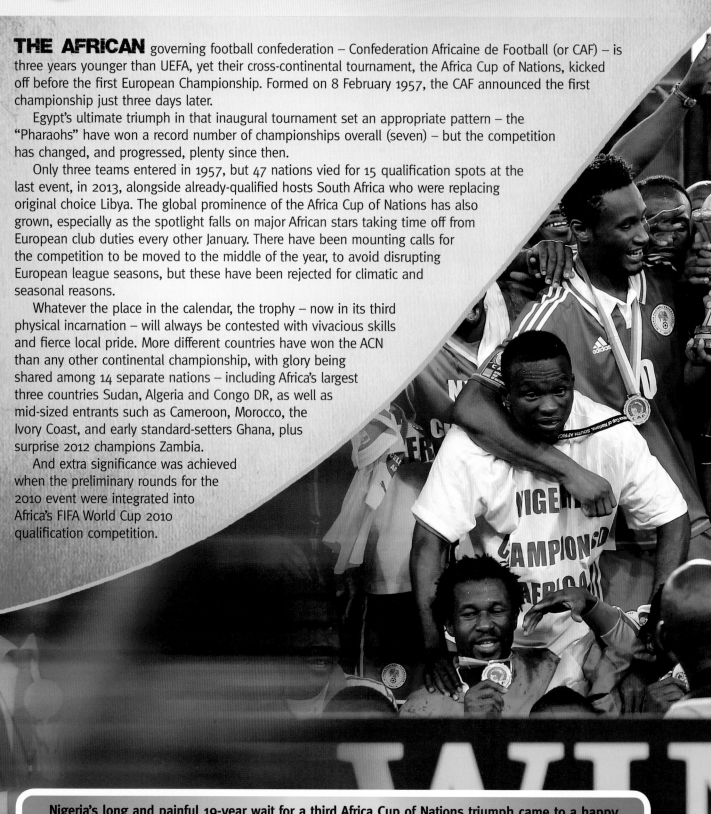

Nigeria's long and painful 19-year wait for a third Africa Cup of Nations triumph came to a happy end when they were crowned champions in 2013, reawakening the optimism of their glory days.

AFRICA CUP OF NATIONS 2013 REVIEW

Nigeria, at last, lived up to their status as one of the powers of African football by winning the Cup of Nations in South Africa. They took happy advantage of the absences of Egypt and Cameroon to claim only their third success in the tournament's 29 finals since 1957. Four of Nigeria's players were in the team of the tournament, Emmanuel Emenike was four-goal joint top scorer and Stephen Keshi became only the second man to win as both player then coach.

HOME COMFORTS

Stephen Keshi survived attempts to sack him on the eve of the 2013 Africa Cup of Nations but then became his country's first Nigerian ACN-winning coach, while picking as many as six squad members plying their trade in their own country's domestic league – unheard of in recent years. The home-based players were joined by such European league stars as Chelsea's **Jon Obi Mikel** and Victor Moses and Villarreal's Ikechukwu Uche, and Keshi did without big names he deemed disruptive – including Newcastle United's Shola Ameobi, Levante's Obafemi Martins and West Bromwich Albion's Peter Odemwingie.

2013 TEAM OF THE TOURNAMENT

GK	Vincent Enyeama (Nigeria)
DF	Bakary Kone (Burkina Faso)
DF	Nando (Cape Verde)
DF	Siaka Tene (Ivory Coast)
DF	Efe Ambroke (Nigeria)
MF	Jonathan Pitroipa (Burkina Faso)
MF	Seydou Keita (Mali)
MF	John Obi Mikel (Nigeria)
MF	Victor Moses (Nigeria)
FW	Asamoah Gyan (Ghana)
FW	Emmanuel Emenike (Nigeria)

BACK, SO SOON?

The Africa Cup of Nations was held in 2013, just a year after the previous tournament, in a deliberate change of schedule to ensure it would never again take place in the same calendar year as the World Cup finals.

GOAL-SHY

Niger were the only team to go home from South Africa without scoring a single goal, though were at least denied the worst defensive record: Ethiopia conceded seven in three matches, while Mali picked the ball out of the net eight times – albeit stretched across six games.

NOT QUITE PLAYING FOR KEEPS

Five red cards were shown at the 2013 Africa Cup of Nations, though one of them – Burkina Faso winger Jonathan Pitroipa's – was later rescinded. One other was shown to a team-mate, along with two flourished to Ethiopia players and one to Nigeria. Ethiopia goalkeeper **Sisay Bancha** was dismissed against Nigeria for two yellow cards earned three minutes apart, in the 82nd and 85th minutes of their first-round clash. The sending-off was Bancha's second in six appearances for his country.

SO NEAR, SO MBA

Scoring the winner for Nigeria in their quarter-final against pre-tournament favourites Ivory Coast made **Sunday Mba** the first man since 1990 to score at an Africa Cup of Nations while playing his league football in Nigeria. The last man to do so was Emmanuel Okocha in 1990. Warri Wolves midfielder Mba then went even better by hitting the only goal of the final against Burkina Faso, five minutes before half-time.

WAITING GAME

The 2013 African Cup of Nations brought to an end long waits for both finalists. Burkina Faso had not won an ACN tournament game on away soil before, a run stretching across 26 matches – not including, of course, their run to the final when hosts in 1998. Their eventual conquerors in 2013, Nigeria, were lifting the trophy for the first time since 1994 – and third time overall – despite being widely perceived as one of the continent's traditional footballing giants.

SEYDOU HAS HIS SAY

Seydou Keita, twice a UEFA Champions League winner with Barcelona but then playing his domestic football in China, won more man-of-the-match awards – four – than any other player at the 2013 Africa Cup of Nations.

SOCCER CITY LIMITS

The stadium formerly known as Soccer City – in that guise it was the venue for the 2010 FIFA World Cup opening game and final – played host to the final of the 2013 Africa Cup of Nations. In the meantime the 85,000-capacity venue had reverted, domestically, to the sponsor-branded name of the original, pre-reconstruction FNB Stadium. The total attendance at the 2013 tournament of 729,000 – an average 22,781 per match - was a record for the event in its 16-team format. The other four host venues were in Durban, Port Elizabeth, Nelspruit and Rustenburg.

CONFED UP

Nigeria's triumph qualified them for the 2013 FIFA Confederations Cup in Brazil, as Africa's representatives at the expense of Zambia. The surprise winners of the Africa Cup of Nations in 2012 departed in the first round 12 months later following three draws out of three against Ethiopia, Nigeria and Burkina Faso.

O COME, O COME, EMMANUEL

Spartak Moscow striker **Emmanuel Emenike** not only took home from South Africa a winners' medal, but also the Golden Boot for his four goals for Nigeria. Ghana's Espanyol midfielder Mubarak Wakaso scored just as many, but could not manage any assists – in contrast to Emenike, who also set up three goals for his team-mates. Three of Wakaso's strikes came from the penalty spot.

EVER-READY TOGO

Togo were not even meant to be compete in the 2013 tournament, having been disqualified for their decision to take time off in 2010 after their team bus had been attacked by militants in Angola – killing three. They won an appeal against their exclusion and qualified for South Africa, where even captain **Emmanuel Adebayor** turned up despite threats to stay away in a pay dispute. The Tottenham Hotspur forward's goal against Algeria helped take Togo out of the first round for the first time, only losing 1-0 to Burkina Faso in the quarter-finals.

2013 OVERVIEW

Total goals:	69 (ave. 2.16 per match)
Penalties awarded:	15
Penalties scored:	10
Most goals scored:	Nigeria, 11
Fewest goals scored:	Niger, 0
Most goals conceded:	Ethiopia, 7
Fewest goals conceded:	Zambia, 2
Highest-scoring match:	Nigeria 4, Mali 1
Most own goals:	Nando (Cape Verde), 1
Oldest scorer:	Didier Drogba (34 years 324 days, Ivory Coast vs Algeria)
Youngest scorer:	Ahmed Musa (20 years 115 days, Nigeria vs Mali)

TEST OF ENDURANCE

The Ivory Coast have won the two highest-scoring penalty shoot-outs in full international history – they beat Ghana 11-10 over 24 penalties in the 1992 Africa Cup of Nations final, and Cameroon 12-11, over the same number of kicks, in the quarter-finals of the 2006 Africa Cup of Nations.

GHANA AGAIN

Ghana's "Black Stars" became the first country to reach the final of four consecutive Africa Cup of Nations, lifting the trophy in 1963 and 1965 and finishing runners-up in 1968 and 1970. They have now reached eight finals in all – a tally matched only by Egypt. The two countries have also staged the tournament four times apiece.

FROM TRAGEDY TO TRIUMPH

Zambia's unexpected glory at the 2012 African Cup of Nations was both fitting and poignant as the setting for their glory was just a few hundred metres from the scene of earlier calamity. The 2012 players spent the day before the final against **Ivory Coast** laying flowers in the sea in tribute to the 30 people killed when a plane crashed off the coast of Gabonese city Libreville on 27 April 1993. Victims that day included 18 Zambian internationals flying to Senegal for a FIFA World Cup qualifier. French coach Herve Renard dedicated the 2012 victory to the dead, after watching his side beat Ivory Coast 8-7 on penalties following a goalless draw after extra-time. Centre-back Stoppila Sunzu struck the decisive spot-kick, after Ivory Coast's Kolo Toure had his penalty saved by Kennedy Mweene and Gervinho blazed his over the bar. Both teams were competing in their third African Cup of Nations final, Ivory Coast having won in 1992 and lost in 2006, while Zambia had finished runners-up in 1974 and 1994. Zambia's success was the climactic surprise of a tournament that produced shocks when traditional powerhouses Egypt, Cameroon, Nigeria and South Africa all failed to even make the finals – then Senegal, Angola and Morocco were knocked out in the first round.

REIGNING PHARAOHS

Egypt dominate the Africa Cup of Nations records. They won the first tournament, in 1957, having been helped by a bye to the final when semi-final opponents South Africa were disqualified, and have emerged as champions another six times since – more than any other country. Their victories in the last three tournaments – 2006, 2008 and 2010 – make them the only country to lift the trophy three times in a row. They have also qualified for a record 22 tournaments, playing 84 matches – 10 more than nearest challenger Nigeria. Egypt have won 51 matches in all, followed by Ghana and Nigeria on 46 apiece, Cameroon on 37 and Ivory Coast on 36.

BAFANA BAFANA

The Africa Cup of Nations has been won by its hosts on 11 separate occasions – including three times by Egypt and twice by Ghana. But perhaps the most surprising host-country triumph was South Africa's in 1996. The country had returned to international football only four years earlier, post-apartheid, when an 82nd-minute penalty by Theophilus "Doctor" Khumalo gave them a win over Cameroon on 7 July 1992. In February 1996, substitute Mark Williams scored both goals against Tunisia as South Africa won the Africa Cup of Nations trophy – lifted by white captain **Neil Tovey**, and handed over by the country's president Nelson Mandela, in Johannesburg's Soccer City stadium. South Africa were not even meant to be hosts, but stepped in for original choice Kenya who were stripped of staging rights after falling behind on new stadium-building.

GIMME GUINEA GIMME

Guinea equalled the record for biggest ever win at an African Cup of Nations when they beat Botswana 6-1 in a first-round match in 2012 – though both teams failed to make it out of Group D. Guinea were also only the third team to score six times in one match at a finals, following Egypt's 6-3 win over Nigeria in 1963 and Ivory Coast's 6-1 defeat of Ethiopia seven years later. The only other game to match the record- winning margin saw Guinea not as the victors but the victims, going down 5-0 to Ivory Coast in 2008.

EQUATORIAL DEBUTANTS

Equatorial Guinea took part in an Africa Cup of Nations finals for the first time in 2012, thanks to co-hosting the tournament with Gabon. Equatorial Guinea had never managed to qualify before while Gabon had reached the finals only four times previously. Botswana and Niger were the 2012 competition's other first-timers. The opening match of the 2012 competition was staged in Equatorial Guinea, in Bata, while the final was played in Gabonese city Libreville. The 2012 event was only the second to be shared between two host nations, after Ghana and Nigeria shared duties in 2000. Libya was awarded the right to host the Africa Cup of Nations, for a second time, in 2013, but turmoil in the country meant it was switched to South Africa, despite Nigeria initially being nominated as first reserve. Morocco has been selected to host their second ACN in 2015, and Libya pencilled in for 2017.

TOURNAMENT TRIUMPHS

7 **Egypt** (1957, 1959, 1986, 1998, 2006, 2008, 2010)
4 **Ghana** (1963, 1965, 1978, 1982)
  Cameroon (1984, 1988, 2000, 2002)
3 **Nigeria** (1980, 1994, 2013)
2 **Zaire/Congo DR** (1968, 1974)
1 **Algeria** (1990)
  Congo (1972)
  Ethiopia (1962)
  Ivory Coast (1992)
  Morocco (1976)
  South Africa (1996)
  Sudan (1970)
  Tunisia (2004)
  Zambia (2012)

TOURNAMENT APPEARANCES

22 **Egypt**
20 **Ivory Coast**
19 **Ghana**
17 **Nigeria**
16 **Cameroon, Zaire/Congo DR, Tunisia, Zambia**
15 **Algeria, Morocco**
12 **Senegal**
10 **Ethiopia, Guinea**
9 **Burkina Faso**
8 **Mali, South Africa, Sudan**
7 **Angola, Togo**
6 **Congo**
5 **Gabon, Kenya, Uganda**
4 **Mozambique**
3 **Benin, Libya**
2 **Liberia, Malawi, Namibia, Niger, Sierra Leone, Zimbabwe**
1 **Botswana, Equatorial Guinea, Mauritius, Rwanda, Tanzania**

FOUR SHAME

Hosts **Angola** were responsible for perhaps the most dramatic collapse in Africa Cup of Nations history, when they threw away a four-goal lead in the opening match of the 2010 tournament. Even more embarrassingly, they were leading 4-0 against Mali with just 11 minutes left, in the capital Luanda's Estadio 11 de Novembro. Mali's final two goals, by Barcelona's Seydou Keita and Boulogne's Mustapha Yatabare, were scored deep into stoppage-time. Mali failed to make it through the first round, while Angola went out in the quarter-finals.

MAGIC CAPE

The only country making their debut in an African Cup of Nations final tournament, in 2013, was Cape Verde. Few expected the newcomers to go beyond the first round, yet they qualified for the quarter-finals where they lost 2-0 to competition veterans Ghana. The first Cape Verde goal at the finals was struck by **Luis Carlos Almada Soares (right)** in their opening 1-1 draw with Morocco – though the player who grew up in the French capital Paris is more popularly known by his nickname, after the France footballing legend: "Platini".

AFRICA CUP OF NATIONS PLAYER RECORDS

🏈 YO, YOBO

Nigeria's legendary **Joseph Yobo** – formerly of Marseille in France and Everton in England, but now playing for Fenerbahce in Turkey – was brought on to acclaim for the final few minutes over their final victory against Burkina Faso, while taking part in his sixth Africa Cup of Nations. He then had the honour of hoisting the trophy above his head as skipper. The record for most Africa Cup of Nations tournaments remains, however, with Cameroon's Rigobert Song – whose appearances in 1996, 1998, 2000, 2002, 2004, 2006, 2008 and 2010 also include an unprecedented 35 games in a row. Ivory Coast goalkeeper Alain Gouamene played at seven tournaments from 1988 to 2000.

🏈 REVOLUTION #9

No player has scored more goals in one Africa Cup of Nations than Zaire's Ndaye Mulamba's nine during the 1974 tournament. Three months later he was sent off at the FIFA World Cup in West Germany, as his team crashed to a 9-0 defeat against Yugoslavia.

🏈 STAR STRUCK

Gabon's Chiva Star Nzigou became the Africa Cup of Nations' youngest-ever player when he took the field against South Africa in January 2000, aged 16 years and 91 days. Gabon lost the game 3-1 and finished bottom of Group B without a win from three games.

🏈 PROLIFIC POKOU

Ivory Coast striker Laurent Pokou scored a record five goals in one Africa Cup of Nations match, as his side trounced Ethiopia 6-1 in the first round of the 1968 tournament. He finished top scorer at that tournament, and the following one – though ended both without a winners' medal. Only modern-day Cameroon star Samuel Eto'o has overtaken his overall Africa Cup of Nations tally of 14 goals.

🏈 OPENING GOAL

The first Africa Cup of Nations goal was a penalty scored by Egypt's Raafat Ateya in the 21st minute of their 2-1 semi-final win over Sudan in 1957. But his team-mate Mohamed Diab El-Attar would soon take over – he not only scored Egypt's second goal that day, but all four goals in the final against Ethiopia.

🏈 TOURNAMENT TOP SCORERS

Year	Player	Goals
1957	Mohamed Diab El-Attar (Egypt)	5
1959	Mahmoud Al-Gohari (Egypt)	3
1962	Abdelfatah Badawi (Egypt) Mengistu Worku (Ethiopia)	3
1963	Hassan El-Shazly (Egypt)	6
1965	Ben Acheampong (Ghana) Kofi Osei (Ghana) Eustache Mangle (Ivory Coast)	3
1968	Laurent Pokou (Ivory Coast)	6
1970	Laurent Pokou (Ivory Coast)	8
1972	Salif Keita (Mali)	5
1974	Ndaye Mulamba (Zaire)	9
1976	Keita Aliou Mamadou 'N'Jo Lea' (Guinea)	4
1978	Opoku Afriyie (Ghana) Segun Odegbami (Nigeria) Philip Omondi (Uganda)	3
1980	Khaled Al Abyad Labied (Morocco) Segun Odegbami (Nigeria)	3
1982	George Alhassan (Ghana)	4
1984	Taher Abouzaid (Egypt)	4
1986	Roger Milla (Cameroon)	4
1988	Gamal Abdelhamid (Egypt) Lakhdar Belloumi (Algeria) Roger Milla (Cameroon) Abdoulaye Traore (Ivory Coast)	2
1990	Djamel Menad (Algeria)	4
1992	Rashidi Yekini (Nigeria)	4
1994	Rashidi Yekini (Nigeria)	5
1996	Kalusha Bwalya (Zambia)	5
1998	Hossam Hassan (Egypt) Benni McCarthy (South Africa)	7
2000	Shaun Bartlett (South Africa)	5
2002	Julius Aghahowa (Nigeria) Patrick Mboma (Cameroon) Rene Salomon Olembe (Cameroon)	5
2004	Francileudo Santos (Tunisia) Frederic Kanoute (Mali) Patrick Mboma (Cameroon) Youssef Mokhtari (Morocco) Jay-Jay Okocha (Nigeria)	4
2006	Samuel Eto'o (Cameroon)	5
2008	Samuel Eto'o (Cameroon)	5
2010	Mohamed Nagy 'Gedo' (Egypt)	5
2012	Pierre-Emerick Aubameyang (Gabon), Cheick Diabate (Mali), Didier Drogba (Ivory Coast), Christopher Katongo (Zambia), Houssine Kharja (Morocco), Manucho (Tunisia), Emmanuel Mayuka (Zambia)	3
2013	Emmanuel Emenike (Nigeria), Mubarak Wakaso (Ghana)	4

TOP KATONGO

Zambian captain **Christopher Katongo** not only lifted the 2012 African Cup of Nations trophy but also took home with him the prize for best player of the tournament. Katonho, who played his club football in China for Henan Construction, had got the final penalty shoot-out off to the perfect start for his team by successfully converting his spot-kick. His younger brother Felix Katongo also scored in the shoot-out, having come on as a 74th-minute substitute. Midfielder Felix had been playing earlier in the year for Libyan club Al-Ittihad but Zambian authorities arranged for a plane to fly him out of the country as civil war raged. Another Zambian forward was awarded the Golden Boot for top scorer – though Emmanuel Mayuka was level on three goals with six other players: strike partner Christopher Katongo, as well as Pierre-Emerick Aubameyang (Gabon), Cheick Diabate (Mali), Didier Drogba (Ivory Coast), Houssine Kharja (Morocco) and Manucho (Angola).

SAM THE MAN

Cameroon's Samuel Eto'o, who made his full international debut – away to Costa Rica on 9 March 1997 – one day short of his 16th birthday, is the Africa Cup of Nations' all-time leading goalscorer. He was part of Cameroon's victorious teams in 2000 and 2002, but had to wait until 2008 to pass Laurent Pokou's 14-goal Africa Cup of Nations record. That year's competition took his overall tally to 16 goals – only for the former Real Madrid and Barcelona striker, now with Italy's Internazionale, to add another two in 2010. In 2005, Eto'o became the first player to be named African Footballer of the Year three years running. He has also won an Olympic Games gold medal with Cameroon in 2000 and the UEFA Champions League three times, with Barcelona in 2006 and 2009 – scoring in both finals – and Inter in 2010.

PITROPIA REPRIEVE

Flying winger **Jonathan Pitroipa** was voted best player of the 2013 Africa Cup of Nations, despite finishing on the losing side when Burkina Faso fell short against Nigeria in the final. He took part in that showpiece game only after a reprieve following a red card in the semi-final victory over Ghana. His second yellow card – for simulation in the 117th minute – was judged harsh by officials at an appeal hearing. Pitroipa, who plays his club football for Stade Rennais in France, struck Burkina Faso's extra-time winner against Togo in the quarter-finals.

AFRICA CUP OF NATIONS ALL–TIME TOP SCORERS

1	Samuel Eto'o (Cameroon)	18
2	Laurent Pokou (Ivory Coast)	14
3	Rashidi Yekini (Nigeria)	13
4	Hassan El-Shazly (Egypt)	12
5	Didier Drogba (Ivory Coast)	11
=	Hossam Hassan (Egypt)	11
=	Patrick Mboma (Cameroon)	11
8	Kalusha Bwalya (Zambia)	10
=	Ndaye Mulamba (Zaire)	10
=	Francileudo Santos (Tunisia)	10
=	Joel Tiehi (Ivory Coast)	10
=	Mengistu Worku (Ethiopia)	10

NO HASSLE FOR HASSAN

Egypt's **Ahmed Hassan** not only became the first footballer to play in the final of four different Africa Cup of Nations in 2010 – he also became the first to collect his fourth winners' medal. Earlier in the same tournament, his appearance in the quarter-final against Cameroon gave him his 170th cap – a new Egyptian record. Hassan marked the game with three goals – one in his own net and two past Cameroon goalkeeper Carlos Kameni – although one appeared not to cross the line.

AFRICA CUP OF NATIONS OTHER RECORDS

AFRICA CUP OF NATIONS: FINALS

1957	(Host country: Sudan) Egypt 4 Ethiopia 0
1959	(Egypt) Egypt 2 Sudan 1
1962	(Ethiopia) Ethiopia 4 Egypt 2 (aet)
1963	(Ghana) Ghana 3 Sudan 0
1965	(Tunisia) Ghana 3 Tunisia 2 (aet)
1968	(Ethiopia) Zaire/Congo DR 1 Ghana 0
1970	(Sudan) Sudan 1 Ghana 0
1972	(Cameroon) Congo 3 Mali 2
1974	(Egypt) Zaire/Congo DR 2 Zambia 2
	Replay: Zaire/Congo DR 2 Zambia 0
1976	(Ethiopia) Morocco 1 Guinea 1 (Morocco win mini-league system)
1978	(Ghana) Ghana 2 Uganda 0
1980	(Nigeria) Nigeria 3 Algeria 0
1982	(Libya) Ghana 1 Libya 1 (aet; Ghana win 7-6 on penalties)
1984	(Ivory Coast) Cameroon 3 Nigeria 1
1986	(Egypt) Egypt 0 Cameroon 0 (aet; Egypt win 5-4 on penalties)
1988	(Morocco) Cameroon 1 Nigeria 0
1990	(Algeria) Algeria 1 Nigeria 0
1992	(Senegal) Ivory Coast 0 Ghana 0 (aet; Ivory Coast win 11-10 on penalties)
1994	(Tunisia) Nigeria 2 Zambia 1
1996	(South Africa) South Africa 2 Tunisia 0
1998	(Burkina Faso) Egypt 2 South Africa 0
2000	(Ghana & Nigeria) Cameroon 2 Nigeria 2 (aet; Cameroon win 4-3 on penalties)
2002	(Mali) Cameroon 0 Senegal 0 (aet; Cameroon win 3-2 on penalties)
2004	(Tunisia) Tunisia 2 Morocco 1
2006	(Egypt) Egypt 0 Ivory Coast 0 (aet; Egypt win 4-2 on penalties)
2008	(Ghana) Egypt 1 Cameroon 0
2010	(Angola) Egypt 1 Ghana 0
2012	(Gabon & Equatrorial Guinea) Zambia 0 Ivory Coast 0 (aet; Zambia 8-7 on pens)
2013	(South Africa) Nigeria 1 Burkina Faso 0

GEDO BLASTER

Egypt's hero in 2010 was Mohamed Nagy, better known by his nickname "Gedo" – Egyptian Arabic for "Grandpa". He scored the only goal of the final, against Ghana, his fifth of the tournament, giving him the Golden Boot. Yet he did all this without starting a single game. He had to settle for coming on as a substitute in all six of Egypt's matches, playing a total of 135 minutes in all. Gedo – born in Damanhur on 3 October 1984 – made his international debut only two months earlier, and had played just two friendlies for Egypt before the tournament proper.

TOGO'S TRAGIC FATE

Togo were the victims of tragedy shortly before the 2010 Africa Cup of Nations kicked off – followed by expulsion from the event. The team's bus was fired on by Angolan militants three days before their first scheduled match, killing three people: the team's assistant coach, press officer and bus driver. The team returned home to Togo for three days of national mourning, and were then thrown out of the competition by the CAF as punishment for missing their opening game against Ghana. Togo were later expelled from the 2012 and 2014 competitions, but this sanction was overturned on appeal in May 2010.

RENARD REDEEMED

Herve Renard, the coach of 2012 champions Zambia, was in his second spell in charge, having previously led them between 2008 and 2010. His decision to resign after a run to the quarter-finals of the 2010 Africa Cup of Nations (to become Angola's coach) meant his return to Zambia in October 2011 wasn't uniformly welcomed. But all was forgiven when Zambia won their first title. Renard's celebrations included carrying injured defender Joseph Musonda on to the pitch – he had limped off after only ten minutes – and handing his winner's medal to Kalusha Bwalya, probably Zambia's greatest ever player. Bwalya had missed the doomed 1993 flight because he was playing club football for PSV Eindhoven in the Netherlands. He later coached Zambia but, by the time of the 2012 triumph, Bwalya was president of his country's football association.

UNFINISHED BUSINESS

Beware – if you go to see Nigeria play Tunisia, you may not get the full 90 minutes. Nigeria were awarded third place at the 1978 Africa Cup of Nations after the Tunisian team walked off after 42 minutes of their play-off, with the score at 1-1. They were protesting about refereeing decisions, but thus granted Nigeria a 2-0 victory by default. Oddly enough, it had been Nigeria walking off when the two teams met in the second leg of a qualifier for the 1962 tournament. Their action came when Tunisia equalized after 65 minutes. The punishment was a 2-0 win in Tunisia's favour – putting them 3-2 ahead on aggregate.

INTERNATIONAL EXILE

South Africa were disqualified from the four-team Africa Cup of Nations in 1957 after refusing to pick a multi-racial squad.

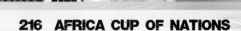

MEET THE NEW (BIG) BOSS, SAME AS THE OLD (BIG) BOSS

Stephen Keshi – known to admiring fans as "Big Boss" – became only the second man to win the Africa Cup of Nations as both player and manager, when leading Nigeria to the title in 2013. He previously lifted the trophy as captain in 1994. The Nigerian football association, for so long mired in corruption and mismanagement claims, had their grudging faith in Keshi vindicated in summer 2013 – though he was their 19th manager in 19 years. Before Keshi, the only man to win the tournament both as a player and manager was Egypt's Mahmoud Al-Gohary – top scorer in 1959 and in charge 39 years later. Hassan Shehata, striker when Egypt finished third in 1970, then won a record-breaking three times as his country's coach.

TUNED IN TO SUDAN

The 1970 Africa Cup of Nations in Sudan marked the first time the tournament was televised. Ghana reached the final for a then unprecedented fourth time in a row, but were beaten 1-0 by the hosts.

RECENT AFRICA CUP OF NATIONS–WINNING COACHES

1988	Claude Le Roy (Cameroon)
1990	Abdelhamid Kermali (Algeria)
1992	Yeo Martial (Ivory Coast)
1994	Clemens Westerhof (Nigeria)
1996	Clive Barker (South Africa)
1998	Mahmoud El-Gohary (Egypt)
2000	Pierre Lechantre (Cameroon)
2002	Winfried Schafer (Cameroon)
2004	Roger Lemerre (Tunisia)
2006	Hassan Shehata (Egypt)
2008	Hassan Shehata (Egypt)
2010	Hassan Shehata (Egypt)
2012	Herve Renard (Zambia)
2013	Stephen Keshi (Nigeria)

LOCK DEFENCE

Liberia's military leader Samuel Doe threatened to jail the national team if they lost at an Africa Cup of Nations qualifier to Gambia in December 1980 – a game that also doubled up as a FIFA World Cup qualifier. The players escaped punishment by achieving a 0-0 draw, though neither side went on to reach either the Africa Cup of Nations or the 1982 FIFA World Cup.

MISSING THE POINT

The absences of Cameroon, Nigeria and reigning champions Egypt from the 2012 African Cup of Nations were surprising – though each could at least comfort themselves on not missing out in quite such embarrassing circumstances as **South Africa.** They appeared happy to play out a goalless draw with Sierra Leone in their final qualifier, believing that would be enough to go through – and greeted the final whistle with celebrations on the pitch. But they were mistaken in thinking goal difference would be used to separate teams level on points in their group, with Niger qualifying instead thanks to a better head-to-head record. South Africa's distraught coach Pitso Mosimane admitted misinterpreting the rules and deliberately targeting his side's tactics towards a draw. The South African football association initially appealed against elimination, claiming goal difference should be the decider – but ultimately decided not to pursue the matter.

DOUBLE FAULTED

Stephen Keshi was not the only coach going into the 2013 Africa Cup of Nations hoping to become only the second to triumph both as player and manager. James Kwesi Appiah, in charge of his native Ghana, was on the winning side in 1982 – the last time his nation were continental champions. This time, however, his luck was out as Burkina Faso prevailed in a semi-final penalty shoot-out.

PART 6:
OTHER FIFA TOURNAMENTS

AROUND three billion people are involved in football in one way or another. The passion and ambition explains just why the international game's competitive structure has expanded to meet demand. The value of all the other FIFA championships is that the competitive structure is devolved down to a regional level – whether in Africa or Europe or Oceania.

That brings world competition down to a local level and increasingly imaginative concepts for tournament hosting means that more and more nations enjoy the opportunity to welcome the world. An obvious example is the FIFA Under-17 Women's World Cup in Azerbaijan – a relatively new member of the world football family – in the autumn of 2012. Such events encourage and acknowledge the work of enthusiasts at grassroots levels across the world. Regional confederations organize international championships for players in a wide range of age groups.

In 1977, FIFA extended its worldwide development programme with the launch of the FIFA World Youth Cup. The Soviet Union beat Mexico in the first final, in Tunisia. Eight years later came the FIFA Under-17 World Cup. Simultaneously, the Olympic Games football tournament became an Under-23 event with an exception for teams in the finals to field up to three over-age players. In 2000, FIFA stepped into the senior club sphere with the launch of FIFA Club World Cup. The establishment of such events at the top of world football encouraged regional confederations to create their own matching tournaments so their teams could take to the world stage and face elite opponents.

Corinthians captain Alessandro with the FIFA Club World Cup after the Brazilians had beaten European champions Chelsea 1–0 in the final in Japan in 2012. South America broke Europe's five-year grip on the trophy.

FIFA U-20 WORLD CUP

First staged in 1977 in Tunisia and known as the FIFA Youth World Championship until 2005, the FIFA U-20 World Cup is the world championship for footballers under the age of 20. It has featured some of the game's most notable names. Staged in alternate years, the tournament's most successful team has been Argentina, who have lifted the trophy on six occasions.

FULL HOUSES

The 2011 tournament saw record crowds, with 1,309,929 fans attending the 52 games at eight venues across eight Colombian cities – meaning the average attendance was 25,191 per match. The overall tally exceeded the 1,295,299 going to games at the finals in Egypt two years earlier, though the average crowd of 36,099 for the 32 games in Mexico in 1983 remains a record too. That 2009 tournament did feature a record 167 goals, two more than in Malaysia 12 years earlier – 3.21 goals per game in Egypt, marginally higher than Malaysia's 3.17. Poor Tahiti helped keep the goal rate high, conceding 21 goals in three group games in Egypt without managing to score for themselves.

SUPER SUB

The Soviet Union became the first winners of the FIFA Under-20 World Cup when they beat hosts Mexico 9-8 on penalties after a 2-2 draw in the 1977 final. Their shoot-out hero was substitute goalkeeper Yuri Sivuha, who had replaced Aleksandre Novikov during extra-time. It remains the only time the Soviet Union won the event, though their striker **Oleg Salenko**, a future 1994 FIFA World Cup Golden Boot winner, took the top scorer award in 1989, with five goals. Two years later, fellow Soviet Sergei Sherbakov also finished top scorer, also with five goals, although his full international career was less successful. He played only twice for Ukraine before injuries suffered in a car accident in 1993 left him in a wheelchair.

DOMINANT DOMINIC

Ghana became the first African country to lift the trophy when they upset Brazil in the 2009 final – despite playing 83 of the 120 minutes with just 10 men, following Daniel Addo's red card. The final finished goalless, one of only two games in which **Dominic Adiyiah** failed to score. He ended the tournament as top scorer with eight goals and also won the Golden Ball prize for best player. Immediately afterwards a further reward was a transfer from Norway's Fredrikstad to Italy's AC Milan. The Silver Ball went to Brazil's Alex Teixeira, even though it was his missed penalty, when the final shoot-out went to sudden death, which handed Ghana victory.

LISBON LIONS

In 1991, **Portugal** became the first hosts to win the tournament with a team that became known as the country's "Golden Generation", featuring Luis Figo, Rui Costa, Joao Pinto, Abel Xavier and Jorge Costa. Portugal's winning squad was coached by Carlos Queiroz, who would later manage the full national side twice, with spells in charge at Real Madrid and as assistant at Manchester United in between. Their penalty shoot-out win over Brazil in the final was played at Benfica's iconic Estadio da Luz in the capital Lisbon. In 2001, Argentina became the second team to lift the trophy on home territory.

CAPTAIN MARVELS

Two men have lifted both the FIFA Under-20 World Cup and the FIFA World Cup as captain: Brazil's Dunga (in 1983 and 1994) and Argentina's Diego Maradona (in 1979 and 1986). Many had expected Maradona to make Argentina's full squad for the 1978 FIFA World Cup but he missed out on selection. He showed his potential by being voted best player at the 1979 youth tournament in Japan.

SAVIOUR SAVIOLA

Javier Saviola has scored more goals in one FIFA Under-20 World Cup than any other player – he managed 11 in seven games at the 2001 competition, as his side Argentina went on to beat Ghana in the final, with Saviola scoring his team's three unanswered goals. Saviola, born on 11 December 1981 in Buenos Aires, was playing for River Plate at the time but joined Barcelona for £15 million not long afterwards – before later signing for the Spanish side's arch-rivals Real Madrid. When Pele picked his 125 "greatest living footballers" for FIFA in March 2004, 22-year-old Saviola was the youngest player on the list.

OSCAR WINNING

Only one player has scored a hat-trick in the final of a FIFA Under-20 World Cup: Brazilian midfielder Oscar, who hit all his side's goals in their 3-2 triumph over Portugal to claim the latest trophy in August 2011. He was further rewarded by making his senior Brazil debut the following month, against Argentina. They were actually Oscar's first goals of the tournament staged in Colombia, with the Golden Shoe going to his team-mate Henrique for five goals in the preceding six matches – including the 200th goal in FIFA Under-20 World Cup history, in a 3-0 first-round victory over Austria.

TOURNAMENT HOSTS AND FINAL RESULTS

1977 (Host: Tunisia) USSR 2 Mexico 2 (aet: USSR win 9-8 on penalties)
1979 (Japan) Argentina 3 USSR 1
1981 (Australia) West Germany 4 Qatar 0
1983 (Mexico) Brazil 1 Argentina 0
1985 (USSR) Brazil 1 Spain 0 (aet)
1987 (Chile) Yugoslavia 1 West Germany 1 (aet: Yugoslavia win 5-4 on penalties)
1989 (Saudi Arabia) Portugal 2 Nigeria 0
1991 (Portugal) Portugal 0 Brazil 0 (aet: Portugal win 4-2 on penalties)
1993 (Australia) Brazil 2 Ghana 1
1995 (Qatar) Argentina 2 Brazil 0
1997 (Malaysia) Argentina 2 Uruguay 1
1999 (Nigeria) Spain 4 Japan 0
2001 (Argentina) Argentina 3 Ghana 0
2003 (United Arab Emirates) Brazil 1 Spain 0
2005 (Holland) Argentina 2 Nigeria 1
2007 (Canada) Argentina 2 Czech Republic 1
2009 (Egypt) Ghana 0 Brazil 0 (aet: Ghana win 4-3 on penalties)
2011 (Colombia) Brazil 3 Portugal 2 (aet)

WHAT A MESSI

Lionel Messi was the star of the show for Argentina in 2005, and not just for scoring both his country's goals in the final – both from the penalty spot. He achieved a hat-trick by not only winning the Golden Boot for top scorer and Golden Shoe for best player, but also by captaining his side to the title. This feat was emulated two years later by compatriot Sergio Aguero, who scored once in the final against the Czech Republic, before team-mate Mauro Zarate struck a late winner. Four other men have finished as both top scorer and as the tournament's best player (as voted by journalists) – Brazil's Geovani in 1983, Argentina's Javier Saviola in 2001, Dominic Adiyiah of Ghana in 2009 and another Brazilian, Henrique, in 2011.

TOURNAMENT TOP SCORERS

Year	Player	Goals
1977	Guina (Brazil)	4
1979	Ramon Diaz (Argentina)	8
1981	Ralf Loose (West Germany), Roland Wohlfarth (West Germany), Taher Amer (Egypt), Mark Koussas (Argentina)	4
1983	Geovani (Brazil)	6
1985	Gerson (Brazil), Balalo (Brazil), Muller (Brazil), Alberto Garcia Aspe (Mexico), Monday Odiaka (Nigeria), Fernando Gomez (Spain), Sebastian Losada (Spain)	3
1987	Marcel Witeczek (West Germany)	7
1989	Oleg Salenko (USSR)	5
1991	Sergei Sherbakov (USSR)	5
1993	Ante Milicic (Australia), Adriano (Brazil), Gian (Brazil), Henry Zambrano (Colombia), Vicente Nieto (Mexico), Chris Faklaris (USA)	3
1995	Joseba Etxeberria (Spain)	7
1997	Adailton Martins Bolzan (Brazil)	10
1999	Mahamadou Dissa (Mali), Pablo (Spain)	5
2001	Javier Saviola (Argentina)	11
2003	Fernando Cavenaghi (Argentina), Dudu (Brazil), Daisuke Sakata (Japan), Eddie Johnson (USA)	4
2005	Lionel Messi (Argentina)	6
2007	Sergio Aguero (Argentina)	7
2009	Dominic Adiyiah (Ghana)	8
2011	**Henrique (Brazil)**	5

TALKING TURKEY

Hosting rights for the 2013 tournament were awarded to Turkey, allowing the country to stage a FIFA tournament for the first time. The 52,000-capacity Turk Telekom Arena in Istanbul was chosen for the final in June 2013. The United Arab Emirates and Uzbekistan had their bids rejected. Peru, Tunisia and Wales were unsuccessful in their bids to stage the 2015 competition, which will be held in New Zealand.

FIFA U-17 WORLD CUP

First staged in China in 1985, when it was known as the FIFA Under-16 World Championship, the age limit was raised from 16 to 17 in 1991 and the competition became known as the FIFA U-17 World Cup from 2007. Staged on a bi-annual basis, the 2009 edition of the event was staged in Nigeria, the defending champions, who, along with Brazil, are the tournament's most successful countries, with three wins each.

WHOSE SHOE?

Sani Emmanuel can boast of being top scorer while also voted best player, after starring in Nigeria's run to the 2009 final – though that last match was the only one he started. He was awarded the Golden Ball for his performances, but had to settle for the Silver Shoe prize – despite scoring five goals, the same tally as Golden Shoe winner Borja. The Spanish striker took the main award because he managed one more assist. Uruguay's Sebastian Gallegos and Switzerland's Haris Seferovic also finished the tournament with five goals apiece. Yuri Nikiforov scored a joint-best five goals for Russia at the 1987 tournament, including one in the final as his team beat Nigeria on penalties – but FIFA awarded the Golden Shoe to Ivory Coast's Moussa Traore, who also hit five but for a lower-scoring side. The Soviet Union scored 21 overall, to the Ivory Coast's nine.

TAKING WING

Nigeria's youth side, the "Golden Eaglets", became the first African nation to win a FIFA tournament when they triumphed at the inaugural Under-16 FIFA World Cup in 1985 (it became an Under-17 event in 1991). Their opening goal in the final against West Germany was scored by striker Jonathan Akpoborie, who would go on to play for German clubs Stuttgart and Wolfsburg.

GOALS FLO

Apart from Cesc Fabregas, the only other man to have won both the Golden Ball and the Golden Shoe is France's **Florent Sinama-Pongolle**, whose nine goals in 2001 set a tournament record for one player. His tally included two hat-tricks in the opening round. Unlike Fabregas, Sinama-Pongolle also ended the final on the winning side. The team goalscoring record is held by Spain, who struck 22 times on their way to third place in 1997. Sinama-Pongolle's scoring record was equalled in 2011 by Ivory Coast striker Souleymane Coulibaly. While Sinama-Pongolle needed six matches, the young Ivorian managed his in just four games as his team reached the second round only – and earned himself a transfer from Italy's Siena to English Premier League club Tottenham Hotspur not long afterwards.

SEOUL SURVIVOR

The final of the 2007 tournament was the first to be hosted by a former FIFA World Cup venue – the 68,476-capacity Seoul FIFA World Cup Stadium in South Korea's capital, which had been built for the 2002 FIFA World Cup. The game was watched by a crowd of 36,125, a tournament record. The 2007 event was the first to feature 24 teams instead of 16, and was won by Nigeria – after Spain missed all three of their spot-kicks in a penalty shoot-out.

GOOD AND BAD BOY BOJAN

Barcelona star **Bojan Krkic** quickly went from hero to villain in the final moments of Spain's semi-final victory over Ghana in 2007 – he scored his team's winner with four minutes of extra-time remaining, but was then sent off for a second yellow-card offence just before the final whistle. His expulsion meant he was suspended for the final, which Spain lost on penalties to Nigeria.

GOLDEN HAUL

West Germany's Marcel Witeczek is the only person to finish top scorer at both a FIFA Under-16 World Championship and the Under-20 version of the event. The Polish-born striker hit eight goals at the 1985 Under-16 tournament, followed by seven more at the Under-20 championship two years later. Brazil's Adriano – a different Adriano to the one who later played for the senior side and Serie A club Internazionale – came closest to equalling the feat: he won the Golden Shoe, for top scorer, after scoring four goals at the 1991 FIFA Under-17 World Cup, then the Golden Ball, for best player, at the Under-20 event in 1993.

LITTLE ITALY

The 1991 tournament was originally scheduled to take place in Ecuador, but a cholera outbreak in the country meant it was switched to Italy instead – though played in much smaller venues than those that had been used for the previous year's senior FIFA World Cup in the country. The 1991 tournament was the first to be open to Under-17s – the first three had been known as the FIFA U-16 World Cup.

TOURNAMENT TOP SCORERS

1985	Marcel Witeczek (West Germany)	8
1987	Moussa Traore (Ivory Coast)	5
	Yuri Nikiforov (USSR)	5
1989	Khaled Jasem (Bahrain)	3
	Fode Camara (Guinea)	3
	Gil (Portugal)	3
	Tulipa (Portugal)	3
	Khalid Al Roaihi (Saudi Arabia)	3
1991	Adriano (Brazil)	4
1993	Wilson Oruma (Nigeria)	6
1995	Daniel Allsopp (Australia)	5
	Mohamed Al Kathiri (Oman)	5
1997	David (Spain)	7
1999	Ishmael Addo (Ghana)	7
2001	Florent Sinama-Pongolle (France)	9
2003	Carlos Hidalgo (Colombia)	5
	Manuel Curto (Portugal)	5
	Cesc Fabregas (Spain)	5
2005	Carlos Vela (Mexico)	5
2007	Macauley Chrisantus (Nigeria)	7
2009	Borja (Spain)	5
	Sani Emmanuel (Nigeria)	5
	Sebastian Gallegos (Uruguay)	5
	Haris Seferovic (Switzerland)	5
2011	Souleymane Coulibaly (Ivory Coast)	9

SWISS SURPRISE

Switzerland were the unexpected winners in 2009, in their first-ever appearance at the tournament. Their 1-0 win over favourites Nigeria in the final, thanks to a Haris Seferovic goal, prevented the Africans from becoming only the second country to retain the trophy. Swiss goalkeeper Benjamin Siegrist, who conceded only four goals in seven games, was given the Golden Glove prize for best goalkeeper. Nigerian preparations for the finals had been disrupted when 15 of their players were found to be over-age and had to be dropped from the squad.

GOMEZ AT HOME

Mexico became the first host country to lift the FIFA U-17 World Cup trophy on home soil, when they beat Uruguay 2-0 in the final in the Azteca Stadium in Mexico City in July 2011. The Golden Ball award for the tournament's best player went to Mexican winger **Julio Gomez,** whose brace against Germany in the semi-final including a spectacular bicycle-kick for the last-minute winner – though he played only ten minutes of the final, as a substitute, after picking up an injury in the previous game.

FAB FABREGAS

Spain's Cesc Fabregas joined Florent Sinama-Pongolle as only two players to win both the Golden Shoe, for top scorer, and the Golden Ball, for best player, at a FIFA Under-17 World Cup. He took both prizes after scoring five goals at the 2003 tournament, despite losing the final to Brazil. He and team-mate David Silva would later be part of the senior Spanish team that won the 2008 European Championship and, two years later, the FIFA World Cup in South Africa. Fabregas, born in Arenys de Mar on 4 May 1987, left Barcelona for Arsenal a month after the 2003 tournament, where he later became club captain.

HOSTS AND FINAL RESULTS

(Host country)

1985	(China) Nigeria 2 West Germany 0
1987	(Canada) USSR 1 Nigeria 1 (aet: USSR win 4-2 on penalties)
1989	(Scotland) Saudi Arabia 2 Scotland 2 (aet: Saudi Arabia win 5-4 on penalties)
1991	(Italy) Ghana 1 Spain 0
1993	(Japan) Nigeria 2 Ghana 1
1995	(Ecuador) Ghana 3 Brazil 2
1997	(Egypt) Brazil 2 Ghana 1
1999	(New Zealand) Brazil 0 Australia 0 (aet: Brazil win 8-7 on penalties)
2001	(Trinidad & Tobago) France 3 Nigeria 0
2003	(Finland) Brazil 1 Spain 0
2005	(Peru) Mexico 3 Brazil 0
2007	(South Korea) Nigeria 0 Spain 0 (aet: Nigeria win 3-0 on penalties)
2009	(Nigeria) Switzerland 1 Nigeria 0
2011	(Mexico) Mexico 2 Uruguay 0

FIFA CONFEDERATIONS CUP

The FIFA Confederations Cup has assumed numerous guises over the years. In 1992 and 1995 it was played in Saudi Arabia and featured a collection of continental champions. From 1997 to 2003 FIFA staged a tournament every two years. The tournament was played in its current format for the first time in Germany in 2005. It is now celebrated throughout the football world as the Championship of Champions.

OVERALL TOP SCORERS

1	Cuauhtemoc Blanco (Mexico)	9
=	Ronaldinho (Brazil)	9
3	Fernando Torres (Spain)	8
4	Romario (Brazil)	7
=	Adriano (Brazil)	7
6	Marzouk Al-Otaibi (Saudi Arabia)	6
7	Alex (Brazil)	5
=	John Aloisi (Australia)	5
=	Luis Fabiano (Brazil)	5
=	Fred (Brazil)	5
=	Vladimir Smicer (Czech Rep.)	5
=	Robert Pires (France)	5

FAB'S FIVE

Brazil's victory over the United States in the 2009 final made them the first country to complete a hat-trick of FIFA Confederations Cup triumphs, following success in 1997 and 2005. But they did it the hard way, needing to come back from two goals down at half-time before winning 3–2 – thanks to a late goal from captain and centre-back Lucio. **Luis Fabiano**, who ended as tournament top scorer with five goals overall, struck the other two goals. His team-mate Kaka was voted best player, with Luis Fabiano second and America's Clint Dempsey third.

TOURNAMENT TOP SCORERS

1992	Gabriel Batistuta (Argentina), Bruce Murray (USA) 2
1995	Luis Garcia (Mexico) 3
1997	Romario (Brazil) 7
1999	Ronaldinho (Brazil), Cuauhtemoc Blanco (Mexico), Marzouq Al-Otaibi (Saudi Arabia) 6
2001	Shaun Murphy (Australia), Eric Carriere (France), Robert Pires (France), Patrick Vieira (France), Sylvain Wiltord (France), Takayuki Suzuki (Japan), Hwang Sun-Hong (South Korea) 2
2003	Thierry Henry (France) 4
2005	Adriano (Brazil) 5
2009	Luis Fabiano (Brazil) 5
2013	Fernando Torres (Spain) 5 Fred (Brazil) 5

FIT FOR A KING

Before being rebranded as the FIFA Confederations Cup, a tournament bringing together the continental champions of the world was known as the King Fahd Cup and was hosted in Saudi Arabia. Copa America holders Argentina reached both finals, beating their hosts in the first in 1992 thanks to goals by Leonardo Rodriguez, Claudio Caniggia and Diego Simeone. Only four teams took part in the 1992 event, with the United States and the Ivory Coast also represented, but world champions Germany and European champions Holland did not participate. In 1995, a six-team version was won by European champions Denmark. The current eight-team format, with two groups and knockout semi-finals, was adopted in 2005.

TON–UP SUPERSTARS

Andrea Pirlo and Diego Forlan both celebrated their 100th international appearance at the 2013 Confederations Cup. Italy playmaker Pirlo scored the *Azzurri's* first goal in their opening 2-1 win over Mexico in Maracana. Forlan marked his own achievement (becoming the first Uruguayan to reach 100 caps) by hitting a brilliant left-footed drive which proved the decisive goal in a 2-1 victory over Nigeria.

NO STOPPING NEYMAR

The 2013 Confederations Cup crowned a memorable six months for Brazilian striker Neymar. In January he had been voted South American Footballer of the Year for the second successive year and in June he agreed to leave Santos and take up a five-year contract with Spanish champions Barcelona. In one of his farewell appearances in Brazil, Neymar da Silva Santos Junior struck the first goal of the Confederations Cup in only the third minute of the tournament's opening match against Japan. Neymar scored in each of Brazil's group matches and then again in the defeat of Spain in the final.

HIGH–TECH INSURANCE

Goal-line technology was used at the Confederations Cup for the first time in Brazil. GoalControl, a German company, won a tender to install its system in all six venues. In fact, it was never needed to decide a goal-scoring issue, but FIFA was satisfied it functioned effectively. Howard Webb, lone English referee at the competition, hailed "the reassurance the system gives us".

BURSTING A SOUTH SEA BUBBLE

Minnows Tahiti suffered the heaviest defeat in Confederations Cup history when they crashed 10-0 to Spain in the 2013 tournament in Brazil. The South Pacific part-timers – including an accountant, a carpenter and a teacher – were not too upset, however. None of them had ever even dreamed of playing in the legendary Maracana or against the world and European champions and now they had done both in one match. The Oceania champions also conceded a cup record 24 goals in their three games, with Jonathan Tehau scoring their historic single goal, against Nigeria, in return. The defeat by Spain equalled the Cup's largest single-match aggregate: in 1999, Brazil thrashed Saudi Arabia 8-2.

BRILLIANT BRAZIL

Brazil's 3-0 demolition of world and European champions Spain in the 2013 final in Maracana enhanced their historical command of the Confederations Cup. Their 12th consecutive win in the competition saw Luiz Felipe Scolari's men become the first nation to land the Cup three times in a row. They scored at least three goals in each of their title match victories and are the competition's only four-times champions. Brazil set a standard off the pitch as well: record ticket sales generated a 16-match aggregate attendance of 804,659 for an average of 50,291 per game. The 68 goals averaged out at 4.25 per match, the most prolific marksmanship over the last six competitions.

CLINT MAKES AMERICA'S DAY

The United States' surprise run to the 2009 final included a shock semi-final win over Spain that ended the European champions' long unbeaten run. Heading into the match, Spain had won a record 15 international matches in a row – and gone 35 successive games unbeaten, a tally shared with Brazil. But their hopes of extending their run to 36 matches were ruined by goals from US striker Jozy Altidore and winger **Clint Dempsey**. The result put the Americans into the final of a FIFA men's senior competition for the first time.

SHARED SADNESS

The 2003 FIFA Confederations Cup was overshadowed by the tragic death of Cameroon's 28-year-old midfielder **Marc-Vivien Foe**, who collapsed on the Lyon pitch after suffering a heart attack 73 minutes into his country's semi-final win against Colombia. After Thierry Henry scored France's golden-goal winner against Cameroon in the final, he dedicated his goal to Foe, who played much of his club career in the French championship. When the trophy was presented at the Stade de France in Paris, it was jointly lifted by the captains of both teams – Marcel Desailly for France and Rigobert Song for Cameroon.

FIFA CONFEDERATIONS CUP HOSTS AND FINAL RESULTS

1997	(Host country: Saudi Arabia) Brazil 6 Argentina 0
1999	(Mexico) Mexico 4 Brazil 3
2001	(South Korea and Japan) France 1 Japan 0
2003	(France) France 1 Cameroon 0 (aet: France win on golden goal)
2005	(Germany) Brazil 4 Argentina 1
2009	(South Africa) Brazil 3 United States 2
2013	(Brazil) Brazil 3 Spain 0

FIFA CLUB WORLD CUP

As is the case with the FIFA Confederations Cup, the FIFA Club World Cup has been played in several different formats since 1960, when Real Madrid defeated Penarol. In its current guise, the competition pits the champion clubs from all six continents against each other. It has been staged on an annual basis in Japan since 2005, apart from 2009 and 2010 when the tournament was held in Abu Dhabi.

CORINTHIAN SPIRIT

Brazilian club Corinthians not only succeeded Barcelona as FIFA Club World Cup champions in 2012 but also equalled the Spanish side's record as two-time winners and with a record of six matches won overall. Peruvian striker Paolo Guerrero scored the only goal of their semi-final victory over Egypt's Al-Ahly, and repeated the feat in the final against England's Chelsea. The Corinthians line-up included goalkeeper and player-of-the-tournament **Cassio**, as well as Danilo and Fabio Santos, a pair who had both won the tournament with Sao Paulo seven years earlier. Defeat for the European champions also prevented newly-appointed Chelsea manager Rafael Benitez from equalling former Barcelona boss Pep Guardiola in winning the tournament twice. Benitez previously lifted the trophy as Internazionale coach in 2010.

WINNERS BY COUNTRY*

- 10 Brazil
- 9 Argentina, Italy
- 6 Uruguay, Spain
- 3 Germany, Netherlands
- 2 Portugal, England
- 1 Paraguay, Yugoslavia

Includes Intercontinental Cup

FIRST INTO DOUBLE FIGURES

Despite Al-Ahly's 2-0 defeat to Monterrey in the 2012 third-place play-off, the game was a landmark for three of the Egyptian club's players: Mohamed Aboutrika, **Wael Gomaa** and Hossam Ashour were all playing in a FIFA Club World Cup match for a record tenth time. Former Al-Ahly coach Manuel Jose de Jesus shares the record for most tournaments as a manager (2005, 2006 and 2008) with Rafael Benitez (2005, 2010, 2012) – though the Portuguese manager's appearances were all with Al-Ahly whereas Benitez's were with Liverpool, Internazionale and Chelsea.

SIX APPEAL

Barcelona's triumph in 2009 made them the first club to lift six different major trophies in one calendar year: the FIFA Club World Cup, the UEFA Champions League, the UEFA European Super Cup, and a Spanish hat-trick of La Liga, Copa del Rey and Super Cup. This made their trophy cabinet one cup heavier than Liverpool's in 2001, when Gerard Houllier's men won the FA Cup, League Cup and Charity Shield in England and the UEFA Cup and Super Cup in Europe.

UAE O.K.

The 2009 tournament was the first of the "new" FIFA Club World Cup events to take place outside Japan – in the United Arab Emirates state of Abu Dhabi, where the tournament was also staged 12 months later. Two stadia shared the workload: the **Al Jazira Mohammed bin Zayed Stadium** and the 60,000-capacity Sheikh Zayed Stadium, the setting for the final each time. The UAE saw off rival bids from Australia and Japan to secure hosting rights for the December 2010 event. However, the competition returned to Japan in 2011 and 2012, with the final played at the Yokohama International Stadium, the venue of the 2002 FIFA World Cup final.

SWITCHING SYSTEMS

From 1960 until 1968, the Intercontinental Cup was settled, not on aggregate scores, but by using a system of two points for a win and one for a draw. This meant a third, deciding match was needed in 1961, 1963, 1964 and 1967. No team that had not been worse off on aggregate after the first two legs had gone on to win the third match, though before losing their play-off 1-0 to Argentina's Racing Club in 1967, Celtic would have won the two-legged tie if aggregate scores and away goals counted. The Scottish side won their home leg 1-0, before losing 2-1 away. From 1980 until 2004, the annual event was a one-off match staged in Japan.

FIGURE OF EIGHT

Manchester United's 5-3 win over Gamba Osaka in the semi-final of the FIFA Club World Cup in 2008 was the highest-scoring single game in the history of the competition in all its forms – bettering the 5-2 victory over Benfica by a Santos team featuring Pele in 1962. Even more amazingly, all but two of the goals in the Manchester United–Gamba game were scored in the final 16 minutes, plus stoppage-time. United were leading 2-0 with 74 minutes gone, before a burst of goals – including two by substitute Wayne Rooney – at both ends. Manchester United became the first team to score five goals in the FIFA Club World Cup's revised format.

LONG-DISTANCE, LONG-RUNNING RIVALRY

The precursor to the modern FIFA Club World Cup was the Intercontinental Cup, also known informally as the World Club Cup and/or the Europe–South America Cup, which pitted the champions of Europe and South America against each other. Representatives of UEFA and CONMEBOL contested the event from 1960 to 2004, but now all continental federations send at least one club to an expanded Club World Cup organized and endorsed by the world federation, FIFA. The original final, in 1960, was between Spain's Real Madrid and Uruguay's Penarol. After a goalless draw in the rain in Montevideo, Real triumphed 5-1 at their own stadium in Madrid – including three goals scored in the first eight minutes, two of them by Ferenc Puskas. The two clubs are among five sharing the record for Intercontinental Cup triumphs, with three victories apiece – the others being Argentina's Boca Juniors, Uruguay's Nacional and AC Milan of Italy. Milan are the only one of these clubs to have added a FIFA Club World Cup to their tally, as the championship was first contested in 2000 (in Brazil) before it was swallowed up by the Intercontinental Cup and was instituted on an annual basis.

SUCCESS IN PHASES

Since FIFA introduced its own, expanded Club World Cup in 2000, with representatives from all the world's continental football federations, Brazilian sides have the best overall record – with Corinthians the first winners. Carlo Ancelotti's AC Milan finally broke the Brazilian stranglehold in 2007, when the trophy was lifted by club captain Paolo Maldini, who had appeared for Milan – alongside Alessandro Costacurta – in five Intercontinental Cup showdowns between 1989 and 2003.

CONGO DANCE

For the first time in unofficial Intercontinental Cup or official FIFA Club World Cup history, an African team contested the 2010 final. TP Mazembe, from the Democratic Republic of Congo, defeated South American champions Internacional, from Brazil, 2–0 in their semi-final. Internacional, winners in 2006, were the first former FIFA Club World Cup champions to compete for a second time. Mazembe achieved the surprise victory despite missing their star striker and captain Tresor Mputu, who was serving a one-year ban for furiously chasing a referee after a match in May 2010. Goalkeeper **Muteba Kidiaba,** sent off during the 2009 FIFA Club World Cup, was man of the match against Internacional a year later. He celebrated the victory by bouncing across the pitch on his bottom.

FIFA CLUB WORLD CUP FINALS (2000–12)

2000	Corinthians (Brazil) 0
	Vasco da Gama (Brazil) 0
	(aet: Corinthians win 4-3 on penalties)
2005	Sao Paulo (Brazil) 1 Liverpool (England) 0
2006	Internacional (Brazil) 1 Barcelona (Spain) 0
2007	AC Milan (Italy) 4
	Boca Juniors (Argentina) 2
2008	Manchester United (England) 1
	LDU Quito (Ecuador) 0
2009	Barcelona (Spain) 2
	Estudiantes (Argentina) 1 (aet)
2010	Internazionale (Italy) 3
	TP Mazembe (DR Congo) 0
2011	Barcelona (Spain) 4 Santos (Brazil) 0
2012	Corinthians (Brazil) 1 Chelsea (England) 0

INTERCONTINENTAL CUP TRIUMPHS (1960–2004*)

3 wins: Real Madrid, Spain (1960, 1998, 2002); Penarol, Uruguay (1961, 1966, 1982); AC Milan, Italy (1969, 1989, 1990); Nacional, Uruguay (1971, 1980, 1988); Boca Juniors, Argentina (1977, 2000, 2003).

2 wins: Santos, Brazil (1962, 1963); Internazionale, Italy (1964, 1965); Ajax, Netherlands (1972, 1995); Independiente, Argentina (1973, 1984); Bayern Munich, West Germany/Germany (1976, 2001); Juventus, Italy (1985, 1996); Porto, Portugal (1987, 2004); Sao Paulo, Brazil (1992, 1993).

1 win: Racing Club, Argentina (1967); Estudiantes, Argentina (1968); Feyenoord, Netherlands (1970); Atletico Madrid, Spain (1974); Olimpia Asuncion, Paraguay (1979); Flamengo, Brazil (1981); Gremio, Brazil (1983); River Plate, Argentina (1986); Red Star Belgrade, Yugoslavia (1991); Velez Sarsfield, Argentina (1994); Borussia Dortmund, Germany (1997); Manchester United, England (1999).

* = not contested in 1975 and 1978

MEN'S OLYMPIC FOOTBALL TOURNAMENT

First played at the 1900 Olympic Games in Paris, although not recognized by FIFA as an official tournament until London 1908, the men's Olympic football tournament was played in strict accordance with the Games' strong amateur tradition until 1984, when pros were allowed to play. The competition is now an Under-23 event – with allowance for three over-age players – to give rising stars the chance of major tournament experience. Since World War 2, however, no Olympic champions have won the FIFA World Cup within 10 years.

CZECH OUT

The climax of the 1920 Olympic Games tournament is the only time a major international football final has been abandoned. Czechoslovakia's players walked off the pitch minutes before half-time, in protest at the decisions made by 65-year-old English referee John Lewis – including the dismissal of Czech player Karel Steiner. Belgium, who were 2-0 up at the time, were awarded the victory, before Spain beat Holland 3-1 in a play-off for silver.

MEN'S OLYMPIC FOOTBALL FINALS

1896 Not played
1900 (Paris, France)
Gold: Upton Park FC (GB) Silver: USFSA XI (France) Bronze: Universite Libre de Bruxelles (Belgium) (only two exhibition matches played)
1904 (St Louis, US)
Gold: Galt FC (Canada) Silver: Christian Brothers College (US) Bronze: St Rose Parish (US) (only five exhibition matches played)
1908 (London, England)
Great Britain 2 Denmark 0 (Bronze: Holland)
1912 (Stockholm, Sweden)
Great Britain 4 Denmark 2 (Bronze: Holland)
1916 Not played
1920 (Antwerp, Belgium) Belgium 2 Czechoslovakia 0
(Gold: Belgium, Silver: Spain, Bronze: Holland)
1924 (Paris, France)
Uruguay 3 Switzerland 0 (Bronze: Sweden)
1928 (Amsterdam, Netherlands)
Uruguay 1 Argentina 1; Uruguay 2 Argentina 1 (Bronze: Italy)
1932 Not played
1936 (Berlin, Germany) Italy 2 Austria 1 (aet) (Bronze: Norway)
1940 Not played
1944 Not played
1948 (London, England) Sweden 3 Yugoslavia 1 (Bronze: Denmark)
1952 (Helsinki, Finland) Hungary 2 Yugoslavia 0 (Bronze: Sweden)
1956 (Melbourne, Australia) USSR 1 Yugoslavia 0 (Bronze: Bulgaria)
1960 (Rome, Italy) Yugoslavia 3 Denmark 1 (Bronze: Hungary)
1964 (Tokyo, Japan) Hungary 2 Czechoslovakia 1 (Bronze: Germany)
1968 (Mexico City, Mexico) Hungary 4 Bulgaria 1 (Bronze: Japan)
1972 (Munich, West Germany) Poland 2 Hungary 1 (Bronze: USSR/East Germany)
1976 (Montreal, Canada) East Germany 3 Poland 1 (Bronze: USSR)
1980 (Moscow, USSR) Czechoslovakia 1 East Germany 0 (Bronze: USSR)
1984 (Los Angeles, USA) France 2 Brazil 0 (Bronze: Yugoslavia)
1988 (Seoul, South Korea) USSR 2 Brazil 1 (Bronze: West Germany)
1992 (Barcelona, Spain) Spain 3 Poland 2 (Bronze: Ghana)
1996 (Atlanta, USA) Nigeria 3 Argentina 2 (Bronze: Brazil)
2000 (Sydney, Australia) **Cameroon** 2 Spain 2
(Cameroon win 5-3 on penalties) (Bronze: Chile)
2004 (Athens, Greece) Argentina 1 Paraguay 0 (Bronze: Italy)
2008 (Beijing, China) **Argentina** 1 Nigeria 0 (Bronze: Brazil)
2012 (London, England) Mexico 2 Brazil 1 (Bronze: South Korea)

BARCELONA BOUND

Future Barcelona team-mates Samuel Eto'o and Xavi scored penalties for opposing sides in 2000, when Cameroon and Spain contested the first Olympic final to be settled by a shoot-out. Ivan Amaya was the only player to miss, handing Cameroon gold.

RETROSPECTIVE MEDALS

Football was not played at the very first modern Summer Olympics, in Athens in 1896, and the football tournaments played at the 1900 and 1904 events are not officially recognized by FIFA. Medals were not handed out to the winning teams at the time – with Great Britain represented in 1900 by the Upton Park club from East London – though the International Olympic Committee has since allocated first, second and third place to the countries taking part.

BLOC PARTY

Eastern European countries dominated the Olympic Games football competitions from 1948 to 1980, when professional players were officially banned from taking part. Teams comprising so-called "state amateurs" from the Eastern Bloc took 23 of the 27 medals available during those years. Only Sweden, in 1948, brought gold medals west of the Iron Curtain. Sweden also collected bronze four years later, before Denmark claimed silver in 1960 and Japan bronze in 1968.

LAPPING IT UP

Until London 2012, Uruguay had a perfect Olympic football record. They won gold on the first two occasions they took part (1924 and 1928). Those Games were seen as a world championship and helped prompt FIFA into organizing the first World Cup in 1930 – also won by Uruguay, who included 1924 and 1928 gold medallists Jose Nasazzi, Jose Andrade and **Hector Scarone** (right) in their squad. Uruguay's 1924 champions are thought to have pioneered the lap of honour.

LONDON CALLING

Mexico were the unexpected winners when **Wembley Stadium** became the first venue to stage two men's Olympic Games football finals as part of London 2012. The stadium hosted the showpiece game when England's capital held the Olympics in 1948 and London is also now the only city to stage three separate summer Olympics, though the football final back in 1908 was played at White City. **Oribe Peralta** scored both goals as Mexico – managed by Luis Tena, assistant coach to the senior team – defeated Brazil 2-1 in the 2012 final. A late reply by Hulk was little consolation for the highly-fancied South Americans - though Brazil's Leandro Damiao did end the summer as six-goal top scorer. London 2012 matches were shared with cities away from the English capital, including Hampden Park in Glasgow, Old Trafford in Manchester, St James' Park in Newcastle and the City of Coventry Stadium. A united British team competed in the Olympic finals for the first time since 1960, featuring English Premier League stars such as Ryan Giggs and Craig Bellamy.

AFRICAN AMBITION

Ghana became the first African country to win an Olympic football medal, picking up bronze in 1992, but Nigeria went even better four years later by claiming the continent's first Olympic football gold medal – thanks to Emmanuel Amunike's stoppage-time winner against Argentina. Nigeria's triumph came as a huge surprise to many – especially as their rival teams included such future world stars as Brazil's Ronaldo and Roberto Carlos, Argentina's Hernan Crespo and Roberto Ayala, Italy's Fabio Cannavaro and Gianluigi Buffon, and France's Robert Pires and Patrick Vieira. Future FIFA World Cup or UEFA European Championship winners to have played at Summer Olympics include France's Michel Platini and Patrick Battiston (at the Montreal Games in 1976); West Germany's Andreas Brehme and Brazil's Dunga (Los Angeles, 1984); Brazil's Taffarel, Bebeto and Romario and West Germany's Jurgen Klinsmann (Seoul, 1988); France's Vieira, Pires and Sylvain Wiltord, Italy's Cannavaro, Buffon and Alessandro Nesta, and Brazil's Roberto Carlos, Rivaldo and Ronaldo (Atlanta, 1996); Italy's Gianluca Zambrotta and Spain's Xavi, Carles Puyol and Joan Capdevila (Sydney, 2000); and Italy's Daniele De Rossi, Andrea Pirlo and Alberto Gilardino (Athens, 2004).

BLUE STARS FIFA
YOUTH CUP

Staged on an annual basis by Zurich club FC Blue Stars since 1939, and granted FIFA's patronage since 1991, the Blue Stars/FIFA Youth Cup tournament has become football's premier youth event and features many teams from around the globe. Several of the game's greatest names – from Bobby Charlton to David Beckham – gained their first taste of international football competition at the event.

RAISING THE BARÇA

No Spanish side took part until Barcelona's involvement in 1988, with a team featuring midfielder **Josep Guardiola** and right-back Albert Ferrer, both of whom would help the club to their first European Cup triumph in 1992.

ABOUT SCHMID

It was third time lucky for FC Zurich when they became 2012 FIFA Blue Stars champions – for the fourth time. The Swiss side had lost on penalties – to Argentina's Boca Juniors in 2010 and FC Porto of Portugal in 2011 – before goals from Fabio Schmid and Ali Imren earned them a 2-0 derby win over Grasshopper Club.

HEART OF THE BLATTER

Long before he was elected FIFA president in 1998, Sepp Blatter was a keen amateur footballer who played centre-forward for Swiss club FC Sierre in the Blue Stars tournament in the early 1950s. He is now an honorary member of FC Blue Stars.

PORTO SPOT ON

FC Porto became Portugal's first FIFA Blue Stars champions in 2011 – just weeks after the club's senior team clinched a treble of domestic league and cup and the UEFA Europa League. The youngsters beat FC Zurich in the FIFA Blue Stars final, 3-0 on penalties following a goalless draw – the second successive year the final went to spot-kicks. It was double disappointment for FC Zurich: 12 months earlier they lost in the same way to Argentina's Boca Juniors.

BRAZIL FORTUNE

Only in 1999 was the tournament won by a non-European club when Brazil's Sao Paulo edged FC Zurich on penalties. Sao Paulo, now with Kaka, won again the next year. Argentina's Boca Juniors became the only other South American winners, in 2010.

BLUE STARS CHAMPIONSHIPS

Manchester United 18
(1954, 1957, 1959, 1960, 1961, 1962, 1965, 1966, 1968, 1969, 1975, 1976, 1978, 1979, 1981, 1982, 2004, 2005)
Grasshoppers 6
(1939, 1956, 1971, 1987, 1998, 2006)
FC Zurich 5
(1946, 1949, 2008, 2012, 2013)
Barcelona 3
(1993, 1994, 1995)
FC Young Fellows 3
(1941, 1942, 1953)
AC Milan 2
(1958, 1977)
Arsenal 2
(1963, 1964)
AS Roma 2
(1980, 2003)
FK Austria Vienna 2
(1947, 1948)
Sao Paulo 2
(1999, 2000)
Spartak Moscow 2
(1991, 1992)
FC Basel 1
(2009)
Boca Juniors 1
(2010)
FC Porto 1
(2011)

BLUE STARS/
FIFA YOUTH CUP 2011

FIFA FUTSAL WORLD CUP

Developed in South America in the 1930s, Futsal – a variant of five-a-side indoor football – has enjoyed a huge surge in popularity, and participation numbers, in recent years. The first FIFA Futsal World Cup was staged in Holland in 1989 and has been contested on a four-yearly basis since 1992. Two teams have dominated the event: Spain (with two wins) and, above all, Brazil (five wins).

FIFA FUTSAL WORLD CUP FINALS (and hosts)

1989 (Hosts: Holland) Brazil 2 Holland 1
1992 (Hong Kong) Brazil 4 United States 1
1996 (Spain) Brazil 6 Spain 4
2000 (Guatemala) Spain 4 Brazil 3
2004 (Chinese Taipei) Spain 2 Italy 1
2008 (Brazil) Brazil 2 Spain 2
      (aet: Brazil win 4-3 on penalties)
2012 (Thailand) **Brazil 3 Spain 2** (aet)

THE FIRST MANOEL

Brazilian Manoel Tobias can claim to be the FIFA Futsal World Cup's most prolific goalscorer, with 43 in 32 appearances. Tobias, born in Salgueiro on 19 April 1971, represented his country in the 1992, 1996, 2000 and 2004 tournaments – only once ending up on the losing side within normal time. He ended both the 1996 and 2000 competitions with the prizes for both best player and top scorer.

CUBAN EMBARGO

Cuba hold the record for the fewest goals scored in a single tournament. They managed only one goal in their three games at the 2000 FIFA Futsal World Cup, while conceding 20 in defeats to Iran, Argentina and eventual champions Spain.

SAMBA SUPREMACY

Predictably for a game relying heavily on swift, deft passing and nimble footwork, Brazilians have excelled at Futsal – an indoor, five-a-side, 40-minute version of the 11-a-side game. Since FIFA inaugurated its Futsal World Cup in 1989, Brazil have won the trophy five times out of a possible seven – finishing runners-up to Spain in 2000 and third behind Spain and Italy four years later. Brazil have ended every tournament as the top-scoring team, hitting the back of the net a record 78 times during eight games in 2000 – at a staggering rate of 9.3 goals per match. Their largest FIFA Futsal World Cup win was a 29-2 trouncing of Guatemala in 2000 – though their best-ever scoreline, an overall record for Futsal, came when they beat East Timor 76-0 in October 2006. Strangely enough, though, their first-ever FIFA Futsal World Cup match ended in defeat – 3-2 to Hungary in the first-round group stage in 1989.

BACK OF THE NETO

The 2012 FIFA Futsal World Cup was the largest yet, with 24 countries taking part in Thailand – four more than the 2008 tournament. Yet it was a familiar story at the climax, with Brazil and Spain contesting the final for the fourth time, and the South Americans again emerged victorious, this time with a 3-2 win after extra time. The winning goal, the second of a brace, was scored by the man voted player of the tournament – Brazil's **Neto** – though Russia's Eder Lima claimed the golden boot thanks to his nine goals across the competition

NINE'S ENOUGH

Russia's Pula may have pipped Falcao to the top scorer prize in 2008 (with 16 goals to 15), but the Brazilian, who had already won both the Golden Ball and Golden Shoe awards four years earlier, was voted player of the tournament. Pula's 16 goals across the 2008 event included nine in one game – an all-time FIFA Futsal World Cup record – as the Solomon Islands were thrashed 31-2.

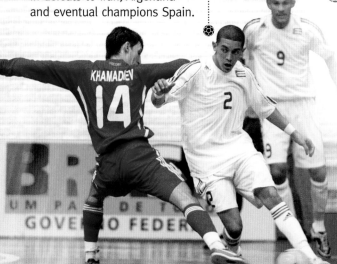

FIFA BEACH SOCCER WORLD CUP

Another variant of the game that can trace its roots to South America, beach soccer is a high-octane, all-action, made-for-TV, goal-crazy version of the game that has enjoyed a rapid surge in popularity in recent years. First contested in 1995 at its spiritual home on Copacabana Beach in Rio de Janeiro, Brazil, the FIFA Beach Soccer World Cup became a biannual event after the 2009 tournament.

ERIC THE KING

Footballer, actor and wannabe poet and philosopher **Eric Cantona** coached the French team that won the 2005 FIFA Beach Soccer World Cup – the first tournament to be staged under the FIFA banner, having previously been known as the Beach Soccer World Championship. However, the former Manchester United striker only allowed himself limited playing time and ended the tournament with a solitary goal to his name – in a 7-4 quarter-final victory over Spain.

FIFA BEACH SOCCER WORLD CUP FINALS

1995 (Host beach and city/country: Copacabana, Rio de Janeiro/Brazil) **Brazil 8 USA 1**
1996 (Copacabana) **Brazil 3 Uruguay 0**
1997 (Copacabana) **Brazil 5 Uruguay 2**
1998 (Copacabana) **Brazil 9 France 2**
1999 (Copacabana) **Brazil 5 France 2**
2000 (Marina da Gloria, Rio de Janeiro) **Brazil 6 Peru 2**
2001 (Costa do Sauipe, Rio de Janeiro) **Portugal 9 France 3**
2002 (Vitoria/Brazil) **Brazil 6 Portugal 5**
2003 (Copacabana) **Brazil 8 Spain 2**
2004 (Copacabana) **Brazil 6 Spain 4**
2005 (Copacabana) **France 3 Portugal 3 (France win 1-0 on penalties)**
2006 (Copacabana) **Brazil 4 Uruguay 1**
2007 (Copacabana) **Brazil 8 Mexico 2**
2008 (Plage du Pardo, Marseille/France) **Brazil 5 Italy 3**
2009 (Jumeirah, Dubai/United Arab Emirates) **Brazil 10 Switzerland 5**
2011 (Ravenna, Italy) **Russia 12 Brazil 8**

MADJER FOR IT

In 2006, Angolan-born Portuguese star **Madjer** set a record for goals in one tournament when he put the ball in the net 21 times – one of the five tournaments he has finished as top scorer. His seven goals in one game, against Uruguay in 2009, broke the record he himself set when scoring six against Cameroon in 2006.

GOAL GLUT

The 2003 tournament was the most prolific, with an average of 9.4 goals per game – 150 in total. Two years earlier had brought the lowest average – 7.2 per match, 144 in total.

FRENCH SELECTION

The 2008 tournament, on the beaches of Marseille in the south of France, was the first to take place outside Brazil. In 2009, it was held in Dubai. Future events will take place two years apart, rather than one, with the next tournament scheduled for 2011.

LIFE SAVING

Brazil's Paulo Sergio was voted best goalkeeper for the first four FIFA Beach Soccer World Cups, but since then the award has gone to Portugal's Pedro Crespo (1999), Japan's Kato (2000), France's Pascal Olmeta (2001), Thailand's Vilard Normcharoen (2002), Brazil's Robertinho (2003) and Mao (2009), Spain's Roberto (2004) and Roberto Valeiro (2008), and Russia's Andrey Bukhlitskiy (2011). There was no goalkeeper prize from 2005 to 2007.

RUSSIAN INVASION

The final of the 2011 FIFA Beach Soccer World Cup was the highest-scoring showdown in the competition's history, as reigning champions Brazil lost 12-8 to a country that might not usually be associated with the most suitable climactic conditions – Russia. Yet the Russians went into the tournament as reigning European champions and clinched their first world title with the help of a hat-trick in the final from Dmitry Shishin and the performances by player of the tournament Ilya Leonov. Brazil's Andre at least had the consolation of the Golden Shoe for his 14 goals.

FIFA INTERACTIVE WORLD CUP

The EA SPORTS FIFA Interactive World Cup, the world's largest football video game tournament, made its debut in 2004 with participants from around the world battling it out on the virtual pitch in FIFA 2005. The inaugural event showcased an eight-player finals tournament in Zurich, Switzerland, and the winner earned a trip to the FIFA World Player Gala in Amsterdam. Since then, the FIWC has expanded its reach to attract entries from all over the world, with 1.3 million players competing to qualify for the finals in 2012. The finals were held in Dubai, with 24 contestants battling for the trophy (plus US$20,000 and two tickets to the FIFA Ballon d'Or Gala) on EA Sports™ FIFA 12 on the Sony PlayStation® 3.

HOW TO QUALIFY

The 2012 FIWC involved a similar qualification process to that of 2011, including two places available apiece from six different monthly "seasons" played online by gamers across the world. Defending champion Francisco Cruz was one of three former winners who made it to the finals – and 2010 winner Nenad Stojkovic provided on-line analysis for the live streams – another FIFA Interactive World Cup first.

FIWC FIRST-TIMERS

Fifteen of the 24 FIWC grand finalists in Dubai in 2012 qualified for the climactic event for the first time. Tassal Rushan's opening match nearly resulted in a shock against defending champion Francisco Cruz, but he lost 2-1. However, only three first-timers reached the quarter-finals.

1.3 MILLION AND STILL RISING

The 2012 FIFA Interactive World Cup had a record 1.3 million players, a huge increase on the near 870,000 who took part in 2011. As recently as 2009, only 420,000 players paticipated.

GRAND CHAMPIONS

There have been seven grand champions in FIFA Interactive World Cup history, with the 2011 winner being the youngest and 2012 seeing a first repeat champion. The inaugural tournament in 2004 was won by Brazil's Thiago Carrico de Azevado. A year later Chris Bullard of England captured the second FIWC title, on home soil. In 2006, Andries Smit, from the Netherlands, captured the championship also in his own homeland, besting the other finalists in Amsterdam. After a blank year in 2007, Spain's Alfonso Ramos won in Berlin in 2008, before France's Bruce Grannec took the 2009 crown and American gamer Nenad Stojkovic emerged triumphant in 2010 – both these latter victories coming in Barcelona. At Los Angeles in 2011, Francisco Cruz became Portugal's first champion, and the youngest ever – aged just 16. Dubai hosted the 2012 tournament and the final ensured there would be the first two-time winner as 2009 champion Grannec fought through to face 2008 winner Ramos. A tense final went to penalties before Real Madrid fan Ramos triumphed.

FIT OF PIQUE

Real Madrid fan **Alfonso Ramos** not only became the first two-times FIFA Interactive World Cup champion in 2012, he also enjoyed victory in a game played at the subsequent FIFA Ballon d'Or celebrations, this time with Barcelona centre-back **Gerard Pique** at the controls as his opponent. Pique predictably played as Barcelona to Alfonso's Real, and not only lost 1-0 but the computer-game "Gerard Pique" was sent off. Ramos – nicknamed "Vamos Ramos" – celebrated both of his 2012 triumphs with a dance inspired by Brazil striker Neymar. Other 2012 Ballon d'Or Guests enjoying some FIFA computer game action included Christian Karembeu, a FIFA World Cup winner with France in 1998, and Italy's Luca Toni, who lifted the trophy in 2006.

SINGING THE BLUES

Despite being an FC Porto fan, Francisco Cruz played as English club Chelsea at the 2011 FIWC – while the opponent he defeated in the final, Colombia's Javier Munoz, competed as Spanish side Real Madrid.

PART 7:
WOMEN'S FOOTBALL

"THE FUTURE IS FEMININE" is a favourite slogan of FIFA president Sepp Blatter and his optimism for the women's game has been borne out by recent surges in participation all around the world. Up to 30 million women worldwide play football, with recruits more than doubling during the past decade. International women's competitions now pull in significant crowds, whose enthusiasm and support has spilled over into national league and cup competitions around the world.

Women's football was first organized in England early in the last century, but was banned by The Football Association in 1921. That led to the creation of an independent women's association with a cup competition of its own. Women's football was developing elsewhere and the surge of interest eventually led, in the early 1980s, to the first formal European Championships and, in 1988, to a FIFA invitational tournament in Chinese Taipei.

FIFA launched an inaugural world championship in 1991, which was won by the United States to claim primacy in the game. The Americans hosted the third FIFA Women's World Cup, which saw a record crowd of 90,185 celebrate their shoot-out victory over China in the final in Pasadena. They underlined their No.1 status by winning the first women's football gold medal at the Atalnta 1996 Olympic Games, taking silver in 2000 and gold again in 2004, 2008 and 2012.

FIFA set up a world youth championship in 2002, initially for players aged Under-19, later amended to Under-20, and added an Under-17 event to the international calendar in 2008.

A professional clubs' league was launched in the USA in 2009. It attracted some of the world's finest players, including Brazil's Marta and England's Kelly Smith, but it suspended operations for the season in January 2012. England introduced its own first semi-professional women's league in April 2011. Later that year the showpiece FIFA Women's World Cup was staged in Germany which had dominated the preceding two tournaments. Surprise winners Japan overcame great odds to claim Asia's first FIFA world title, and demonstrated that new boundaries are still being broken.

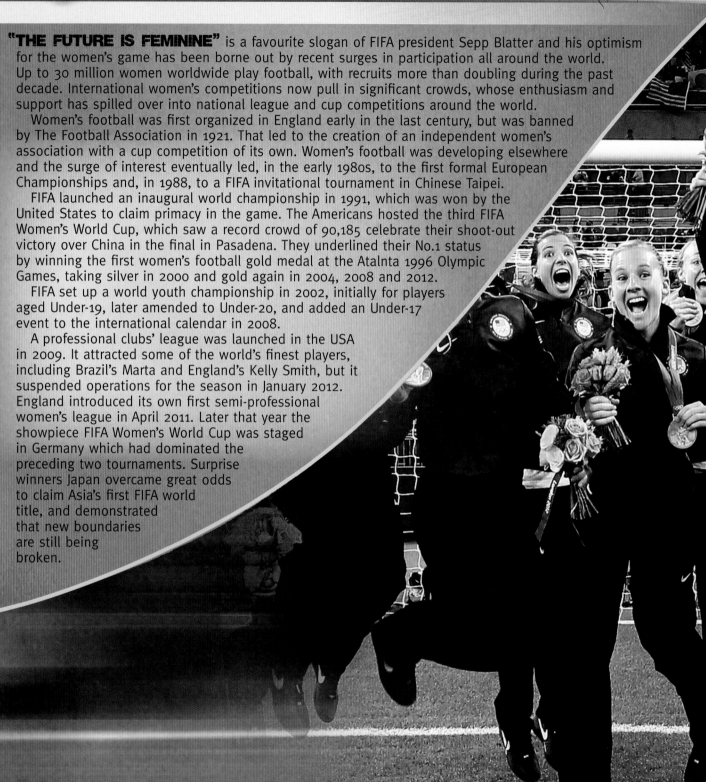

United States players celebrate at Wembley after winnning their fourth women's Olympic Games Football gold medal at London 2012. The USA have reached all five finals and lost only to Norway at Sydney 2000.

FIFA WOMEN'S WORLD CUP

The first FIFA Women's World Cup finals were held in China in 1991. Twelve teams, divided into three groups of four, took part, with the top two in each group, plus the two "best losers" going through to the knockout quarter-finals. The tournament was expanded in 1999 to include 16 teams, divided into four groups of four, with the top two in each group progressing to the quarter-finals. That is the current format, although an expansion of the tournament to 24 teams is still under consideration.

HAVELANGE'S DREAM COMES TRUE

The FIFA Women's World Cup was the brainchild of former FIFA president João Havelange. The tournament began as an experimental competition in 1991 and has expanded in size and importance ever since. The success of the 1999 finals in the United States was a turning point for the tournament, which now attracts big crowds and worldwide TV coverage. The USA and Norway – countries in which football (soccer) is one of the most popular girls' sports – dominated the early competitions. The Americans won the inaugural competition and the 1999 tournament. Norway lifted the trophy in 1995. Germany became the dominant force in the new century, winning the trophy in 2003 and retaining it in 2007. The recent emergence of challengers such as Brazil, China and Sweden underlined the worldwide spread and appeal of the women's game.

IMMENSE DEFENCES

The 2011 FIFA Women's World Cup in Germany had the lowest goal average since the competition was first held in 1991 with an average of just 2.69 goals per game – or 86 overall. The most prolific was the 1999 tournament, boasting 123 goals – the equivalent of 3.84 each match.

US CELEBRATE FIRST ACHIEVEMENT

The USA's victory in the inaugural FIFA Women's World Cup in 1991 made them the first USA team to win a world football title. The USA men's best performance came when they reached the semi-finals in 1930, losing 6-1 to Argentina.

ASIA MAJORS

Japan's women became the country's first football side to claim a FIFA world title when they upset the odds to win the 2011 FIFA Women's World Cup, beating favourites USA 3-1 on penalties after a 2-2 draw. Player of the tournament Homare Sawa had levelled the scores with just three minutes of extra-time remaining, before **Saki Kumagai** struck the winning spot-kick in the shoot-out. Japan had failed to win in the two teams' previous 25 meetings, losing 22 and drawing three. The Japanese women's previous best FIFA World Cup performance had been reaching the quarter-finals in 1995. The 2011 generation's triumph was all the more moving, as they dedicated the victory to victims of the devastating tsunami that had struck Japan in March that year.

FIFA WOMEN'S WORLD CUP FINALS

Year	Venue	Winners	Runners-up	Score
1991	Ghuangzhou	USA	Norway	2-1
1995	Stockholm	Norway	Germany	2-0
1999	Los Angeles	USA	China	0-0
USA won 5-4 in penalty shoot-out				
2003	Los Angeles	Germany	Sweden	2-1 (aet)
2007	Shanghai	Germany	Brazil	2-0
2011	Frankfurt	Japan	USA	2-2 (aet)
Japan won 3-1 in penalty shoot-out				

THIRD–PLACE PLAY–OFF MATCHES

Year	Venue	Winners	Losers	Score
1991	Guangzhou	Sweden	Germany	4-0
1995	Gavle	USA	China	2-0
1999	Los Angeles	Brazil	Norway	0-0
Brazil won 5-4 in penalty shoot-out				
2003	Los Angeles	USA	Canada	3-1
2007	Shanghai	USA	Norway	4-1
2011	Sinsheim	Sweden	France	2-1

FOUR GAIN DOUBLE MEDALS

Four of the USA's 1991 winners were in the team that beat China on penalties in the 1999 final: **Mia Hamm** (left), Michelle Akers, Kristine Lilly and Julie Foudy.

WINNERS KEEP SQUAD TOGETHER

Six Germany players appeared in their 2003 and 2007 final wins: **Kerstin Stegemann**, Birgit Prinz, Renate Lingor, Ariane Hingst and Kerstin Garefrekes started both games, while Martina Muller came on as a substitute both times.

GERMANS SET DEFENSIVE RECORD

In 2007, Germany became the first team to make a successful defence of the FIFA Women's World Cup. They also set another record. They went through the tournament – six games and 540 minutes – without conceding a single goal. As a result, their goalkeeper Nadine Angerer overhauled Italy keeper Walter Zenga's record of 517 minutes unbeaten in the 1990 men's finals. The last player to score against the Germans was Sweden's **Hanna Ljungberg**, who scored in the 41st minute of the 2003 final.

TWICE AS NICE

China are the only country to have been awarded the Fair Play prize at two separate FIFA Women's World Cups – in 1999 and 2003. Yet, in a major surprise, they failed to even qualify for the 2011 edition – the first time they have missed out on the tournament. Brazil, Germany, Japan, Nigeria, Norway, Sweden and the United States remain the only teams to have taken part every time.

LA FINALE BEATS THEM ALL

The 1999 finals in the USA were the best attended of the five tournaments to date. A total of 3,687,069 spectators watched the matches, at an average of 24,913 per game. The final, between hosts USA and China – at the Rose Bowl, Los Angeles on 10 July – drew 90,185 spectators, a world record for a women's match. The programme that day also included the third-place play-off between Brazil and Norway.

TOP TEAMS

Country	Winners	Runners-up	Third
Germany	2	1	-
US	2	1	3
Norway	1	1	1
Japan	1	-	-
Brazil	-	1	1
Sweden	-	1	2
China	-	1	-

TOP TEAM SCORERS

1991:	USA	25
1995:	Norway	23
1999:	China	19
2003:	Germany	25
2007:	Germany	21
2011:	USA	13

TOP ALL–TIME TEAM SCORERS

1	USA	98
2	Germany	91
3	Norway	77
4	Brazil	55
5	Sweden	54

THE FIRST GAME

The first-ever game in the FIFA Women's World Cup finals was hosts China's 4-0 win over Norway at Guangzhou on 16 November 1991. A 65,000 crowd watched the game.

THE REGULAR EIGHT

Eight teams have played in all five finals tournaments – the USA, Germany, Norway, Brazil, China, Japan, Nigeria and Sweden.

NORWAY POST LONGEST WIN RUN

Norway, winners in 1995, hold the record for the most consecutive matchtime wins in the finals – ten. Their run started with an 8-0 win over Nigeria on 6 June 1995 and continued until 30 June 1999 when they beat Sweden 3-1 in the quarter-finals. It ended when they lost 5-0 to China in the semi-finals on 4 July.

UNBEATEN CHINA SENT HOME

In 1999, China became the only team to go through the finals without losing a match, yet go home empty-handed. The Chinese won their group games, 2-1 against Sweden, 7-0 against Ghana and 3-1 against Australia. They beat Russia 2-0 in the quarter-finals and Norway 5-0 in the semi-finals, but they lost on penalties to the USA in the final after a 0-0 draw. In 2011, Japan became the first team to lift the trophy despite losing a match in the first-round – as had runners-up the USA.

FIFTEEN ON TARGET FOR NORWAY

Norway hold the record for scoring in the most consecutive games – 15. They began their sequence with a 4-0 win over New Zealand on 19 November 1991 and ended it with a 3-1 win over Sweden in the quarter-finals on 30 June 1999.

THE LOWEST CROWD...

The lowest attendance for any match at the finals came on 8 June 1995, when only 250 spectators watched the 3-3 draw between Canada and Nigeria at Helsingborg.

CHAMPIONS RUN UP 11

The biggest victory margin in the finals was **Germany's** 11-0 win over Argentina in Shanghai on 10 September 2007. Argentina keeper Vanina Correa punched a Melanie Behringer corner into her own net after 12 minutes. Birgit Prinz and Sandra Smisek scored hat-tricks, with Germany's other goals coming from Renate Lingor (2), Behringer and Kerstin Garefrekes.

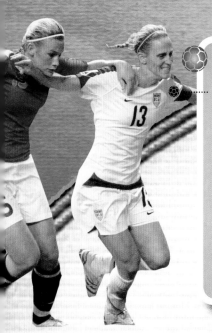

FIVE FIVE–STAR STARS

Five players have been to five different FIFA Women's World Cups. The USA's **Kristine Lilly** was the first to achieve this feat, as part of her record 340 games for her country – scoring 129 goals. She is also the oldest scorer in finals history, being 36 years and 62 days old when she netted the third in a 3-0 quarter-final victory over England in September 2007. Norway goalkeeper Bente Nordby was a squad member in 1991 but did not play any games, but did get on to the field in the four tournaments that followed. Three players joined the five-tournament honours board in 2011: Brazil's Formiga, Germany's Birgit Prinz and Brazil's Marta.

QUICKEST RED AND YELLOW

The record for the fastest red card is held by Australia's Alicia Ferguson, who was sent off in the second minute of their 3-1 defeat by China in New York on 26 June 1999. North Korea's Ri Hyang Ok received the quickest yellow card, in the first minute of their 2-1 defeat by Nigeria in Los Angeles on 20 June 1999.

THE FASTEST GOAL

Lena Videkull of Sweden netted the fastest goal in finals history when she scored after 30 seconds in their 8-0 win over Japan at Foshan on 19 November 1991. Canada's **Melissa Tancredi** struck the second-fastest goal – after 37 seconds – in their 2-2 draw with Australia in Chengdu on 20 September 2007.

PRINZ SEIZES FINALS CHANCE

In 2007, Birgit Prinz became the first player to appear in three FIFA Women's World Cup finals. She was also the youngest player to appear in a FIFA Women's World Cup final. The Germany forward was 17 years 336 days when she started in the 2-0 defeat by Norway in 1995. Team-mate Sandra Smisek was just 14 days older. The oldest finalist was Sweden's Kristin Bengtsson, who was 33 years 273 days when her side lost to Germany in the 2003 final.

HOT SHOT AKERS SETS THE STANDARD

US forward Michelle Akers (born in Santa Clara on 1 February 1966) hold the record for the most goals scored in a single finals tournament – ten in 1991. She also set a record for the most goals scored in one match, with five in the USA's 7-0 quarter-final win over Taiwan at Foshan on 24 November 1991. Akers grabbed both goals in the USA's 2-1 victory in the final, including their 78th-minute winner. Judges voted her as FIFA's Women's Player of the 20th Century.

THE FASTEST SUBSTITUTIONS

The fastest substitutions in finals history were both timed at six minutes. Taiwan's defender Liu Hsiu Mei was subbed by reserve goalkeeper Li Chyn Hong in their 2-0 win over Nigeria in Jiangmen on 21 November 1991. Li replaced No. 1 keeper Lin Hui Fang, who had been sent off. Therese Lundin subbed for the injured Hanna Ljungberg, also after six minutes, in Sweden's 2-0 win over Ghana at Chicago on 26 June 1999.

DANILOVA THE YOUNGEST SCORER

The youngest scorer at the finals was Russia's Elena Danilova. She was 16 years 96 days when she scored her country's only goal in the 2003 quarter-final against Germany at Portland on 2 October. The Germans scored seven in reply.

MORACE HITS FIRST HAT–TRICK

Carolina Morace of Italy scored the first hat-trick in finals history when she netted the last three goals in Italy's 5-0 win over Taiwan at Jiangmen on 17 November 1991.

NEW STARS DOMINATE THE FINALS

The FIFA Women's World Cup has been dominated by a series of great players. American attackers Michelle Akers and Carin Jennings starred in the opening tournament in 1991. Playmaker **Hege Riise** and top scorer Ann-Kristin led Norway to victory four years later. Another American great, Mia Hamm, was at the top of her form when the USA triumphed for a second time in 1999. That tournament marked the emergence of the best-ever Chinese player, Sun Wen, who finished joint top scorer and won the Player of the Tournament award. Birgit Prinz of Germany was Player of the Tournament and top scorer when Germany won for the first time in 2003. The Brazilian forward, Marta, matched that feat in 2007, though, unlike Prinz, she found herself on the losing side in the final. Hamm, Prinz and Marta are the only winners of FIFA Women's Player of the Year award, introduced in 2001. Hamm took the prize in 2001 and 2002. Prinz won it in 2003, 2004 and 2005. Marta came top of the voting list in 2006, 2007, 2008 and 2009. Japan captain Homare Sawa took both the best player and top scorer prizes at the 2011 tournament, as well as lifting the main trophy itself, before being voted 2011 FIFA Women's Player of the Year.

FIFA WOMEN'S WORLD CUP
PLAYER OF THE TOURNAMENT

Year	Venue	Winner
1991	China	Carin Jennings (USA)
1995	Sweden	Hege Riise (Norway)
1999	USA	Sun Wen (China)
2003	USA	Birgit Prinz (Germany)
2007	China	Marta (Brazil)
2011	Germany	Homare Sawa (Japan)

FIFA WOMEN'S WORLD CUP FINALS TOP SCORER

1991	Michelle Akers (USA)	10
1995	Ann-Kristin Aarones (Norway)	6
1999	Sissi (Brazil)	7
2003	Birgit Prinz (Germany)	7
2007	Marta (Brazil)	7
2011	Homare Sawa	5

ALL–TIME TOP SCORERS

1	Birgit Prinz (Germany)	14
=	Marta (Brazil)	
3	Abby Wambach (USA)	13
4	Michelle Akers (USA)	12
5	Sun Wen (China)	11
=	Bettina Wiegmann (Germany)	
7	Ann-Kristin Aarones (Norway)	10
=	Heidi Mohr (Germany)	
9	Linda Medalen (Norway)	9
=	Hege Riise (Norway)	

FIFA WOMEN'S WORLD CUP WINNING CAPTAINS

1991	April Heinrichs (USA)
1995	Heidi Store (Norway)
1999	Carla Overbeck (USA)
2003	Bettina Wiegmann (Germany)
2007	Birgit Prinz (Germany)
2011	Homare Sawa (Japan)

MOST FINALS APPEARANCES (BY GAMES)

30	Kristine Lilly (USA)
25	Birgit Prinz (Germany)
24	Julie Foudy (USA)
23	Joy Fawcett (USA)
	Mia Hamm (USA)
22	Bente Nordby (Norway)
	Hege Riise (Norway)
	Bettina Wiegmann (Germany)

TEAM PLAYERS

Only four players have been named in the tournament all-star teams at two separate FIFA Women's World Cups: China's Wang Liping, Germany's Bettina Wiegmann, Brazil's Marta, and the USA's Shannon Boxx – despite Boxx being unfortunate enough to miss a crucial spot-kick in the 2011 final's penalty shoot-out.

MARTA'S FINAL AGONY

Brazil's Marta may have been the star of the 2007 tournament, but she was heartbroken in the final after Germany goalkeeper Nadine Angerer saved her penalty that would have put Brazil level. Germany won the match 2-0.

LAST–DITCH FIRST

Japan's 2011 success was bittersweet at the last for defender **Azuza Iwashimizu**, whose red card in stoppage-time of extra-time against the USA made her the first player to be sent off in a FIFA Women's World Cup final. Her punishment was for a foul on American attacker Alex Morgan, just minutes after Japan had equalised at 2-2.

THE FIRST SENDING OFF

Taiwan goalkeeper Lin Hui Fang was the first player to be sent off in finals history. She was red-carded after six minutes of Taiwan's 2-0 win over Nigeria in Jiangmen on 21 November 1991.

SUN RATTLES THE MEN

In 1999, Shanghai-born **Sun Wen** became the first woman player ever to be nominated for the Asian Footballer of the Year award, following her performances in China's run to the 1999 FIFA Women's World Cup final. Three years later, she won the Internet poll for FIFA's Women's Player of the 20th Century.

OTHER WOMEN'S TOURNAMENTS

OLYMPIC RINGING THE CHANGES

Germany forward Birgit Prinz was the only player to score in all of the first four Olympic women's finals tournaments but missed out on London 2012 because her country did not qualify. That allowed Brazil's Cristiane to push ahead as all-time top scorer, adding two to take her tally to 12. Prinz's Olympic haul of ten goals was also equalled in 2012 by Canada's Christine Sinclair.

WOMEN'S OLYMPIC FINALS

Year	Venue	Winners	Runners-up	Score
1996	Atlanta	USA	China	2-1
2000	Sydney	Norway	USA	3-2
	Norway won with a golden goal			
2004	Athens	USA	Brazil	2-1 (aet)
2008	Beijing	USA	Brazil	1-0 (aet)
2012	London	USA	Japan	2-1

THIRD-PLACE PLAY-OFFS

Year	Venue	Winners	Losers	Score
1996	Atlanta	Norway	Brazil	2-0
2000	Sydney	Germany	Brazil	2-0
2004	Athens	Germany	Sweden	1-0
2008	Beijing	Germany	Japan	2-0
2012	London	Canada	France	1-0

MEDALLISTS

Country	Gold	Silver	Bronze
USA	4	1	-
Norway	1	-	1
Brazil	-	2	-
China	-	1	-
Japan	-	1	-
Germany	-	-	3
Canada	-	-	1

WOMEN'S OLYMPIC TEAM TOP SCORERS

1996:	Norway	12
2000:	USA	9
2004:	Brazil	15
2008:	USA	12
2012:	USA	16

WOMEN'S OLYMPIC INDIVIDUAL TOP SCORERS

1996:	Ann-Kristin Aarones (Norway)	
	Linda Medalen (Norway)	
	Pretinha (Brazil)	4
2000:	Sun Wen (China)	4
2004:	Cristiane (Brazil)	
	Birgit Prinz (Germany)	5
2008:	Cristiane (Brazil)	5
2012:	Christine Sinclair (Canada)	6

CRISTIANE'S TREBLE DOUBLE

Brazil striker **Cristiane** is the only player to score two hat-tricks in FIFA Olympic history. She netted three in a 7-0 win over hosts Greece in 2004 and added another treble in a 3-1 win over Nigeria in Beijing four years later. Birgit Prinz is the only other hat-trick scorer, with four goals against China in 2004.

HOSTS WITH THE MOST

The FIFA Under-20 Women's World Cup is held every two years, in contrast to the four-yearly senior tournament – but since 2010, the younger players' event held a year before a FIFA World Cup is hosted by the same nation. That meant 2011 FIFA Women's World Cup hosts Germany staged the FIFA Under-20s Women's World Cup a year earlier, when they became the first hosts to also win the tournament. The 2012 hosts Japan could not emulate such a feat, instead seeing Germany beaten 1-0 in the final by the United States thanks to a goal by Kealia Ohai. The Germans had beaten the Americans 3-0 in their first-round group game. Japan's Kim Un-Hwa finished top scorer, on seen, while Germany's Dzsenifer Marozsan – whose father Janos Marozsan played for Hungary – was voted best player.

GERMANS CHALK UP BIGGEST WIN

Germany hold the record for the biggest win in the Olympic finals. They beat China 8-0 at Patras on 11 August 2004, with Birgit Prinz scoring four times. The Germans' other goals came from Pia Wunderlich, Renate Lingor, Conny Pohlers and Martina Muller. Yet, in a major surprise, Germany failed to qualify for the women's football tournament at the 2012 Olympic Games in London. The 2011 FIFA Women's World Cup was used as UEFA's qualifiers, meaning beaten quarter-finalists Germany fell short. Semi-finalists Sweden – including their most-capped player Therese Sjogran – and France, whose stars include midfielder **Louisa Necib** (right), went through to the 2012 event instead.

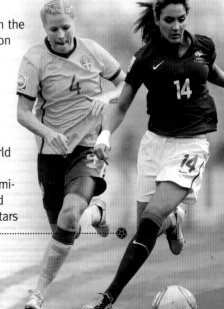

LATE STARTS, LATE FINISHING

Carli Lloyd scored the winning goal for the USA, against Brazil, to clinch Olympic gold in 2008 – then struck the decisive brace in the London 2012 final, as her team beat Japan 2-1. Other memorable moments of the women's football tournament at London 2012 included Alex Morgan's winner for the USA against Canada in the semi-final – she made it 4-3 three minutes into stoppage-time at the end of extra-time, the latest goal in Olympic history. Hosts Great Britain fielded a team for the first time and although they finished top of their first round group with a perfect three wins from three, without conceding a goal, they were beaten 2-0 by Canada in the quarter-final and missed out on a medal.

ROMANE EMPRESS

Mana Iwabuchi was named best player at the 2008 FIFA Under-17s World Cup, despite her Japan team reaching only the quarter-finals. However, North Korea's Yeo Min-Ji in 2010 and France's Griedge Mbock Bathy two years later could enjoy both individual and team glory. France took the 2012 title by beating defending champions North Korea 7-6 on penalties, after a 1-1 draw. French goalkeeper Romane Bruneau was the shoot-out heroine, saving two of the Koreans' eight spot-kicks.

KOREA CHANGE

Two years after North Korea won the inaugural FIFA Under-17 Women's World Cup, neighbours South Korea lifted the trophy the second time around, this time in Trinidad and Tobago. The final on 25 September was the first to go to penalties, with South Korea beating Japan 5-4 in the shoot-out after a thrilling 3-3 draw. South Korea had recovered to reach the final despite a 3-0 first-round defeat to Germany, who scored 22 goals in three games before losing a quarter-final 1-0 to North Korea.

US DOMINATE OLYMPIC GOLDS

The USA have dominated the Olympic football tournament since it was introduced at the 1996 Games in Atlanta. They have won four gold medals and finished runners-up in the other final. Norway and China were the Americans' early challengers, with Brazil, FIFA Women's World Cup holders Germany and Japan proving their toughest rivals in the past three Olympics (2004, 2008 and 2012). The tournament has rapidly grown in popularity, attracting record crowds at the 2008 Olympic Games in Beijing. FIFA have added two worldwide competitions for younger teams, too. The FIFA U-20 Women's World Cup was staged for the first time in 2000 and the first edition of the Under-17 event followed in 2008. Once more, the USA have been prominent, though they have faced a strong challenge from North Korea in recent years.

FIFA U-20 WOMEN'S WORLD CUP

FINALS

Year	Venue	Winner	Runners-up	Score
2002	Edmonton	USA	Canada	1-0 (aet)
2004	Bangkok	Germany	Chile	2-0
2006	Moscow	North Korea	China	5-0
2008	Santiago	USA	North Korea	2-1
2010	Bielefeld	Germany	Nigeria	2-0
2012	Tokyo	USA	Germany	1-0

TOP SCORERS

2002	Christine Sinclair (Canada)	10
2004	Brittany Timko (Canada)	7
2006	Ma Xiaoxu (China),	
	Kim Song Hui (North Korea)	5
2008	Sydney Leroux (USA)	5
2010	Alexandra Popp (Germany)	10
2012	Kim Un-Hwa (Japan)	7

FIFA U-17 WOMEN'S WORLD CUP

FINALS

Year	Venue	Winner	Runners-up	Score
2008	Auckland	North Korea	USA	2-1 (aet)
2010	Port of Spain	South Korea	Japan	3-3 (aet)
	(South Korea won 5-4 on penalties)			
2012	Baku	France	North Korea	1-1 (aet)
	(France won 7-6 on penalties)			

TOP SCORERS

2008	Dzsenifer Marozsan (Germany)	6
2010	Yeo Min-Ji (South Korea)	8
2012	Ri Un-Sim (North Korea)	8

CONTINENTAL CONQUERORS

Nigeria have dominated African women's football with eight out of 10 triumphs in the CAF African Women's Championship – Equatorial Guinea claiming the other two, including the latest in 2012. The European equivalent has been won a record seven times by Germany, the Asian title eight times by China, South America's version five times by Brazil and once by Argentina, and Oceania's three times apiece by New Zealand and Australia.

SINCLAIR HITS FIVE

Christine Sinclair of Canada and Alexandra Popp of Germany share the record for most goals scored in a single FIFA Under-20 Women's World Cup. Each struck 10, Sinclair in 2002 and Popp eight years later. Sinclair also holds the record for the most goals in one game. She netted five in Canada's 6-2 quarter-final win over England at Edmonton on 25 August 2002. But Popp is the only player to score in all of her country's six games at a tournament. Only Sinclair and Popp have won both the Golden Ball for best player and Golden Shoe for top scorer. Sinclair finished the 2012 Olympics as six-goal top-scorer in the women's football tournament. Her tally included a hat-trick – in vain – in Canada's 4-3 semi-final defeat to the US.

KIM GRABS ONLY HAT-TRICK

North Korea's **Kim Song-Hi** netted the only hat-trick in any final of the FIFA Under-20 Women's World Cup. It came in their 5-0 win over China on 3 September 2006.

THE WORLD GAME enters party mode every January when FIFA hosts the annual gala at which it hails a range of achievements and achievers from the previous 12 months.

The January 2012 event had Argentina and Barcelona's Lionel Messi and Team USA superstar Abby Wambach as its "headline" acts. Messi collected the FIFA Ballon d'Or as the world player of the year again but was far from being the only personality who could take pride in a memorable year. Wambach succeeded the first Asian player to win a world player award, Homare Sawa of the FIFA 2011 Women's World Cup winners, Japan.

The awards presentations also featured a multi-million-euro collection of 11 players comprising the 2012 "dream team" – Iker Casillas (Spain), Dani Alves (Brazil), Marcelo (Brazil), Gerard Pique (Spain) and Sergio Ramos (Spain) in defence; Xabi Alonso (Spain), Andrés Iniesta (Spain) and Xavi Hernández (Spain) in midfield; and Cristiano Ronaldo (Portugal), Radamel Falcao (Colombia) and Lionel Messi (Argentina) up front. Only Marcelo, Dani Alves, Sergio Ramos, Xabi Alonso and Radamel Falcao didn't feature in the team chosen 12 months earlier.

The two coaching awards went to the winners of international competitions, with 2010 FIFA World Cup and 2012 UEFA European Championship-winning Vicente Del Bosque of Spain scooping the award in the men's game and Pia Sundage, who led the United States to Olympic Games gold before returning to her native Sweden taking the women's prize.

A two-times European Footballer of the Year and the only man to win the FIFA World Cup as a captain (1974) and a coach (1990), Franz Beckenbauer of Germany – the man who oversaw the 2006 tournament in his homeland – received the Presidential Award. Miroslav Stoch of Turkish club side Fenerbahce was recognised as the scorer of the goal of the season – a stunning volley in a league fixture against Genclerbirligi – and received the FIFA Ferenc Puskas Award. The Uzbekistan Football Federation received the FIFA Fair Play Award to complete the major honours at world football's gala night.

> **Every man selected in the 2012 FIFA/FIFpro World XI team play their club football in Spain and six of them (Iker Casillas, Gerard Pique, Xavi, Andres Iniesta, Cristiano Ronaldo and Lionel Messi) were also in the 2011 team.**

FIFA PLAYER OF THE YEAR 2012

LIONEL MESSI

No-one argued when Argentina's **Lionel Messi** was hailed by all of world football in collecting a record-breaking fourth consecutive FIFA Player of the Year crown at the world federation's Ballon d'Or Gala.

Messi had concluded 2012 by scoring a professional record 91 goals. He also finished top scorer in the UEFA Champions League 2011–12 season with 14 goals. Yet, just to prove that football is a team game, he had ended the year with "only" one trophy, the Spanish King's Cup.

"This is unbelievable," marvelled Messi after becoming the first player to win four successive FIFA Ballon d'Or awards, emulating the achievement of old France hero Michel Platini, the UEFA president. "I'd like to thank my colleagues from Barcelona, my friends with Argentina, coaches, staff, family, friends ... also my wife and my new son."

Messi's remarkable year had seen him overcome his major perceived weakness, a lack of goals for his country. Captain Messi scored 12 goals for Argentina, including his first two national team hat-tricks, to fire them towards a place at the 2014 World Cup finals.

But, in the club world, Messi and Barcelona had finished behind old rivals Real Madrid in La Liga and their UEFA Champions League campaign had ended in a semi-final defeat by Chelsea.

Liga success was the consolation for Madrid's Cristiano Ronaldo, who finished FIFA runner-up. Messi collected 41.6 percent of the votes in the poll conducted among the coaches and captains of the world's national teams and a media panel. Ronaldo claimed 23.68 percent and Barcelona's Andres Iniesta 10.91 percent.

This was the third time in a row since FIFA's Player of the Year of the Year merged with *France Football*'s Ballon d'Or that the podium had been shared by three La Liga players. They were not alone. Another Barcelona hero, playmaker Xavi, was fourth with Atletico de Madrid's Radamel Falcao fifth.

Africa's only representative on the 23-player shortlist was Didier Drogba, who was eighth after his decisive, penalty-converting role in Chelsea's UEFA Champions League Final win over Bayern Munich in the German club's home stadium.

Even with the World Cup around the corner, Brazil's only representative was the Santos striker Neymar. He was 13th in the 23-player list with 0.61 percent of the vote. The five-times world champions have not had a player in the final three since Kaka won the award in 2007.

Hence the only Brazilians to make it on to the Gala stage, to assist with the presentations, were national coach Luiz Felipe Scolari and World Cup mascot Fuleco, a giant armadillo.

PREVIOUS WINNERS

1991 Lothar Matthaus (Germany)
1992 Marco van Basten (Netherlands)
1993 Roberto Baggio (Italy)
1994 Romario (Brazil)
1995 George Weah (Liberia)
1996 Ronaldo (Brazil)
1997 Ronaldo (Brazil)
1998 Zinedine Zidane (France)
1999 Rivaldo (Brazil)
2000 Zinedine Zidane (France)
2001 Luis Figo (Portugal)
2002 Ronaldo (Brazil)
2003 Zinedine Zidane (France)
2004 Ronaldinho (Brazil)
2005 Ronaldinho (Brazil)
2006 Fabio Cannavaro (Italy)
2007 Kaka (Brazil)
2008 Cristiano Ronaldo (Portugal)
2009 Lionel Messi (Argentina)
2010 Lionel Messi (Argentina)
2011 Lionel Messi (Argentina)

FIFA WOMEN'S PLAYER OF THE YEAR 2012

ABBY WAMBACH

The year 2012 saw **Abby Wambach**, surprisingly considering the United States' status, become the first American to win the FIFA Women's World Player of the Year award in a decade.

Wambach followed in the footsteps of Mia Hamm, who won in 2001 and 2002. She collected 20.67 percent of the 2012 vote, ahead of Brazil's Marta and fellow American Alex Morgan on 13.50 percent and 10.87 percent, respectively.

This triumph reflected the most outstanding year in Wambach's highly successful career. She led the US to gold medal success at the London 2012 Olympic Games and took home the golden ball as the best player, as well as finishing second, behind Christine Sinclair of Canada, in the scoring charts, with five goals. Uniquely, Wambach scored in all of the first five matches at London 2012 and was the only US player to start all the national team's 32 games during the year.

"I'm very, very surprised," she said. "I really don't think of myself as the best player in the world, just a player who plays on the best team in the world."

Wambach and Morgan, between them, had accounted for 55 goals in one of the most profilic years in US women's history. Together they equalled a record for a US strike duo set back in 1991 by Michelle Akers (39) and Carin Jennings (16). Wambach's 27 goals had lifted her to a career tally of 152 in nearly 200 games while Morgan contributed 28 goals with 21 assists.

Sunil Gulati, the US Soccer president, said: "The contributions Abby Wambach has made to US Soccer and women's sports in general are far-reaching and significant. Her play on the field during her entire career and her leadership year in helping capture the gold medal were both inspirational and consistently world-class.

"As a person and a player, she has represented her country and her teammates for more than a decade with tremendous professionalism."

Wambach, also an Olympic champion at the Beijing 2008 Games, had been hailed five times as US Soccer's Female Athlete of the Year.

PREVIOUS WINNERS

2001	Mia Hamm (United States)
2002	Mia Hamm (United States)
2003	Birgit Prinz (Germany)
2004	Birgit Prinz (Germany)
2005	Birgit Prinz (Germany)
2006	Marta (Brazil)
2007	Marta (Brazil)
2008	Marta (Brazil)
2009	Marta (Brazil)
2010	Marta (Brazil)
2011	Homare Sawa (Japan)

OTHER FIFA AWARDS

In conjunction with the FIFA World Player of the Year awards (for both men and women), and tournament-specific prizes for best player, top scorer and top goalkeeper, in recent years the game's governing body has handed out other prizes at its end-of-year gala: the presidential award, the fair play award, a development prize, and recognition to the best rankings mover of the year and the team of the year.

The achievements of **Vicente Del Bosque** – defying the fashion for charismatic, media-magnetic managers – do his talking for him. Thus Spain's national team boss, having guided his national team to 2010 World Cup and 2012 European Championship glory, was also hailed as FIFA's Coach of the Year for 2012.

The one-time Real Madrid player and coach secured 34.51 percent of the vote, ahead of José Mourinho, Real Madrid's Portuguese coach, with 20.49 percent and Pep Guardiola, who received 12.91 percent for his continuing achievements with Barcelona.

Herve Renard, who had led Zambia to a poignant and highly unlikely win at the African Nations Cup, and Tite, coach of South American and world club champions Corinthians, both failed to make the shortlist of 10 coaches.

Pia Sundhage led the FIFA World Coach of the Year for Women's Football category with 28.59 percent, ahead of Norio Sasaki (23.83 percent), coach of the Japanese team who collected silver at the London 2012 Olympic Games – the winner of the award in 2011 – and France team coach Bruno Bini (9.02 percent). The United States' gold medal success made amends for their defeat by Japan in the 2011 FIFA Women's World Cup Final.

Slovakia striker Miroslav Stoch carried off the FIFA Puskas Award for the "most beautiful goal" of the year as voted by more than five million fans on FIFA.com, FIFA on YouTube and francefootball.fr. That was the Fenerbahce star's reward for his spectacular strike in a league against Gençlerbirligi in March 2012.

Veteran German captain, manager and director Franz Beckenbauer received the FIFA Presidential Award in recognition of his service to the game while the Fair Play Award went to the Uzbekistan Football Federation for its teams' exemplary behavioural record. Iran were runners-up.

Finally, Lionel Messi received an extra accolade – to add to his world player prize – when he was named in the FIFPro World XI selected by a poll of the international players union's 50,000 members. Messi was one of five players from Barcelona to be named to the team, but proof of the worldwide respect in which La Liga – Spain's top tier of football – can be seen that the other six players also came the competition, five from Real Madrid and the other, Radamel Falcao, from Real's cross-city rivals, Atletico.

FIFA Awards 2012:

Men's Player of the Year: Lionel Messi (Argentina, Barcelona)
Women's Player of the Year: Abby Wambach (US)
Men's Football Coach of the Year: Vicente Del Bosque (Spain)
Women's Football Coach of the Year: Pia Sundhage (USA/Sweden)
FIFA Ferenc Puskas Award (outstanding goal): **Miroslav Stoch**
(for Fenerbahce, v Genclerbirligi, Turkish League)
Presidential Award: **Franz Beckenbauer** (Germany)
Fair Play Award: **Uzbekistan Football Federation**

FIFA/FIFpro World XI: Iker Casillas (Spain), Dani Alves (Brazil),
Marcelo (Brazil), Gerard Pique (Spain) and Sergio Ramos (Spain)
in defence; Xabi Alonso (Spain), Andres Iniesta (Spain) and Xavi
Hernandez (Spain) in midfield; and Cristiano Ronaldo (Portugal),
Radamel Falcao (Colombia) and Lionel Messi (Argentina) up front.

1991
Fair Play award: Real
Federacion Espanola de Futbol
(Spanish FA), Jorginho (Brazil)

1992
Fair Play award: Union Royale
Belge des Societes de Football
Association

1993
Fair Play award: Nandor
Hidgekuti (Hungary)*, Football
Association of Zambia
Top Team of the Year: Germany
Best Mover of the Year:
Colombia
*award presented
posthumously*

1994
Top Team of the Year: Brazil
Best Mover of the Year: Croatia

1995
Fair Play award: Jacques
Glassmann (France)
Top Team of the Year: Brazil
Best Mover of the Year: Jamaica

1996
Fair Play award: George Weah
(Liberia)
Top Team of the Year: Brazil
Best Mover of the Year: South
Africa

1997
Fair Play award: Irish
spectators at the FIFA World
Cup preliminary match versus
Belgium, Jozef Zovinec (Slovak
amateur player), Julie Foudy
(United States)
Top Team of the Year: Brazil
Best Mover of the Year:
Yugoslavia

1998
Fair Play award: National
associations of Iran, the United
States and Northern Ireland
Top Team of the Year: Brazil
Best Mover of the Year: Croatia

1999
Fair Play award: New Zealand
football community
Top Team of the Year: Brazil
Best Mover of the Year:
Slovenia

2000
Fair Play award: Lucas Radebe
(South Africa)
Top Team of the Year: Holland
Best Mover of the Year: Nigeria

2001
Presidential award Marvin Lee
(Trinidad)*
Fair Play award: Paolo Di
Canio (Italy)
Top Team of the Year:
Honduras
Best Mover of the Year:
Costa Rica
award presented posthumously

2002
Presidential award:
Parminder Nagra (England)
Fair Play award: Football
communities of Japan and
Korea Republic
Top Team of the Year: Brazil
Best Mover of the Year:
Senegal **2003**
Presidential award: Iraqi
football community
Fair Play award: Fans of Celtic
FC (Scotland)
Top Team of the Year: Brazil
Best Mover of the Year:
Bahrain

2004
Presidential award: Haiti
Fair Play award: Confederacao
Brasileira de Futebol
Top Team of the Year: Brazil
Best Mover of the Year:
China PR
Interactive World Player:
Thiago Carrico de Azevedo
(Brazil)

2005
Presidential award: Anders
Frisk (Sweden)
Fair Play award: Football
community of Iquitos (Peru)
Top Team of the Year: Brazil
Best Mover of the Year:
Ghana
Interactive World Player: Chris
Bullard (England)

2006
Presidential award: Giacinto
Facchetti (Italy)*
Fair Play award: Fans of the
2006 FIFA World Cup
Top Team of the Year: Brazil
Best Mover of the Year: Italy
Interactive World Player:
Andries Smit (Holland)
award presented posthumously

2007
Presidential award: Pele (Brazil)
Fair Play award: FC Barcelona
(Spain)

Top Team of the Year:
Argentina
Best Mover of the Year:
Mozambique

2008
Presidential award: Women's
football (presented to the
United States women's team)
Fair Play award: Armenia,
Turkey
Development award: Palestine
Interactive World Player:
Alfonso Ramos (Spain)
Top Team of the Year: Spain
Best Mover of the Year: Spain

2009
Presidential award: Queen
Rania
Al Abdullah of Jordan [co-chair
of 1Goal: Education for All]
Fair Play Award:
Sir Bobby Robson (England)*
Development prize:
Chinese Football Association
Interactive World Player:
Bruce Grannec (France)
Top Team of the Year: Spain
FIFA Ferenc Puskas Award
(outstanding goal):
Cristiano Ronaldo
(Manchester United v Porto)
award presented posthumously

2010
Coach of the year (men): Jose
Mourinho (Internazionale,
then Real Madrid)
Coach of the year (women):
Silvia Neid (Germany women)
FIFA Ferenc Puskas Award
(outstanding goal): Hamit
Altintop, Turkey v Kazakhstan
Presidential award: Archbishop
Desmond Tutu, South Africa
Fair Play Award: Haiti Under-17
women's team

2011
Coach of the year (men): Pep
Guardiola (Barcelona)
Coach of the year (women):
Norio Sasaki (Japan women)
FIFA Ferenc Puskas Award
(outstanding goal): Neymar,
Santos v Flamengo
Presidential award: Sir Alex
Ferguson, Manchester United
Fair Play award: Japan Football
Association

APPENDIX 2: FIFA/COCA-COLA WORLD RANKINGS

Germany were at No. 1 when FIFA's world rankings system was first calculated and published in December 1992. Brazil took over at the top before the 1994 FIFA World Cup – which they, of course, went on to win. Latterly Spain have commanded the table. The system, simplified after the 2006 FIFA World Cup, provides a monthly statistical insight into the rise and fall of fortunes for traditional footballing giants and aspiring minnows alike. The tallies are based on results in international A matches and consider match status, goals scored, strength of opposition and regional balance – based on matches played over a four-year period, rather than the eight years used until 2006. The rankings are issued every month.

Spain line up for the photographers before the 2013 FIFA Confederations Cup final. They may have lost the match to Brazil, but still retained a commanding lead at the top of the FIFA/Coca-Cola World Rankings.

FIFA/COCA-COLA WORLD RANKINGS 2013

The FIFA/Coca-Cola World Ranking offers a snapshot of fooball's world order, in this case as of July 2013, taking particular account of the FIFA Confederations Cup which ended days before the new standings were computed. Spain, despite losing to Brazil in the Confederations Cup Final, remained commanding leaders. Brazil moved up to ninth from a lowest-ever 22. The five-times former world champions had slipped down because, as 2014 World Cup hosts, their results lacked competitive value. For example, Colombia ranked third because of their progress in the South American section of the 2014 FIFA World Cup qualifying competition. No change, sadly, for Bhutan, San Marino and the Turks & Caicos Islands who remained joint bottom – as they were in July 2012.

Seven wins in 12 matches in qualifying for the 2014 FIFA World Cup have seen Colombia, spearheaded by **Radamel Falcao,** rise four places to third in the FIFA/Coca Cup world rankings.

RANKINGS (as at July 2013)

Pos.	Country	Pts	(Change)
1	Spain	1532	(0)
2	Germany	1273	(0)
3	Colombia	1206	(4)
4	Argentina	1204	(-1)
5	Netherlands	1180	(0)
6	Italy	1142	(2)
7	Portugal	1099	(-1)
8	Croatia	1098	(-4)
9	Brazil	1095	(13)
10	Belgium	1079	(2)
11	Greece	1038	(5)
12	Uruguay	1016	(7)
13	Cote d'Ivoire	1009	(0)
14	Bosnia-Herzegovina	995	(1)
15	England	994	(-6)
16	Switzerland	987	(-2)
17	Russia	979	(-6)
18	Ecuador	932	(-8)
19	Peru	898	(11)
20	Mexico	880	(-3)
21	Chile	872	(4)
22	USA	865	(6)
23	France	838	(-5)
24	Ghana	830	(-3)
25	Norway	801	(4)
26	Czech Republic	797	(-2)
27	Denmark	788	(-7)
28	Mali	774	(-5)
=	Montenegro	774	(-3)
=	Ukraine	774	(11)
31	Sweden	765	(-4)
32	Hungary	749	(1)
33	Romania	732	(1)
34	Algeria	730	(1)
35	Nigeria	723	(-4)
36	Venezuela	704	(1)
37	Albania	689	(1)
=	Japan	689	(-5)
39	Costa Rica	688	(9)
40	Australia	671	(7)
41	Serbia	661	(-5)
42	Burkina Faso	656	(9)
43	Korea Republic	642	(-3)
44	Republic of Ireland	639	(-3)
45	Slovenia	634	(10)
46	Wales	630	(-1)
47	Tunisia	627	(-5)
48	Paraguay	622	(-4)
49	Cape Verde Islands	620	(23)
50	Scotland	610	(24)
51	Panama	601	(-8)
52	Bulgaria	596	(-6)
=	Iran	596	(15)
54	Austria	595	(22)
55	Honduras	582	(-3)
=	New Zealand	582	(2)
57	Turkey	573	(-3)
58	Uzbekistan	563	(0)
59	South Africa	558	(1)
60	Zambia	554	(-11)
61	Guinea	545	(24)
62	Egypt	543	(9)
63	Slovakia	542	(-7)
64	Israel	540	(-2)
65	Finland	537	(19)
66	Armenia	534	(23)
67	Equatorial Guinea	532	(-3)
68	Bolivia	528	(-15)
69	Haiti	522	(-6)
70	Libya	518	(-1)
71	Cameroon	517	(-6)
72	Togo	511	(1)
73	Iceland	499	(-12)
74	Senegal	497	(25)
75	Poland	493	(-10)
76	Jordan	489	(-1)
77	Jamaica	484	(-28)
78	Belarus	482	(-11)
79	Morocco	470	(-2)
80	Uganda	466	(13)
81	Gabon	459	(1)
82	Cuba	458	(9)
83	Sierra Leone	443	(-13)
84	Congo DR	434	(-5)
85	United Arab Emirates	432	(2)
86	Estonia	423	(3)
87	Trinidad and Tobago	419	(-6)
88	Canada	413	(-5)
89	Central African Republic	398	(-30)
90	Congo	396	(-10)
=	Dominican Republic	396	(4)
92	FYR Macedonia	395	(-14)
93	Guatemala	388	(-5)
94	El Salvador	382	(-8)
95	Ethiopia	381	(11)
96	Angola	380	(-5)
97	New Caledonia	377	(0)
98	Georgia	369	(-2)
99	Oman	361	(2)
100	China PR	339	(-5)
101	Iraq	335	(-3)
102	Mozambique	326	(1)
103	Liberia	324	(-3)
104	Lithuania	321	(1)
105	Saudi Arabia	315	(3)
106	Tajikistan	314	(6)
107	Niger	313	(0)
108	Malawi	312	(1)

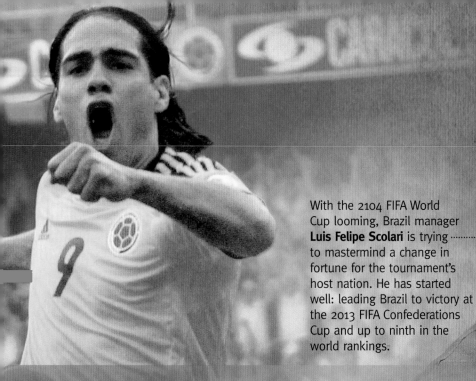

With the 2104 FIFA World Cup looming, Brazil manager **Luis Felipe Scolari** is trying 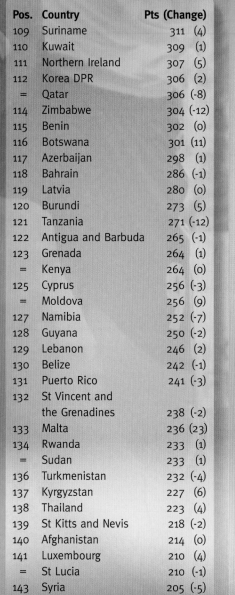 to mastermind a change in fortune for the tournament's host nation. He has started well: leading Brazil to victory at the 2013 FIFA Confederations Cup and up to ninth in the world rankings.

Pos.	Country	Pts (Change)
109	Suriname	311 (4)
110	Kuwait	309 (1)
111	Northern Ireland	307 (5)
112	Korea DPR	306 (2)
=	Qatar	306 (-8)
114	Zimbabwe	304 (-12)
115	Benin	302 (0)
116	Botswana	301 (11)
117	Azerbaijan	298 (1)
118	Bahrain	286 (-1)
119	Latvia	280 (0)
120	Burundi	273 (5)
121	Tanzania	271 (-12)
122	Antigua and Barbuda	265 (-1)
123	Grenada	264 (1)
=	Kenya	264 (0)
125	Cyprus	256 (-3)
=	Moldova	256 (9)
127	Namibia	252 (-7)
128	Guyana	250 (-2)
129	Lebanon	246 (2)
130	Belize	242 (-1)
131	Puerto Rico	241 (-3)
132	St Vincent and the Grenadines	238 (-2)
133	Malta	236 (23)
134	Rwanda	233 (1)
=	Sudan	233 (1)
136	Turkmenistan	232 (-4)
137	Kyrgyzstan	227 (6)
138	Thailand	223 (4)
139	St Kitts and Nevis	218 (-2)
140	Afghanistan	214 (0)
141	Luxembourg	210 (4)
=	St Lucia	210 (-1)
143	Syria	205 (-5)

Pos.	Country	Pts (Change)
144	Philippines	203 (0)
145	Vietnam	182 (-12)
146	India	178 (1)
147	Barbados	175 (2)
148	Hong Kong	173 (-1)
=	Liechtenstein	173 (10)
150	Kazakhstan	172 (-4)
151	Palestine	167 (0)
152	Bangladesh	166 (0)
153	Aruba	163 (-3)
154	Maldives	147 (3)
=	Tahiti	147 (-16)
156	Singapore	146 (9)
157	Bermuda	139 (4)
158	Nicaragua	138 (4)
159	Malaysia	136 (0)
160	Chad	134 (-6)
161	Lesotho	133 (-8)
162	Solomon Islands	132 (4)
163	Myanmar	129 (-8)
164	Gambia	126 (-2)
165	Dominica	124 (2)
166	Sao Tome e Principe	120 (-7)
167	Pakistan	114 (1)
168	Indonesia	112 (2)
169	Nepal	106 (2)
170	Yemen	96 (3)
171	Sri Lanka	95 (1)
172	Mauritania	94 (2)
173	Laos	87 (-5)
174	Faroe Islands	81 (-12)
175	Chinese Taipei	77 (0)
176	Guam	70 (2)
177	Montserrat	66 (-1)
178	Curacao	65 (0)
179	Swaziland	60 (-1)

Pos.	Country	Pts (Change)
180	Guinea-Bissau	58 (1)
181	Bahamas	53 (-5)
182	Brunei Darussalam	52 (3)
=	Mauritius	52 (3)
=	Timor-Leste	52 (3)
185	Madagascar	51 (-1)
186	Mongolia	49 (-4)
187	Samoa	46 (1)
=	US Virgin Islands	46 (6)
189	Tonga	43 (1)
=	Vanuatu	43 (2)
191	Comoros	41 (1)
=	Fiji	41 (-9)
193	British Virgin Islands	34 (2)
194	Cayman Islands	33 (2)
195	American Samoa	30 (2)
196	Eritrea	24 (2)
197	Papua New Guinea	23 (-3)
198	Cambodia	20 (-9)
=	South Sudan	20 (2)
200	Seychelles	19 (-1)
201	Somalia	14 (1)
202	Macau	12 (0)
203	Djibouti	11 (1)
204	Cook Islands	9 (-3)
205	Andorra	8 (0)
206	Anguilla	3 (0)
207	Bhutan	0 (0)
=	San Marino	0 (0)
=	Turks and Caicos Islands	0 (0)

INDEX

PICTURE CREDITS

The publishers would like to thank the following sources for their kind permission to reproduce the pictures in this book. The page numbers for each of the photographs are listed below, giving the page on which they appear in the book and any location indicator (C-centre, T-top, B-bottom, L-left, R-right).

Action Images: /Matthew Childs: 95BR, 230BL

Getty Images: 161TL; /2010 FIFA World Cup Organising Committee: 183L; /2010 Qatar 2022: 182R; /AFP: 55C, 119TL, 119BL, 163BR, 171L, 192BR, 197R, 204BL, 206L; /Eitan Abramovich/AFP: 5TL, 102TR; /Vanderlei Almeida/AFP: 5BL, 146-147; /Odd Andersen/AFP: 33R, 73C; /Rodrigo Arangua/AFP: 114R, 158TL; /Brian Bahr: 150BR; /Dennis Barnard/Fox Photos: 107TL; /Scott Barbour: 132BL; /Lars Baron: 107B, 173B, 231TR, 231BR; /Juan Barreto/AFP: 116T; /Robyn Beck/AFP: 68BR, 179TR; /Sandra Behne/Bongarts: 136BL; /Fethi Belaid/AFP: 123BR; /Bentley Archive/Popperfoto: 78C, 79BL, 169BR; /Martin Bernetti/AFP: 117BR; /Gunnar Berning/Bongarts: 177BL; /Monirul Bhuiyan/AFP: 154-155, 185B; /Bongarts: 36L, 167BL; /Shaun Botterill: 8-9, 13BR, 44BL, 61BL, 74C, 84TR, 128TR, 162L, 170L, 177TR, 178BR, 185TR, 194BR, 223R; /Cris Bouroncle/AFP: 220T; /Gabriel Bouys/AFP: 33TL, 42B, 176C; /Clive Brunskill: 113R; /Simon Bruty: 80BR, 116BR; /Rodrigo Buendia/AFP: 103BL; /Martin Bureau/AFP: 23TR; /Eric Cabanis/AFP: 158R; /Jose Cabezas/AFP: 156TR; /Giuseppe Cacace/AFP: 5C, 35T; /Felipe Caicedo/LatinContent: 251TL; /David Cannon: 18L, 39R, 40BR, 50BR, 55BR, 74BR, 106TR, 145TR; /Mario Castillo/Jam Media/LatinContent: 148BR; /Central Press: 77BL; /Central Press/Hulton Archive: 62BR; /Andre Chaco/FotoArena/LatinContent: 181BL; /Graham Chadwick: 74TR; /Chung Sung-Jun: 161TR; /Robert Cianflone: 28TL, 81T, 83L, 133TR; /Timothy A Clary/AFP: 153BR; /Thomas Coex/AFP: 165R; /Fabrice Coffrini/AFP: 61R, 156BR; /Chris Cole: 109BR; /Phil Cole: 57BR, 86C, 96R, 122B, 148BL; /Yuri Cortez/AFP: 152BR; /Anesh Debiky/Gallo Images: 211BR, 217TL; /Stephane de Sakutin/AFP: 185L, 213BR; /Carl de Souza/AFP: 173TR; /Adrian Dennis/AFP: 79C, 194TR; /Philippe Desmazes/AFP: 142TL, 184TR; /Khaled Desouki/AFP: 122TR, 215BL, 217C; /Dimitar Dilkoff/AFP: 52BL, 68L; /Kevork Djansezian: 151C; /Nikolay Doychinov/AFP: 50C; /Denis Doyle: 10-11, 43BR, 46L; /Stephen Dunn: 126BR; /Paul Ellis/AFP: 27C; /Darren England: 158BL, 158BR; /Francisco Estrada/LatinContent: 138BR; /Evening Standard: 134; /Franck Fife/AFP: 21BR, 23BR, 107TR, 125TR, 198TR, 212TC; /Julian Finney: 62L, 234-235; /Stu Forster: 15TL, 56C, 73BL, 92BL, 93BL, 105TL; /Stuart Franklin: 61T, 242-243; /Romeo Gacad/AFP: 58C; /Daniel Garcia/AFP: 202BR; / Paul Gilham: 47TL, 128C, 171B, 178TR; /Georges Gobet/AFP: 59BR; /Sergio Goya/AFP: 202C; /Sebastian Granata/LatinContent: 118B; /Otto Greule Jr: 150TR; /Laurence Griffiths: 2, 13C, 42R, 56L, 76TR, 87C, 135R, 145L, 164T; /Alex Grimm: 47BR, 69TR; /Gianluigi Guercia/AFP: 31R, 186BL, 214B; /Jack Guez/AFP: 190TR; /Steve Haag: 211C; /Valery Hache/AFP: 118C, 141R, 177C, 196BL; /Ronny Hartmann/AFP: 88TR, 190B; /Alexander Hassenstein: 233, 245BR, 247TL; /Alexander Hassenstein/Bongarts: 22TR, 29R, 136L; /Haynes Archive/Popperfoto: 160TR, 161B, 203BL; /Richard Heathcote: 38BR, 105BL; /Scott Heavey: 16L, 51TL; /Alexander Heimann/Bongarts: 153BL; /Alfredo Herms/LatinContent: 110BR; /Marcelo Hernandez/LatinContent: 113TL; /Patrick Hertzog/AFP: 19BR, 22R, 41BR, 90TR, 160BL; /Mike Hewitt: 25T, 63BR, 65BR, 111BL, 226L, 229L; /Antonia Hille: 98C; /Boris Horvat/AFP: 38BL, 195T; /Hulton Archive: 14TC, 63TR, 160BR, 168BL; /Karim Jaafar/AFP: 129L, 132C, 135BL, 137TR, 138L; /Liu Jin/AFP: 168TL; /Alexander Joe/AFP: 120-121, 215TL; /Hannah Johnston: 156L; /Jose Jordan/AFP: 46BR; /Jasper Juinen: 14TL, 14C, 44C, 45TL, 194L, 221BR, 227TR, 248-249; /Yuri Kadobnov/AFP: 76C; /Gorm Kallestad/AFP: 66BL; /Nicholas Kamm/AFP: 151TL; /Keystone: 18TR, 62BL, 77BR; /Keystone/Hulton Archive: 31BL, 45BL; /Saeed Khan/AFP: 156BL; /Ian Kington/AFP: 16TR; /Ross Kinnaird: 172TR; /Pedro Kirilos/LatinContent: 185R; /Glyn Kirk/AFP: 229BR; / Toshifumi Kitamura/AFP: 50T, 130-131, 159C, 218-219, 226TR; /Joe Klamar: 57L, 67TR; /Christof Koepsel: 30C, 57TR, 112TR, 225C, 226BL, 244L, 246; /Mark Kolbe: 133TL; /Patrick Kovarik/AFP: 97C; /Jimin Lai/AFP: 136TR; /LatinContent: 200-201; /David Leah: 175TL; /David Leah/Mexsport: 148TR; /Christopher Lee: 82TR, 83TR, 85C; /Bryn Lennon: 65TR, 72TR; / Francisco Leong/AFP: 24TR, 77C; /Matthew Lewis: 68TR; /Alex Livesey: 20R, 43TR, 58TR, 59T, 77TL, 85TL, 92C, 127C, 139BR, 157TR, 169R, 199TR, 224L, 251TR; /John MacDougall/ AFP: 75BR; /Pierre-Philippe Marcou/AFP: 44TL, 126TL, 170TR; /Francois-Xavier Marit/AFP: 179TL; /Tony Marshall: 4BR; /Clive Mason: 26L, 55BL, 89BL, 91BR, 127TL, 165BL, 174TL; / Jamie McDonald: 38T, 56BR, 62TR, 72C, 127BR, 149C, 223BL; /Chris McGrath: 103TR, 178TL; /Miguel Medina/AFP: 19TR; /Buda Mendes/LatinContent: 109TR, 115TR, 182L, 205TR; / Philippe Merle/AFP: 119R; /Aris Messinis/AFP: 60BL; /Damien Meyer/AFP: 27R, 188-189; /Douglas Miller/Keystone: 12BL; /Sandra Montanez: 239T; /Filippo Monteforte/AFP: 94C; / Olivier Morin/AFP: 247BR; /Dean Mouhtaropoulos: 100-101; /Peter Muhly/AFP: 96BL, 191L; /Jonathan Nackstrand/AFP: 197L; /Hoang Dinh Nam/AFP: 140BL, 150C; /Mark Nolan: 133BR; /Kiyoshi Ota: 247R; /Jeff Pachoud/AFP: 193C; /Pascal Pavani/AFP: 89BR; /Valerio Pennicino: 31TL; /Doug Pensinger: 14BR, 180BL; /Ryan Pierse: 94BL, 144TR, 152L, 174B; /Vincenzo Pinto/AFP: 176BR; /Jan Pitman/Bongarts: 180TR; /Hrvoje Polan/AFP: 52C; /Joern Pollex: 5L, 24BL, 28R, 58BL, 125C, 222C; /Joern Pollex/Bongarts: 29TL; /Popperfoto: 20BL, 26BR, 28BL, 29B, 51BR, 64BL, 84C, 93T, 110L, 113BL, 137L, 140R, 141T, 143B, 151BL, 159BR, 167BR, 169L, 192BL, 196TR, 198B, 205BL, 206BR, 228BL; /Anne-Christine Poujoulat/AFP: 71BR, 232BL; /Savo Prelevic/AFP: 99B; /Craig Prentis: 149TR; /Gary M Prior: 110TR, 139C, 174C; /Ben Radford: 49TR, 49BR, 111C, 135T, 175BR; /Roslan Rahman/AFP: 143TR; /Aizar Raldes/ AFP: 118C; /David Ramos: 244BR; /Patricio Realpe/LatinContent: 117L; /Michael Regan: 12TR, 17TR, 90B, 93BR; /Chris Ricco/Backpagepix: 217BR; /Rafa Rivas/AFP: 45R; /Miguel Rojo/ AFP: 104TL, 119TR, 207TL; /Rolls Press/Popperfoto: 15B, 33B, 108TR; /Quinn Rooney: 241BC; /Clive Rose: 81BL, 91BL, 106BL; /Martin Rose: 21C, 245TL; /Martin Rose/Bongarts: 89TR, 94BR; /STR/AFP: 99TR; /Jewel Samad/AFP: 40TL, 71TR, 176BL; /Mark Sandten/Bongarts: 124BL; /Issouf Sanogo/AFP: 125BL, 129TR, 210B; /Genia Savilov/AFP: 69L; /Roberto Schmidt/ AFP: 164BL, 181TR, 187TL; /Antonio Scorza/AFP: 111R, 115BL; /Abdelhak Senna/AFP: 216; /Lefty Shivambu/Gallo Images: 128L, 210L, 212TR, 213TR, 215C; /Torsten Silz/AFP: 171TR; / Christophe Simon/AFP: 7, 167TR; /Janek Skarzynski/AFP: 199BLL; /Javier Soriano/AFP: 163L, 183B, 195BR; /Cameron Spencer: 168TR; /Jamie Squire: 123TL, 172BL; /Michael Steele: 51T, 84BL, 163TR, 186TR; /Srdjan Stevanovic: 81R; /Patrik Stollarz/AFP: 4R, 26TR, 97BL, 187BR; /Boris Streubel: 88L; /Graham Stuart/AFP: 78TR; /Henri Szwarc/Bongarts: 116L, 193B; /Mehdi Taamallah/AFP: 5BC; /Bob Thomas: 32BL, 32BR, 34B, 48TR, 51BL, 64TR, 65C, 65BL, 69BR, 70TR, 72BL, 78L, 83BR, 92TR, 92BR, 97R, 104BR, 105C, 108BL, 112BL, 115BR, 123TR, 137BR, 168BR, 180C, 184B, 186BR, 191TR; /Bob Thomas/Popperfoto: 4T; /Mark Thompson: 66TR, 212BR; /John Thys/AFP: 50BL, 51R, 54TR; /Atsushi Tomura: 142BR; /Omar Torres/AFP: 138TR, 166TR, 207BR; /Pedro Ugarte/AFP: 162R; /Pius Utomi Ekpei/AFP: 4TR; /VI Images: 37TL, 37TR, 41T, 191B; /Robert van den Brugge/AFP: 48BL; /Manus van Dyk/Gallo Images: 210C, 214L; /Jean-Christophe Verhaegen/AFP: 95TR; /Claudio Villa: 32TL, 35BL, 98BR; /Claudio Villa/Grazia Neri: 34TR; /Friedemann Vogel: 236C; /Nigel Waldon: 67BL; /Ian Walton: 18BR, 39BL, 208-209, 211TR, 215R; /Koji Watanabe: 228TR; /Andrew Yates/AFP: 129B; /Rick Yeatts: 149BR; /Jung Yeon-Je/AFP: 170BR

Press Association Images: 16BL, 80TR, 104R, 204BR, 229TR; /ABACA Press: 165TL; /AP: 166BL; /Matthew Ashton: 109C, 133C, 144BL, 153TR, 238BR; /Greg Baker/AP: 237BL; /Jon Buckle: 239BR; /Felice Calabro/AP: 178BL; /Roberto Candia/AP: 237TL; /Barry Coombs: 60TR; /Malcolm Croft: 159TL; /Claudio Cruz/AP: 224C; /DPA: 22L, 27TL, 37B, 132TR, 162BL; / Adam Davy: 236B; /Sean Dempsey: 25BR; /Paulo Duarte/AP: 70L, 70C; /Mike Egerton: 152TR; /Paul Ellis/AP: 76BL; /Denis Farrell/AP: 182B; /Dominic Favre/AP: 86BR; /Gouhier-Hahn-Orban/ABACA: 86TR; /Michel Gouverneur/Reporter: 222BL; /Jae C Hong/AP: 145B; /Intime Sports/AP: 60C; /Silvia Izquierdo/AP: 232L, 232R; /Julie Jacobson/AP: 238TL, 241BR; / Lee Jin-Man/AP: 238TR; /Ross Kinnaird: 205C; /Tony Marshall: 34L, 39TL, 88B, 108TL, 167TL, 203TR, 221TL, 224TR, 225TR, 230TR; /Cathal McNaughton: 12C; /Phil O'Brien: 30BL; / Panoramic: 222R; /Eraldo Peres/AP: 231BL; /Natacha Pisarenko/AP: 206C; /Nick Potts: 19BL; /Duncan Raban: 106BR; /Peter Robinson: 25L, 35BR, 36TR, 64C, 78BR, 80L, 82BL, 91TR, 102L, 114BL, 124TL, 220BL, 220BR; /S&G and Barratts: 13T, 15TR, 17B, 70BR, 73BR, 176TR; /SMG: 79TC; /Ariel Schalit/AP: 124R; /Murad Sezer/AP: 23C; /Matthias Schrader/AP: 240BR; /Sven Simon: 108BR; /Neal Simpson: 51BL, 75TR, 87BR, 204T; /Michael Sohn/AP: 240TR; /Jon Super/AP: 227BR, 237TR; /Topham Picturepoint: 71BL, 85BL, 96TL, 102B; /John Walton: 105TR; /Aubrey Washington: 67C; /Witters: 179B

Every effort has been made to acknowledge correctly and contact the source and/or copyright holder of each picture and Carlton Books Limited apologises for any unintentional errors or omissions that will be corrected in future editions of this book.

ABOUT THE AUTHOR

Keir Radnedge has been covering football for more than 40 years. He has written countless books on the subject, from tournament guides to comprehensive encyclopedias, aimed at all ages. His journalism career included the *Daily Mail* for 20 years, as well as the *Guardian* and other national newspapers and magazines in the UK and abroad. He is a former editor of *World Soccer,* generally recognized as the premier English-language magazine on global football. In addition to his writing, Keir has been a regular analyst for BBC radio and television, Sky Sports and the American cable news channel CNN. He also edited a tournament newspaper at the FIFA World Cup tournaments of 1982, 1986 and 1990. He has also scripted video reviews of numerous international football tournaments. He is also the London-based editor of SportsFeatures.com, the football and Olympic news website.